THE SEMINARY AT
100

REFLECTIONS ON THE JEWISH THEOLOGICAL SEMINARY AND THE CONSERVATIVE MOVEMENT

From the original architectural designs for the third and current home of the Seminary at 122nd Street and Broadway (circa 1925).

THE SEMINARY AT
100

REFLECTIONS ON THE JEWISH THEOLOGICAL SEMINARY AND THE CONSERVATIVE MOVEMENT

Edited by

Nina Beth Cardin
and
David Wolf Silverman

Published by

The Rabbinical Assembly and
The Jewish Theological Seminary of America

Copyright © 1987 by The Rabbinical Assembly

All rights reserved.

Library of Congress Cataloging-in-Publication Data

The Seminary at 100.

   1. Jewish Theological Seminary of America—
Congresses. 2. Conservative Judaism—United States—
Congresses. 3. Judaism—Study and teaching—
United States—Congresses. 4. Faith and reason (Jewish
theology)—Congresses. I. Cardin, Nina Beth.
II. Silverman, David Wolf. III. Jewish Theological
Seminary of America. IV. Rabbinical Assembly.
V. Title: Seminary at one hundred.
BM90.J56S46   1987   296.8′342′0973   87-20781
ISBN 0-916219-04-6 (clothbound)
ISBN 0-916219-05-4 (paperback)

Cover Design by Nina Gaelen
Production by The Town House Press

Table of Contents

Introduction: Centering Judaism
    David Wolf Silverman and Nina Beth Cardin xiii

Preface
    Ismar Schorsch 1

SECTION ONE: THE RELIGIOUS CENTER
THE SEMINARY AND ITS SPHERES OF INFLUENCE

Introduction to Section One
    John S. Ruskay 7

A. THE MAKING OF AMERICAN RABBIS

Training Rabbis in the Land of the Free
    Elliot N. Dorff 11

Authority and Autonomy in Rabbinic Education Today
    Arthur Green 29

The Next Generation of Conservative Rabbis:
An Empirical Study of Today's Rabbinical Students
    Aryeh Davidson and Jack Wertheimer 33

A Personal Look at Self, Judaism and the Seminary
    Bradley Shavit Artson 47

A View from the Inside: September 1986
    Debra Reed Blank 51

Toward Shared Religious Practices
    Samuel Weintraub 57

B. THE MAKING OF LAY LEADERSHIP

The Jewish Theological Seminary and Conservative
Congregations: Limited Associates or Full Partners?
    Rela Geffen Monson 63

A Red Brick Building, an "Educated Layperson," and
Thoughts of a Future
    Francine Klagsbrun 73

On Creating an Educated Laity
    Miriam Klein Shapiro 81

C. SPHERES OF INFLUENCE

The University of Judaism
    David L. Lieber 87

The Renewal of the Cantor
    Morton L. Leifman 97

Ramah at Forty: Aspirations, Achievements, Challenges
    H. A. Alexander 105

From Camper to National Director: A Personal View of the Seminary and Ramah
    Burton I. Cohen 125

The Impact of the Seminary on Israeli Religious Thought
    Reuven Hammer 135

Seeing the Future through the Light of the Past: The Art of the Jewish Museum
    Emily D. Bilski 143

The Seminary and "Havurah Judaism": Some Thoughts
    Robert Goldenberg 155

The Jewish Theological Seminary and the Academic Study of Judaism
    Michael Panitz 165

SECTION TWO: SYMPOSIUM ON SCHOLARSHIP AND BELIEF

Introduction to Section Two
    Raymond Scheindlin 175

A. BIBLE

History and Religion: A Reflection on Ralbag's Torah Commentary
    Edward L. Greenstein 179

Religion and Secular Study
    Yochanan Muffs 187

B. EDUCATION

On the Training of Rabbis: Scholarship, Belief and the Problem of Education
    Barry W. Holtz 195

Jewish Education and Jewish Scholarship:
Maybe the Lies We Tell are Really True
    Joseph Lukinsky 205

C. HISTORY

The Jewish Historian and the Believer
    Ivan G. Marcus 215

Reflections of a Jewish Historian
    Joel E. Rembaum 223

D. LITERATURE

"My God, Who Is Without Ending":
Modern Hebrew Literature as a Mode of Religious Quest
    Anne Lapidus Lerner 231

On Account of Two Hats
    David G. Roskies 239

E. PHILOSOPHY

A Philosopher's View on the Problem of Scholarship and Belief
    Gordon Tucker 251

F. PRACTICAL RABBINICS

Scholarship and the Rabbinate: A Vital Symbiosis
    Gilbert S. Rosenthal 261

Teaching Conservative Judaism
    Yaakov G. Rosenberg 271

G. TALMUD

An Unscientific Postscript
    David Weiss Halivni 275

Halakhah and History
    Joel Roth 281

SECTION THREE: THE SELF DEFINED

Introduction to Section Three
    Kassel Abelson 293

A. HOW OTHERS SEE US

Reflections on the Conservative Movement
    Jacob J. Staub 297

"His Majesty's Opposition," As It Were
    Eugene B. Borowitz.. 305

B. QUESTIONS OF DEFINITION

Toward a Conservative Theology
    David Novak... 315

Rituals, Myths and Communities
    Neil Gillman... 327

Pluralism in the Conservative Movement
    Ronald Price... 345

C. RESPONDING TO FEMINISM

Kol Isha: A New Voice in Conservative Judaism
    Amy Eilberg... 349

A Woman in the Mirror: Conservative Judaism Faces Feminism
    Leonard Gordon... 361

Feminism in the Conservative Movement
    Paula E. Hyman... 373

D. THE NEXT FIFTY YEARS

Masorti Judaism in Israel: Challenge, Vision and Program
    Lee Levine... 381

Conservative Judaism in Israel: Problems and Prospects
    Theodore Friedman... 391

The Next Step
    Benjamin Z. Kreitman... 399

Looking Toward the Next Century
    Franklin D. Kreutzer... 405

Dreams are Realized in Accordance with Their Interpretation
    Selma Weintraub... 411

The Rabbi for Me
    Jules Porter.. 423

A New Image of the Rabbinate
    Alan Silverstein.. 427

Fifty Years Hence
    Howard A. Addison... 433

The Seminary and the Declining Synagogue
    Elliot B. Gertel.. 441

Between Two Worlds: Or Why the Peacock Doesn't Fly
  Benjamin Edidin Scolnic 451
Some Notes on the Future of Conservative Judaism
  Elliot Salo Schoenberg 459

The Contributors 467

Between the Texts: A Pictorial Reflection

From the original architectural designs for current home of the
  Seminary (circa 1925).. ii
Sabato Morais, JTS founder and first President, 1886–1897............. xviii
H. Pereira Mendes, JTS founder and acting President, 1897–1902..... xviii
Solomon Schechter, first President of the reorganized Seminary,
  1902–1915 xviii
Cyrus Adler, founder and President of the Seminary, 1915–1940........ xviii
Louis Finkelstein, President, then Chancellor of the Seminary,
  1940–1972 10
Gerson D. Cohen, Chancellor of the Seminary, 1972–1986............... 10
Ismar Schorsch, Chancellor of the Seminary since 1986................... 10
Seminary students with Professor Joshua A. Joffe, 1897.................... 50
First faculty and graduation class of the Teachers Institute................. 86
Mordecai Kaplan and Solomon Schechter greet each other at a train
  station (circa 1910).. 96
Members of the Board presenting Louis Marshall with congratulatory
  speech on the occasion of his 70th birthday (1926).................... 104
View from the quadrangle of the entrance to the Seminary and the
  tower (1985)... 134
Alexander Marx, Librarian and Professor of History, 1903–1953....... 142
Louis Ginzberg, Professor of Talmud, 1903–1953......................... 142
Abraham Joshua Heschel, Professor of Jewish Ethics and Mysticism
  at the Seminary, 1945–1973.. 164
Saul Lieberman, Rector of the Seminary, with H. L. Ginsberg,
  Professor of Biblical History and Literature........................... 164
The old Library Reading Room in the Schiff Building at 122nd Street.. 178
A promotional poster of the Seminary's structure and programs from
  the early 1940's.. 186
A promotional guide to Seminary activities from the late 1960's.......... 204
The ashes of books consumed on their shelves in the devastating
  library fire of April 1966... 230
Massive efforts to salvage the books damaged by water in the library
  fire... 230

List of Illustrations xi

From the Seminary's Rare Book collection of Genizah fragments:
    The oldest surviving Hebrew manuscript with musical notation.... 250
    A letter signed by Moses Maimonides.................................. 280
The present campus of the University of Judaism in Los Angeles........ 314
The Seminary Sukkah... 344
Adele Ginzberg coordinated the lavish Sukkah decorations............... 344
At Camp Ramah, 1969... 360
At Camp Ramah, 1986... 372
Studying at Neve Schechter, 1986... 390
Erica Lippitz and Marla Rosenfeld Barugel, the first women to receive
    the diploma of Hazzan from JTS (1987).............................. 398
View of the Seminary quadrangle and new library building (1985)...... 410
Treasures of the Jewish Museum:
    Seder plate by Ludwig Wolpert (Frankfurt, 1930).................... 422
    Torah finials by Jeremias Zobel (Frankfurt, 1720).................. 422
Treasures of the Jewish Museum:
    The Talmudists by Max Weber (1934).............................. 440
    The Holocaust by George Segal (1982).............................. 440
School Children at the Jewish Museum's archaeology exhibition
    (1987).. 450

Introduction: Centering Judaism

David Wolf Silverman and Nina Beth Cardin

The Seminary at one hundred is a robust institution. Its combined schools, in New York, Jerusalem and Los Angeles, boast a total enrollment of 575 students engaged in the study of rabbinics, *hazzanut* (the cantorial arts), undergraduate as well as advanced graduate work in such diverse fields as education, art, music, counseling, and *torah lishmah* (that is, study for its own sake). At present, its faculty numbers 100. It is completing a multi-million dollar campus expansion project, including the new library building which houses more than a quarter of a million volumes, comprising one of the largest Judaica collections in the world. Its rabbis are the spiritual leaders of over one and a half million Conservative Jews. Its graduates are numbered among the faculties of over 200 university departments of Judaic Studies. On the indices of academic, physical, financial and human resources, therefore, the Seminary is more successful than ever before.

Yet the Seminary is not at rest. The changes and challenges it has embraced over the past few years have given it a new vibrancy. Even more, they have given a particular urgency to the need to explain again what the Seminary, and hence the Conservative movement, is all about. They have led the Seminary to engage in the healthy, at times difficult, at times painful, most often satisfying process of self-examination. This book is part of that self-examination.

The Seminary at 100 does not focus on the past or the present, but directs itself towards the future. Among the questions raised in the following pages are:

— What will be the goals of the Seminary in the coming decades?

— How should the Seminary best prepare rabbis to be religious leaders in an era of ever-accelerating change?

— What will be the impact of its historic decision to ordain women as rabbis and confer the title of cantor upon women?

— To what extent can and should the Seminary remain *American* and at the same time strengthen the Masorti movement in Israel?

— What should be the Seminary's relationship with the other arms of the movement—*primus inter pares* or formally and functionally the leader of the Conservative movement?

— What will be the movement's relationship with other denominations within Judaism?

We do not present here an historical overview of the Seminary's first one hundred years as we might have done. Nor do we linger on outstanding personalities, institutional achievements or exceptional academic contributions made by the Seminary. Others at a greater critical distance than we must do that.

This book is a family portrait reflecting the state of the Seminary and the movement in this centennial year. Like a portrait, it unkindly crops the images too close to the frame, and freezes that which is fluid. Still, it allows us to pause and consider what we think of ourselves, and what we want to be. It is a book about the Jewish Theological Seminary and the Conservative movement. Why both? Because one cannot exist without the other.

The Seminary is more than a school designed to provide the Conservative movement with a cadre of professional leaders. It is the source of the movement; that which gave birth to it, and which continues to nurture it. The Chancellor of the Seminary is the "Rabbi" of the movement. The Rabbinical Assembly, the United Synagogue, Women's League, Camps Ramah, Leaders Training Fellowship, the Foundation for Masorti Judaism all issued from and are part of the Seminary matrix.

Part one of the book, "The Religious Center: The Seminary and Its Spheres of Influence," is therefore devoted to views of the Seminary, its relationship to the movement and its broader impact. The question which delicately and deliberately weaves its way through each of the articles is: *how shall the Seminary continue to lead the movement?* Until very recently, and to some degree even today, the Seminary has led from afar, simply by being, by doing or by representing a position. Officially, the Seminary's jurisdiction extends only as far as its academic gates. Yet unofficially, its influence pervades the movement.

Should then, the Seminary join with the United Synagogue and the Rabbinical Assembly to provide religious guidance to individual congregations? Should the Seminary, as it makes decisions and determines policies which affect the movement as a whole, reach out to its Conservative constituency both to offer explanations and to consider their responses? In fact, the forthcoming publication of the faculty papers on the ordination of women upon which the 1983 vote was based hints at a more activist approach.

In the popular mind, the Seminary as an institution pursues two programs simultaneously: the religious, which entails the training of spiritual leaders; and the academic, classically known as *Wissenschaft des Judentums*, which entails the pursuit of the scholarly investigation of the Jewish past in all its complexity. Conceivably, these two tasks carried out by a single faculty, can coexist under one roof. At the Seminary, scholarship and professional skills have long been taught in one and the same classroom. For a century, the Seminary has fashioned religious, communal and educational leaders on the wheel of critical scholarship. But, has the mode of critical study created and nourished the religious spirit? Does this synthesis work? If it does, how is it sustained? Do the same assumptions which led to its past success continue to hold true today? If they are no longer valid, how should this affect the curriculum of rabbinic training?

These and related questions were posed to Seminary faculty members. Their responses appear in the second section of this book, "Symposium on Scholarship and Belief." They describe, both on a professional and a personal level, their own reconciliation of the academic objectivity required by critical scholarship with the ultimate concerns of belief. Do their studies affect their religious lives? If so, how? Can and should "presuppositionless" scholarship be pressed into the service of developing and nurturing religious minds? If so, how?

The answers to these questions, both perennial and contemporary, have ramifications beyond the training of rabbinical students. The answers reveal how the Seminary as the leader of the Conservative movement must respond to the needs of the fourth generation of American Jews.

Finally, in its third section, "The Self Defined," this book plumbs the wisdom of various leaders, both within and without the movement. They present their visions of the Conservative movement in the decades to come: its challenges, its contours, its limits, its concerns. What are the projections for our growth? What programs and enterprises must be undertaken to achieve them? How shall we respond to the calls for a fully articulated self-definition? What should be the role of the Conservative movement in strengthening Israel as state and community? Is there a distinctive Conservative style? How shall we define our role as God's covenantal partner?

Our eagerness, creativity and confidence in approaching these tasks will determine our future.

Acknowledgments

Every book is the creation of a team of artisans: authors, editors, advisors, technical assistants, production personnel and artists. How much more so this book with over fifty contributors. The editors would like to acknowledge our indebtedness to these friends, old and new, who offered so much, so generously, to make this book a reality. In particular, we would like to thank the contributors themselves, who graciously and capably answered our invitations. We owe special thanks to Ivan Marcus, who first suggested the idea for this book. We are indebted to the Editorial Board of *Conservative Judaism*, under whose auspices this book was created, for its steady vision which helped focus the book's structure, themes and content. Alvin Schultzberg, president of The Town House Press, has, as always, offered more than production services. We are grateful for his helpful guidance and advice. The photographs which so movingly give us a glimpse of the Seminary over the past one hundred years could not have been assembled and identified without the kind and extensive cooperation of Marjorie Wyler and the Communications Department of the Seminary.

From the very beginning, the Rabbinical Assembly and the Seminary warmly endorsed this project. They provided us with continual support and sustaining encouragement.

Sabato Morais, JTS founder and first President, 1886–1897.

H. Pereira Mendes, JTS founder and acting President, 1897–1902.

Solomon Schechter, first President of the reorganized Seminary, 1902–1915.

Cyrus Adler, founder and President of the Seminary, 1915–1940.

Preface

Ismar Schorsch

As Jews, we are not in the habit of taking survival for granted. Every holiday is greeted with a *sheheḥeyanu,* a prayer of thanksgiving for having reached yet another religious haven. A history of precariousness has taught us to value intervals of tranquility.

The Seminary's centennial brings to mind the stark fact that its Breslau forerunner — the first modern rabbinical school in the world — lasted but eighty-four years. In the fall of 1938, as Louis Finkelstein in New York bravely set about to launch his experiment in interfaith dialogue, the seminary founded by Frankel in Breslau, along with hundreds of synagogues and organizations, fell victim to Nazi barbarism. In a century of unprecedented genocide, Jewish survival became ever less certain. For this reason, the centenary of the school opened by Sabato Morais in January 1887 resonates with political as well as religious significance. It bespeaks a society that affords Jews the right to be different, individually and collectively. It symbolizes the fulfillment of George Washington's depiction of America in his celebrated letter to the Jews of Newport upon his assumption of the presidency in 1790. The intersection of the Seminary's centenary with the centennial of the Statue of Liberty and the bicentennial of the national constitution accentuates the nexus between religious opportunity and political freedom.

Millennia ago a signal was sent into the world from Sinai that continues to reverberate with undiminished strength. The Seminary is one of the great transmitters of Jewish history designed to recharge and disseminate that signal to the four corners of the Jewish world. Over the last one hundred years, the Seminary has grown into a veritable Jewish university to which no medium of Jewish expression is alien. A panoply of schools, institutes, and programs spans the globe and touches every aspect of the Jewish experience. Besides a full-time faculty of fifty professors and over five hundred students, the Seminary comprises a rabbinical school that has shaped the modern rabbinate, the largest graduate school of Jewish studies outside Israel, a college that pioneered undergraduate Jewish education, a new library building worthy of its unique holdings, the finest Jewish museum in America, and a network of Ramah camps that has changed the face of American Judaism. Above all, the Seminary has never deviated from a standard of Jewish scholarship which at one and the same time inspired the religious allegiance of the Conservative movement and the academic respect of the American university.

But what is the sound of the signal emitted from the Seminary? What is the character of the Judaism being transmitted? The Seminary stands for a Judaism mediated through the Hebrew language and rooted in the sacred texts of the biblical canon and rabbinic literature. Though necessary, translation is never deemed sufficient. Hebrew is the umbilical cord to our Jewish heritage and its treasures are studied in the original, for continuity is a function of medium as well as message. At the same time, it is a Judaism that does not compel intellectual submission. The study of our religious legacy is carried out in an integrated fashion. The wisdom of our age—its scientific and humanistic learning—is honestly brought to bear on the meaning of our classical texts. Belief is not pitted against knowledge, but reserved for those vast realms that lie beyond human grasp.

The Seminary stands for a Judaism grounded in the sacred soil of the Jewish State. The founders of Breslau were Zionists before the formation of a Zionist movement and our fidelity to the ineradicable national core of Judaism has never wavered. The creation of a just society is the ultimate challenge of Judaism, a mission imbedded in the revolutionary act of the Exodus itself. It is also a Judaism that makes demands upon us as individuals. It sets boundaries and curbs appetites. Its religious discipline constantly reminds us that we do not live by bread alone. The great test for American Jewry in the coming century will be whether it can endure its affluence and security. We have more experience at handling adversity.

The Seminary stands for a Judaism that has never become fossilized, a Judaism unafraid to confront the challenges of any age. What earlier generations may have effected unconsciously, we are fated to forge in the inhibiting glare of self-consciousness: the adjustment of ancient loyalties to changing sensibilities without doing violence to our religious integrity. And finally, it is a Judaism determined not to let the remembrance of the Holocaust turn into a world-view. For all the anguish conjured up by the Holocaust, we are not consumed by

Preface

hatred, anger, and resentment toward non-Jews. The extermination of six million Jews and the establishment of Israel have not muted the universal strains in the Jewish message.

In sum, the Judaism of the Seminary is an authentic yet modern, vibrant yet balanced, clear yet multifaceted expression of an eternal religion. Our determined quest for a genuine synthesis of the old and the new, the Jewish and the secular, the rational and the emotional, the parochial and the universal makes the Seminary the most important religious institution in the contemporary Jewish world. The fate of Judaism in America may well ride on its continued success.

Section One

THE RELIGIOUS CENTER: THE SEMINARY AND ITS SPHERES OF INFLUENCE

The Making of American Rabbis
The Making of Lay Leadership
Spheres of Influence

Introduction to the First Section

John S. Ruskay

The primary purpose of the Jewish Theological Seminary in its first century was to create and sustain a high quality academic institution for the training of rabbis and later cantors, Jewish educators, and lay leaders. This was accomplished in its four schools—The Rabbinical School, the Teachers Institute (later the Seminary College and recently re-named List College of Jewish Studies), the Graduate School and finally the Cantors Institute/Seminary College of Jewish Music. Over the years, fulfillment of this primary goal increasingly required the Seminary to extend its role to include leadership of the Conservative movement. Many Seminary programs—Camps Ramah, Leaders Training Fellowship, OMETZ (the college outreach program of the Conservative movement), Eternal Light Radio and TV, the Melton Center for Jewish Education, the Institute for Religious and Social Studies, the Institute on Ethics—responded to community needs, and reflected a strong commitment to extend the Seminary role far beyond the walls of the academy.

In the collection of essays which comprises this section, both Seminary missions and their interdependency are evident throughout. Each article about the Seminary's four schools extends beyond the "school agenda." Each discusses the dialectic between the training of rabbis, cantors, and Jewish educators and the Conservative movement. Several articles grapple with the demand to study and master Jewish tradition and the simultaneous need to be prepared to serve and lead living Jewish communities. It is in the nexus of these curricular issues that the relationship and tension between the Seminary's role as an academic institution committed to the critical study of Judaism and its role as an institution which trains communal professionals is most acutely evident.

Professors Davidson and Wertheimer explore the changing characteristics of those who enter Rabbinical School and what this entails for the future of both the Conservative rabbinate and the movement. Francine Klagsbrun provides the reader with a moving account of how the Seminary College affected her personal development; and several recent students—Bradley S. Artson, Debra Reed Blank, Samuel Weintraub—indicate that that impact is still very much present. Several articles, such as Miriam Klein Shapiro's, encourage the Seminary to extend its learning environment to far larger segments of the American Jewish community. Elliot Dorff provides fresh insights into the identity problems of young Jews—even rabbinical students.

In their articles on Camp Ramah, Burton Cohen and Hanan Alexander provide the reader with substantial background on the initiative which is, arguably, the Seminary's most successful effort in enriching the leadership of the Conservative movement.

While the Seminary's four schools remain its institutional backbone, the broad impact of diverse Seminary programs is revealed in several articles. The development, animating spirit, and present programs which have made the Jewish Museum the preeminent institution in its class are set forth in Emily Bilski's contribution, while David Lieber's account of the University of Judaism, the Seminary's West Coast affiliate, describes how the Seminary contributed mightily to the shaping of the Jewish community in California. Writing of the Seminary's youngest academic divisions, Morton Leifman describes the expanded role of the cantor, and the demands which this has placed on the Cantors Institute. Reuven Hammer writes about the impact of the Seminary on religious thought in Israel and emphasizes the enormous potential of Conservative/Masorti Judaism to influence Israeli society. The Seminary, as mediated through Camp Ramah, provided a model of "participatory" Judaism which became a major tenet of the Havurah movement. Robert Goldenberg's article documents this important product of the Seminary's first 100 years.

Michael Panitz in his discussion of the institutionalization of academic training and Arthur Green in his article on authority and autonomy in rabbinical training have brought the continuing dilemmas into focus. Rela Monson confronts directly the tension between scholarship and congregational life and questions whether resolution of this conflict is a Seminary responsibility. Taken together, these articles illumine the Seminary's impressive contribution to American Jewish life. Its scholarship has been a major force creating the field of Jewish studies. Its rabbinical alumni have shaped the modern American synagogue and style of Jewish religious observance. Its pioneering work in Jewish camping, curriculum development, radio and TV, interfaith relations and Jewish art have established models which others have emulated. In the aggregate, they have shaped the American Jewish community during the past 100 years.

Ranging over broad terrain, and assuming different points of departure, the articles return to the complex set of interrelated issues involved in thinking through how the curriculum of the Rabbinical School should be structured. The need for a rabbinate capable of both transmitting Jewish tradition and responding to the spiritual, emotional, and educational needs of the Conservative laity continues urgent. Determining the appropriate curriculum is no easier today than in 1886/7, when recognition of the need to create a new Rabbi, suitable for the American context, was one of the major factors which led to the establishment of the Jewish Theological Seminary. The context has changed but the challenge remains urgent. These articles give robust testimony to what the Seminary has accomplished in its first century, and to the continuing struggle which assures us that the second century will be equally rich for the Seminary, the Conservative movement, and the entire American Jewish community.

Louis Finkelstein, President, then Chancellor of the Seminary, 1940–1972.

Gerson D. Cohen, Chancellor of the Seminary, 1972–1986.

Ismar Schorsch, Chancellor of the Seminary since 1986.

Training Rabbis in the Land of the Free

Elliot N. Dorff

> We hold these truths to be self-evident, that all men are created equal, that they are endowed by their Creator with certain unalienable Rights, that among these are Life, Liberty, and the pursuit of Happiness . . . That to secure these rights, Governments are instituted among Men, deriving their just powers from the consent of the governed.
>
> *United States Declaration of Independence*

> See, this day I set before you blessing and curse: blessing, if you obey the commandments of the Lord your God that I enjoin upon you this day; and curse, if you do not obey the commandments of the Lord your God . . .
>
> *Deuteronomy 11:26-28*

American Jews are the product of two cultures, one American and one Jewish. Nowhere is the conflict between them stronger than in the issue of authority. Am I, as the Declaration of Independence proclaims, a creature born with inalienable rights, or am I, as Deuteronomy would have it, a person born into a host of obligations? The two are not mutually contradictory, but they certainly present two very different ways of thinking of oneself.

Rabbinical students, of course, are no more immune to the conflict than anyone else. By and large they grow up in the same environments as other Americans. Moreover, the vast majority of the people they will serve have deep roots in American individualism and much shallower roots in the authoritarian assumptions of much of the Jewish tradition. How, then, are these future rabbis supposed to reconcile their congregants' and, most likely, their own thinking based on rights with the Jewish tradition's assumptions of rabbinic authority to interpret and apply obligations?

The problem is especially characteristic of the Conservative movement, although it exists in a more diluted form in all of the other American movements as well. Conservative Judaism is at once strongly traditional and unequivocally modern. Other forms of Judaism combine both elements, but in different doses. Each of the other movements in American Judaism, then, resolves the conflict between Judaism and Americanism by suppressing one or the other. It is in Conservative Judaism, which is committed to integrating the traditional with the modern while preserving the integrity of both, that the conflict arises most poignantly.

This essay will address the problem first from a theoretical perspective and then from a practical one. It will explore some of the philosophical ways in which American democracy and Judaism are variously at odds, complementary, or identical. It will then discuss how these varying relationships between Judaism and Americanism manifest themselves in the training of Conservative rabbis. In so doing, it will not erase the tension felt by American Jews who choose to be Conservative rabbis, but hopefully it will make that tension more intelligible and creative.

Judaism and Americanism in Concept

Forms of Democracy

"Democracy" is hard to define. Since the word has acquired a highly emotive, positive charge, people find it useful to apply it to their favorite form of government, from Western democracies to communist governments like that of the "Democratic People's Republic of [North] Korea." The only safe thing that can be said of the word is that it is used to denote a form of government by the people, "people" being defined radically differently in various forms of "democracy" and even in the same government at different times.

When Americans think of democracy, they generally have in mind something like the American form of government. It is important to recognize at the outset, though, that there are two general forms of democratic theory. One form, following Jean Jacques Rousseau, speaks of government by the *collective* will of the people, such that it is downright undemocratic to oppose or impede a government acting with the people's mandate. Popular sovereignty is therefore compatible with the starkest forms of majoritarian tyranny and the total denial of individual rights, as the aftermath of the French Revolution amply demonstrates. While such communitarian forms of "democracy" in their modern communist and socialist forms pose vexing theoretical and practical problems for Jews, the specific conflicts between American democracy and Judaism follow from the other form of democratic theory, following John Locke, which emphasizes individualism and protects minority rights through a system of checks and balances.

Conflicts between Judaism and Liberal Individualism

The clashes between Judaism and American democratic theory appear in several forms. The first concerns the assumptions that I as a human being and a citizen make about myself and others. If rights are the primary reality of my being, the burden of proof rests upon anyone who wants to deprive me of those rights or restrict them. Since other people are born with the same rights, there are times when my rights are legitimately restricted, and there are even times when I have a positive duty to others. In each case, however, the duty arises out of a consideration of the other person's rights. If, on the other hand, the prime fact of my being is that I have obligations, as it is in Judaism, then the burden of proof rests upon me to demonstrate that I have a right against another person as a result of his or her duties to me. My rights exist only to the extent that others have obligations to me, not as an innate characteristic of my being.

The source and purpose of my obligations also divide Judaism from American democracy. It is "We, the people" who create the Constitution of the United States; the government must be "of the people" and "by the people" in Lincoln's words, not just for them. The reason for that is the underlying assumption already articulated in the passage from the Declaration of Independence with which we began: "To secure these rights, Governments are instituted among Men, deriving their just powers from the consent of the governed." Rules are instituted to secure rights; American individualism can be set aside only by American pragmatism, in this case the practical need to ensure that all can enjoy what is theirs by right. The source of authority of the law is the consent of the governed, who presumably see the practical need for imposing a law which restricts freedom.

For Judaism, the author of the commandments is God, not the governed. The Bible delineates several reasons to obey God's laws. These include: to avoid divine punishment and/or receive divine reward; to fulfill the promises of our ancestors and abide by the Covenant, promises to which we too are subject; to have a special relationship with God, thereby becoming a holy people; and to express our love for God. None of these aims, however, is to secure rights. Judaism and American democracy differ completely, then, in the initial assumptions of the legal system (rights or obligations), the source of the law, and its goals.

Moreover, the way in which a person views the world in the two systems of thought is different. In the one, I owe God; in the other, the world, or, at least, the government, owes me. In Judaism I begin with the assumption that things can be expected of me; in the American system, I begin with the assumption that I have "an unalienable right" to "life, liberty, and the pursuit of happiness" which the government is established to secure. President John F. Kennedy said, "Ask not what your country can do for you; ask what you can do for your country"; but those inaugural lines are memorable precisely because they are so surprising in an American context.

All of these differences between Jewish and American ideology derive at least in part from disparate, basic assumptions about the nature of the individual. With the exception of some right-wing, Orthodox groups, all modern Jews see the world through Enlightenment glasses in which the individual is the fundamental reality. All individuals are independent agents who may or may not choose to associate themselves with others for specific purposes. Religious congregations, for example, are voluntary associations to which individuals belong and from which they may dissociate themselves at any time. That is one manifestation of the enduring individuality of existence in this system of thought, for even when people join groups, they do not lose their primary identity and privileges as individuals. That is why Locke's and Jefferson's rights are "unalienable" by any government. Another corollary of this view is that even if other people happen to belong to a group to which I too belong, what they do is none of my business unless it has a direct effect on me.

This metaphysic stands in stark contrast to the traditional, Jewish view in which the individual is defined by his or her membership in the group. Membership in the group is not voluntary and cannot be terminated at will; it is a metaphysical fact over which those born Jews have no control. This indissoluble linkage between the individual and the group means that each individual is responsible for every other[1] and that virtually everything that one does is everyone's business. As the Talmud puts it:

Whoever is able to protest against the wrongdoings of his family and fails to do so is punished for the family's wrongdoings. Whoever is able to protest against the wrongdoings of his fellow citizens and does not do so is punished for the wrongdoings of the people of his city. Whoever is able to protest against the wrongdoings of the world and does not do so is punished for the wrongdoings of the world.[2]

At the same time, the communal view of traditional Judaism does not swallow up the individual's identity; it actually enhances it by linking it to the larger reality of the group. Milton Konvitz has expressed the resulting viewpoint well:

> The traditional Jew is no detached, rugged individual. Nor is his reality, his essence, completely absorbed in some monstrous collectivity which alone can claim rights and significance. He *is* an individual but one whose essence is determined by the fact that he is a brother, a *fellow Jew*. His prayers are, therefore, communal and not private, integrative and not isolative, holistic and not separative . . . This consciousness does not reduce but rather enhances and accentuates the dignity and power of the individual. Although an integral part of an organic whole, from which he cannot be separated, except at the cost of his moral and spiritual life, let each man say, with Hillel, "If I am here, then everyone is here."[3]

These legal and philosophical differences between American democracy and Judaism make it difficult for American Jews to integrate the two parts of their identity.

Points of Convergence between Judaism and American Democracy

On the other hand, Jewish and American practice and ideology are remarkably congenial in certain ways.

On a practical level, Jews have fared much better politically and economically under American democracy than they have under the corporate, stratified societies of the Middle Ages and most of the dictatorships of past or present. Jews in America have been legally protected from infringement in the free exercise of their religion, and they have enjoyed unprecedented political, cultural, and economic opportunities here. Assimilation and intermarriage are major, contemporary headaches for the Jewish people, but from one perspective they are simply the negative proof of Jews' success at being accepted as part of the larger American society.

There are a number of theoretical affinities between Judaism and democracy as well. Although Judaism places strong emphasis on the community, it went a long way to protect individuals and minorities. The Torah depicts each individual as the creature of God. Rabbinic Judaism respects the rights of non-Jews to live as such, as long as they obey the seven laws given, according to tradition, to the descendants of Noah.[4] In several passages the Bible boldly proclaims equality in law between Jew and alien; for instance, "There shall be one law for you and for the resident stranger; it shall be a law for all time throughout the ages. You and the stranger shall be alike before the Lord; the same ritual and the same rule shall apply to you and to the stranger who resides among you."[5] Although the attitude of Jews toward non-Jews varied according to the specific conditions of their interaction, and although there were exceptions to the general principle of equal treatment, the rabbis applied the principle not only to the ritual context in which it appears most often in the Bible, but to broad areas of civil legislation as well.[6] Furthermore, Judaism does not missionize, except by example.[7] It even reserves a place for righteous gentiles in the world to come.[8] In all these ways, Judaism protects the rights of individual gentiles, who constituted perhaps the most vulnerable minority in biblical society; and later, rabbinic Judaism continued these protections of individuals and minorities.

Jewish law also protects the rights of individual Jews and of minorities within the Jewish community. Treatment of the poor in Jewish law and in actual practice was truly remarkable in its level of service and humanity.[9] Jews were enjoined from tormenting the handicapped by, for example, insulting the deaf or placing a stumbling block in front of the blind and, with the exception of a few functions which specific handicaps made it impossible to perform, the handicapped were treated in Jewish law like everyone else.[10] In addition to protecting individuals and minorities from physical abuse or abandonment, Jewish law, like American law, safeguards an individual's right to express his or her own opinion, however unpopular. While Judaism does not recognize the right of Jews to adopt another religion, it does preserve the other First Amendment rights—and, for that matter, many of the privileges embodied in the other sections of the Bill of Rights.[11] These rights were not only theoretical; they were broadly used. Thus those reading the Talmud from the perspective of other cultures are often amazed at the high degree of tolerance in the Jewish tradition for questioning and disagreement. Ultimately a rule of law had to be established, but individuals were free to question it and argue against it, and all "were the words of the living God."[12]

These similarities between Judaism and the United States are rooted in a broader doctrine which they share: specifically, that we are human beings first and citizens second. The Declaration of Independence refers to "all men" and the Bill of Rights applies to all "people," not just to citizens. Similarly, in the Bible, God creates the progenitors of all human beings in the divine image long before establishing a special relationship with the Jewish People through the Covenant. Both traditions are thereby asserting the inherent dignity of all human beings independent of membership in a nation. Their shared, moral affirmation is that people are not merely means for some social or theological goal; they are ends and are to be treated as such.[13] It is no accident, then, that both traditions seek to protect individuals and minorities, and both cherish and vigorously exercise individual freedoms.

Another important manifestation of the sanctity of the individual in both ideologies is the overpowering emphasis that they both put on the rule of law. Kings, presidents, military leaders, and even individual judges do not determine the rules: there is a law by which even they must abide.[14] To ensure that judges are not lured into thinking that they are the source of the law, ordained judges, although authorized to judge cases on their own, are advised by the Mishnah not to do so. As Rabbi Ishmael, son of Rabbi Yose, said, "Do not judge by yourself, for there is only One who [appropriately] judges by Himself."[15]

Insistence that the law must govern has engendered great effort in both systems to extend it to cover every contingency. Jewish law became, as the Talmud put it, a veritable sea, and American law is now even more extensive. According to lawyer and legal philosopher Milton Konvitz, the United States is the only nation in the world which has centered its civilization around law as much as the Jews have.[16]

There are even some similarities in the sources of the law. As indicated earlier, one major distinction between American democracy and Judaism is that the former assumes that the source of the law and its ultimate claim to authority are the people, while the latter declares it to be God. While that difference is real, one should not exaggerate it. After all, according to the Declaration of Independence, governments are instituted among men to secure rights given them by their Creator. Government in this theory is thus not only a pragmatic mechanism to take care of the practical needs of the society; it is rather an instrument to accomplish divine purpose. Conversely, while classical Judaism understands God to be the author of the law, the judges of each generation have both the right and the obligation to interpret and apply it — even to the extent of revising it outright. Over the centuries those judges have been guided significantly, and sometimes openly, by the needs and customs of the people.[17] Thus American law cannot be reduced to populism, and Jewish law cannot be reduced to authoritarianism. Both traditions involve both elements — albeit in significantly different degrees.

Underlying these similarities are some commonalities of vision between Judaism and American democracy. American individualism has always been accompanied by American idealism and pragmatism, and those elements are at the heart of Judaism as well.

American idealism appears in the very first documents of the nation. It is clearly not "self-evident" that all men are created equal; it is, in fact, patently false. Similarly, it is not the case that all human beings enjoy the "unalienable" rights of life, liberty, and the pursuit of happiness. Jefferson knew this, but he inserted these lines in the Declaration of Independence to articulate the ideals for which this new nation would strive. The Jewish people also have such statements, descriptions of a time in which there would be neither want nor war, in which all nations would learn of God's word from Jerusalem and follow it.

Although these statements in both traditions do not describe realities, they are not empty dreams, either, for both ideologies are marked by a heavy dose of pragmatism. That is part of the reason for the emphasis on law in both societies; law is understood as one instrument to achieve an ideal society. As Simon Greenberg has pointed out, the Declaration of Independence is to the Constitution very much as the Aggadah is to the Halakhah; in both cases the first element is the ideal which the second endeavors to articulate in real terms.[18]

But the law is only part of the story; Americans and Jews constitutionally take an aggressive attitude toward improving life. It is at least partly for this reason that, as Konvitz notes, Americans and Jews are the only nations on earth who feel it necessary to justify their existence as nations. Other nations simply exist, but these two live in pursuit of ideals by which they and others measure them.[19]

The combination of idealism and pragmatism that characterizes and unites Judaism and Americanism is ultimately rooted in a positive attitude toward the material in life, an attitude which assumes that physical conditions can and should be improved. The Declaration of Independence itself speaks most about the colonists' specific grievances against the king, including many economic concerns. Moreover, Jefferson altered Locke's formula, making "pursuit of happiness" a prime goal of the American social contract. Similarly, in Judaism, a person will have to give an account on the day of judgment of every good, permissible thing which he might have enjoyed and did not.[20] Thus, contrary to significant strands within Christianity and other cultures embracing a bifurcation between body and soul, Jewish and American ideology and practice have instead tried to infuse the physical with the ideal, seeing the physical as much as any other aspect of existence as the creation of God. This positive attitude toward the world lies at the bottom of the idealism and pragmatism which the two traditions share,[21] and those features, in turn, motivate both systems' emphasis on law.

Conservative Rabbinic Training for American Jews

Lay vs. Rabbinic Integrations of Judaism and Americanism

The similarities in philosophy between Judaism and American ideology, together with the practical benefits which Jews have enjoyed in America, make Jews feel a strong kinship to the United States. They commonly adopt American democratic theory and Judaism with little thought of their differing assumptions and goals. Many lay Jews understand religion just as Locke did, *i.e.*, as a source of piety and morality—and, for some, ethnic identity—but not of binding law.

Conservative rabbinical students, however, do not have that option. Although they often come from backgrounds and assumptions identical to those of most lay Jews, they soon learn that Conservative Judaism understands halakhah to be binding. They discover that in times past Jewish law was actually enforced in court, with penalties including fines, lashes, excommunication, and even capital punishment. That, of course, is no longer true in the American context, but rabbinical students must confront the fact that Jewish law still intends to obligate, whether the obligations are enforced or not.

Stages and Objects of the Conflict

The dissonance appears in two distinct arenas at two different stages of a rabbinical student's studies. It is first a matter of personal concern, and it then becomes a professional problem.

In the first year or two, most rabbinical students, especially those not accustomed to abiding by Jewish law, are primarily interested in finding a way to reconcile Judaism and Americanism in their own belief systems and patterns of life. How should they understand *themselves* as American Jews? Why should they take upon themselves the obligations of Jewish law in an American environment which values maximal freedom?

Later the issue shifts ground. In the last portion of rabbinical training, students face the prospect that the vast majority of laypeople whom they will be serving do not think of Jewish law as a binding regimen. Moreover, they come to realize that the laity's lack of observance is not only a function of ignorance, to be solved by more effective educational techniques; it is also, and perhaps fundamentally, a product of an ideological barrier to be overcome. Rabbis cannot simply teach people how to be observant; they must show them why — and in a context that militates against restricting oneself any more than necessary. As students think about their future congregants, the issue which was at first personal now becomes professional.

Strategies to Help Students Resolve the Personal Problem

In the last ten years or so, as more and more people have come to rabbinical school at least in part to find themselves as Jews, the rabbinical programs at the Jewish Theological Seminary of America and the University of Judaism have taken steps to help them do that. Candidates for admission generally follow the dictates of Jewish law, but often that is a new pattern of behavior which is not deeply rooted in their lives or thought. In most cases, entering rabbinical students speak about the personal meaningfulness of obeying the commandments but have little if any sense of being obligated by them. Their entrance essays are especially vague on the relationship between God and the commandments. Put simply, these students are almost all children of the Enlightenment more than of the Jewish tradition. Following Jewish law is what they now choose to do as individuals, not what they must do as Jews. For such people rabbinic education cannot rely on informal discussions alone to impart a sense of *commandment*; programs to do that must be consciously inserted into the rabbinical school experience.

That, of course, is not easy. It is not simply a matter of recognizing an intolerable gap in our graduates' fund of information or skills and filling it with another course or examination. It is rather a matter of communicating an entirely new mindset. To borrow an expression from another setting, that is something which is caught, not taught — at least not directly.

At first, our efforts were entirely on an extracurricular basis. These varied over the years, but I will describe some of them to give the reader an idea of how we tried to deal with this educational challenge. I will talk most of the rabbinical program at the University of Judaism, where a student may take the first two years of rabbinical school, since I have directed that program since 1971 and know it best.

Ranging from occasional Sunday evening sessions in the homes of faculty members in the early 1970s to weekly sessions over lunch at school later on, we first tried to address our students' concerns in extracurricular settings. Students were encouraged to question instructors about their personal patterns of observance, including not only what they observed, but how and why they decided to adhere to Jewish law in this specific way and why they were religiously Jewish in the first place. The agenda also included questions concerning relationships. How, for example, could rabbinical students from non-observant backgrounds maintain friendships with people who neither knew nor understood their new way of living? How should they relate to their parents? The questions revolved not only around ritual matters, like observing the dietary laws in such circumstances, but also more personal issues. For instance, how do they convince friends from earlier in their lives that, despite their decision to become rabbis, they are still real people, capable of enjoying movies, sports, parties, and, yes, even a dirty joke now and then? And how can they balance personal and professional relationships with their future congregants?

People define themselves and their convictions not only by analysis of their own traditions, but also by seeing how they compare to those of others. Partly for that reason and partly to learn how the majority population of the United States thinks and lives, since 1973 rabbinical students at the University of Judaism have taken part in the Interseminarians Conference, sponsored by the National Conference of Christians and Jews. From 2:00 P.M. Sunday until 2:00 P.M. Monday, Catholic, Protestant, and Jewish seminarians from throughout California meet together at a kosher camp in Malibu to discuss each other's beliefs, practices, and training and to witness each community's form of worship. The event has a powerful effect on students, for it demonstrates to them more clearly than anything else what it means to be a Jew, especially one bound by halakhah.

Students pressed for yet other ways to confront the issue: it clearly was a deep-seated conflict for them. They did not necessarily express their concern as the dissonance between liberty and authority; they often asked instead for more spiritual guidance. There are aspects of that quest which do not reduce to the issue of this essay, but there is great overlap; for when students search for the spiritual meaning of Judaism, they are generally trying to discover why *they personally* should abide by Jewish law and belief. "Spiritual meaning" as used in this context rarely denotes something communal; it is almost always individual and idiosyncratic, why *I* should be committed to Judaism. For most, this is not the quest of the kabbalist; it is rather American individualism and freedom asserting itself against Jewish authority and obligations in a new form.

To meet these needs, in 1983 we established the Beit Midrash program.[22] At first it met each school day for an hour in the late morning, but we have now cut it back to three sessions a week. Students are required to attend, but there are no assignments or examinations. One session each week is devoted to the colloquium, in which rabbis and others doing important things in Jewish life talk with the students about their work and their own personal reactions to it. The colloquium is also the format for discussing the Jewish and personal aspects of being rabbinical students and rabbis. The other days of the Beit Midrash are spent in *Torah lishma*, study for its own sake. The topics chosen each year are designed to speak to the students' spiritual needs. So, for example, this past year one session each week concerned the rationales and meanings for the commandments; another sought to elicit spiritual meaning from the weekly Torah reading; and another dealt with creating one's own system of beliefs. Next year we plan to include a meeting each week on the prayerbook. In each case, the goal is not to cover text or to impart a skill; it is rather to discover how to relate personally to aspects of the Jewish tradition.

In all of these efforts, we have effectively accepted the liberalism of the American environment as the given. Although we speak the language of commandment (*mitzvah*) and obligation (*ḥiyyuv*), the effort is unabashedly to convince students to integrate Jewish law into their lives on personal grounds. That is not only unorthodox; it is logically backwards. As the rabbis who spoke of the structure of the *Shema* recognized, first one must accept the yoke of the Kingdom of God and then the yoke of the commandments.[23] At the same time, there is a long history within Judaism, beginning with the Bible, of suggesting other rationales for obeying the commandments.[24] While these were generally assumed to be supplementary to the primary reason of obeying God's command, the very existence of other rationales demonstrates that our ancestors also sought to make Jewish law intelligible to themselves in personal and practical terms. Consequently, while the current appeal to the personal meaning of Jewish law is based on the assumption that in America it is ultimately optional to obey it, the hope is that, as rabbinical students integrate it into their convictions and lives, they will accept it in its own, legally obligatory terms. As the rabbis of the Talmud put it, "From doing the commandments for the wrong reason one may come to do them for the right reason."[25]

Toward that end in recent years we have given greater attention to this issue in formal classes as well. Some Talmud and codes professors at the University and the Seminary address issues of the philosophy of Jewish law in their class discussions and correlative readings but, as one might expect, the primary place where the issue is treated is in courses in philosophy. The curriculum in place since 1976 includes one course in which the grounds for the authority of Jewish law are discussed in the works of others and another course in which students must articulate and defend their own views. As a result, students increasingly have been aided in the classroom as well as in extracurricular activities in reconciling their American, libertarian backgrounds with the theological dimensions of the obligations of Jewish law.

Strategies to Help Students and Graduates Solve the Professional Problem

In their last years of rabbinical school, students face the fact that many of their future congregants do not abide by Jewish law. Since nobody has found a way to solve this problem in its entirety, rabbinical training does best by exposing students to both the practical and theoretical efforts which have worked to some degree in various settings. Aside from the steps taken to help students resolve the issue in their own minds and lives, Seminary training includes some time for an internship, in which a student sees how at least one rabbi helps congregants integrate their American and Jewish identities. Some of this is also treated in practical rabbinics courses.

This is clearly not enough, but rabbinical school probably cannot do more. The extent to which an individual rabbi will or will not prove effective in this area depends crucially upon the degree to which he or she can model a halakhic, yet modern, form of Judaism in his or her own life and influence others to do likewise. As long as rabbinical school helps students resolve their own conflicts between their Jewish and American identities and gives them some training as to how to motivate and help their congregants do the same, it has done about all that it can.

What *is* necessary is continued, in-service work on this issue. As rabbis find new ways to treat this problem in their work, they should share the fruits of their efforts with others. The Rabbinical Assembly through its publications and conferences, thus has an important educational role to play here on both the theoretical and practical planes.

And so do the Seminary and the University of Judaism. In their capacity as academic institutions, they can and should sponsor philosophical, sociological, and educational research on this topic. That will not only help rabbis with their congregants; it will also help with the training of rabbis in the first place. For all American Jews face this conflict.

Epilogue: From Conflict to Complement

Although the ideological conflicts between America's secular and religious ideologies will probably never be resolved with total philosophical adequacy, there are good reasons to believe that the mutually confirmatory aspects of the relationship between America and her primary religious groups will prevail. For one thing, the history of this country has demonstrated a close relationship in practice between national and religious principles. To a certain extent that is because the structure of religious freedom built into the American system of government affords both the government and America's religions independent identities so that they can continually criticize each other's weaknesses and fortify each other's strengths.

But part of the reason for the history of harmony between religion and the American government is that Americans from the time of the Founding Fathers have expected rapport. James Madison argued strongly for religious freedom precisely because it would strengthen both the state and religion.[26] George Washington thought that "reason and experience both forbid us to expect that national morality can prevail in exclusion of religious principle."[27] Whether they were right or not is immaterial; the fact is that American consciousness from the very beginning *thought* that religion and government should complement each other, and that went a long way toward guaranteeing that they would. It has been a self-fulfilling prophecy.

But perhaps the primary reason for the complementary relations between religion and state in this country is that religion touches on areas of life beyond the Constitutional mandate of government. As Simon Greenberg has put it, the goals set by the Declaration of Independence and the Preamble of the Constitution,

> . . . broad as they are, do not include all aspects of the individual's life. We are not merely citizens of a body politic. We are also children, parents, neighbors, members of identifiable, self-conscious, historically and often biologically determined ethnic, religious, and cultural groupings. In addition, we share with all human beings the well-nigh daily necessity of confronting tragedy, pain, distress; of living with the awareness of the awesome mysteries of life and death—with the psychologically almost unbearable fact that we know not whence we came and whither we are going.[28]

And if America needs its religions, religions need effective government: "Pray for the welfare of the government, for without the fear of it people would swallow each other alive."[29]

The mutual gains which religion and state afford each other, and the commonalities which they share, thus form a strong basis for an integrated American Jewish identity. American rabbinical students and other American Jews must work out the frictions in the American and Jewish viewpoints; but history, expectation, and the separation of functions of religion and government in this country all bode well for their success. American Jews can learn much from their Americanism and their Judaism independently and from their conflicting and complementary relations. American rabbinical students must therefore be taught how to integrate the American and Jewish parts of their identity so that they can help other American Jews, the largest group of Jews in the world, benefit fully from the unique gift that is America.

NOTES

1. *Mishneh Torah, Laws of Repentance* 3:4. Cf. *Rosh Hashanah* 17a.

2. *Shabbat* 54b. Along with Jeremiah (31:29-30) and Ezekiel (18:20-32), this offends our sense of justice, but that is only because we are so used to thinking in individualistic terms.

3. Milton R. Konvitz, *Judaism and the American Idea* (New York: Schocken Books, 1978, 1980), pp. 143, 150; and cf. Chap. 5 generally. Hillel's words are in *Sukkah* 53a.

4. Cf. *Tosefta, Avodah Zarah* 8:4; *Sanhedrin* 56a; *Seder Olam*, ch. 5; *Gen. R.* 16:6, 34:8; *Canticles R.* 1:16; *Mishneh Torah, Laws of Kings* 9:1. For a thorough description and discussion of this doctrine, cf. David Novak, *The Image of the Non-Jew in Judaism* (New York: Edwin Mellen Press, 1983).

5. Numbers 15:15-16; cf. Exodus 12:49; 22:20; Leviticus 24:22; Numbers 9:14; 15:29; Deuteronomy 24:14-15; etc. A stranger had recourse to Israelite courts: Exodus 22:21; 23:9; Deuteronomy 24:17; 27:19. One must even "love" the stranger and treat him as a citizen; Leviticus 19:33-34; cf. Deuteronomy 10:18.

6. *Gittin* 5:8-9; *Mekhilta Pisha*, 15; *Gittin* 61a; *Bava Metzia* 70b; *Bava Batra* 113a; Maimonides, *Commentary to the Mishnah, Kelim* 12:7; *Mishneh Torah, Laws of Sale* 18:1. Cf. "Gentile," *Jewish Encyclopedia*, 5:615-626; "Gentile," *Encyclopaedia Judaica* 7:410-414.

7. On not missionizing: *Yevamot* 47a-47b; P.T. *Kiddushin* 4:1 (65b); *Mishneh Torah, Laws of Forbidden Intercourse* 13:14-14:5; *Shulhan Arukh, Yoreh De'ah* 268:2. Cf. "Proselytes," *Encyclopedia Judaica* 13:1182-1194. An example to other nations: Isaiah 2:2-4; 11:10; 42:1-4; 49:6; *Gen. R.* 43:7; *Lev. R.* 6:5; etc.

8. *Tosefta, Sanhedrin* 13:2; *Bava Batra* 10b; *Mishneh Torah, Laws of Repentance* 3:5. According to Samuel, on the Day of Judgment there is no distinction between Jew and gentile; P.T. *Rosh Hashanah* 1:3 (57a).

9. *E.g.*, Deuteronomy 24:10-22; cf. also Exodus 22:21-26; 23:6; Leviticus 25:25-55; Deuteronomy 15:7-11. Biblical law condoned slavery to pay debts, but it restricted the length and conditions of servitude; cf. Exodus 21:2-11, 20-21, 26-27; Deuteronomy 15:12-18; 23:16-17. For one poignant example of Jewish provision for the poor in the Middle Ages, cf. S. D. Goitein, *A Mediterranean Society: The Jewish Communities of the Arab World as Portrayed in the Documents of the Cairo Geniza* (Berkeley: University of California

Press, 1971), Vol. II, pp. 139-142; cf. also p. 128. Cf. also my paper, "Jewish Perspectives on the Poor" (New York: American Jewish Committee, 1986) for a general treatment of the topic.

10. Leviticus 19:14. Cf. Carl Astor, *Who Makes People Different* (New York: United Synagogue Youth, 1985).

11. Cf., for example, Aaron Kirschenbaum, *Self-Incrimination in Jewish Law* (New York: Burning Bush Press, 1970); Norman Lamm, *Faith and Doubt* (New York: Ktav, 1971), chaps. 10, 11; Milton R. Konvitz, ed., *Judaism and Human Rights* (New York: W. W. Norton, 1972).

12. *Eruvin* 13b. But cf. its correlative in *Sotah* 47b.

13. Milton R. Konvitz has emphasized this point; cf. his *Judaism and the American Idea*, Ch. 1, esp. pp. 33-41.

14. Deuteronomy 17:18-20; II Samuel 11-12; I Kings 21. Cf. also the talmudic story of the confrontation between Simeon ben Shetah and King Alexander Yannai; *Sanhedrin* 19a-19b.

15. *Avot (Ethics of the Fathers)* 4:10.

16. Konvitz, *Judaism and the American Idea*, pp. 53-55; the quotation is from p. 55.

17. For rabbinic sources and further discussion on these points, cf. my article, "Judaism as a Religious Legal System," *Hastings Law Journal*, 29:6 (July 1978), pp. 1331-1360; and my *Conservative Judaism: Our Ancestors to Our Descendants* (New York: United Synagogue Youth, 1977), Ch. 3, Section C.

18. Simon Greenberg, *The Ethical in the Jewish and American Heritage* (New York: Jewish Theological Seminary of America, 1977), pp. 223-224, and chap. 4 generally. Cf. also *ibid.*, p. 99 and chap. 2 generally, in which he shows how the Declaration came to be interpreted as the goal for American history and law against which individual acts and laws could be appropriately judged.

19. Cf. Konvitz, *Judaism and the American Idea*, pp. 15-18, 50-51.

20. P.T. *Kiddushin* 4:12 (66d). Cf. also Rabbi Isaac's sarcastic question, "Are not the things prohibited in the Torah enough for you that you want to prohibit yourself other things?" in P.T. *Nedarim* 9:1 (41b). Voluntary asceticism was actually classified as a sin; cf. *Nedarim* 10a; *Nazir* 3a, 19a, 22a; *Bava Kama* 91a; *Ta'anit* 11a; etc. Cf. also *Mishneh Torah, Laws of Attitudes (De'ot)* 3:1.

21. Cf. Konvitz, *Judaism and the American Idea*, pp. 21; 31; and Chap. 7.

22. The Beit Midrash program was primarily the creation of Rabbi Robert Wexler.

23. *Berakhot* 2:2. Maimonides is especially clear about this logical progression, placing belief in God as the first of "The Laws of the Fundamental Principles of the Torah," to be followed by all of the other provisions of his code.

24. Cf. Yitzhak Heinemann, *Ta'amei Hamitzvot B'sifrut Yisrael (Rationales for the Commandments in the Literature of Israel)* (Jerusalem: Jewish Agency, 1942, 1966), 2 vols. (Hebrew).

25. *Pesaḥim* 50b.

26. Cf., for example, "A Memorial and Remonstrance (1785)," *The Papers of James Madison,* William T. Hutchinson and William M. E. Rachal, eds. (Chicago: University of Chicago Press, 1973) 8:298–304.

27. Washington's Farewell Address, quoted in Simon Greenberg, *The Ethical in the Jewish and American Heritage,* p. 154.

28. *Ibid.,* pp. 154–155.

29. *Avot (Ethics of the Fathers)* 3:2.

Authority and Autonomy in Rabbinic Education Today

Arthur Green

The issue of authority and autonomy in Jewish life lies right at the heart of Judaism's problematical relationship with life in the democratic and "open" society of the contemporary West. It is also the issue that creates essential divergence between the various Jewish religious groups, a divergence that now threatens the ultimate unity of the Jewish people. For both reasons, no issue is more crucial to the Jewish future.

Classical rabbinic Judaism is a tradition of authority. The essential task of the Jew is to live in accord with the will of God, a will revealed in the Torah but made clear in all its myriad detail only by the teachings of the rabbis. The rabbis, or the rabbinic court, as interpreters of the divine law, have the right to punish anyone who violates the law, contravenes their decisions, or questions their right to legislate in God's name. This is not to forget, of course, that rabbinic jurisprudence was often guided by legislative principles (and legal scholars) marked by exceptional humanity and sensitivity, nor is it to ignore the fact that through most of Jewish history in Diaspora, rabbinic courts had but partial control over Jewish lives and were usually the much preferred alternative to the "justice" of Europe's kings and princes. But the intent of rabbinic Judaism as a legal system, with all its goodness and all its limitations, was to achieve the absolute hegemony of the law, as taught and administered by the rabbis, over the lives of all Jews.

The Reconstructionist view of authority and autonomy in Judaism today begins with the realization that we live in a *post-revolutionary* situation. The Jewish people, with the exception of its Orthodox minority, has over the past hundred years clearly and unequivocally rejected the authority of rabbinic law. This was no less the case for our largely non-ideological forebears who came to America than it was for their cousins who settled in Eretz Israel and created that radically new version of Jewish identity known as Zionism. Whether opting for assimilation and economic success in capitalist America, socialist activism among laborers in Warsaw, or Zionist pioneering among the early Eretz Israel settlers, Jews leaving the shtetl in the early part of this century had in common a rejection of the old way of life of the Jewish people, including the authority of rabbi and law.

As Reconstructionists we believe that this was both an inevitable and essentially healthy rebellion, and we would have no desire to turn back the clock. The authoritarian/corporate structure of traditional Jewish society stood too much in contrast to the values of individual liberty, universalism, and scientific progressivism for it to withstand the pressures of life in an increasingly open society. Living where and when they did, most thinking Jews of the late nineteenth and early twentieth centuries necessarily saw the authority of tradition as an outmoded impediment to progress, and the rabbinate as a bastion of reaction.

Liberal Jewry today stands on the other side of that great revolutionary divide. Much has changed since the heyday of rebellion, but the essential new facts created by it have not. Most of Jewry still stands outside the law's authority and shows little desire to go back to it. This holds for the relatively "good" tradition-loving family in the Conservative synagogue as well as for the left-wing Reformer. True, we have learned to think of Jewry again in corporate terms, and many of the dreams that led Jews away from the community have been consumed in the fires of Auschwitz or Hiroshima. Assimilation to the point of disappearance has become as disreputable among Jews in the wake of the Holocaust as anti-Semitism has become among Christians (though both, of course, continue to exist!). The new faith so many Jews shared in the coming universal nationhood of all humanity to be brought about by the "liberating" truth of science is by now mostly a relic. Many have in fact returned to the Jewish community and are again willing, thanks largely to the influence of Israel, to view Jewry as a single body. But the vital core of Jewish corporate existence, as Ahad Ha-Am and Kaplan knew so well, is Jewish *peoplehood,* not Jewish law. Jews continue to live as a creative national entity with a language, culture, and land of our own. The essential character of this culture is, to be sure, religious; in this lies our national distinctiveness. The circumstances of Jewish life in America also dictate that here the religious will play a dominant role in our survival as a people, while elsewhere this may be less the case. But the future of this religion will be determined by the Jewish people as a whole, not by rabbinic authority. It is all of us together, rabbinic and "lay" (a term terribly alien to our tradition), educated and ignorant, committed and indifferent who, consciously or not, are daily shaping the Jewish future.

This does not mean, however, that anything Jews decide to do can be called Judaism. We are part of an evolutionary process, though one drastically speeded up by the fast pace and resulting impatience of contemporary living. Evolution means that the past is always present in determining the course of the future, the emergent new forms of the future embodying the past within them. As we enter a new age in Jewish history, we need to re-commit ourselves to that process. If there is to be real historic continuity with the Jewish past, which is to say that if Israelis are to be more than Hebrew-speaking goyim or American Jews are to be more than WASPs with bar mitzvahs, the Jewish people needs to engage collectively in intelligent self-examination. This involves serious study of the Jewish past, including both the tradition and the Jewish historical experience, and honest dialogue about the meaning of that legacy and its place in determining our future.

Such is the role of rabbis in our time. A rabbi is a Jew who has devoted his/her life to the study of Judaism and who serves as a cultural resource to the Jewish community, an ambassador, if you will, from the tradition to the Jewish people. The rabbi's task is to *present* the tradition in all its richness, to *interpret* it so that it is meaningful and spiritually compelling to contemporary Jews, and to work *with* a community, as its leader and most fully committed member, toward the creation of a Jewish lifestyle that calls forth the best in that community. By personal example he/she should set standards of Jewish intensity that always stand as a challenge to others; such challenges may be in the realm of piety, of learning, or of activism, depending on the particular rabbi and community. A rabbi should also work to lead a community toward *normative* behavior — toward setting standards for itself and making demands on its members. This is the most difficult task in our entirely voluntaristic Jewish community, whose leaders are often too afraid that people will be turned away if serious demands are made on them. For at least a significant minority of Jews, the opposite is true: they long for demands, for a sense that Judaism makes a real claim on their lives, for the richness that comes only of discipline.

It is when they see that we are too weak or fearful to make such demands that some of these turn to Orthodoxy, even if they continue to disbelieve in its intellectual foundations.

Yes, the rabbi must be trained to be a leader, but a leader who works from *within* the community. The real decisions will be made by *klal Yisrael*, hopefully with good rabbinic guidance, not by the rabbis themselves. Of course any rabbi worth his/her salt/pepper must have *personal* standards of behavior and lines that he/she will not cross. This is part of education by example. But we must never delude ourselves into thinking that any battles have been won or issues resolved because the community has *allowed* the rabbi to maintain a certain standard. Jews love to use vicariousness as a way out of their own commitments, and we should be wary of that unhealthy trap. The real job is that of educating, cajoling, persuading the community itself to become more deeply Jewish in whatever ways will be appropriate to it.

The generations that rebelled against the authority of halakhah rejected also the language of religious faith and the sense that Judaism had anything important to say about questions of ultimate meaning. This was especially true for East European Jews, for whom religion seemingly had to stand or fall in its entirety. The spiritual climate of more recent times is one of much greater openness to religion in its ultimately spiritual sense; there is a hunger in contemporary life, not only in America, for inwardness and for a sense of the divine. On the social plane too, such diverse experiences as those of black America, Poland, South Africa, and the current anti-nuclear movement have shown that religion can stand at the forefront of positive societal change. Both of these changes create tremendous opportunities for us as Jews, and our rabbinic leadership must become a part of them. *Only a rabbi who has a rich spiritual life of his/her own will be able to serve as a facilitator for others.* Such things are not given to mere professionalism. But the rabbi who is not attuned to the great spiritual hunger of our day will not, in this area, succeed. Similarly, only a *personal* commitment to Israel, to racial equality, to Soviet Jewry, world peace, or any other cause will work to persuade others. A rabbi who cannot exhibit such commitment will make a sorry showing.

Our authority is gone. All we have left to give is ourselves; all we have left to teach with is the example of our own lives. But — come to think of it — isn't that all we ever had?

The Next Generation of Conservative Rabbis: An Empirical Study of Today's Rabbinical Students*

Aryeh Davidson and Jack Wertheimer

While the controversy over the ordination of women as rabbis has generated much publicity during the past decade, other far-reaching changes in the Rabbinical School of the Jewish Theological Seminary of America have gone virtually unnoticed outside of the institution. These include a significant revision of the school's curriculum; changes in policies that define which faculty members may teach rabbinical students; the hiring of approximately two dozen new, and mainly young, faculty members; and most important of all, the admission of rabbinical students whose characteristics differ considerably from those of their predecessors.

This essay addresses the last of these recent developments by analyzing the present cohort of rabbinical students at the Seminary. Who are today's rabbinical students? What is their familial and educational background? What motivates them to aspire to become rabbis? What types of rabbinic work do they wish to undertake? And what is their outlook as Conservative Jews?

In order to answer such questions, the authors of this essay conducted an exploratory survey in the fall of 1985 when all matriculants in the Seminary's Rabbinical School and its affiliated programs at the University of Judaism in Los Angeles and Neve Schechter in

---

*The authors acknowledge with appreciation financial support received from the Maxwell Abbell Research Fund of the Jewish Theological Seminary of America which defrayed the costs of research expenses. We benefited from the cooperation of the Seminary's Provost, Raymond Scheindlin, and Dean of the Rabbinical School, Gordon Tucker, as well as from our discussions with Professors Paul Ritterband and Nathalie Friedman.

Jerusalem were asked to complete a questionnaire anonymously. Over seventy-five percent of this population (110 out of 143 students) responded. The questionnaire asked students about their personal backgrounds, perceptions of the rabbinic role, occupational preferences within the rabbinate, personal religious standards and practices, and assessments of the current curriculum. While the data we collected are sufficient to present a descriptive portrait of today's rabbinical students, we have been particularly interested in identifying changes over time, and accordingly have tried to place our findings into an historical framework. Fortunately, a few studies were conducted in the past—two by Arthur Hertzberg in 1943 and 1955, and one by Charles Liebman in 1967 as part of his larger inquiry into the training of American rabbis.[1] Whenever possible, we will compare our findings concerning the present cohort of rabbinical students with the results of these three earlier surveys. When such comparisons are not feasible due to a dearth of data, we will limit ourselves to a description of current students.

The Current Student Body

Familial Characteristics

In the fall of 1985, 143 students were enrolled in the Rabbinical School, of which 26 were women. The vast majority of students were born and raised in the United States, mainly on the East Coast (51%), while smaller numbers came from West Coast and midwestern states (20% from each area), thereby reflecting fairly accurately the geographic distribution of American Jewry.[2] The students ranged in age from a few who were in their early twenties to one who was sixty-one years of age. Approximately half, however, were in their early thirties, and therefore as a group current students are somewhat older than their predecessors (Liebman, pp. 11-12). Unlike earlier populations, many present-day students do not begin rabbinical studies immediately upon completing their undergraduate education. Furthermore, the Seminary is now attracting a small number of rabbinical students who either have worked in other careers and are now retraining for the rabbinate, or are women who could not study for the Conservative rabbinate prior to 1983.

The presence of women and older students provides visible evidence of changes in the population of the Rabbinical School. Contemporary students also differ in less overt, but far more significant ways from their predecessors. To begin with, their familial backgrounds are different. Three-quarters of all rabbinical students today are the children of American-born parents. (Let us note that this figure would be even higher were it not for the fact that the Seminary trains Latin American and other foreign students who will eventually serve as rabbis in their homelands.) By contrast, in 1943 barely 7% and in 1955 only 20% of rabbinical students reported that both their parents were born in the United States (Hertzberg, p. 312). And even as recently as 1967, only 55% of students were the sons of American-born fathers (Liebman, p. 12). Clearly, then, the Conservative rabbinate is no longer drawing most of its members from the children of immigrants, as had been the case from the founding of the Seminary until mid-century. Instead, rabbinical students of the present generation are the grandchildren of immigrants: all students surveyed had at least one set of foreign-born grandparents.[3] While this shift is not surprising given that the mass migration of Jews from Eastern Europe to the United States came to an end over sixty years ago, it highlights the distance between today's students and their immigrant forebears, ancestors who had a direct personal exposure to the traditional Jewish societies of the Old World.

A second shift in familial background concerns the occupations of the fathers of rabbinical students.[4] Continuing a trend that mirrors patterns in the Jewish community at large, there has been a steady rise in the number of students whose fathers are professionals, from 34% in the 1940s to 85% today (Hertzberg, p. 318). Significantly, there has been a corresponding decline in the number of fathers employed as professionals serving the Jewish community. In 1943 over one-third of all students were the sons of rabbis or Jewish educators, and as recently as 1967, close to one-fifth of students came from homes where the father was a Jewish professional (Hertzberg, p. 318; Liebman, p. 12). Today, only 7% of parents (fathers and mothers) are Jewish professionals. At the present time, it is impossible to assess the consequences of this shift. But we note that the children of Conservative rabbis and other professionals working in the Jewish community are not following in the career paths of their parents. An examination of rabbinic families in other denominations, and indeed of American clergy in general, may reveal that this lack of generational continuity is the norm. Our data suggest, however, that the tradition of service to the Jewish community that characterized many rabbinic families in the past is disappearing in the Conservative movement.

The most important changes in the familial backgrounds of rabbinical students pertain to the denominational affiliations of their parents. To understand this shift, let us begin with the broader pattern that has been developing during the past three decades. Prior to the middle of the century, the Seminary had recruited students who for the most part grew up in Orthodox homes. Writing in the mid-fifties, Arthur Hertzberg demonstrated that this pattern was changing; he noted that "the Conservative movement, which was in 1943 largely dependent upon the Orthodox group for its rabbinic candidates, is at present producing almost half its own rabbis" (p. 311). By the mid-sixties, Liebman reported that "most fathers of JTS students were affiliated with Conservative (69%), some with Orthodox (19%), and none with Reform synagogues" (p. 13). Today, two-thirds of all rabbinical students still come from Conservative homes. What has changed is that virtually none (merely 3%) come from Orthodox families, while 19% grew up in Reform and 12% in unaffiliated homes. (The latter category includes some rabbinical students who have converted to Judaism, and therefore listed their families as unaffiliated.)

Educational Backgrounds

The formal education of Seminary students prior to their enrolling in the Rabbinical School also differs markedly from the educational backgrounds of earlier cohorts. Although 92% of current students received a Jewish education on the elementary school level, only a small minority attended day schools. (Again, we must note the presence in this population of some converts to Judaism who, of course, as children did not have a Jewish education.) In contrast to the 41% of students in 1967 who had received most of their childhood education in day schools, only 22% of current students did so (Liebman, p. 15). This decline is even more noteworthy when we observe that the Conservative movement's Solomon Schechter Day Schools were proliferating at precisely the time when these students were of school age—and yet only a small fraction attended these or any other day schools. Instead, the majority of current students attended Hebrew Schools under Conservative auspices. Interestingly, close to half of the current student body rated their elementary level Jewish education as only "somewhat effective" or "ineffective." And when asked which institution had the greatest positive influence on their Jewishness during their childhood years, only 22% cited their Jewish school, as compared to youth groups, summer camps, and synagogue programs. Thus, the quality of Jewish education experienced by current students at the elementary level was neither very intensive nor perceived as particularly effective. For the most part, rabbinical students did not receive a better Jewish education during their high school years: in fact, 35% of all current students received *no formal Jewish education* during their high school years; and only 8% attended day schools on the secondary level.[5]

For the vast majority of rabbinical students, the most important experience of Jewish education came during their college years rather than earlier. The overwhelming majority (83%) engaged in Jewish study at the college level, particularly in Jewish Studies programs. Here we have hard evidence of the much vaunted, but rarely demonstrated, contribution of Judaic studies programs at colleges to the strengthening of Jewish identity in students. Almost one-third of current rabbinical students majored in Jewish Studies, and another 30% took at least several courses. When we add to this group the population of students who studied formally in Israel and in other programs outside of their colleges, we have clear evidence of the critical importance of the college years as a time of decision-making and education leading to the rabbinic vocation. That the college years are crucial in identity formation is a commonly observed phenomenon, but our data suggest that the availability of courses and programs of Jewish study on campuses enables Jewish students to pursue their new-found interests. (We have no information as to whether these courses sparked such interest or simply attracted students who were searching for information on Jewish life.) Not surprisingly, most rabbinical students decided only during their college years to become rabbis.

In noting changes in the educational backgrounds of rabbinical students, we must draw attention to shifts in their experiences of informal Jewish education, as well. Whereas in 1967 over two-thirds of rabbinical students reported that they had been members of United Synagogue Youth or its Leadership Training Fellowship, only 36% of current students had been members of USY (Liebman, pp. 16–17). An even smaller percentage attended Ramah Camps—barely a quarter of all who attended any Jewish camp and under 15% of all current rabbinical students. Thus, the most important institutions for informal Jewish education of the Conservative movement—Ramah camps and the United Synagogue Youth—no longer serve as significant feeders for the Rabbinical School. It appears that the institutions of the Conservative movement are shaping the outlook of future Conservative rabbis far less than they did in the past.

Career Choices and Expectations

In order to gain a more rounded picture of the current student body of the Rabbinical School, our questionnaire posed a series of attitudinal questions concerning career choices and expectations. Unfortunately, there is virtually no information from earlier studies that would enable us to place the attitudes of current students into a comparative framework. Moreover, since our own survey represents only an exploratory stage of research that we hope to build upon with subsequent questionnaires, we cannot yet provide longitudinal data on this cohort of students as it makes its way through the Rabbinical School and into the field. Given these limitations, we will confine our remarks in this section to a brief description of students' attitudes and pose a number of questions that arise from our findings.

In assessing the present generation of rabbinical students, it is critical to understand how these students perceive the rabbinic vocation. What do they regard as the most important aspect of rabbinic work? What, in their opinion, does a rabbi need to do? To elicit information on these issues our questionnaire asked students to rate the relative importance of seventeen different skills and activities commonly associated with the rabbinic profession. Students rated as "extremely important" skills that related to teaching (86%) and counseling (77%). They also emphasized the importance of serving as a model of spirituality (66%), living as an halakhic Jew (50%) and a religious person (67%), speaking comfortably in public (53%), and demonstrating concern for the social issues of the time (50%). In contrast, a large proportion of students viewed the following items as moderately important: administrative skills (49%), actively supporting the local Federation (46%), promoting the study of Hebrew (45%), promoting improved relations between Jews and non-Jews (48%), understanding other religions (46%), and promoting Zionism (44%). Support for the policies of the Israeli government was viewed as unimportant by 45% of respondents. While women tended to view the understanding of other religions as more important to the rabbinic profession than men, there were no major differences in outlook between men and women, or junior and senior students concerning the most important activities of rabbis.

To understand the statistical relationships between the various items concerned with the role of the rabbi, a factor analysis was conducted. Our analysis revealed three underlying constructs: the role of the rabbi was perceived as that of 1) a religious and public leader; 2) educator and counselor; and 3) *talmid ḥakham*. From a statistical standpoint, the first role has the greatest explanatory power. It describes a leader concerned with communal issues, relations between Jews and gentiles, the welfare of Israel, and the rabbi's public persona as leader and model of spirituality and religiosity. Of minor importance to this role is the mastery of Jewish texts and living as an halakhic person. The second role stresses the importance of the rabbi as counselor and educator, who is not particularly concerned with halakhic or spiritual issues. And the third role type perceived by students is concerned with study, spirituality, and Jewish law.

While these types are by no means mutually exclusive, they suggest that rabbinical students today are not monolithic in their approach to the rabbinic vocation. (It is doubtful that any cohort of rabbinical students at the Seminary ever was.) Given this clear evidence of heterogeneity within the student body and the perception of students that there are distinct role types, can rabbinic training at the Seminary better guide students to meet their individual career expectations? Could such guidance in rabbinical school help slow the rate of attrition in the Conservative rabbinate? Students who are most attracted to the *talmid ḥakham* model, for example, could be steered already in rabbinical school toward a career as educators or academicians. Alternatively, students most attracted to the counseling model could be steered to rabbinic work where such skills are most appropriate—for example, Hillel work and positions in helping agencies. While this might necessitate a track system (about which more below), it also would require an effort to aid students to become aware of their career expectations and to match those expectations with actual positions. The result might well be a more effective rabbinate.

Our questionnaire also asked students to identify the people and experiences that influenced their decision to enter rabbinical school. Over eighty percent of respondents cited the role of influential individuals, including family members, professionals in the Jewish community, professors of Judaica, and friends. While a few students cited their own synagogue rabbis, a far larger group were inspired by charismatic Jewish personalities whom they encountered outside of their synagogues. These individuals range across the Jewish ideological spectrum, but share the ability to project spirituality. Among the individuals mentioned were: Rabbis Ben Zion Gold, Arthur Green, Max Ticktin, on one end of the spectrum; and Rabbis Brovender and Dovid Din, the Rebbetzin Jungreis, and local Lubavitch representatives, on the other. It is noteworthy that after exposure to these charismatic and spiritual types of individuals, students nonetheless enroll at the Seminary, which offers a more rationalistic approach to the study of Judaism. The impact of such individuals, none of whom is positioned at the center of the Conservative movement, suggests the need to reevaluate the ability of programs within the movement to inspire and excite young people. Put differently, does the movement's emphasis on the critical study of Judaism, and its discomfort with charismatics attract young people to Conservative Judaism and rabbinic work, or do we only preach to those who have been "converted" by others?

Unquestionably, the common experience shared by the highest percentage of rabbinical students (49%) was study in Israel. Two-fifths of all rabbinical student studied in Israel for at least a semester, and in some cases for up to two years *prior* to enrolling in the rabbinical school. Although only half of these rabbinical students viewed their experience in Israel as crucial in their decision to prepare for the rabbinate, there is reason to think that such programs may decisively influence an even greater number of students given the large numbers who were educated in Israel. Until the Six Day War, study in Israel was relatively uncommon for rabbinical students. (Liebman never even raised the question in his essay of 1968.) In our own time, study in Israel is as noticeable a factor in the educational backgrounds of rabbinical students as day school attendance was in past decades. It appears that Israeli study programs are now the decisive training ground for many future Conservative rabbis that day schools were twenty years ago.

Finally, we turn to the personal career goals of current students. Respondents were asked to rate fifteen different occupations most often associated with the rabbinate. The vast majority (87%) of students are most interested in becoming pulpit rabbis, and are considerably less interested in serving as administrators in Jewish institutions, educators, or chaplains. Women students were more interested than men in pursuing careers as rabbis of small congregations

(300 families and less), as well as directors of Hillel programs. Whether these preferences reflect the true aspirations of women or their assessments of what positions will realistically be open to them is not clear. It appears that the type of Jewish education students received affects their career goals: students with little formal Jewish education were not attracted to the field of Jewish education, whereas graduates of day schools considered becoming principals of such schools. Significantly, close to fifteen percent of current students are either highly or moderately interested in careers unrelated to their rabbinical training.[6]

These findings, though hardly surprising, raise a series of questions that deserve further exploration: Since the career goals of men and women differ, will certain fields of rabbinic work become associated with women and others with men? Will women, who in our survey indicate a greater preference for positions that involve more interpersonal work, eventually select jobs that entail such activities? And if not, will they adjust their career goals and experience frustration? And more broadly, does the diversity of career goals among rabbinical students suggest that the rabbinic career will undergo increased specialization? In other fields, such as law, medicine, and business, professional schools have provided students with tracks to prepare for specialties. Has the time come for rabbinic education to plan for specialization, as well? Is it advisable to educate the rabbi as a *kol bo* (generalist) or to train students for specific rabbinic roles?

Implications

For the Rabbinical School

Having examined some of our most important findings about current rabbinical students, we conclude this essay with a discussion of some implications arising from our study. We begin by rejecting one possible inference that might be drawn from our discussion of shifts in the demographic, familial, and educational backgrounds of students — namely that today's students are less able than those of the past. In pointing to the differences between contemporary students and their predecessors, it has not been our intention to bemoan decline, but to identify change. There is no evidence that current students are any less gifted, open to education, or committed to serving the Jewish community than their predecessors. On the contrary, the Rabbinical School continues to admit students only selectively, and is recruiting candidates from the finest private and state universities in the country.

Furthermore, there is no reason to assume that the less intense preparation in Judaica of current students necessarily predicts a lack of religious observance and greater latitude regarding halakhah. While much more research needs to be done on the religious observances of students, we have some information on their religious outlook that derives from a dozen questions posed regarding Conservative standards and practices. Seventy-one percent of students responded negatively when asked whether they "would drive to the synagogue on Shabbat"; and approximately forty percent oppose either strongly or moderately permitting congregants to drive to the synagogue on Shabbat, despite the Rabbinical Assembly's ruling permitting this practice. Similarly, three-quarters of respondents opposed abolishing the second day of Yom Tov. Ninety-five percent opposed permitting rabbis to officiate at intermarriages. And only seven percent approved "accepting as Jewish someone whose father, but not mother, is Jewish." By contrast, over ninety percent approved the ordination of women as rabbis and close to sixty percent approve the acceptance of women as witnesses for religious ceremonies. What seems to emerge from these responses is a pattern of traditionalism in areas of religious ritual combined with strong support for change when it comes to the traditional status of women. It will be important to monitor the changing religious practices and attitudes of students as they progress through rabbinical school and enter the field. But at the present time students show evidence of fidelity to halakhah and traditional observances.

Our findings, however, do confirm the perceptions of many faculty members and other observers of the Seminary who have noted that today's students differ from those of twenty years ago, let alone from those of forty years ago, in the intensity of their prior Judaic preparation. Many students enter the Rabbinical School with only an elementary knowledge of Hebrew, relatively little exposure to rabbinic texts, and a limited knowledge of practical halakhah. Yet the curriculum, with all the changes of recent years, still focuses mainly on providing students with the tools to master rabbinic texts, and thereby assumes that students are fluent in Hebrew and knowledgeable about Jewish practices and skills. If the goals of the curriculum are to remain the same, many students will require considerable work in basic Jewish skills and knowledge prior to matriculating in the Rabbinical School. Like medical students who must obtain a solid background in biology and chemistry before entering medical school, rabbinical students will have to demonstrate their acquisition of linguistic and textual skills before embarking on rabbinical-studies. This would, of course, lengthen the number of years of post-graduate study from 5-6 years to perhaps 6-7 years, thereby raising the financial and psychic costs of rabbinic education, and encouraging some potential students to enroll in other, less demanding, rabbinical schools.

An alternative to requiring incoming students to demonstrate a minimum of Judaic learning is to reconsider the goals of the Rabbinical School's curriculum. Is it still desirable to focus rabbinic education mainly on the mastery of classical texts? And if so, should the curriculum permit students to focus on one type of text by permitting them to major in Bible, or Talmud, or Codes, or modern Hebrew literature? The advantage of introducing a major requirement is that students would develop a sense of mastery in at least one area of Jewish learning, whereas today's students with their smattering of knowledge in all fields are not entirely at home in any field. The disadvantage is that students will leave rabbinical school with only a passing familiarity with several areas of classical Jewish learning. Let us note that these proposals are not necessarily mutually exclusive: with some fine tuning, the curriculum could still focus on the breadth of Judaic knowledge while permitting specialization.

For the Movement

The differences between current and earlier cohorts of students recruited by the Rabbinical School raise important questions for the Conservative movement as a whole. It is noteworthy that three-quarters of current students grew up in Conservative families, yet only small numbers participated in the youth and camping programs sponsored by the movement. Significantly, the Conservative movement also eliminated two important programs that had originally been designed to recruit future leaders — the United Synagogue's Leaders Training Fellowship (disbanded in 1971) and Ramah's Mador (terminated in 1980). To solve the long-term recruitment needs of the Rabbinical School, the Conservative movement will have to rethink how it develops its future leaders. Presently, most rabbinical students are not nurtured by the movement's institutions.

Shifts in the student body of the Rabbinical School also raise questions regarding recruitment to the Conservative movement at large. It is clear from our data that the Conservative rabbinate no longer holds any attraction for children of Orthodox Jews. We must ask whether this holds true among the laity as well. Will Conservative synagogues attract young Jews from Orthodox homes as they did in the past? Or will the bulk of lay people attracted from outside of the movement come from Reform and non-affiliated families, as is the case with rabbinical students? For much of this century, the Conservative movement has gained most of its adherents from among the dissatisfied children of Orthodox Jews; perhaps the time has come to recognize that Orthodoxy today is retaining the allegiance of its young, but the Reform movement is not as successful. As the Reform movement embarks on an aggressive campaign to attract intermarried couples and others on the periphery of Jewish life, perhaps the Conservative movement ought to appeal to more traditional members of the Reform laity, just as the Seminary is attracting rabbinical students from this population. Such a campaign would require the leaders of the Conservative movement to sharpen the distinctions between themselves and leaders of the Reform movement, distinctions that often have been blurred in the effort to form political alliances with Reform rabbis.[7]

Finally, we must explore the consequences of shifts in the student body of the rabbinical school for relations between the Seminary and the movement. Much has been written by partisans of the movement, as well as academic observers such as Marshall Sklare and Charles Liebman, on the gap separating the ideology and observances of the elite from the Judaism of the laity. As the percentage of rabbis raised in the movement continues to climb, will that gap narrow? Or are current students as likely as their predecessors to be lonely champions of halakhah and Conservative ideology?

By raising a series of questions that cannot be answered on the basis of our present knowledge, it has been our purpose to highlight how much research remains to be done. It is ironic that the Conservative movement, which takes justifiable pride in its commitment to history and scientific research, has expended so little energy to document its own history and examine its present condition. In the field of social scientific inquiry, for example, far more surveys were conducted between 1930 and 1955, than in the past quarter-century.[8] Ongoing research is necessary to preserve the historical record of the movement, as well as to plan coherently for the future. In the case of the Rabbinical School, we need to study the impact of rabbinic education as students make their way through the Seminary; then we must trace the experiences of rabbis in the field in order to evaluate the effectiveness of rabbinic education and to identify the factors leading to personal growth in the rabbinate, as well as burn-out. As the Jewish Theological Seminary begins its second century of training rabbis, a great deal needs to be learned about the students it is recruiting and how it can best prepare them to serve the American Jewish community.

NOTES

1. Arthur Hertzberg, "The Conservative Rabbinate: A Sociological Study," in *Essays On Jewish Life and Thought in Honor of Salo W. Baron,* Joseph L. Blau, et al., eds. (New York: Columbia University Press, 1959), pp. 309-332. Charles S. Liebman, "The Training of American Rabbis," *American Jewish Yearbook,* 1968 (New York: American Jewish Committee) pp. 3-112. Page citations from the Hertzberg and Liebman studies appear within parentheses in the text of this essay.

2. In fact, Jewish communities from the sunbelt states are underrepresented and those in midwestern and West Coast states are somewhat overrepresented in the Rabbinical School. On the geographic distribution of American Jewry, see Alvin Chenkin and Maynard Miron, "Jewish Population in the United States, 1979" in the *American Jewish Yearbook,* 1980 (New York: American Jewish Committee), p. 163.

3. Data on the birthplace and denominational affiliations of the parents and grandparents of students were obtained in a follow-up survey of sixty-five randomly selected students enrolled in the Rabbinical School.

4. Our data indicate that over 75% of current students have mothers employed outside the household. They are mainly engaged in teaching (35%), self-employment (23%), and clerical work (15%). No data are available in earlier surveys on the occupations of mothers, and therefore it is difficult to judge the significance of our findings on the employment of mothers.

5. In comparing the Jewish educational experiences of male and female rabbinical students, several important differences emerge. A greater proportion of female students: a) received a day school education; b) attended Orthodox schools; c) rated their previous Jewish education as effective. Women admitted to Rabbinical School during these first years, at least, seem to have enjoyed a more intensive and satisfying education than their male counterparts.

6. In order to determine how students perceive their career choices in relationship with their career preparations, it will be necessary to conduct interviews. It would be interesting to know whether the sixteen students (15%

of respondents) who indicate that they are interested in pursuing careers unrelated to rabbinic training intend to complete rabbinical school. Did earlier cohorts of students at the Seminary also have students who did not plan to practice as rabbis? How do career aspirations relate to attrition in the rabbinate?

7. It will also be of interest to learn whether students of a Reform or unaffiliated background differ from their classmates in their religious outlooks. An initial examination of this question based on our population sample indicates that students from Reform homes lean to the left in their religious practices and attitudes. The unaffiliated, on the other hand, tend to fit the pattern of the *baal teshuvah* (one who returns to Judaism). The former tend to perceive the rabbi as a spiritual leader, whereas the latter favor the *talmid ḥakham* model. But given the small samples and the limited data we have, such findings are inconclusive and the entire issue warrants further study.

8. For bibliographic citations to many of the earlier surveys, see Jack Wertheimer's essay on the Conservative synagogue in a volume he has edited entitled, *The American Synagogue in Historical Perspective* (forthcoming, Cambridge University Press, 1987).

A Personal Look at Self, Judaism, and the Seminary

Bradley S. Artson

(for Rabbi Ben-Zion Gold, with love)

Our sense of self is both our most fluid and our most resistant attribute. As with any living thing, a self acts defensively to keep external influences outside in order to preserve its own nature. But that same self, the soul, also aspires to growth, since to be alive is to be dynamic and ever-changing. This openness to development keeps us in touch with others and with our surroundings. Being a living person requires a dual commitment to exclusion and to inclusion, to integrity and to flexibility, to tradition and to change. We are all, if you will, *mayim hayyim,* living waters. We course and flow throughout our lives, unaware of our final end, essentially involved in our own movement and fluidity.

Judaism is the way we channel and direct the dynamics of our souls. We strive, ultimately, to be able to unify the four corners of our lives — intellect, emotions, spirituality, and physicality — into a single outpouring of living. To do that, we require a way of life which is at once a pattern of behavior, an insight into being human, a dialogue with the Holy, and a framework of study. That blend is Judaism.

Judaism, like self, is something dynamic, yet defined. This presents a possible contradiction, or at least a tension. To be dynamic implies a constant state of change, to be never again exactly what one was before. Yet to have a sense of self is simultaneously to be defined, to perceive some essential traits which must be retained for a continuity of identity. In order to thrive, Judaism and self require both characteristics.

Continuity and change are not easy values to maintain. Individuals often prefer the solid, unchallenging verities of a simpler response. Out of fear, they opt for the fixed and the monolithic. Or, fearing the bond of commitment and relationship, they compulsively break all previous traditions and restraints. Mediating between those two extremes becomes the task of Judaism — to teach that traditions are collective reflections of the human soul in community. Those reflections are naturally dynamic — maintaining an essential core while adapting to changing circumstances and knowledge. Judaism is that mediating power which draws individuals into community, that permits innovation in the midst of tradition and continuity in partnership with meaning.

Judaism is the *etz hayyim,* tree of life, always stretching forth new leaves which didn't exist before, shedding old leaves once they no longer help the tree thrive, thickening its bark to survive in the world, extending its roots deeper and in new places. Judaism teaches the courage and the wisdom of openness to change and of insistence on integrity. Judaism is physician and therapist not just to psyche or to body, but to the whole person.

Berakhot 8b relates that both of the tablets of the law, the ones shattered by Moses in his anger and their unbroken replacements, were placed side by side in the ark together. Both were sacred; both were necessary for *shleimut,* wholeness.

We are the broken tablets, but we are also the whole tablets. In the course of living, each of us is scarred, each of us is bruised. We all carry with us shattered dreams and hopes of childhood, fears and passions of adolescence, and frustrations and resignation of adulthood. Significant parts of our selves lie shattered and in pieces. But we are also whole. We still dream, still act, and still cherish our passions. Unlike stone, we are able to grow anew. Like living water, we cover over our old sores, we shift our direction to compensate for our own limitations and for life's disappointments. And we go on. Our shattered self connects us to our past and preserves the fullest range of our own personality through time. Our unbroken self gives us the courage to go on dreaming and living and caring. The two join together to form the ark of our soul, strengthening us to blend the learning and experience of our past with the hope and energy of our being.

The Jewish Theological Seminary is the community which helps us to fuse Judaism and self into one organic creation, so that we will, with God's help, reflect the sanctity of Torah and Torah will continue to respond to the needs, hopes, and concerns of today. We remake ourselves in the Image so that the Image can work through us. Here as students we are taught to lovingly internalize the experiences and perceptions of our ancestors: women and men who grew and who worked to make holiness a part of their being and their communities.

Here we are taught to place ourselves in the center of the currents of our heritage, to see that we are a part of this continuity, this living thing, this Torah. We learn to become sensitive to quiet, to the rhythm of Shabbat and week, holy days and seasons, to months which circle the moon. We learn to awake to speak to the Holy Ancient One and to fall asleep after praising that Oneness. Our tables become altars; our minds and hearts, tools—however clumsy—for experiencing and sharing the wisdom of the ages and of our age.

Being a rabbi is not simply communicating texts, although those texts are an indispensable part of being a rabbi. Wanting to be a rabbi reflects a desire to share our humanity, after molding our humanity to incorporate the wisdom and perspectives of Midrash and Jewish philosophy, after extending our behavior to internalize the patterns and privileges of halakhah, after including in our sense of ourselves four thousand years of Jewish history and literature. Only after making these all a part of ourselves can we then offer to the seeking Jew a haven, a challenge, a way.

Our authenticity as rabbis depends upon this renewed and renewing self: a self that is the product of the Torah, Talmuds, Codes, Midrash, contemplation, and millennia of history. That new self is a self with something to give.

The ability to give, which springs from a recognition of ourselves and our congregants as dynamic, coupled with a knowledge of Judaism's past, its texts, its thoughts and its songs, present the rabbi with a special vision. It is not only the perspective of the scholar, which is one of erudition and learning, nor only that of the social worker, which is one of organization and concern. The unique role of the rabbi is *involvement*. We involve our Jewish learning in our congregants' lives, we approach them as fellow-travelers, and we offer them access to what is already theirs—would that they only possessed the tools. We present them with their own inheritance. The authenticity of the rabbi emerges to the extent that he or she teaches and practices a *Torat ḥesed*, a Torah of kindness.

Introspection, growth, integrity, community—these are precious gifts which our traditions cultivate. We who are, or have been, blessed to learn this *Torat ḥesed* at the Jewish Theological Seminary act, indeed, as its daughters and sons when we enable Jews to live by the dynamic Torah of kindness which is our special tradition. We then not only enliven and vitalize our selves, but we do honor to our Seminary and to our God.

Seminary students with Professor Joshua A. Joffe, 1897.

A View from the Inside: September 1986

Debra Reed Blank

As I prepare these comments for this volume I am profoundly aware of history and my own role in it. To be involved actively in the Seminary's centennial celebration, to be standing alongside her on the brink of a new century while at the same time pondering the previous one, underscores in my mind just how important our individual roles are in history.

This is the second point during my short sojourn at the Seminary that I have felt historically self-conscious. The first was when I entered rabbinical school as a member of the first class to include women. Pervading all my emotions at that time was a sense of wonder at my great luck for being (for once!) "in the right place at the right time."

There is no question that I have benefited thus far from my education at the Seminary. The required curriculum is well-rounded and succeeds in satisfying my love for the tradition (through courses in Bible and Rabbinics), in preparing me for my chosen profession (via courses in homiletics and counseling), and in improving my general competence in Jewish Studies (by requiring me to take courses which I might otherwise not take, e.g., Modern Hebrew Literature). The Rabbinical School curriculum is, however, the object of no little criticism. The nature of the criticism suggests to me that the curriculum is, ironically, the victim of its own laudable goals. The curriculum intends to produce a rabbi who is in command of the whole of Jewish tradition in addition to being a master of pastoral skills. The curriculum is therefore ambitious and, in turn, demands a corresponding ambition from the individual student. The ambition of the former leads to an inevitable superficiality in many courses; the ambition of the latter leads to course-overload and burnout.

I suspect that students accuse of superficiality those courses which they most value. The student who wishes to master our textual tradition perceives that Bible and Rabbinics are given short shrift in the curriculum; the student who places most value on the development of his or her practical skills finds that courses in counseling, education, and homiletics are insufficiently developed. Thus it seems that the curriculum—by having as its aim the formation of a "super-rabbi"—is producing rabbis who are jacks of all the rabbinic trades, but frequently the masters of none.

The overloaded students' primary goal quickly becomes freedom from the pressures of too many unsatisfying classes. The unfortunate consequence is a mad rush to get out of rabbinical school. And who can blame them: in addition to a remarkably heavy course load, they are frustrated, feeling that their primary area of interest is not accorded the depth it deserves, while at the same time feeling forced to take courses of little or no interest to them. The joys of learning for learning's sake are, too often, soon lost.

What the curriculum is trying to provide, it seems to me, is the sort of rabbi which today's American Jewish community wants: a representative and teacher of the Jewish tradition who is also prepared to serve as an orator, a therapist, a spokesperson for the Jewish community, an administrator, a chaplain, and a director of programming. Is this asking too much of the average individual? And is this, in fact, what a rabbi should be? Some would say that a rabbi is primarily an interpreter and teacher of the Jewish tradition. Others would argue that mastery of the tradition means nothing if a rabbi cannot deal with Jews in need. Others will even argue that an ability to respond humanely and effectively to needs is more important than talmudic expertise. This tension is played out in the curriculum, and my classmates and I struggle with the definition in our classes, in our self-images, and in our lives. The question becomes—where on the continuum between talmudist and social worker does the rabbi lie?

All of this notwithstanding, I believe more and more each day that the general dissatisfaction with the curriculum is the result of its having been designed according to an earlier philosophy which is at odds with today's rabbinical student. Earlier classes of rabbinical students came mostly from traditional Jewish backgrounds. The curriculum then served to introduce their Jewish learning—much of it already firmly in place—to the critical methods of Western education. In contrast, today's student arrives—almost without exception—already familiar with the methodologies of secular, western education and is looking to acquire a traditional Jewish education. On the average, today's rabbinical student has only an afternoon Hebrew School education at best, sometimes complemented by a smattering of college-level Jewish Studies courses. His or her early home-life is not likely to have been more than minimally observant. Thus he or she comes to the Seminary expecting to be instructed in a Jewish way of life. What he or she finds, however, are a faculty and a curriculum which race the student through a rapid succession of textual survey and "skills-building" courses, with the sole purpose of arriving at its raison d'être, textual criticism. In a very short time, most students can be found rebelling under the yoke of these required courses entitled, "Critical Methodologies of Bible", "Critical Methodologies of Talmud", "Critical Methodologies of Midrash", etc., and can be heard demanding "More *text*! More meaning!"

An unfortunate consequence of this situation is a communication gap between professor and student: the latter cries for more textual exposure while the former eagerly tries to introduce the wonders of textual criticism, without which the professor deems the student unable to fully appreciate the text. The professor—even while objectively knowing quite the contrary—teaches as if the student's Jewish "learning" were firmly in place. Inevitably the professor becomes disappointed in the student's poor command of text, and the student becomes disillusioned with the professor's "obsession" with textual criticism.

Despite this fundamental problem, the dissatisfaction with the curriculum—at least on my part—is not as deep as one might expect. A tremendous amount of education occurs in the Rabbinical School: in addition to our classes, organized channels exist for students to perform charitable actions, to participate in social action programs, and to give *tzedakah*. A twice-weekly luncheon program introduces rabbinical students to speakers from both within and without the Seminary on a wide array of Jewish topics, including theological and social issues, music, sermon ideas, and holiday preparation. Moreover, we all benefit from interaction with our classmates and teachers: here is where ideas, fears, struggles and solutions are shared.

But the Rabbinical School—no matter the quality of its curriculum, no matter the additional programs it sponsors, no matter the extent of the camaraderie it provides—can *never* completely prepare a student for the rabbinate. The finishing touches obviously come from working with a community, for I will only truly become a rabbi when someone addresses me as "Rabbi."

What effects the transition from student to rabbi eludes me. For example: although I came to rabbinical school with a relatively solid Jewish background, and I believe that I am getting an excellent education, I wonder how it will be that one day I will wake up a *rabbi,* whose opinion on Jewish issues should be sought and respected, who should be qualified to serve as a community leader and spokesperson for the Conservative movement. Even on my more self-confident days, I fear that I will never feel as comfortable representing Conservative Judaism as I imagine my colleagues who grew up in the movement will feel. Moreover, how do I weather the periods of profound doubt which plague me—doubts about God, doubts about whether Conservative Judaism can survive, doubts about my own integrity?

It is usually at this point that I borrow some vocabulary from my friends and acquaintances in the Christian ministry: I draw upon a certain degree of "faith" that I have a "calling" to fulfill a "mission." Yes, I am well aware of the theological differences prevailing between the rabbinate and the Christian ministry. But did I not feel from the very beginning indescribable certitude about my decision to apply to rabbinical school? Did I not feel inexplicable certitude that I would be accepted—that this is truly what I was destined to do? This is exactly how I have heard Christian ministers speak of their "faith" in their "calling"! And do I not, despite my occasional feelings of doubt, feel confidence in the worth and integrity of Conservative Judaism and trust in what it has to offer Jews and society as a whole? And do I not believe that I can somehow contribute to Conservative Judaism? This is exactly how I have heard some Christian ministers speak of their "faith" in their "mission"! Certainly (I assure myself) there is more to the making of a rabbi than one's *yiḥus,* more than the number of Talmud pages studied, more than the number of sermons written! But I have never heard any of my classmates or teachers use this vocabulary, nor does the Seminary offer a course on "The Mission of the Rabbi." So this source of self-confidence gets checked sooner or later.

What I *can* assert comfortably amongst my peers is that I believe that I have "something to offer," that I can make a contribution to Conservative Judaism.

Many point to the fact that I am a woman and suggest that any contribution I will make will stem from this arena: that I and my female colleagues will change the Conservative rabbinate because we are women. I am not so certain that women qua women will profoundly change the rabbinate, given what I have observed in the fields of medicine, law, and business, as well as the Reform rabbinate. In the past decade there has been a tremendous influx of women into these fields, and women seem more to have conformed to the "male" demands of these fields than to have effected revolutionary "female" changes.

No, I do not see any unique contribution that I might make coming from my gender; rather, I imagine it coming from my various ideas about how the Conservative movement can improve.

The first idea concerns my dream to establish a yeshiva, open to high school graduates who wish to spend a year or two studying texts in a non-academic setting where Jewish observance is taken seriously. I imagine the yeshiva in New York City, possibly having some relationship with a local synagogue. In addition to daily study and prayer, students would enjoy periodic "Shabbat field trips" which would not only expose them to the various faces of Conservative Judaism in New York, but to other varieties of Judaism as well. My yeshiva, the yeshiva of the Conservative movement, might attract some of the many young people "returning" to their Judaism, but it might also be an attractive option to the graduates of Ramah and USY. Most of all, this yeshiva might be an important step toward adding to the ranks of our Jewishly educated adult laity, which is vital for the strength of our movement.

It is with respect to the institution of the yeshiva that I feel that Conservative Judaism has missed the boat. That we have not established one is perhaps an indication of how we have suffered from our otherwise commendable emphasis upon critical scholarship. We lose too many of our youth to the Orthodox movement, which knows the yeshiva to be a tried and true means of educating and inspiring the rank and file. People who attend a yeshiva are interested in developing a close relationship to text and tradition, not in receiving an academic degree in Judaica. Only a yeshiva can offer a program of intense study for study's sake within an atmosphere of religious inquiry. The yeshiva is part of our Jewish legacy, and it is too educationally valuable to be overlooked any longer.

My second goal is to strengthen the movement's influence, through education, on individual personal observance. Why are we not educating all Conservative Jews regarding the decisions of the Committee on Jewish Law and Standards? Why is not each Conservative Jew provided with details on decisions regarding certain foods, women's ritual roles, and the like? If the movement provided individual Jews with such direction, every rabbi's role as *posek* would be enhanced, a role which has been deplorably undermined if not completely forgotten by our communities.

My third goal is to work for Conservative Judaism's independence from the Orthodox movement. As long as we are dependent upon them for kashrut, mikvah, and milah, we will always seem less religious, less valid, less authoritative—both in their eyes and (inevitably) in our own.

Ultimately I hope to help Conservative Judaism fulfill its "mission" of preaching the golden mean of Judaism. I was originally attracted to Conservative Judaism by virtue of this golden mean: I found within it ideals of religious observance which are challenging but not blindly fanatic, a relationship to Israel which is loyal but not naive, an admirable emphasis upon social justice, a spiritual appreciation of study, and encouragement of intellectual openness. Conservative Judaism *must* continue on this path amidst, and in spite of, the prevailing tides of religious fanaticism and reactionism. As a rabbi, I hope to exemplify and preach this golden mean.

Toward Shared Religious Practices

Samuel Weintraub

With many of my teachers and fellow students at JTS, I mourn the loss, among many Jews today, of knowledge and appreciation of traditional Jewish religious practices. I feel this way because, to me, the central strength, beauty and uniqueness of the Jewish religion is its concretization of our emotional striving, spiritual aspirations, biological and psychological needs, ethical ideals, *et al.* into a rich repertoire of religious practices. *Shiva* rituals, building booths, *tefilah**, Shabbat rest, giving a percentage of one's income to charity, saying *hamotzi***, burning leaven and other observances—these allowed Jews to develop rich personal lives. Moreover—and especially in the pre-modern social context—Jewish religious practice and Jewish communities enjoyed a dialectical relationship. To the extent that rituals were observed popularly and meaningfully, they strengthened the institutional structures and psychological and spiritual bonds which create community. Conversely, these practices gained holiness and beauty as they were cherished in communities.

Religiously speaking, over the last 200 years, major Jewish population centers have lost most of the practice, and most of the community. The radical events which precipitated that loss include the Emancipation, the Holocaust, the Soviet suppression of Judaism, and the displacement of many traditional Sephardic communities. In our own North American communities—and despite a dynamic "civil religion"—the complex politics of emancipation have created Jews mostly indifferent, uninformed or even hostile towards traditional religious practice.

In promoting these practices today, Conservative rabbis and activists find themselves starting from scratch. We are—as Rabbi Zalman Schachter has commented in a different context—at Yavneh, and Yavneh, for all of its later romanticization, was a very anxious

---
*prayer   **the blessing said before eating bread

period. Like Yochanan and his students, we grope for an effective and multi-dimensional response to the loss of old, sanctified religious institutions. For Conservative Jews, that response should involve an imaginative re-translation of traditional Jewish practices, in order to re-enlist the hearts, minds and practical commitments of American Jews. Unfortunately, the principal Conservative practice-defining body, the Rabbinical Assembly Committee on Jewish Law and Standards, mostly discusses what attenuation of ancient and medieval legal prescriptions may be permissible due to modern exigencies. Our need, however, is to develop a positive, manageable set of religious duties and rituals in which the modern Jew may be trained. In doing so, we can only hope that we will exhibit the same clever intuition and radical innovativeness of the talmudic rabbis. And we should also expect, and not be frustrated, if our final goal, a reconstituted, caring community emerges as slowly and unconsciously as theirs did.

Following, then, are some suggestions for re-establishing community religious practice:

1. As Gerson Cohen celebrated in his seminal essay, "The Blessing of Assimilation in Jewish History", there is a fine, age-old Jewish tradition of Judaizing the secular interests and identifications of Jews. Thus, for example, Passover and Shavuot are, partially, Judaized versions of ancient Near Eastern harvest festivals; Saadiah Gaon and Moses Maimonides espoused Jewish beliefs through Aristotelian methods in the Arabic language; Hasidic *niggunim* are often Judaized versions of Russian folk songs; and political Zionism is the Jewish response to nineteenth century European nationalism.

We need today to re-adopt such an integration in order to excite and empower a now passive laity. Our synagogue rituals ought to involve the best efforts of the musicians, psychologists, technicians, family educators, writers *et al.* in our midst. It has, and can be done. In Sudbury, Massachusetts, at Temple Beth El, a mainstream Reform congregation, two women—a professional writer and an educator—led the congregation's Ritual Committee in writing and publishing *V'Taher Libenu,* a superb modern siddur, combining the intimacy of hasidic *kavvanot* with the inclusiveness of modern feminism. Arthur Waskow and the anti-nuclear Shalom Center in Philadelphia have developed *Sukkat Shalom,* an ingenious adaptation of the rituals and midrash of Sukkot to teach Jewish traditions about peace, ecology and conflict resolution, and to bring Jewish insights to the American debate about nuclear arms. Developing similar, integrated expressions will relieve the alienation modern Jews feel between their Jewish and other identifications, and lend new vigor to religious practices.

2. We owe to the havurah movement an appreciation of the need to decentralize religious activities. Our synagogues should begin to integrate havurot structurally, each havurah comprising ten or twenty people, and devoted to performing some specific practice, e.g., *tefilah, niḥum aveilim* (comforting mourners), Shabbat dinner, community political action, synagogue beautification, etc. Every synagogue member above the age of four should be required, in a manageable fashion, to join a havurah. In order to foster vital, sentient connections among Jews, the havurot should be as interactive, experiential and body-involving as possible. Further, these havurot should be multi-generational, as synagogues too often mirror the ubiquitous age-segregation of American life, with its disastrous social and ethical consequences.

To make this suggestion specific, and to share a personal vision, let me propose a programmatic direction for American synagogues. It seems to me that synagogues would inspire more heartfelt, energetic religious involvement if they undertook to farm a small piece of land on their grounds. Multi-generational havurot would do the plowing, seeding, tending and harvesting, and also study and observe the many rites and blessings associated with agriculture in our tradition. The produce of the farm would be used religiously, especially in connection with our major festivals, which reflect our agricultural origins and traditions. Similarly, because of the historical meaning of the festivals, this farm work would promote an intellectual as well as visceral appreciation of our national history. Caring for nature also inspires the sense of *kedushah* so profoundly absent in modern life. Farm work would involve the body, arouse the emotions, and engage males and females of all ages. It would also be fun. Around the farm we could institute praying outside, which is beautiful, and family education, which is critical. Moreover, it would attract nonknowledgeable and unaffiliated Jews who may feel uncomfortable or incompetent in the standard sanctuary services. Indeed, this relatively small gesture — a 1500 square foot garden of squash and tomatoes — would help counteract the individual alienation and communal disaffiliation which plague synagogues today.

3. This re-translation of religious practices must also respond in-

telligently to the complicated, modern identities of the men, women and children in our congregations. The world they inhabit — psychologically and externally — fundamentally differs from the medieval, orthodox world in which our religious mores were centralized and codified. American Jews today, like most moderns (including their rabbis), *choose* aspects of their material lives and personal identities which were in the past more socially determined: place of residence, occupation, religious commitments, spouse, *et al.* While they strongly identify with Jewish peoplehood and history, they also build their sense of self around other definitions — professional, manual worker, parent, feminist, volunteer worker, etc. They are terribly imbued with the modern delegitimization of supra-human and supernatural authority. They question religious and other social conventions which do not satisfy some personal psychological, spiritual or physical need.

However, these modern Jews also have a spiritual yearning for meaning in their lives. Rabbis should see and feel that yearning, which is ultimately more profound and powerful than the indifference or cynicism which laypeople may exhibit towards traditional Judaism. They do not know what *kedushah* means, but they want it badly.

A new Conservative community practice, then, must realistically confront the psychology, spiritual aspirations, and potential religious commitments of today's laity. I would suggest, for example, that we develop a three- or four-hour Shabbat day ritual, involving an abbreviated *tefilah,* short family education, and *seudah* (festive meal). A regular, imaginative, family-centered ritual would benefit both now-uninvolved laity and the synagogue itself. While this proposal may seem limited, any more thoroughgoing community practice will only proceed from initial steps which are workable.

Speaking more attitudinally, we need to correct a fruitless tendency among Conservative rabbis to focus on the "ignorance" and nonobservance of laypeople. Instead, we should begin, positively, to appreciate the personal commitments and problems of laypeople as deserving of Jewish attention. If they come to the rabbi because their children leave home, or their jobs dehumanize them, or their marriages sour, then we ought to prepare our rabbis with better counseling, or at least referral, skills. If women are being liberated, and men are feeling threatened, our liturgies and educational programs should encourage proud female and male expressions such as female God-language, Jewish men's discussion groups, the study of Jewish women's history. If the laity like to use their bodies, we ought to subsidize more Jewish folk artists, singers and dancers, and include more physical expression in our liturgies and rituals.

A constructive attitude towards the laity should also include a sensible program of engagement towards the tens of thousands of Conservative-reared and/or -identified Jews who have married non-Jews. From having worked with the intermarried, most recently through a pilot JTS "outreach" project, I share three central impressions. Firstly, many intermarried individuals as well as couples want to learn about Judaism and participate in Jewish life. Secondly, for exogamous couples, as for endogamous couples, it is the onset of pregnancy and children which most critically promotes their religious agenda. Among mixed couples, there are thousands wherein the non-Jewish partner has no present plans to convert, but joins his/her spouse in a sincere decision to raise their children as Jews. While this scenario presents great religious and psychological problems, it is also important that the many potential Jews from these unions not be lost.

Finally, from my experience with the JTS project, I feel that there is great value in a specifically Conservative outreach program. Many intermarried Jews come from Conservative or Orthodox backgrounds. When they return to Judaism for their own or their new family's sake, they realize that they don't feel comfortable in Reform environments. Also, many Jews and non-Jews in mixed relationships are attracted to the traditionalist, Conservative emphasis on concrete religious practice. Clearly, among the intermarried Jews there are many with traditional backgrounds or proclivities whom our movement might productively engage.

4. The re-translation of traditional practice to meet modern realities should also prompt changes in the role of the Rabbi. Today, many Conservative rabbis still exercise a predominant if not exclusive control over the religious life of their congregation. That situation is outdated, because of democratic advances, and dangerous, because it reinforces the isolation of the rabbi, and the passivity and Jewish ignorance of too many laypeople. We need instead to transform the role of the Rabbi, and to spread Jewish knowledge and creativity throughout the congregation. The latter could be achieved through havurot, and perhaps also through specially trained, lay "pararabbinics," as proposed by Rabbi Harold Schulweis of Los Angeles.

The new rabbinic role would involve a mixture of old and new functions. The role will be traditional as the rabbi advocates certain religious practices, explains their history and meaning, and guides in their implementation. The role will be new as the rabbi acts as a peripatetic resource person, visiting the havurot, training lay assistants, and providing traditional insights for various religious practices whose ultimate formation lies outside of his/her exclusive control. In short, the rabbi will be less distant and authoritarian, but more intimate and facilitating.

5. Finally, some notes of caution. It is likely that we will feel awkward during the period in which we begin to re-translate communal religious practices. We should accept that self-consciousness as natural for a group which addresses the need to redefine its shared rituals, language and social relationships. The short history of Jewish feminism is already a case in point. Moreover, during this initial period, we should tolerate and even value a high degree of diversity and experimentation in religious practice. It will be years, perhaps generations, before such practices become uniform and widely accepted. Again, that is necessary and positive in the process of communal re-definition.

One cannot predict what the new repertoire of Conservative religious rights and responsibilities will look like, any more than Yochanan could have imagined the world of the late talmudic rabbi, Jose bar R. Bun. But it is clear that we need to develop new religious concepts, ritual expressions, and leadership models. These new forms will call upon traditional values, like the integration of non-Jewish influences, and the importance of regular, cross-generational ritual. They should also incorporate new advances, like feminism and religious democracy. If successful, re-translated religious practices will help establish, in modern form, the best features of the traditional, premodern community. These would include a network of rituals and responsibilities in which children and adults regularly participate, and an organic, communal consensus about important values and customs. It is to be hoped that this task of rebuilding practicing communities will excite Conservative leaders in the movement's second century.

The Jewish Theological Seminary and Conservative Congregations: Limited Associates or Full Partners?

Rela Geffen Monson

Those seriously engaged in the debate over the future of the Conservative movement cannot help but ponder the nature of the linkage between the Jewish Theological Seminary and the congregations which are its major structural embodiment on the American scene. What should be the nature of their relationship? Should it be one of non-interference and independence or of mutuality and interdependence? If one of interdependence, should the relationship be symmetrical or uneven? If uneven, what should the balance of power be? Central to the whole debate is the relationship of the lay leadership of the congregations to the professional leadership of the Seminary. Is it the responsibility of the Seminary to foster and train a lay leadership cadre? Should the Seminary originate a theory and practice model for the Conservative movement as a whole? Should the Seminary, through its faculty and administration, encourage the observance of mitzvot among the laity and be the final arbiter of Jewish law for the movement? Should the professional leadership of the Seminary somehow be held accountable for current levels of observance in Conservative homes? If the Seminary is currently elitist in thrust, and chooses to remain so, then who is responsible for educating the Conservative masses? All of these issues arise out of a historical context and a legendary aura surrounding the Seminary symbolized for many by the image of the bush that was not consumed.

Let us take a moment to examine the view of some of the founders of the movement and some later analysts as to the relationship between the Seminary and the congregations that now are connected to it. Robert Gordis (1945) wrote in an early essay that:

> . . . a small group of English-speaking rabbis of traditional sympathies decided to create a theological seminary which, in contradistinction to the Hebrew Union College in Cincinnati, would stand four-square on the program of loyalty to traditional Judaism . . . For a few years its doors were closed, but meanwhile, as the stream of Jewish immigration from eastern Europe became a flood, it grew increasingly clear that there was a great service the Seminary could render these immigrants and their native-born children, from the American as well as from the Jewish point of view.

In his pioneering work on the Conservative movement, Marshall Sklare (1972) cites an early appeal sent to potential supporters from the Hon. Joseph Blumenthal, then president of JTS, which stated: "The equipment of such missionaries, the training of rabbis who though fitted by culture and scholarship to occupy positions in the pulpits of the most cultivated congregations shall also be able to successfully undertake such work among their humbler coreligionists, is indeed, an object that ought to secure the support of Jews" (p. 164). These early lay leaders clearly saw the connection between the Seminary and satellite congregations. For instance, Dr. H. Pereira Mendes wrote:

> The future of American Judaism will be powerfully affected by the Russian Jews . . . These congregations will be either the fame or the shame of American Judaism . . . Our own interests require that they shall be supplied with ministers who shall be acceptable to them . . . Yet we need not the Seminary for the sake of supplying the spiritual wants of the Russian congregations only. We, indeed, require it for our own spiritual needs and for our own children's spiritual well-being.

According to Sklare's analysis, the connection between the Seminary and Conservatism came about because the congregations in the area of third settlement hired their rabbis from JTS. He feels that Seminary policy was such that its graduates were better suited to act as the spiritual leaders of these congregations than those graduated from other rabbinical schools. They were suited on a number of grounds. First, they spoke English. Second, because they usually were clean shaven and dressed in contemporary American clothing while the European trained rabbis clung to old world garb and beards, they were perceived to be willing to compromise on religious observance, even in their personal lives. To their congregants, this symbolized their modernity. Third, they were willing to tolerate low levels of observance among their congregants, but projected a traditional image without being so *"frum"* as to be offensive to them. Finally, they were open to interaction with the non-Jewish world. Exposure to *Wissenschaft,* notes Sklare, had led them to intellectual liberalism.

Thus, to begin with, the connection between the Seminary and the congregations was instrumental—the Seminary produced the rabbis who fit these congregations. The Seminary did not call itself Conservative. Though the congregations did perceive themselves as part of a new stream in Judaism, for many years, Seminary professors and administration deliberately blurred the lines between themselves and the Orthodox. Mordecai Waxman (1958, p. 175), in his introduction to an essay by Cyrus Adler, notes that:

> He was insistent that the Seminary was primarily an institution of higher learning rather than the proponent of a new viewpoint in Judaism. He assiduously avoided the idea that there was a Conservative movement or party and clung to the notion of a Conservative tendency. This position enabled him to receive support for the Seminary from people who did not personally share the Conservative viewpoint. However, it impeded the emergence of a well-organized Conservative movement and limited the development of the Conservative ideology.

This, of course, caused great ambivalence for the pulpit rabbis— those human links between the school and the shul. The young JTS graduate was trained to perpetuate the ideal of the classic role of the rabbi as a model of Torah living and master of Jewish law. One way to fulfill this role was to support the Seminary as a bulwark of Torah by solidifying its financial base. By strengthening the Seminary, says Sklare:

> . . . the practitioner creates a center of rabbinical learning—one where the older values can be conserved in spite of the impact of the environment. While the rabbi cannot but feel somewhat alienated from the local Conservative synagogue (it is after all the province of the layman), the Seminary can give him a sense

of expansiveness, for here a type of rabbinical culture is being preserved safe from the influence of the uninitiated (p. 188).

Unfortunately, however, the reverence of the graduates was often not reciprocated by respect from their teachers. The professors played upon the guilt evoked by the compromises made by their students, and even implied that they were not real rabbis—only the Seminary teachers could be true spiritual leaders. (During the crisis provoked by the decision to ordain women, the Union for Traditional Conservative Judaism further narrowed this definition by asserting that the Talmud faculty alone embodied traditional rabbinic authority.) In spite of their "love-hate" relationship with the Seminary, the rabbinic alumni continued to function as the link between the school and the shul. In a parody of their own relationship with their teachers, the rabbis preferred to keep the reality of the Seminary remote from the laity, thus preserving a mystique about the institution. The rabbi wanted the Seminary to preserve what might be lost in his own scholarship and even practice. Hence the anomaly of the separate seating in the Seminary synagogue. A congregant who visited the Seminary had difficulty in relating to this service and might refer to the faculty as Orthodox. (While in South Africa this summer under the aegis of the Kaplan Centre for Jewish Studies at the University of Capetown, I had the opportunity to spend some time with Mr. Mendel Kaplan, its sponsor. After ascertaining that I was a Conservative Jew, he confided to me that as a student at Columbia University's business school some thirty years ago, he had *davened* at the Seminary synagogue for a full year. It was only upon his return to South Africa that he learned, somewhat to his chagrin, that he had not been praying at an Orthodox synagogue!)

Thus, the Seminary gave spiritual leadership to the rabbis, and they in turn ministered to their congregations. This led to a tenuous, indirect link. In this regard Waxman (1975, p. 256) has written that:

> Conservative Judaism . . . is not a mass movement despite its numbers. Its one million members have not made or basically affected the thinking or the emphases of the movement. They are, rather, a response to the ideas proposed and implemented by the rabbinic leaders of the movement over the last fifty years. The aims and the intellectual orientation of Conservative Judaism have been provided by a kind of elite which sought to mold the

community without itself being molded.

This is not merely fortuitous. It has been a basic policy which is in consonance with the traditional theory of authority in Jewish life. The prominent political scientist, Daniel J. Elazar and his school (see for instance Woocher: 1982) have postulated that one constitutional principle of the *Edah* (Jewish body politic) throughout Jewish history has been leadership through a kind of aristocratic republicanism. This trusteeship system stems from a belief that the form and character of Judaism are properly the concern of those who are both learned and interested. Within the Conservative movement this practice has led to a particularly high concentration of influence and policy determination being vested in the Seminary and its scholars as against congregational rabbis and/or lay leaders. It has also, according to Waxman (1975, p. 257), "made it possible for the more traditional elements in individual congregations to exercise a greater control over synagogue patterns than they would be entitled to by their numbers. [Thus,] the Conservative movement has, in the past, successfully operated on the assumption that if guidance were forthcoming and properly communicated, it would be accepted."

This view of the layperson as the privileged recipient of Torah from his or her teachers/rabbis who should be honored to provide the fiscal support for the institutions which will preserve Jewish learning in America has been institutionalized and is counterproductive, according to critics from within and outside the movement. Jacob Neusner, for instance, one of the more scathing critics of this dynamic, has written that:

> The Conservative movement was called into being to provide a firm basis of support for the Seminary. It has assumed its own momentum, however, because the ideas and principles originally advanced as the basis for the institutions have been taken seriously by many quite remote from the movement . . . The place of the layman in the Conservative movement does not yet reflect these realities. In both the synagogues and the central institutions, the interest of the lay supporter is cultivated not for Conservative Judaism but for the institution that serves it. The center of interest is the maintenance of budgets not the creation of a movement. The lay leader is a leader because he can give and raise money. His words are solicited only when he can tell us

how to realize the most practical necessities. A lay leader need not even adhere to Conservative Judaism, and the virtues of his leadership do not necessarily include his wisdom, understanding [or] concern (1975, p. 274–5).

While Neusner surely overstates his case, the alienation of the leadership of many congregations and in particular of United Synagogue lay leadership from the Seminary is well known. This alienation is the product of years of "benign neglect." In the short run, this disattention isolated the Seminary from the necessity to be pragmatic. There could be little pressure from a lay public that didn't understand, or a rabbinate that treated the faculty with veneration. Indeed, Waxman contends that the clerical elitism of the movement has been a basic policy.

But the Seminary and the movement have paid a considerable price for this policy. Because of it, laypeople have often been discouraged and even precluded from dealing with ideology and basic policies. While enhancing the influence of the Seminary and its scholars, this has also led to abandonment of ritual observances by a majority of the laity. Laypeople felt that their rabbis should be public models of piety, while their own private practice could lapse. Thus, while the rabbi should strictly observe kashrut and Shabbat, for instance, the officers of the congregation need not.

This policy may even have prevented inculcation of a sense of personal responsibility for fulfilling mitzvot to this same majority. Without grounding in Jewish law, without a sense of its relevance or power to give meaning and personality to their everyday lives, the laity have often been content to be a silent majority. Ironically, those who get involved — to the left, to the right or in the middle — are sometimes moved to remove themselves from the establishment Conservative congregations. Thus, some of the successful products of Ramah, United Synagogue Youth and the Solomon Schechter Schools may say, "I am too passive in this movement and in its synagogues; deal me out." They then go on to found havurot, the Union for Traditional Conservative Judaism or even leave for modern Orthodoxy. In this sense, the UTCJ is no different in its call for lay observance of mitzvot than the founders of the Havurah movement who stressed *guf* (person) over *mamon* (money), requiring their members to personally commit themselves to regular communal worship, study and celebration. It may seem ironic, but both groups argue that the laity must reclaim its power through real rather than delegated participation in religious life, whether it be through leading worship or visiting the sick.

Today there is a need for a reevaluation of the Seminary mystique, with regard to the relationships between the Seminary, its students and alumni; the Seminary and lay leaders of the movement; and the Seminary and the congregations on a local level. The chart (page 70) shows one schematic model listing possible reciprocal relationships between the Seminary and Conservative congregations in the future. It is a model which implies a lessening of distance between the institutions and the professional and lay leaders who head them.

In the proposed model, the Seminary would have five major functions *vis à vis* the congregations. Four flow from the Seminary: training of professionals; training of adult lay leaders; providing education for future generations; and promoting the Israel programs of the movement. The Seminary would fulfill these functions by: maintaining and enhancing the library, the undergraduate, graduate and professional schools; creating educational materials for children and adults; training and sending out teachers to the congregations; bringing lay leaders to it or its retreat centers for study; publishing guidebooks for Jewish living for use by the laity; providing guidance for major educational institutions such as Ramah Camps, Solomon Schechter Day Schools and regional high schools. The fifth flows toward it: engaging in fundraising from the congregations to enable the accomplishment of all these goals. (Ideology has not been mentioned as a major function, except insofar as the Seminary would act as a mechanism to diffuse the ideology of the movement. Ideology is central, but it should be formulated through an interaction of the scholars at the Seminary, the leadership of the Rabbinical Assembly and educated lay leaders.)

The model shows the Seminary reaching out to congregations through mediating instrumentalities. These might include: the rabbis, cantors and educators; outreach of the faculty and administration through personal visits and creative use of the media; regular meetings of regional movement councils; and a movement-wide magazine.

Congregants, in turn, in addition to being recipients of services from the Seminary, would participate in an interactive process which would help shape the movement. For instance, they would raise issues of special concern through the regional councils. They would interface with the Council of Jewish Federations and the World Zionist

A SCHEMATIC MODEL OF POSSIBLE RELATIONSHIPS BETWEEN THE JEWISH THEOLOGICAL SEMINARY AND CONSERVATIVE CONGREGATIONS

Roles of The Jewish Theological Seminary

Training Professionals	Training Adult Lay Leaders	Israel Programs	Education For Future	(Fundraising)
• Rabbis • Cantors • Formal & Informal Educators • Social Workers • Academics	• Organizational Skills • Torah Study • Pararabbinics • Develop & Disseminate Course on Ideology • Run Conference Centers • Establish Standards of Practice for Leaders	• Mercaz • Kibbutz Hannaton • Tali Schools • Seminary for Judaic Studies	• Guidance for Day Schools • United Synagogue Youth • Prozdor High School • Ramah Camps • Melton Center	

Mediated Through These Liaisons to Congregations

- Pulpit Rabbis
- Seminary Administration
- Outreach Faculty and Media
- Regional Councils with Professionals and Lay Leaders
- Movement-Wide Magazine

Roles of Congregational Leaders and Members

- Tell Leaders What Real World is Like
- Raise Issues of Concern
- Support Conservative Educational Institutions in US and in Israel
- Financial Support & Business Expertise
- Send Their Children to Ramah & Schechter Schools
- Study & Pray Regularly
- Observe Ethical Mitzvot
- Enforce Standards for Leaders
- Interface with Federation and World Zionist Organization

Organization on behalf of the movement. They would provide fiscal support and business and professional expertise where needed to help movement institutions in North America and in Israel. They would participate in developing a set of standards for congregational leaders combining observance of ethical and ritual mitzvot. They would write articles and letters to the editor to the movement-wide magazine. They would help educate their children to become practicing Jews by sending them to Ramah, Schechter day schools, and on movement-sponsored Israel programs, and encouraging their participation in United Synagogue Youth. Finally, lay leadership would be in constant dialogue with their fellow congregants on the one hand, and with rabbis and Seminary faculty and administration on the other. In these dialogues, they would reflect on the reality of life in their communities and the contribution that Judaism could make to the issues they face—from business ethics to bioethics and from nuclear disarmament to Jewish unity.

Would this close interfacing destroy the mystique so carefully cultivated for decades? I would argue that for many Conservative Jews it is already gone. Veneration and fascination have been replaced by intermittent curiosity on special occasions. The Seminary is seen by many as a remote institution which makes financial demands and gives little to enrich their lives. In the absence of a well-respected spiritual leader who is fervently attached to his or her alma mater, even the financial claim becomes just one more in a sea of such demands from the Jewish community. Surely we have little to lose and much to gain through consideration of a renewed relationship between school and shul, based on a more open model.

NOTES

Robert Gordis, *Conservative Judaism: An American Philosophy* (New York: Behrman House, 1945).

Jacob Neusner, "Conservative Judaism in a Divided Community", in Jacob Neusner, ed. *Understanding American Judaism, Volume Two, Sectors of American Judaism: Reform, Orthodoxy, Conservatism, and Reconstructionism* (New York: Ktav Publishing House, Inc., 1975).

Marshall Sklare, *Conservative Judaism: An American Religious Movement* (New York: Schocken Books, 1972).

Mordecai Waxman, ed. *Tradition and Change: The Development of Conservative Judaism* (New York: Burning Bush Press and Rabbinical Assembly of America, 1958).

Mordecai Waxman, "The Ideology of the Conservative Movement", pp. 259-278 in Jacob Neusner, ed. *Understanding American Judaism, Volume Two, Sectors of American Judaism: Reform, Orthodoxy, Conservatism, and Reconstructionism* (New York: Ktav Publishing House, Inc., 1975).

Woocher, Jonathan, "How the American Jewish Community Governs Itself", *Face-To-Face: An Interreligious Bulletin,* Fall 1982, pp. 14-19.

A Red Brick Building, an "Educated Layperson," and Thoughts of a Future

Francine Klagsbrun

For almost an hour my friend Naomi and I sat on a bench and stared at the red brick building across the street. We had never seen anything quite like it. We knew it was called Schechter's Seminary, but we didn't know who Schechter was and we weren't really sure what a seminary did. The building looked so unJewish; it seemed so *American*. The Hebrew school we were used to was the tiny Brooklyn day school, Shulamith Institute for Girls, in Boro Park, where we had both grown up. That building was nondescript, dingy at best, its strongest asset being a sturdy side wall against which we banged Spalding balls in relentless games of king and handball.

But this building was imposing, intimidating, grownup. This was a serious school. We had heard that famous professors taught here, although the only name familiar to us was Saul Lieberman's, and we only knew of him because his wife, Judith, was the principal of our Shulamith Institute. Once she had invited our class to her home for an informal dinner and her husband had forgotten to pick up the hot dogs. When he finally arrived with the food, hours late, we had all laughed at him and felt a little sorry for this absent-minded husband of a brilliant woman. Looking at the building now we wondered what he did there. We wondered what Conservative Judaism meant. We wondered what it might be like to go to school in "the city," in Manhattan, when our entire lives so far had been spent in Brooklyn, and even the higher education we were about to pursue would be at Brooklyn College.

We sat and stared at the red brick building, fearful of entering it. The fears were justified, for when we finally did cross the street and walk into that building, we walked into a world far removed from the sheltered world of our little day school. This was a world that challenged us to question what we thought we knew, to reexamine what we thought we believed, to test our minds in ways they had never been tested before. Eventually that world proved to be more than Naomi had bargained for, and she left it after a year or so. But I remained, to graduate from the Seminary College, to work in the Seminary Library for a few years, to stay connected—in a thousand different ways—to Seminary thought and action.

What was it about life in that red brick building at that time that spilled over to shape my entire life outside it? We're speaking now of the late 1940s and early 1950s, the post-World-War-II-McCarthy-silent generation era I inhabited during my teen and young adult years. More than anything there was the excitement of discovery and self-discovery—not just for me, but for every student there. Outside, society may have been repressed and troubled, but within the walls of our classrooms, we felt energized and enlightened as our professors probed ideas we had simply learned and accepted when taught by other teachers in other schools:

Here is Professor Abraham Halkin analyzing a prophecy by Isaiah in the book of Kings and showing that it had to be written after the prophet actually lived because it refers to events that did not take place until two hundred years later. And here am I stunned at such an analysis. "But Professor," I say, recalling the clearcut teachings of my Shulamith school days, "Isaiah was a *prophet*. He could see far into the future because God showed him what was going to happen." His smile is both sweet and sardonic. "Aliza" (the name by which I am known at the Seminary), he replies, "if you believe that, please, by all means, don't pay attention to me. I am presenting the *critical* view of the text. You must decide on your own beliefs." I decide only that there is a way of looking at a text that I had never heard of before, a way of synthesizing history and archaeology into what I had been taught was purely a matter of faith. I decide that I must know more and more of the texts and of the history and archaeology, the philosophy and poetry my professors are masters of.

I never thought of my Seminary education as something to be put to practical use. I did not study to become a Jewish educator, nor did I plan to devote my life to Jewish scholarship or to the rabbinate. In any event, the last two career choices were not open to girls in those days. The Seminary was, for me, a fountain of knowledge from which I could refresh myself again and again. It was my intellectual home, and eventually its extension, Camp Ramah, became my home away from home. So significant was the Seminary College in my life that when my graduation from it conflicted with my graduation from Brooklyn College, neither my parents nor I hesitated for a moment in choosing to attend the Seminary graduation. We all knew that my secular education would probably be the basis for whatever occupation I chose in life, but that no matter what else I did, my soul belonged to the Seminary.

Ironically, for all that I learned at the Seminary, I learned very little about Conservative Judaism or Solomon Schechter or the ideology of the movement. That is, I absorbed the perspective and viewpoints of Conservative theology, but I don't remember ever having formal classes or even discussions about the philosophy or tenets of the movement. I was religiously apolitical. Many of us were, I suppose, because the Jewish community was not as religiously polarized then as it is today. Nor within the movement did I think of myself as part of the "laity." In classes, in camp, in discussion groups or on dates, my friends and I made few conscious distinctions between those who would seek professional roles in the Jewish community and those who would not. We were all committed Jews, absorbed in our learning and in each other.

All that changed when I moved away from New York and the Seminary. In Chicago, where my husband (whom I met at Camp Ramah) attended medical school, I began working as an editor for an encyclopedia. For the first time in my life I met Jews on my job who were embarrassed — not to mention ignorant — about their Jewishness; for the first time I met non-Jews who had never met a Jew like me. Because I didn't know how to be self-conscious about my Judaism I was open about it, and after a while my openness seemed to encourage other Jewish staff members to become more comfortable and more open themselves.

My position and self-image had shifted now — from being a Seminary kid to being an "educated layperson" (although that heavy-handed term is not one I would have thought to use). I was far from the fountain, the source that had nourished me, and I had to learn to sustain myself. I learned to subscribe to Jewish intellectual journals and to read them avidly, to follow Seminary events through its publications, to keep up, as much as possible, with growing numbers of Jewish scholarly books. And whereas the philosophy and ideology of the movement had not concerned me as a Seminary student, they now became of deep interest and urgency to me. I *had* to know the nuances of differences between various branches of Judaism because people asked me. I *had* to know the legal rationales for positions held by the Conservative movement because I had to explain them to others. In my circle of friends, Jews who rarely, if ever, went to synagogue or spoke to rabbis turned to me for information and knowledge. I became the true Conservative Jew, one foot in the secular world and one firmly planted in tradition, always balancing myself between the two.

That balancing act, and more especially, the role of the "educated layperson" (although I *still* don't use that term) remained an essential part of my identity long after I returned to New York and put encyclopedia editing behind me. Many of my friends now are writers like myself and many of them, although Jewish, are Jewishly uninformed. I have become the person the others turn to when they grow curious about their tradition, when they want to become more connected, when they have complaints against God, when they feel frustrated about ever reconciling Judaism and feminism. They see me as "authentic" because my beliefs and practices are based on knowledge. Some of that knowledge comes from my earliest background and education. Much of it comes from my continuing study of Jewish texts and teachings. But the "authenticity" about my knowledge comes mostly from its rootedness in the critical approach of an Abraham Halkin, in the meticulousness of an H. L. Ginsberg, in the profundity of an Abraham Joshua Heschel, in the unbounded curiosity of a Gerson Cohen. What I absorbed at the Seminary, when I was learning for the sake of learning, has shaped my identity, both in the essence of my own being and in the being that I present to the outside world. What would my life have been like without that education?

I am certainly not the only graduate of the Seminary College who cherishes her education; if asked, each would have his or her own story to tell. But what of the vast majority of Conservative Jews who did not attend the Seminary College or have an equivalent Jewish education? What connections should they have with the Seminary; what connections should it have with them? I know the Conservative laity well because they often make up the audiences for lectures I give around the country. I know them — many of them — as secularly-educated people, but not Jewishly so. I know that many, although not all, respond to appeals for money for the Seminary, that some maintain contact with the Seminary through the Women's League, the Men's Clubs, the United Synagogue. But I know, also, that more would feel themselves involved if they had closer ties to the Seminary, if the Seminary education, so rich and vital at its center, could spread far beyond itself. There are, of course, many educational programs emanating from many branches of Conservative Judaism. But shouldn't it be possible to turn every Conservative Jew into an "educated layperson"? Shouldn't it be possible for the thousands of Conservative congregants who have never set foot inside the Seminary to feel, as I who spent years there feel, that this is my school, my movement, my identity? Here are some thoughts and some dreams for those possibilities:

I would like to see a national dialogue on Conservative ideology take place in Conservative synagogues everywhere similar to the dialogue that is beginning to take place within the Seminary itself. Seminary task forces have been appointed and scholars have been talking and writing about the need to articulate a Conservative philosophy. The need is real. I learned little about ideology and philosophy when I studied at the Seminary because the necessity for formalizing Conservative thought was not pressing then. But today, as religious fundamentalism pushes to extremes, it is crucial for us to know and make known who we are and what we stand for. It is crucial for us to present ourselves not as the middle ground, some place between Reform and Orthodoxy, but as a positive movement whose ideals and purposes stem from the very core of our tradition. So it is time, then, for the Seminary leadership to embark on an ideological self-examination. But it is time, also, for the laity to be involved, for this examination to be a communal one.

How should this be done? Let the word go out from the Seminary that such a dialogue is beginning. Let meetings be held in every synagogue, led by rabbis, educators, or lay leaders—not one meeting, but many, for months, perhaps a year. What is the Conservative ideology? What do we stand for? How do we see ourselves now? What do we want for the future? Let congregants prepare background materials and reading lists. Let there be discussion and dispute, but let there be dialogue and engagement. I sat on the Commission for the Study of Women in the Rabbinate, and later I attended meetings in which laypeople, men and women, testified to voice their opinions and describe their personal experiences. Although some people maintain that the issue of women rabbis was a divisive one, I would argue that those months of discussion throughout the community were among the most vibrant and creative in the history of the movement. Congregants were involved—passionately, lovingly, angrily involved. With such involvement, ideology becomes real and meaningful, not something abstract, handed down from on high. Let's have involvement and discourse between the Seminary and the laity on the ideals and principles of our movement.

Let's have, along with a renewed look at ourselves, a renewal of study of our texts, under the centralized direction of the Seminary. In what way? First, I would like to institute a *Daf Yomi* (that is, a page [of Talmud] a day) program—a daily recorded lesson, available over the telephone, sponsored by the Seminary. When I tried to join such a program organized by an Orthodox institution in Brooklyn I was laughed off the phone. "What, a woman wants to learn Talmud?" a voice barked. "What do you know? You have to *know* to be part of this." Well, in the Conservative movement we recognize that anyone can learn and *know* if she or he wants to. Let's make learning accessible by having a recorded half-hour lesson a day available by phone through an "800" number at the Seminary. Anyone could call the *Daf Yomi* number any time or several times a day and learn from the recorded lesson. But those people interested in a more intensive approach could sign up, for a minimal fee, to receive a curriculum outline and a year's worth of texts in Hebrew and English to follow day by day.

Then, I would institutionalize a practice that has informally been taking place in many parts of the community: study groups in the workplace. In law firms, hospitals, investment companies and other unlikely grounds, small groups of men and women are meeting to study Bible, Talmud and other source material. The Seminary can expand that program throughout the Conservative community by preparing a "brown-bag curriculum," a program to be used for lunch-hour study sessions for working people. A rabbi or—if available—learned community member would lead once-a-week sessions at some centralized location (I know of only one or two rabbis who do this at present), and class members might use the curriculum materials to continue studying in small groups at their own offices between larger sessions if they wish. Yes, this is a form of adult education, but one that would capture the imaginations of many people who do not ordinarily attend adult education courses.

My next suggestion in this area of study is directed both at the Seminary and the rabbis it graduates. Why not turn weekly Shabbat sermons into textual lessons? So many sermons in so many synagogues begin with the portion of the week, then lead into a lecture on some current events issue. Don't misunderstand — many of those lectures are excellent. Yet, what an opportunity for learning is missed when a text is used as a takeoff point rather than the center of a sermon! I can picture a year-round curriculum developed at the Seminary as resource material for rabbis, a curriculum built around some part of the text of the week, and including critical interpretations and commentaries, both old and new. The "sermon" would be truly a teaching session, with congregants participating or not as the rabbi wished, but with Torah being taught for itself. Do you think laypeople are uninterested, that they prefer to sit back and listen to a sermon without having to think too hard? Don't underestimate our congregants. There is a hunger out there for real knowledge of sources, for real grappling with texts. People will respond enthusiastically if their rabbi enthusiastically announces and follows through on a weekly program of study rather than sermonizing.

I've referred several times to curriculum development at the Seminary. The curricula, I believe, would have to be prepared by a separate department — a department for external affairs, or something equivalent — headed by a Seminary scholar and devoted to the creation of materials for the purposes outlined above.

A different form of community study I hope to see in the future is an intensive outreach program by the Seminary to the uneducated Jewish intellectuals in our midst — that community of writers, poets, reporters, editors and opinion makers who are Jewish but have little Jewish background or knowledge. I attended a session at which Adin Steinsaltz, the Israeli talmudist and sometime guru, spoke to just such a group. He discussed the most basic of ethical issues, used the simplest of talmudic texts to make his point, and his audience was enthralled. That hunger, the same hunger for real Jewish knowledge that I sense throughout the community, was gnawing away here too. Let's feed that hunger with real teaching sessions led by some of the most dynamic Seminary scholars, beginning in New York, perhaps, but spreading to other cities as well. It takes only one or two contacts in intellectual circles to gather such a group; it would take only one or two good meetings — preferably in the homes of well-known writers — to generate the excitement necessary to keep the program going. The Seminary would benefit, group members would benefit, and the Jewish community at large would benefit by being represented by writers and artists who know whereof they speak on Jewish matters.

And here are suggestions for other kinds of outreach:

- A program originating at the Seminary that could be duplicated at other centers to train people for second careers in Jewish education. These days retired people usually have many productive years ahead of them. What better way for the Jewishly-committed to spend them than in studying and then teaching adult education or even synagogue high-school courses?

- Traveling exhibits from the Seminary library to major Conservative Jewish centers throughout the country. There are manuscripts and books in the Seminary collection that have dramatic and exciting histories few people know about. A traveling exhibit — much the way museums circulate their exhibitions — would spread knowledge about Jewish books and spread excitement about the Seminary's collection. Seminary rabbinical students might accompany exhibits in some major locations to lecture about the works displayed.

- An automatic subscription to *Conservative Judaism* for every member of a Conservative congregation. Why cannot synagogue dues be increased the small amount required to include a subscription to the journal? Contributors to UJA-Federation automatically receive *The Jewish Week* and other such papers; Conservative Jews should be reading *Conservative Judaism*.

Finally, in the realm of dreamland — a Seminary-sponsored cable TV show that would include interviews and discussions with Seminary scholars, historical information and dramas, debates on current Jewish issues, readings by Jewish authors and so on. The networks have continually cut back the time they allot for public service religious programs such as the *Eternal Light*. Surely we can find contributors in the Jewish community who are willing to support a Seminary-directed educational TV show. I like to think so, anyway.

When I sat and stared at the red brick building on the other side of the street so long ago I never dreamed that one day I would be pondering and planning how to extend its teachings to thousands of others. I thought I was entering another Hebrew school. I found instead a new universe. Let's open that universe wide during the next hundred years, spreading its glow of learning to Jews everywhere.

As for me, I'm so glad I crossed that street.

On Creating An Educated Laity

Miriam Klein Shapiro

When, during my freshman orientation at Barnard, I told my roommate that I was going to the Seminary to register for a full program in Judaic studies in addition to my course of studies at Barnard, she was incredulous. Why would a seemingly sane and normal college freshman want to take a double program? It would cut into my study time, affect my grades, destroy my social life, and be of no earthly use toward my credits at Barnard. I had to admit that I really had not given it much thought; it had simply been automatic. Throughout my life, I had always carried a double program—afternoon Hebrew school after grade school, Hebrew high school after public high school, and now, Hebrew college after college seemed to be the next step. All my friends from Ramah were doing the same thing and none of us had really questioned it. Now I did stop to think. I tried my best to explain to my roommate that while my studies at the Seminary would be of little career use (I had planned to become a social worker), they would be of great personal benefit helping me become the kind of human being I hoped to be. They were part of my inner self, of what made me "me". While the courses I planned to take at the Seminary College of Jewish Studies would not teach me social work skills, they would help me develop the kind of sensitivities that would lead me to want to be a social worker. (Later, I was to write my master's thesis at the Columbia School of Social Work on the congruence of Jewish values with social work values.) I stressed that I was continuing my Jewish education at the Seminary for my personhood.

My years at the Seminary were very happy ones. In those days, it formed an important part of my social life as well. "Everyone" ate Friday night dinner at the Seminary. Often there was a program following dinner. Professors invited us to their homes. Everyone lived near the Seminary—the professors in the surrounding neighborhood, the rabbinical students in the dormitory or, if married, across the street. We enjoyed each other's company and, most importantly, felt that we were part of a community.

Yet, if I were asked — as in fact I have been for this article — if my original goals for going to the Seminary were realized, I have serious questions. I went originally simply to become an educated Jew. Part of my definition of being an adult Jew was to be an educated one. I am still in contact with many of my friends from that period. It is interesting to look at that group to see how many used their education to function as educated laypeople. Few of us are lay leaders or even just ordinary members of a Conservative synagogue. Basically, we divide into four groups. A large group of us have become professionals in the Jewish community, such as rabbis, academics, cantors, agency personnel, and educators. I myself, though trained originally in another field, am now a professional Jewish educator. Many had originally planned to become Jewish professionals, but for others there were subtle inducements and encouragements to enter fields in which they originally had no interest. Another large group has settled in Israel and they, too, tend to work professionally for the Jewish community in education or with Jewish organizations. A third group makes no active use of their knowledge and do not lead identifiably Jewish lifestyles. A fourth group are those who have left our movement. A very small number remain to fill the ranks of our laity. Of those few, almost none have reached positions of leadership and power.

Although no longer a true layperson, I am involved with a number of lay arms of the Conservative movement. The leaders and indeed members of these arms — Women's League, United Synagogue, Men's Clubs, etc. — are by and large not educated at the Seminary. To put it succinctly, when I attend a meeting of the Jewish Educators Assembly, I find many fellow alumni with whom to share memories; when I attend a meeting of the National Board of the United Synagogue (as a JEA representative), I find almost none. There is a real dichotomy between lay leadership and Seminary graduates.

This should give us pause for concern. If the graduates of the Rabbinical School all chose other professions or left the rabbinate at a young age, we would surely investigate. We would check both the curriculum of the Rabbinical School and the situation in the rabbinate at large. We should do the same thing in the area of lay leadership. It is a many-faceted question. Why do the constituent organizations of our movement and individual synagogues not consider Seminary graduates as top candidates for leadership positions? Why do those who are best prepared for that leadership not see it as a goal worthy of their attention? Are we preparing students to look at membership in a synagogue or a leadership position as something which requires education? Are we preparing those with the education to look at synagogue leadership as a worthy goal, or is it subtly denigrated? Is our only definition of *haosek b'tzorkhei tzibbur* (a communal activist) a professional one? Should the Seminary curriculum teach Practical Lay leadership much as the Rabbinical School teaches Practical Rabbinics? I recently asked a friend with an educational background similar to mine who belongs to a Conservative synagogue in a small town why she was not more active in the movement. "Why should I be?" she asked. When I pressed her to explain, she said, "They are not looking for what I have. Jewish education is not a road to Jewish leadership." This sums up the two sides of the problem. She did not see Jewish Leadership in our movement as a goal to pursue; those who knew of her background did not see it as making her worthy of pursuing.

There are a number of reasons why the Seminary and its related institutions should emphasize providing professional leadership for the community. The most obvious one is the great need for functionaries in our movement and indeed, in all of the American Jewish world. Rabbis, educators, agency heads, are all in short supply. It is natural to turn to those educated by the Seminary to fill those gaps. There is a constant pressure on those with this education to use their knowledge to serve the Jewish community as professionals. My own case is an example of this. I originally taught Hebrew school as a means of raising funds while in college. This was easy to do because there were many positions for inexperienced students. Later, I lived in a community where Judaic studies teachers were simply not to be found, and when my background was discovered, I was asked to teach. Still later, when my children were growing older and I was contemplating a change in career plans, I was specifically asked to return to the Seminary and make education my profession.

We even go one step further. Anticipating the shortfall in candidates for professional positions, we recruit our young people from Ramah and USY to come to the Seminary to be educated specifically to fill those gaps. Our particularly fine and promising young people are encouraged to enter the ranks of the professionals in our communities. There is no such emphasis on being a layperson within a synagogue setting. One might argue that this is all that one should ask of the Seminary, that it provide the functionaries to educate the young of our movement and thus provide for an educated laity. Yet, I think that this is not enough. First and most basic, educators and rabbis leave the field because of the frustrations of dealing with uneducated laity. We hear the sad story over and over: the loneliness of living in a community with no peers; the guilt at bringing up children to be "odd-balls," the only children in the community to keep Shabbat and kashrut; the difficulty of being the only "Jew" in town; the terrible sense of futility when one seems to be working alone for something little understood. My professors at the Seminary often complained of their pain that while they wrote many fine scholarly works they knew that they had few if any readers "out there." We cannot continue to create musicians but train no one to appreciate music.

A second problem is our denigration of laypeople. We often tend to think that knowledge may be a dangerous thing in laypeople, that it is easier to deal with less powerful and thoughtful laypeople. They cause less trouble. We do not think of the nonprofessional area as a place for our best and our brightest. "It is better to keep them in the dark" is the philosophy. The opposite is true. It is only with a well-informed and educated laity that the professional can function. We have been extraordinarily successful in preparing rabbis, academics, educators, and agency personnel. We must be equally successful in preparing the people with whom they must work. Our laypeople are bright and sincere and they need the advanced knowledge of the sort that only an institution such as the Seminary can give. Other academic institutions cannot fill the bill because they, by definition, must be neutral. Our laypeople should be educated within the framework of our own institution with our own unique combination of scholarship and philosophy.

I would suggest several levels on which to proceed. One would be in terms of the recruitment and "care" of the students we have now. Some courses should be more general, more geared to real life than either to research or the professions. These should prepare the future professional for the real world in which he or she must live by giving them an overview of the future layperson with whom they will work. What if an engineering school developed only scholars and teachers of engineering? The professional should be taught how to deal with laypeople—not only in the political sense, as important as that is, but in the educational sense. How does one develop returning Ramah, USY, JTS graduates into a powerful positive element in one's synagogue? How does one develop programs to bring them into leadership positions? However, more important than individual courses is a specific atmosphere. This involves areas of personal counseling, advisor programs, extra-curricular events, dormitory life—in general, those things which make up the life of the student. To those who are educated, we must make clear that to be an active lay member of our movement is a worthwhile endeavor. For both the professional-to-be as well as the layperson-to-be these are the areas which should be geared to help the student integrate that which is learned into a personal lifestyle as well as a professional one.

On the other hand, we should be doing more to educate the leaders we have at present on a level consonant with their general education and background. Serious thought should be given to reaching those who are already committed to devoting their time and energies to the leadership of our movement and to Jewry in general. Serious effort should be given to asserting our belief that in Judaism knowledge is not the secret prerogative of the few but the common inheritance of the many. We should have faith in our laypeople and provide them with opportunities to learn, high level courses, and most clearly, an emphasis on our belief that learning is an important activity for them. This implies a two-pronged program. The first, at the Seminary, would involve both more active recruitment as well as some change of focus. The second, in the field, would involve outreach on an unprecedented scale.

Both on the level of the present student and the present layperson, then, the job is twofold: to be vigorous in our conviction that it is worthwhile to be a layperson and that a layperson requires proper education. The Seminary is uniquely qualified both to advance that proposition and to provide the education. In our first one hundred years, the Seminary succeeded in the yeoman task of providing professional and academic leadership for a new land and a new time and circumstance. Our task as we begin the next one hundred years is to provide for a broad-based constituency for that leadership. Our challenge is to ensure that this constituency is educated in a manner appropriate to the task.

First faculty and graduation class of the Teachers Institute. Faculty (center four clockwise from top left): Elias Solomon; Mordecai Kaplan, dean; Moshe Levin; and Mrs. Barnett Brickner.

The University of Judaism

David L. Lieber

At a special convocation in 1945 commemorating the thirty-fifth anniversary of the Teachers Institute of the Jewish Theological Seminary, Mordecai M. Kaplan, the founding dean, called on the Seminary to reorganize itself as a University of Judaism.[1] Its mission would be to train not only rabbis and teachers, which the Seminary already did, but all types of professional and lay leaders to meet the needs of American Jewish life.

Kaplan's proposal was accorded a warm reception. Chancellor Louis Finkelstein was particularly impressed, Kaplan noted in his journal, with its broad sweep. It seemed to offer a way to extend the Seminary's influence and to put its stamp on the entire American Jewish community.

Within a relatively short period of time a number of the elements in Kaplan's blueprint were adopted. The Leaders Training Fellowship was established to reach out to high school youngsters; the Institute of Religious and Social Studies expanded to provide "a meeting ground for representative thinkers and teachers of all faiths and trends in American life";[2] and the Jewish Museum enlarged to encourage Jewish artistic activity. Some items were deferred, such as the establishment of a school for communal service and a research institute to study the contemporary Jewish scene, probably for financial reasons.

What the Seminary did not, and could not, accept was Kaplan's rationale for such a university. In his view, the synagogue could not serve as the unifying force in Jewish life since it was fragmented and many Jews were alienated from it. What was required was the formation of an organic Jewish community, consisting of all who wished to identify as Jews, regardless of their religious affiliations. Such a community would be democratically run and would employ rabbis, teachers and other communal workers to meet the needs of its members. To train these professionals a university was a desideratum, since by its very nature it was open to new cultural and intellectual currents, and was prepared to engage in experimentation. Unlike a seminary, which concentrated mostly on the study of the classics of the Jewish past, a university would also examine the contemporary conditions of Jewish life and devise strategies to deal with them.

Understandably, there was no great enthusiasm for this approach on the part of the Seminary faculty, who did not share Kaplan's view of Judaism. However, Finkelstein grasped the appeal that the idea of the University of Judaism might have to the larger Jewish community. When the Seminary received an invitation to join with the Bureau of Jewish Education in Los Angeles to establish a school for teacher training and adult education, the time seemed right to try out Kaplan's proposal, in the hope that it might attract community-wide support.

It was a very modest school, meeting at first in some classrooms of Sinai Temple. It had no full-time faculty or administration. All those associated with it, however, were very distinguished people. Dr. Simon Greenberg, who commuted from New York, was its part-time director; Dr. Samuel Dinin, the director of the Bureau of Jewish Education, its dean; Dr. Jacob Kohn, the rabbi of Sinai Temple, the dean of its graduate programs; and Rabbi Jacob Pressman, also of Sinai Temple, its registrar. Furthermore, the school enjoyed the support of some very prominent lay leaders of the community, all of whom recognized the need for an institution of higher Jewish learning in the rapidly developing Pacific-Southwest. Despite the diversity of their religious affiliations or lack of them, they joined with the Seminary in establishing the University. At first they hoped that it would receive the support of the Reform community as well, but even when it became apparent that this would not happen, they remained loyal to the University and were among its first supporters.[3]

A year after the school opened, Louis Rabinowitz, a friend and supporter of the Seminary, happened to be in Los Angeles. Urged by Dr. Greenberg to visit the school, he was very much impressed with its potential and leadership. He also realized that it could not become an independent institution unless it had quarters of its own. Without any prompting, he bought a charming four-bedroom house in the vicinity of Sinai Temple and presented it to the University as its first home. There the school remained until 1957 when it moved into a spacious ten-story building on Sunset Boulevard. During those years, the school grew in size and reputation, with hundreds of students attending its classes and participating in its programs, which included not only courses in every aspect of Judaica, but workshops, performances and exhibits in the arts. To add luster to the school's very competent part-time faculty, the Seminary arranged to have visiting professors spend one or two semesters in Los Angeles. Among them were members of its own renowned faculty, as well as people like Elias Bickerman, Martin Buber and Ernst Simon.

The University quickly became the hub for most of the west coast activities of the Conservative movement. Physically, it housed both the United Synagogue and the Women's League. It also provided them with leadership and assistance as Max Vorspan, the part-time director of the United Synagogue, became the school's first full-time registrar and director of its extension programs. Under his skillful guidance, both organizations grew in size and quality as he helped new congregations come into existence. Together with Dinin, he was instrumental in organizing Camp Ramah in California and in involving both laypeople and rabbis in its leadership.

In less than a decade, it was obvious that the University had outgrown its quarters, and had become too large to be operated by part-time staff. It did boast two full-time faculty members—Vorspan, who had been appointed in 1953, and Louis Shub, in 1955, to run the growing library. But more people were needed and so Simon Greenberg, now named president, arranged to spend longer periods of time in Los Angeles. Samuel Dinin was prevailed upon to resign from the Bureau to serve as the University's full-time dean and direct its day-to-day programs.

The twenty years the University remained on Sunset Boulevard saw it transform from a southern California school to a west coast institution. This was the result of a conscious effort on the part of the University to reach out to communities all over the west. Through lectures and consultations, weekend institutes and scholar-in-residence programs, faculty and staff members were brought to major west coast cities, ranging from San Diego to Vancouver. Hundreds of campers attended Camp Ramah in California, now under the direction of the University, from congregations in Phoenix, Tucson and San Francisco, while dozens of leaders of Conservative congregations all over the west participated in leadership weekends on the camp grounds. Close contact was established with each of the rabbis, who, with rare exception, responded with warmth and cooperation. Gradually, also, University graduates began to assume teaching positions in western communities, further strengthening their bonds with the school.

Meanwhile, the University developed close ties with other educational arms of the Conservative movement in Los Angeles and helped forge them into a network of schools. Ramah was central to this process since it not only conducted a large summer program, but offered weekend institutes for children of all ages who attended the afternoon schools. Ramah also worked with the Los Angeles Hebrew High School, which was affiliated with the United Synagogue, as well as with USY to reach the teenage population. Under the University's leadership and in cooperation with the Bureau of Jewish Education, they joined with representatives of the elementary schools in organizing a regional council on Jewish education to coordinate all of their efforts. The University also assumed the leadership in establishing the first Solomon Schechter day school in the city, which became a model for those which were subsequently established. By 1975, a chain of Conservative Jewish educational institutions existed in Los Angeles encompassing children and adults of all ages, with the active participation and leadership of University faculty and staff.

During the years on Sunset Boulevard, two other major developments also took place which enabled the University to expand its operations. The first was a decision by the Board of the Seminary to grant the University operating autonomy with responsibility for its own budget and staff appointments. An independent Board of Directors was established to run the University's affairs within very broad guidelines. Under the energetic and far-sighted leadership of chairmen like Julius Fligelman and Jack Ostrow,[4] this ultimately resulted in a major development program which saw the building of new campuses both for Ramah and the University and the reorganization of the latter as a self-governing affiliate of the Seminary.

The second historic step was the introduction of the School of Judaica program, with Dr. Finkelstein's approval. This meant that the University could now offer the equivalent of the first two years of the Rabbinical School.

While at first this did not involve more than a handful of students, it meant formal recognition by the faculty of the Seminary that the training in Los Angeles was on par with that in New York. This was a significant factor in strengthening the morale of the younger faculty members and encouraging other promising young scholars to join them. It was also a vote of confidence in the administration and lay leadership by the elders of the Seminary, strengthening them in their determination to build a great institution of higher Jewish learning.

The Sunset Boulevard years were very productive. Under Shub's dedicated direction, the library grew from 2500 to 90,000 volumes. Simon Greenberg and Sam Dinin brought national renown to the school, while the younger faculty members won for it a reputation for great teaching and creative scholarship. For a while, too, the arts flourished as Max Helfman, and later Erwin Jospe, headed the School of Fine Arts. As for Ramah, it became a model camp under the skillful leadership of Walter Ackerman, an educator of note, who also served as the dean of the Teachers Institute. At first, the adult education programs, too, maintained their great popularity. Then the numbers began to decline as similar programs developed in other sections of the city. With the increasing move of the Jewish population westward and northward and the decline of the Hollywood area, the location of the University appeared more and more to be a detriment to its further growth.

The administration realized that it would not be long before the other programs would be affected as well. At the same time, the building was no longer adequate. Large as it was, it had become too small for the University's needs and, being in poor physical condition, required a great outlay of money to put it into proper shape. After much discussion, the decision was taken to find another site in the western part of the city, which would be in the neighborhood of UCLA and more readily accessible to the Jewish residents. Fortunately, such a site became available in the Santa Monica mountains close to a major freeway, making it easily accessible to all population centers. It was also large enough to support a campus, though hundreds of thousands of cubic yards of earth had to be moved. The start of construction had to be put off twice, however—first to build a new conference center where Ramah could be housed, since the old camp was no longer habitable, and second, to join with the community in supporting Israel in the aftermath of the Yom Kippur war. Finally, the University's time came with groundbreaking exercises taking place in the spring of 1973. In 1977, the classroom building was ready and the move from Sunset Boulevard effected.

In the nine years that have elapsed, the campus has been almost completed. In addition to the classroom building it includes an administration building with a dining center, an acoustically excellent auditorium, an art gallery, a gift and book shop, an educational resource center and a mikvah. It also includes a sculpture garden and residence halls, with housing for some two hundred students and visiting faculty. What remains to be built is a library building to house the present collection of some 180,000 volumes and the documentation center, comprising more than 800,000 articles and newspaper clippings on contemporary Jewish life. Recreation facilities for students also have to be provided, though the classroom building does contain dance, music, art and sculpture studios. The net effect of the campus is impressive, and many visitors speak enthusiastically about its beauty.

Even more important are the programs it has permitted the University to offer. The best attended are those connected with continuing education. No fewer than 1500 adults a week come to the campus for formal classes. These include not only content courses in Hebrew, Bible, Talmud and the like, but also workshops in dance, drama, painting and sculpture. There is also an Introduction to Judaism program, which is extremely popular, largely directed to non-Jews who are considering the acceptance of Judaism. Additionally, the Program for the Enrichment of Jewish Family Living offers training for para-professionals who serve synagogues and community agencies as trained volunteers in group work and counseling. The auditorium is the home not only for concerts by world renowned artists, but also for Jewish cultural presentations and, most recently, for a children's theater. The art gallery also serves an educational purpose, rotating exhibits of local Jewish artists monthly and encouraging them in their work. Of special interest is the Elderhostel program which has brought hundreds of seniors from all over the country to spend a week at the school, attending eighteen hours of lectures on Judaic subjects and participating in traditional Sabbath services. This is an addition to the Ramah Academy,[7] which brings scholars and teachers from all over the world for weekend institutes in the Conference Center in Ojai. The University also brings together rabbis, Jewish communal workers and other professionals for seminars and workshops in their respective areas. Nor should we overlook the monthly lecture series attended by audiences of well over a thousand and the scholar-in-residence programs the University sponsors for west coast communities, or the University Papers which are written by faculty members on themes of broad Jewish interest and widely disseminated.

At the core of the school remain the academic programs. With the exception of the MA in Talmud or in Judaic studies which attract a few students, all of the graduate programs are professional in nature. The School of Education, which is well attended, prepares students for careers in Jewish education, both as teachers and administrators. It conducts a model school, as well as an educational resource center, and places its graduates in positions all over the country. The MBA program trains people for management posts in congregations, centers, federations and other Jewish agencies. It has a highly sophisticated part-time faculty, largely drawn from the ranks of the Graduate School of Management at UCLA. The School of Judaica program continues its direct association with the Seminary's Rabbinical School and is highly successful not only in the level of its teaching, but in its positive reinforcement of the students in their own sense of vocation.

The newest program, the Lee College,[8] a full four-year undergraduate school, offers a BA in four majors in addition to Judaic studies. All students are enrolled in a core curriculum which integrates the study of Jewish and western civilization with an emphasis on the critical reading of texts in English translation. Freshmen and sophomores under the age of twenty-one are required to live on campus where they are encouraged to participate in Jewish activities, including the celebration of the Sabbath and holidays.

The underlying purpose of the Lee College is to educate the next generation of American Jewish leadership. It emphasizes the importance of knowledge, critical intelligence and the Jewish religious heritage in dealing with the world and enhancing personal development. It offers a perspective on contemporary Jewish life by providing students with an understanding of how Jewish and western cultures have interacted in the past to their mutual enrichment. Since they also learn how to engage in disciplined thinking and express themselves clearly and cogently, they are well prepared for advanced training. Some will enter the Jewish professions. Most will not. It is hoped that they all will play an active role in the Jewish community and that a number of them will occupy positions of leadership in American society as well.

Linked with the degree programs are two others which are now being developed. One is the establishment of a policy research center to examine issues facing American Jewry. A distinguished professorship has already been endowed in this area, and the staff is in the process of interviewing candidates and considering various proposals for structuring the center. A junior-fellow program is also being funded, offering stipends to a small number of promising young scholars in Judaica who are interested in spending a year or two at the University to complete their doctoral research and gain deeper grounding in the classical Jewish texts.

This brings us back to Kaplan's original vision of a University of Judaism for the training of the professional and lay leadership of the Jewish community. Essentially it continues to be the mission of the University, though it has departed from his original "blueprint."[9] More important, however, is that it takes seriously his view that a university, unlike a seminary, is a pluralistic institution which not only tolerates diversity but encourages it. It is a University of *Judaism* because its purpose is to teach the Jewish culture, religion and history in all of its manifestations. It is a *University* of Judaism, because it does so in a spirit of critical inquiry and encourages individual freedom of thought. That is why care is exercised in selecting full-time faculty to seek out the best possible scholars and teachers in their fields of specialization, without reference to their religious affiliation, so long as they are personally committed to a Jewish future. Far from being detrimental, it is the considered judgment of the administration that it is good for students to be exposed to a variety of reasoned approaches to Jewish living. This forces them to examine their own positions and to think them through on the basis of study and reflection. In this they are aided by a dedicated core of scholars who act as models of learned, caring, committed Jews and teachers whose studies are always open to them and who welcome them into their homes. They also are given an opportunity to experience the beauty of Jewish living in a variety of programs and settings. If they do not leave the University having thought through all of the issues of Jewish life, they do go away with an appreciation of the depth of the Jewish tradition and of its value system. They also take with them the ability and the desire to keep on learning, the ultimate prize any school of higher learning can confer on its students.

NOTES

1. Cf. "The Reorganization of the Jewish Theological Seminary of America" reprinted in *Higher Jewish Learning,* Los Angeles, 1963. The address was delivered on February 4, 1945. He repeated the call in a closing chapter in *The Future of the American Jew* (New York: Macmillan, 1948), though he did not mention the Seminary by name.

2. *Ibid,* p. 23.

3. A monograph is currently being prepared by Arthur Hoffnung surveying the history of the University. It is scheduled to appear in the Fall of 1987, when the school will complete its fortieth year.

4. Julius Fligelman, then chairman of the Board of Overseers, helped organize the Board of Directors, with Jack Ostrow as its first chairman.

5. These included Elliot Dorff, Joel Rembaum, Elieser Slomovic and somewhat later, Ziony Zevit, Robert Wexler and Ron Wolfson.

6. These programs have grown considerably under the direction of Jack Shechter.

7. The Academy was established by Alvin Mars, then director of Camp Ramah.

8. The original curriculum was developed with an NEH grant under the leadership of David Gordis. Arnold Band of UCLA was chairman of the committee and Theodore Raab of Princeton a special consultant.

9. "The University of Judaism — A Compelling Need" in *Higher Jewish Learning,* p. 31.

Mordecai Kaplan and Solomon Schechter greet each other at a train station (circa 1910). Kaplan joined the faculty of the Seminary as the first Dean of the newly-established Teachers Institute in 1909. During his five-decade tenure at JTS, he served as Professor of Homiletics, Midrash and Philosophies of Religion.

The Renewal of the Cantor

Morton Leifman

Probably more has been written about cantors in the general North American press in the last two years than in the previous twenty. Interest in the shortage of ḥazzanim and in their profession—its problems, its achievements, its future—has assumed proportions that could not have been predicted. Perhaps some of this can be attributed to the combination of a general interest in things Jewish that we are experiencing in America and to the fact that the possibility of women assuming sacerdotal functions elicits intense responses—positive and negative—from gentiles as well as from Jews.

There is, though, much that is generally left unsaid. The cantorial profession is a complicated and still developing one. There is disagreement about the function of the hazzan and about how he or she should be trained. Cantors' responsibilities vary from congregation to congregation, and even their self-image, their view of their role, varies.

This paper can, at best, skim a surface or two. It will focus on some aspects of the current scene and on cantorial training in the Conservative movement. It will try to examine where we are now.

In May 1987, the Seminary presented the Diploma of Hazzan and an academic degree in sacred music to eight graduating seniors of the Cantors Institute-Seminary College of Jewish Music. Among the eight were two women. Women had previously been awarded music degrees by the Seminary, but never before had they graduated with a diploma certifying, as it were: "This is a hazzan who can lead a Jewish religious service."

Until four years ago, the Seminary's sole official synagogue separated men and women for prayer and, needless to say, did not permit women to lead a service, read from the Torah or, for that matter, be counted towards a minyan. Today the Seminary maintains two official synagogues—a completely traditional gender-segregated one and a new fully egalitarian one housed in the Seminary Library's former reading room. This March, the Cantors Institute student body conducted a Shabbat service at the egalitarian minyan with four student cantors (including one woman) leading *P'sukei d'Zimra, Shaḥarit, Hotza'at Hatorah* and *Musaf* services. Men and women students shared the Torah and *Haftarah* honors and a mixed choir of fourteen voices sang choral selections from a repertoire of nineteenth- and twentieth-century Eastern and Central European liturgical composers.

It would all seem to be obvious and simple. The sensitivities of the right-wing faculty members and students are respected and a fully traditional minyan operates daily. Women who accept Dr. Joel Roth's approach to ritual obligations and who agree to take on the time-bound mitzvot can lead a service at the egalitarian minyan. As of May 1987, women graduates of the Cantors Institute can, with the Seminary's blessing, do professionally what for a number of years many women have done at the Seminary as "amateurs." The Cantors Institute chorus can participate at a Shabbat service to the great spiritual uplift of all present.

But it's not that simple. For even some of those who have no questions about the propriety of the halakhic decision allowing women to act as *shliḥot tzibbur* fear the possible feminization of the cantorial profession. Hebrew Union College's Cantorial School already graduates more women than men. A formal choir at an egalitarian minyan does not create concern about women's participation in the service, but does concern many about the possible future diminution of participation of *congregants* when there is a choir at a service. And a "formal" service in an age of increased informality disturbs some people. All of this raises more issues.

The Cantors Institute accepted its first group of students in 1952. Ambivalence existed even then among Seminary administrators and teachers about the propriety of teaching musicians at the Seminary at all. The attitude reflected an old prejudice among some Judaica scholars against music in general, and especially about *ḥazzanut.* There was a fear that unless the hazzan was truly pious and learned, a mockery would be made of the prayer experience, and it was felt that few, if any, bright and pious Jews would waste time on music if one could study Talmud instead. The prejudice persisted for years.

From the beginning of its existence, the Cantors Institute's Nusah Department was headed by Hazzan Max Wohlberg. This was fortuitous. Hazzan Wohlberg came to personify—both for the Rabbinical School authorities and for the Cantors Institute faculty that he helped to assemble—all that was proper, indeed excellent, in a cantor. His encyclopedic knowledge encompassed not only the fields of religious and secular music, but also those of rabbinic literature, Hebrew, Yiddish and general European culture as well. His gentle manner was endearing, and he was naturally pious and unpretentious.

Another piece of good fortune was in the choice of Dr. Hugo Weisgall as Chairman of the Faculty. A renowned composer and conductor, Weisgall was the son of one of America's most eminent and scholarly cantors. He thus came to the Seminary not only with outstanding musical credentials, but with a commitment to Jewish life and culture. He saw to it that Cantors Institute graduates were broadly educated and sensitive to high musical and Jewish religious standards.

These magnificent goals were not easily attainable. The school did not become large enough to support a full-time faculty. Students came with varying levels of music, of Jewish text knowledge and of general education. Since there was little interaction between cantorial and rabbinical students, morale became a problem. It took many years before music students began to feel that they were accepted as equals by the "others" and, further, that the education which they were receiving, excellent though they felt it was, could guarantee them a decent and respectable livelihood upon graduation. It has only been in the last few years that conditions have changed rather dramatically.

Beginning with the appointment of a dean for the Cantors Institute in 1973 by Dr. Gerson Cohen, then Chancellor of the Seminary, emphasis was placed on curriculum evaluation and revision, as well as on building student morale. Requirements in Jewish studies were dramatically increased and eventually another year was added to the program—a year devoted almost totally to the study of Hebrew language, liturgy, Midrash, Talmud and Bible. The year was spent at Neve Schechter in Jerusalem, together with rabbinical students who were also spending their required year abroad. Upon returning to New York, Jewish text study was continued.

The New York Seminary dormitories were opened to Cantors Institute students, who until then were unable to make use of the facilities which rabbinical students had taken for granted. Some courses at the Seminary were integrated to include rabbinical, cantorial and graduate students so that they were able to see each other in common academic frameworks. The Cantors Institute faculty was increased and rebuilt. *Nusaḥ,* the traditional chanting of the prayers, is the nucleus of cantorial training. A team teaching approach to *Nusaḥ* was instituted, allowing each student the benefit of three instructors — one for theory, one for practicum and a third for *ḥazzanut* coaching. Training for a ḥazzan is complicated and requires the acquisition of many special skills. The student must be prepared in the field of general music (sight-singing, ear training, harmony, piano, composition, choral directing, music history); Jewish music (cantillation, *Nusaḥ,* bibliographic resources, Hebrew school methods and materials); and Jewish texts, laws and customs (the siddur and *Maḥzor,* Bible, *minhag* and halakhah, some Talmud and Bible). But there is more. Many cantors enjoy being, and have discovered the importance of becoming, pastors and want to share the burden and the mitzvah with the rabbi. Cantorial students and graduates now regularly visit hospitals and hospices, sometimes with a guitar, singing for and with patients, counselling the sick and dying and their families. Working with bar and bat mitzvah pre-adolescents who may have personal and/or religious problems, has opened up a whole new framework for the cantor, and students can now choose to take classes in pastoral psychology together with their rabbinical student peers. One summer, recently, a special course in the problems of adolescence was set up by the pastoral psychology department at the Seminary primarily for cantorial students, since so many student cantors were teaching kids from broken or one parent homes and needed guidance in how to relate to these youngsters.

The Cantors Institute is now almost completely a post-graduate school. High school graduates without college training are accepted only in very special circumstances, and almost every student arrives with at least a B.A. and often an M.A. Some come very broadly educated, indeed. The profession and the Jewish people are increasingly being served by cantors who are not only well-trained musicians, but more and more Jewishly educated, articulate and committed Jews.

There is a shortage of cantors. New graduates can choose geography and can begin their careers with excellent salaries. Positions are open all over the United States and in many European communities. A cantor can and often must be multifunctional and experimental. Congregations have different needs and often both the congregation and the cantor must make some accommodation to the needs and talents of the other.

There are plenty of problems. Some congregants no longer respond to or even understand the traditional music of the synagogue and want something new. New music is not necessarily good music. Congregational tunes do not always achieve the liturgical or musical levels to which a trained musician and sensitive religious spirit aspire. Some cantors complain that they are not permitted to really sing, and they do not want to be "song leaders." The rabbi-cantor relationship still requires clarification. Yet, most cantors, rabbis and ritual committees have worked out a *modus vivendi*, which, while not completely satisfactory to all parties, satisfies most needs. Perhaps the ideal would be to agree that congregational singing is desirable, and more congregational participation should be encouraged with the "tunes" chosen to exclude the vulgar. Some "concert" *hazzanut* should be a part of every service, but should not tax the patience of the congregation. Certainly, educating the congregation to the liturgy, both words and music, must become a priority. The establishment of synagogue choirs should be encouraged and music from the best repertoires available should be heard as part of regular congregational services. The small number of decent synagogue choirs in America is scandalous.

It remains to be seen how the granting of diplomas to women will affect the profession and Jewish life. There has been some protest from a few members of the Cantors Assembly about the Seminary's decision, some on halakhic grounds, others on psychological and emotional grounds. Many requests for information keep coming into the Cantors Institute office from women who want admission to the school. Some have excellent credentials and are already active in the liturgical life of their communities. Whether Conservative synagogues, in the long run, will hire women cantors remains to be seen. There is some concern that potential male candidates will stop applying for admission, should women constitute the majority in the school. The special talents that women bring are already obvious in the school. Aside from being able to have a chorus that sings four-part music, some of the women have brought great warmth and some superior musical training to the school. But feminization of the profession is a possibility, and the implications of that have yet to be studied or understood.

The Cantors Assembly is the organization of Conservative hazzanim. Interestingly, it was not established as an alumni association of the Jewish Theological Seminary, since as an organization it pre-dates the Cantors Institute. In fact, it was the Assembly that gave the impetus for the establishment of a school to train hazzanim. With the destruction of the European Jewish communities in World War II, the pool of European hazzanim, trained mostly by an apprenticeship system, disappeared. Cantors serving American congregations in the mid-1940's were by and large Hungarian, Polish, Rumanian, Austrian or German-born men. It became apparent that the apprenticeship approach to teaching hazzanim would not take hold in North America, and if there was to be a cantorate in the future, a school had to be established to train cantors. The Cantors Assembly had other immense responsibilities. It was an overwhelming task to try to create an atmosphere of professionalism when there were few standards, few precedents and almost no training facilities for the future professionals. The leadership of the Assembly undertook to establish standards of professionalism, to publish materials and to arrange for the placement of hazzanim. It had to encourage the concept of full-time cantors and to convince congregations of the necessity of paying full-time salaries. It was necessary to develop new music resources and it was necessary to help in the recruitment of cantorial students. The Assembly has achieved its goals with varying degrees of success in each of these frameworks.

Still, cantors often express concerns about the uneducated laity that finds it difficult to relate to both the words and the music of a rich liturgy. Cantors, like rabbis, are frustrated when they feel that they are neither understood nor appreciated, and that the years spent in learning the "real *davening*" seem wasted. The debate continues about the relative importance of the formal prayer mode chant versus the congregational sing-along. Until there is a recognition that both are necessary for a satisfying service for Jews in the late twentieth century, there will probably be congregational unhappiness and cantorial frustration.

The cantor-rabbi relationship often remains undefined and is always potentially explosive. Perhaps, as the cantor becomes consistently better educated, more sophisticated and more Jewishly committed, the rabbi will recognize him or her as a partner to share the pulpit and responsibilities, rather than as a potential competitor for the attention and affection of the congregation. And perhaps the cantor will better understand the pressures that constantly bedevil the rabbi and will be more understanding of the rabbi's position.

It is more and more understood that the properly trained cantor provides a combination of liturgical, musical, pastoral and educational services that add up to more than a full-time job. A part-time hazzan may be the only option available for a small, financially troubled congregation, but the requirements, even of a medium-size congregation presuppose a well-trained, full-time professional.

To the surprise of some who have predicted the demise of *hazzanut,* there is a remarkable renewal of interest in cantorial music. *Hazzanut* concerts are regularly presented in large cities all over North America to overflowing houses. The last few years, choral pieces of Rossi, Lewandowski, Sulzer and Naumberg are being rediscovered and sung. Cantorial records and tapes sell well. There is also a developing sense of pride in the profession that could not have been predicted twenty years ago. This is, perhaps, the result of a new consciousness in the communities of the potential for spiritual and religious growth that Jewish liturgical music provides and the increasingly higher level of training that the teaching institutions are providing. Such progress gives us hope that more young people will be attracted to a developing and fascinating profession and more Jews will have the experience of inspired liturgical singing.

Members of the Board presenting Louis Marshall with congratulatory speech on the occasion of his 70th birthday (1926). Board members (from left to right): Nathan Straus, Felix Warburg, Louis Marshall, David Brown, Solomon M. Stroock, and Cyrus Adler.

Ramah at Forty:
Aspirations, Achievements, Challenges

H. A. Alexander

Ramah began in 1947 as a small summer camp at Conover, Wisconsin and has blossomed into an international educational movement, boasting six residential summer camps in North America, two in South America, a day camp in New York, a year-round educational conference center in California, summer programs in Israel for North American youngsters, day camps in Israel for Israeli youngsters, and a national winter staff training retreat. Through these programs, Jewish educational experiences are offered to thousands of children each year, including those with special needs, as well as to families and adults.

Ramah is now forty. What has it tried to achieve? To what degree of success? What has it accomplished that was unanticipated? What lies ahead? These questions are not easy to answer. There are three reasons why. First, Ramah is diverse. Its programs are scattered around the globe. They serve the needs of divergent populations and reflect the interests of local leadership. Second, the existing historical, anecdotal, and statistical data concerning the results of these programs are limited and exclusively North American. Third, these data reflect the diversity of the movement. They share few common evaluative standards and record slices of different programs, places, and periods.

Nevertheless, a review of the literature reveals three sorts of aspirations which Ramah programs have shared, at least in North America where the movement began. The first is concerned with *what* Ramah transmits to children, its curriculum; the second with *how* it does so, its pedagogy; and the third with *why*, its mission. We will consider each of these before turning to accomplishments and challenges which lie ahead.

Ramah's Curriculum: Living, Language, and Learning

When the well-known Jewish educator Henry Goldberg was appointed the first director of the camp, he worked with his assistant Hillel Silverman and with representatives of The Jewish Theological Seminary, Sylvia Ettenberg in particular, to build a program around three principles: Jewish living, Hebrew language, and Jewish learning (Schwartz, 1976).

Living. One of the most important concepts which the early leaders of Ramah learned from the Jewish educational camping movement founded by Samson Benderly was the importance of creating a natural environment in which to experience Jewish life. Young Jews of non-Orthodox families who did not remain in overwhelmingly Jewish neighborhoods or who did not attend day schools had no context in which to place the ideas and practices they learned in Jewish schools. Influenced by Dewey, according to whom formal instruction is meaningful only as an extension of informal social experience, Benderly recognized that the summer offered an ideal opportunity to create such an informal social setting for Jewish youth in America.

Thus, Ramah became one of the first places outside of the synagogue where Judaism could be experienced according to the Conservative tradition, where the unique orientation to Jewish law and life developed by the Seminary and its graduates was put into practice. In this environment, Conservative philosophies of halakhah were tested and translated into practice. Questions regarding the order of the prayer service, dietary practice, Sabbath observance, as well as ethical matters all took on new urgency when faced with the growing educational movement which required answers in order to prepare programming.

In the words of Stephen Lerner (1971), in "its hothouse atmosphere, it could implement those ideas which rabbis, at best, would laud. Youngsters *lived* all the slogans which seem so empty in Hebrew school back home. Ramah appropriated the most enduring aims of Conservative Judaism—the importance of Jewish study in Hebrew, regular prayer, significant . . . observance of Sabbath and *Kashrut,* concern for one's fellowman, identification with Israel—and made them work."

Language. Ramah favored a progressive pedagogy for teaching language. It never embraced Hebrew as an end in itself, but rather as a means to the greater ends of Jewish identification and personal growth.

Joseph Lukinsky (1968:102-103) put it this way: "All the Camps Ramah are officially Hebrew speaking camps. What this means is that official communication is in modern Hebrew and that the language is used as much as is meaningful otherwise . . . Announcements in the dining room are in Hebrew, as are most administrative and routine program matters." However, "in classes, discussions, and other programs, when it is felt that understanding is crucial and that deep communication is impossible in Hebrew, the language is never allowed to be a barrier. Dramatic presentations are in Hebrew, but here attempts are made to prepare campers in advance with the necessary vocabulary. Many programs use a great deal of English; some are entirely in English. Campers speak in English almost always among themselves. Counselor-camper interpersonal relations are largely in English."

This approach reflects not only the commitment of Conservative Judaism to Hebrew and Zionism (Dorff, 1977:199-204), but also a distinctively Deweyan approach to the significance of language in the transmission of culture. Dewey held that language, as the product of shared cultural experience, is intimately tied to social experience. Words of one language communicate ideas and feelings that may be completely absent from another. Hence, Dewey (1916:32) believed that language has "unrivaled significance" as a means of cultural transmission. But, this can never be accomplished at the expense of the child whose growth cultural content is intended to serve. Language is vitally important in the transmission of culture, but not more important than the child.

Learning. Although many Jewish camps stressed the importance of Jewish living, few have emphasized formal learning (see, for another example, Furie, 1946). From its inception, however, Ramah included classroom studies as part of its program, though the classroom may have been the shade of a tree or the porch of a camp building.

One reason for this emphasis on formal learning stems from Ramah's relationship with the Jewish Theological Seminary which has always stressed formal study. Another reason grows out of Conservative ideology which is rooted in Jewish texts. A third reason is more practical.

Ramah was intended to be a Hebrew-speaking camp for youngsters in the supplemental school system sponsored by Conservative synagogues. Painfully aware of the shortage of time in six-hour-per-week Hebrew schools, Ramah's founders sought to reinforce this system with intensive summer experiences (Ettenberg, 1982). Thus, a formal program of study in both Judaica and Hebrew language became basic to the Ramah program. In most camps, everyone who attends, campers and staff alike, must be enrolled in a program of formal Judaic study back home. Once at camp, everyone studies, from the camp directorate to the youngest campers.

Thus, each camp employs not only counselors, division heads, and specialists to provide a wholesome camping program, but a full formal educational staff as well, including trained Judaica and Hebrew teachers and a director of education who, together with the camp director, plans and supervises this aspect of the Ramah program. In addition, because of its relationship with the Jewish Theological Seminary, and its western affiliate, the University of Judaism, Ramah has developed a unique program of professors-in-residence. Each camp hosts a faculty member of the Seminary or the University every summer who teaches staff and models devotion to the study of Torah.

Ramah's Pedagogy: Individuality, Character, and Responsibility

When Louis Newman was appointed the third director of Camp Ramah in Wisconsin in 1951, he recognized that the Judaic and Hebraic content of the Ramah curriculum was only half of the educational equation and advocated that the other half of the equation, the child, be taken as seriously as the curriculum. This educational tone became a hallmark of Ramah (Cohen, 1984). Newman focused on the individuality of the child. His successor, Seymour Fox, built on this work with the assistance of Joseph Schwab by emphasizing character development. In the mid-sixties, Joseph Lukinsky expanded these ideas still further by addressing the importance of responsibility.

Individuality. Newman's most original contributions to Ramah (1951:196) grew out of two of his goals and the methods he advanced for achieving them, (1) "to create living situations through which all people, campers, counselors, and all workers will become better human beings," and (2) "to transmit to our campers the knowledge of traditional Jewish values."

By becoming better human beings two things were intended, (a) to "expand one's ability to enjoy life, and to develop and use one's innate capacities," and (b) to "be sympathetic to other human beings, interested in seeing others enjoy life and capable of fulfilling such interests through proper action." He also held that through traditional Jewish values, campers should learn "to act less out of habit and unconsidered impulse, and more on the basis of independent reflective judgement and conscious deliberation."

To accomplish these ends, Newman argued that it was desirable "to get young people to behave now as we wish them to behave as adults, the reward being intrinsic in the act, and extrinsic group approval being incidental." The place to begin, he suggested, is through sympathy, that is, "the capacity of getting out of one's own skin and sensing the world through another's desires, pains, pleasures, fears and anxieties."

The counselor, then, was to accept the youngster and, through caring and concern, to assist her in becoming the best that she was able to be. The subject matter, Jewish tradition and Hebrew language, became means in addition to being ends. The growth of the child, the increased ability of the educated to decide intelligently and to act independently, these were the ultimate ends. This emphasis on individual needs had a profound impact on the Ramah program. In addition to required lessons in Hebrew and Judaica, campers were given choices of activities such as sports, drama, arts, music, hiking, and camping, enabling them to build portions of their programs with the guidance of their counselors (Cohen, 1984:28-33).

Character. Seymour Fox became Newman's successor at Wisconsin and the first national head of the movement. Influenced by the well-known educational theorist Joseph Schwab, he argued that Ramah's pedagogy ought to emphasize the development of character. To this end, he arranged for two sorts of activity groups in camp, those oriented toward achievement and those toward support. The tension created in the former was to place psychological demands on the youngster that could be addressed within the latter. This process would foster social interaction and coping skills that are important to character development. Thus, Newman's interest groups became the core of the achievement-oriented program in camp while the bunk became a "home haven" and the counselor, a surrogate parent (Farago, 1972:62-64, cf. Dorph, 1976:191-194). As a result, both counselors and achievement-activity leaders were to serve as role models who could inspire character development within a Judaic context.

Responsibility. Joseph Lukinsky, another pioneer of the Deweyan pedagogy in Ramah, was appointed director of the American Seminar at Nyack, New York in 1965. The Seminar was designed for seventeen year olds as an alternative to the Ramah Seminar in Israel. During his years as the director of the American seminar, Lukinsky expanded Newman's emphasis on responsibility (Farago, 1972:62) by stressing social action within the non-Jewish community as well as camper involvement in programming and behavior management. He (1968:ii) viewed responsibility "as a component of moral autonomy," which derives from "confrontation of the wisdom of the past and inquiry into experience in the present."

These ideas were implemented in three areas of camp life. (1) In *the formal classes,* topics and texts were chosen which illustrated the message of responsibility. (2) In *the camp community* an atmosphere of relative freedom was relied upon which allowed the camp as a whole, specific bunks, or individuals to think through their responsibilities in any given setting and act accordingly (Lukinsky, 1968:137-141). (3) In the *informal educational program* involvement was encouraged in the "wider community around the camp," such as the Rockland State Hospital, the New York Rehabilitation Center, the Nyack recreation program, and the Head Start program in Nyack.

Ramah's Mission: Leadership, Laity, and Community

Having discussed *what* Ramah has attempted to transmit and *how* it has set about doing so, we turn now to the question of *why* this curriculum and this pedagogy? Three reasons are discussed in the literature: (1) to train Jewish *leaders,* (2) to educate Conservative *laity,* and (3) to preserve the traditional Jewish *community* (cf. Schwartz, 1976). Let us consider each in turn.

Leadership. "When the experiment of Camp Ramah was first undertaken," said Gerson Cohen (1973), "the unspoken aim of its founders was to create a native American elite for the Jewish community. That elite would be patterned very much after the polities of leadership, both lay and professional, in earlier Jewish communities . . . " Simon Greenberg (in Schwartz, 1976:8) pointed out that "it is no coincidence that the Leaders Training Fellowship and the Ramah Movement both came into being at the same time. They were both conceived as possible answers to this pressing question [of how the Conservative movement could find and train future leaders]."

Ramah, then, was seen from the outset as a response to a crisis of leadership. It was intended "to train an indigenous Conservative leadership—both lay and rabbinical—and thereby insure the perpetuation of the movement" (Sklare, 1972, cf. Marshall, et al., 1951 and Schwartz, 1976:9). In the early years, this orientation toward leadership was achieved through the camp program itself. The number of campers that could be accommodated was limited and only a small staff was required. This enabled directors to select campers and counselors with the greatest Hebraic and Judaic background or with the greatest motivation to learn. The program that Ramah could provide with such a population was itself enriching and inspiring. As Ramah grew, however, it became necessary to devise a more systematic approach to leadership training.

The Mador was founded in Wisconsin in 1959 as a national leadership training program. Only high school graduates were admitted. Bringing promising young people together from around the country made it possible to develop a sense of movement among the future staffs of the various camps (Cohen, 1984:35). In addition, it enabled the Ramah directorate to continue a pattern of selectivity in fulfilling its leadership aims while opening the camps to increasingly larger numbers (Farago, 1972:389-390).

Mador studies probed "Jewish learning and literature, psychology and creative arts, in addition to theory and practice of camp leadership. Formal classes, observation of camp activities and discussions with camp administrators" were combined "with the responsibilities of planning and carrying out actual counselor duties" ("To the Heights," 1963). Participants devoted half of their time to study and half to supervised work with children. Formal classes were divided between education, Hebrew, and Judaica. This balance made it possible to transmit Ramah's pedagogic orientation while at the same time perpetuating its commitment to Hebrew language and Jewish learning (cf. Brown, 1973).

Laity. If leadership development was a primary mission of Ramah in its early years, by the time the movement had reached the age of twenty-five, the function of Ramah had become "not so much to create a limited elite leadership for the community as to fashion a broad base of young people who will serve as pillars of the community and change the character of that community through its collective leadership" (Cohen, 1973, cf. Alexander, 1983 and Cohen, 1983).

As early as 1964, Raphael Arzt presented a paper to staff counselors in Connecticut in which he argued that Ramah ought to play a crucial role in the training of "citizens" of the Jewish tradition. Arzt was critical of the tendency of the Schwabian influence on Ramah to emphasize issues of general character development without adequately considering specifically Jewish aims (Farago, 1972:64). Hence, he stressed *Jewish* citizenship.

Arzt held that a citizen Jew ought to be knowledgeable, sensitive, and action oriented; *knowledgeable* in the sense of being rooted in the materials of Jewish tradition and committed to ongoing study, *sensitive* in the sense of being involved in the process of sharpening the soul to respond appropriately to the world and to people about us, and *action oriented* in the sense that "the Citizen (*sic*) Jew is one who feels the impetus to Act, with his tradition playing a significant role in his decision-making process" (Arzt, 1964).

These ends are to be accomplished through the use of the entire camp environment. "Each staff member then must see himself as an environmentalist: one who is actively and consciously organizing components of the camp environment (people, places, things) in order to bring about what we are calling the Citizen-of-Judaism." Two sorts of staff members contribute to this endeavor, those who are primarily, though not exclusively, integrators and interpreters such as camp directors, division heads, and bunk counselors, and those who are specialists such as education directors, teachers, and arts counselors (Arzt, 1964).

Sheldon Dorph (1976:194–202), a former director of Ramah in the Berkshires and in California, summarized this development in Ramah's mission when he wrote (1976:202) that "Ramah wishes to foster increased Jewish behavior and commitment in the camper when he returns home from camp. Beyond this, Ramah hopes to change the young person's concept of adult life style and behavior (college years and beyond) to include a viable Jewish component."

Community. Implicit in both the leadership and laity dimensions of the Ramah mission is a desire not only to maintain but also to transform Jewish life, first in America and later abroad as well. Following Dewey (1899, 1916), the educational aim of Ramah has been not only to *transmit* but also to *transform* culture—or better, to transmit culture by transforming it—that is, to reformulate the ideas and values of the past so that they can meet the ever-changing needs of each generation.

The idea of creating a model Jewish community was present from the inception of Ramah. Cohen (1973:3) put it this way: "Ramah . . . gave a structured model to which a young person might aspire when transferring to his home and community the kind of life that could be translated into American Jewish terms."

The New England Leaders Training Fellowship (LTF) program under Arzt's directorship in the late sixties was among the most concerted efforts to realize this aspect of Ramah's mission, if not also the most controversial. Arzt emphasized the role of camp in changing the Jewish community by developing new ideologies and practices and mobilizing campers to become change agents. The continuity between camp and city life was thought to be crucial. Hence, Arzt developed LTF, which was originally conceived as a national high school, into a youth movement. LTF became a division in camp as well as a youth program in the city (Farago, 1972:71).

Within LTF Arzt followed Lukinsky's lead in granting unprecedented degrees of freedom to campers and encouraging them to take seriously the responsibility associated with that freedom. Unfortunately, many of the excesses associated with the youth rebellion of the sixties crept into the Arzt experiments and the New England camp was closed for a short time after its 1970 season (see Lerner, 1971). According to Cohen (1973:4), year-round programming in Ramah "remains one of the unsolved problems of our generation."

In the early years, the communal dimension of Ramah's mission was focused exclusively on American Jewry. There were even debates in the early fifties over whether the Israeli flag should be raised over the Poconos camp (Schwartz, 1976:41–42). However, as Israel moved into the center of the American Jewish scene, Ramah developed a more openly Zionist stance as well. Thus, Farago (1972:61) cites Arzt as viewing Ramah as "Zionistic in the religious vein" and Dorph (1976:209) suggests aliyah to Israel as one of a number of ways of fulfilling Ramah's "image of adult Jewish life style and commitment."

This then is the Ramah platform, a curriculum stressing Jewish living, language, and learning, a pedagogy emphasizing individuality, character, and responsibility, and a mission aimed at Conservative leadership, laity, and community.

Ramah's Achievements: Curriculum, Pedagogy, and Mission

What of this agenda has Ramah accomplished? And what has it achieved that was unanticipated? Although the available data are incomplete, they do leave us in a position to reflect on some of Ramah's achievements.

Curriculum. In the area of Jewish living, Dorph (1976: 221–305) reports that Ramah is only a "partial success." He administered a survey to 458 students of the Prozdor (the Hebrew High School of the Jewish Theological Seminary) and the Los Angeles Hebrew High School in 1973. His population was divided into those who attended Ramah, other Jewish camps, and no Jewish camps in each location. The questionnaire covered inventories of personal and family observance, general information and background, and perceptions of Jewish summer camp.

He concluded that Ramah has had a greater impact on the attitudes and self-definitions of participants than on their religious behavior. The fact that other camps exerted less influence on attitudes than Ramah is an indication of the latter's success. The fact that its effect on behavior was less than anticipated was disappointing. Still, a small percentage of participants whose families were less observant of Jewish religious practice than Ramah did develop more observant patterns when the socio-cultural environments in which they lived outside of camp were supportive.

Farago's findings for the 1969 season in New England tend to validate Dorph's conclusions, though they suggest some significant differences concerning the perceptions of campers about previous years. He collected behavior and attitude inventories from 250 campers before camp and 186 afterwards. An additional 140 campers responded to questions administered eight months later. Thirty of these were the subjects of observation while at camp. A control group of 35 Hebrew high school students in the Boston area were also questioned. Twenty responses were received.

Farago (1972:301–303) concluded that the 1969 summer at Ramah in New England had a more lasting effect on values and attitudes than on religious behavior, that "many campers who acquire a repertoire of religious practices wish to continue to observe them at their home, but abandon them after a while because their environment fails to support them." In fact, many campers perceived that "in 1969 camp had a less positive effect on religiousness, and particularly on religious observance, than in previous years." Eighty-two percent of the campers felt that the camp had had a positive influence on their religious observance in past years. Only 14% felt that its impact was negative. Forty-five percent of the campers reported a positive effect on observance for the 1969 season, and the same percentage a negative effect (Farago, 1972:300).

This discrepancy between the perceived impact of camp before and during its 1969 season might be seen merely as the result of the experimental programs in New England during that season. The fact, however, that Dorph's 1973 findings tend to reinforce those of Farago in 1969 rather than the perceptions that campers had about earlier years might suggest that the impact of Ramah on religious observance may have declined in the early seventies, perhaps as a result of the culture of the sixties.

Both Dorph and Farago found that Ramah had the greatest impact when either family or external sociogeographic environments reinforced the religious behavior patterns learned in Ramah. Moreover, the Liebman-Shapiro report (1979) suggests that if we take dietary practice as an indicator, observance in Conservative families declines by age. If this is an accurate indicator of not only family practice, but the social environment as well, then it might be argued that there were fewer influences outside of Ramah working to reinforce its program in the seventies than in the fifties and early sixties (cf., *e.g.*, Himmelfarb, 1975).

It might also be argued that such a decline in Ramah's impact on religious behavior is related to the rapid growth of the movement during this period. Lerner (1971) reported, for example, that "both (Seymour) Fox and (David) Mogilner suggested . . . that perhaps Ramah had only enough proper staff for five camps instead of seven." In addition he cites Dorph, then director of the Berkshires camp, as noting that while "kids don't come back from Ramah the way they did ten years ago . . . kids don't come to Ramah with the backgrounds of ten years ago" because of the growth of the movement.

A third explanation of this phenomenon has been found in the decline of the supplemental Hebrew school system which was originally to be the partner of Ramah (Himmelfarb, 1975 and Ackerman, 1980). Even the best prepared campers that arrived at Ramah during this period may not have been as well prepared as those who arrived a decade earlier. Thus, concluded Lerner (1971), "Ramah has been less able to maintain a high level of Hebraic learning." And Hebrew is essential for the style of intelligent observance characteristic of Ramah.

Alexander (1985) proposed a fourth interpretation of these data which is not inconsistent with the above. Based on qualitative data collected at Ramah in the Berkshires in 1982, Alexander argued that an important cultural theme in the camp during that season involved transforming the suburban, American identity of campers to make room for a Jewish component (cf. Farago, 1972:330-341). According to this view, any indications that campers view Judaism as a significant locus of identification should be counted as a success of the implicit curriculum even when more explicit aims are not achieved. In this connection, Farago's observation (1972:344) is relevant that *"evaluating the long-range effect of camp by comparing the Jewish subidentity of the campers before the season and eight months after, almost twice as many campers underwent positive change in various dimensions on their Jewish identity than negative change* (39% as compared to 22%) while 29% recorded no change, on the average." (Emphasis his.)

As far as language and learning are concerned, the data reveal little about what campers have actually achieved through the Hebrew and study programs at Ramah. However, Farago did ask New England campers before and after the 1969 season how they felt about Hebrew. Eighty-one percent before and 95% after expressed positive feelings. Seventeen percent before and 21% after had no special feeling while 2% before and 4% after had negative feelings. In contrast, the control group, which did not use Hebrew at all during the summer, reported an even stronger negative change with 28% before as compared with 52% after indicating no special feeling. Given that Farago observed only limited use of Hebrew in camp during this season, the growth in positive feeling toward the language is quite surprising. It seems that at least at this point in its history, Ramah's emphasis on love of Hebrew rather than speaking it at all costs paid off (see, Alexander, 1985:248-249).

Dorph collected data concerning attitudes toward and intensity of Jewish study. Of the six groups, those who attended no Jewish camp, other Jewish camps, and Ramah in both New York and Los Angeles, the New Yorkers who did not go to camp exhibited the highest level of Jewish study followed by the New York Ramahniks. "One might *theorize*," wrote Dorph, "that the NJC (no Jewish camp) group, *lacking the strong peer group and identity definition of a camp, has taken the intellectual aspect of Judaism — as represented by the Hebrew High School — as a key behavior area for expressing Jewish identification.* It would seem that the Hebrew High School experience and general intellectual environment are the effective variables in levels of Jewish study — certainly NOT camp." (Emphasis his.)

Lukinsky's (1968:173-174) observation in this connection may suggest another interpretation of these data. He pointed out that, at least in 1966, Ramah Seminar participants "had not found their academic Jewish studies very meaningful even though they were willing to bear a minor irritation for the sake of participating in other camp activities . . . If it could not be stated that many had negative views of Jewish learning, they certainly did not hold the view that it had anything specific to do with life. It was clear that they had to be won over . . . " My own experience with adolescent feelings about Jewish learning from teaching Hebrew high school in the mid-seventies and from directing the Mador program in California more recently has not suggested that a great deal has changed in the twenty years which have passed. Clearly this ambivalence toward study stems from forces in American Jewish life which originate beyond the boundaries of Ramah Camps (cf., *e.g.,* Schoem, 1979, 1980). It would be surprising indeed were Ramah able to overcome these forces.

Pedagogy. It is interesting to note that a healthy tension exists between the perennialist character of Ramah's curriculum, which emphasizes the formal study of timeless Jewish values on the one hand, and its progressive approach to pedagogy, which focuses on the needs of the child on the other. The fact that since the Newman revolution, Ramah as a movement has consistently avoided giving way to either horn of this dilemma is one of its most significant educational achievements. Lukinsky (1968:176) called this "the tension between framework and freedom" in teaching responsibility. Dewey (1902) referred to it as the tension between the child and the curriculum.

The desire to communicate Jewish content should not be allowed to overshadow the person to whom the content is being transmitted. Neither, however, can the needs of the child be allowed to completely overshadow curricular content. As Lukinsky (1968:208-210) put it, "the responsible person in the long-range view would make his own decisions about what in his heritage he considers relevant for his life. This can't be determined for him. But since the decision in any meaningful sense depends upon his exposure to *some* heritage or heritages — he can't be exposed to *all* — the educator who plans an educational experience to teach responsibility . . . has the right to choose heritage materials . . . Autonomy, personality, character, and responsibility don't exist 'in general.' Rather the general and universal are clothed, paradoxically, in particular, real, and sometimes unique forms."

Ramah's commitment to this balance is seen in the fact that it made room for the experimentation of Lukinsky and Arzt in the late sixties but did not throw out the baby with the bathwater when the youth rebellion helped to push these innovations too far. Rather, attempts were made to restore the freedom/framework, child/curriculum balance by reemphasizing the religious orientation of the camps in both theory and practice.

Mission. That Ramah has served as a training ground for numerous communal leaders, rabbis, and educators is a commonplace of Conservative Judaism. At one point in the mid-seventies, it was believed that as many as one-half of all students in institutions of higher Jewish learning in the United States had been to a Ramah camp and as many as 75% of all rabbinical students at the Jewish Theological Seminary came out of Ramah ("To The Heights," 1963).

One need only consider the case of Los Angeles to gain a more recent sense of the role that Ramah has played in fostering leadership. Of the four largest Conservative synagogues, two are staffed by senior rabbis and two by educators who were involved with Ramah as youths and young adults. The president, vice presidents, provost, undergraduate dean, director of education programs, dean of students and several members of the faculty of the University of Judaism have all been involved with Ramah either as campers or staff. The director, assistant director, coordinator of school services, and several consultants of the Bureau of Jewish Education have all been involved in one or more of the Ramah camps as campers or staff. The present and past principals of the Conservative Los Angeles Hebrew High School, were active in Ramah before coming to L.A. The current directorate of Ramah in California, as with the movement on the national level, in Israel and at each of the six resident camps, has had significant Ramah experience. Los Angeles is currently the second largest Jewish community in North America. If it is any indication of Ramah's influence, certainly many of those in key professional positions have been involved with Ramah as have numerous members of the lay boards which govern these institutions.

This, of course, does not tell us about the ways this involvement influenced those individuals mentioned. It does suggest, however, that Ramah trains leaders as much through the opportunities it offers its staff to develop dynamic Jewish educational programs as it does through the benefit which its campers receive from the programs which are developed. To reinforce this suggestion we need only consider the current status of a few of the alumni of the first Mador leadership program in 1959. Among them are present and past professors of Judaica or Jewish education in American and Israeli universities, curriculum writers for the Melton Research Center in New York, directors and staff members of bureaus of Jewish education, rabbis, and leaders of the Coalition for Alternatives in Jewish Education.

Be that as it may, we cannot leave the topic of leadership without mentioning the tensions involved in this plank of the Ramah platform (cf. Alexander, 1983; Cohen, 1983; Schwartz, 1976:34–42). As the movement grew and economies of scale required that the doors of Ramah be opened to increasing numbers of campers, conflicts developed between standards of acceptance for both campers and staff which would preserve the elitist quality of the project on the one hand and the need for numbers on the other. Eventually, the desire of directors to keep their best alumni at home in order to preserve the quality of local staffs militated against sending representatives to a national leadership training program and one of the last vestiges of the elitist orientation, the National Mador Program, was closed in 1980. Hence, the populist tendency has come to dominate the elitist.

As far as the impact of Ramah on creating a Conservative Jewish laity is concerned, the findings have been mixed. In 1979, Liebman and Shapiro (for a discussion of the biases of this study, see Schulweis, 1980) surveyed a random sample of about 8% of United Synagogue families. Twenty-eight percent were completed and returned. They found that 10% more Ramah alumni joined synagogues than those who attended no camp, 8% more of them joined Conservative synagogues, and 6% more joined Orthodoxy while 3% fewer former Ramah campers affiliated with Reform Judaism.

By way of comparison, 20% more USY alumni joined synagogues than those who never joined a Jewish youth group. Seventeen percent joined Conservative synagogues, 4% fewer affiliated with Orthodoxy and 1% fewer joined the Reform movement. The trend toward more traditional affiliation is even more dramatic among children of respondents who attended Jewish schools. About 12% more of those who attended afternoon Jewish schools affiliated with Conservative and Orthodox congregations than those who attended no Jewish school (11% Conservative and 1% Orthodox), and almost 32% more of those who attended day schools joined more traditional shuls (14% Conservative and about 18% Orthodox) (cf. Pomerantz, 1980).

Although none of these findings take into account interactions between camp, youth group, school, home, and sociogeographic environment, they nevertheless reinforce the observations of Farago and Dorph. Ramah does have an impact on religious observance and sensibility as measured both in terms of behavior and attitude inventories and in terms of synagogue affiliation. Children who attend Ramah are more likely to join traditional, especially Conservative, synagogues than those who do not. Yet, programs which carry these values into the life of the child in the city such as USY, afternoon schools, and day schools, appear to have an even greater impact. It seems as though some combination of these may be our most powerful educational tools (cf. Bock, 1977, Himmelfarb, 1975, Ackerman, 1980).

This brings us to the influence of Ramah on the preservation of Jewish communal life. Let us distinguish between the American and Israeli Jewish communities. As far as the former is concerned, apart from its influence on the leadership and laity of American Jewry, perhaps the most significant communal outcome of the Ramah movement has been a result of its interaction with the leadership of the early havurot. Havurat Shalom, for example, was founded in 1968 in Somerville, Massachusetts, as "a community of Jewish learning" which viewed itself as an alternative to the modes of Jewish education "presently extant in the United States" which "do not present themselves as viable options for many religiously sensitive individuals" (*Response* Editors, 1968:36-37). Farago (1972:381) reports that "some of the founders of the Havurah had a previous relationship to Ramah, particularly to the camp in New England. The religious search which brought forth the idea of the Havurah might have been particularly stimulated by their experiences as campers or staff members at Ramah."

The importance of the Havurah movement in American Jewish life in the seventies and eighties need not be rehearsed here. In addition to the various popular publications, such as the *Jewish Catalogue* series that it inspired, many of the same individuals who were involved in Havurat Shalom and other similar communities around the country became involved in the Jewish Students Network which in 1973 called for the first Conference on Alternatives in Jewish Education at Brown University. This conference blossomed into the Coalition for Alternatives in Jewish Education which has become a significant agent for change in American Jewish education. In a different connection, in response to the pioneering efforts of Harold Schulweis, the concept of small subcommunities or havurot within large synagogues has become one of the more significant attempts to both humanize and personalize synagogue life. Ramah is certainly not responsible for these developments. It is, however, one of a number of important institutions in American Jewish life that has contributed to them.

With respect to Israel, both Farago (1972:321) and Dorph (1976:267), observed that Ramah had a significant impact on campers' and staffs' plans to visit, study, and even live in Israel. Clearly, wrote Dorph, "when FRB (*f*amily *r*eligious *b*ehavior) is high, the influence of Ramah has a major reinforcing effect on the plans of young people to study and live in Israel." The creation of the Israeli version of Conservative Judaism, the Masorti movement, has no doubt been influenced by the Ramah movement as has Garin Nitzan, the first community committed to founding a Conservative settlement in Israel, Kibbutz Hanaton.

Conclusion: Challenges Facing Ramah

Although the data concerning Ramah's accomplishments are sparse, their message is relatively consistent. First, as part of a consortium of educational institutions, Ramah can contribute to increased commitment to Jewish living, more positive feelings about Hebrew language, and greater willingness to become involved in Jewish learning. Second, when its programs focus on a small group of especially committed young people, Ramah can provide the camaraderie, skills, and inspiration for them to pursue leadership positions in the Jewish community. Thus, of the challenges facing Ramah as it approaches a half-century of operation, two are especially significant: fostering more extensive coordination with other Conservative educational agencies, and creating a more productive balance between its elitist and populist aims through systematic leadership development.

BIBLIOGRAPHY AND REFERENCES

Ackerman, W. (1980), "Jewish Education Today," *American Jewish Yearbook*, 80:130–149.

Alexander, H. A. (1983), "Ometz: A New Conception of Leadership Development for the Conservative Movement," *The Melton Journal*, 15:4, 25.

―――― (1985), *The Qualitative Turn in Evaluation: An Ecumenical Analysis*, doctoral dissertation, Stanford University. Ann Arbor: University Microfilms.

"An Experience Called Ramah" (1970). New York: National Ramah Commission.

Arzt, R. (1964), "Concept of a Citizen of Judaism," unpublished manuscript.

Bardin, S. (1946), "The Brandeis Camp Institute," *Jewish Education*, 17, 3:24–26.

Bock, G. (1977), "Does Jewish Schooling Matter?" New York: American Jewish Committee.

Brown, S. (1973), *Mador Manual*. New York: National Ramah Commission.

Cohen, B. I. (1983), "Leadership Development Programs in the Conservative Movement: A Response," *The Melton Journal*, 16:20–21.

―――― (1984), "Louis Newman's Wisconsin Innovations and Their Effect on the Ramah Camping Movement," in *Studies in Jewish Education and Judaica in Honor of Louis Newman*, A. M. Shapiro and B. I. Cohen (eds.). New York: Ktav.

Cohen, G. (1973), "The Goals of Camp Ramah," unpublished manuscript.

Davis, M. (1946), "Report on LTF," *Proceedings of the Rabbinical Assembly*, 10:180.

Dewey, J. (1899), *The School and the Society*. Chicago: University of Chicago Press.

―――― (1902), *The Child and the Curriculum*. Chicago: University of Chicago Press.

―――― (1916), *Democracy and Education*. New York: Macmillan.

Dorff, E. N. (1977), *Conservative Judaism: Our Ancestors to Our Descendants*. New York: United Synagogue Youth.

Dorph, S. A. (1976), *A Model for Jewish Education in America*, doctoral dissertation, Teachers College, Columbia University. Ann Arbor: University Microfilms.

Ettenberg, S. (1982), unpublished interview (July 12, 1982).

Farago, U. (1972), *The Influence of a Jewish Summer Camp's Social Climate on the Camper's Identity*, doctoral dissertation, Brandeis University. Ann Arbor: University Microfilms.

Furie, W. B. (1946), "Yavneh," *Jewish Education,* 17, 3:28f.
Gannes, A. P. and Shoshuk, L. (1949), "The Kevutzah and Camp Achvah," *Jewish Education,* 20, 3:61-66.
Golub, J. S. (1946), "Bibliography on Camping," *Jewish Education,* 17, 3:36-44.
Goodman, P. (1946), "The Jewish Home Camp," *Jewish Education,* 17, 3:30-35.
Gribetz, B. (1973), "Jewish Educational Camping: Toward a History," unpublished manuscript.
_____ (1974), "The Rise of Jewish Educational Camping," unpublished manuscript.
Himmelfarb, H. (1975), "Jewish Education for Naught," *Analysis,* 51. Washington, D. C.: Institute for Jewish Policy Planning and Research of the Synagogue Council of America.
Isaacson, D. (1966), "Jewish Educational Camping," *American Jewish Yearbook,* 67:245-252.
Kronish, R. (1979), *The Influence of John Dewey on Jewish Education in America,* doctoral dissertation, Harvard University. Ann Arbor: University Microfilms.
_____ (1983), "John Dewey's Influence on Jewish Education in America: The Gap Between Theory and Practice," in *Studies in Jewish Education,* 1. Jerusalem: Magnes Press.
Lerner, Stephen C. (1971), "Ramah and Its Critics," *Conservative Judaism,* 25, 4:1-28.
Liebman, C. and Shapiro, S. (1979), "The State of the Conservative Movement," *United Synagogue Review,* 32,2.
Lukinsky, J. (1968), *Teaching Responsibility: A Case Study in Curriculum Development,* doctoral dissertation, Harvard University. Ann Arbor: University Microfilms.
Marshall, J. *et al.* (1951), "The Crisis of Moral and Intellectual Leadership," *Proceedings of the Rabbinical Assembly,* 15:156-178.
Mogilner, D. (1972), "Ramah is My Pulpit," *Your Child,* Winter:2-5.
Newman, L. (1951), "My Views on Counselorship," in *Studies in Jewish Education and Judaica in Honor of Louis Newman,* A. M. Shapiro and B. I. Cohen (eds.). New York: Ktav.
Pomerantz, S. (1980), "Conservative Movement Surveyed Again," *United Synagogue Review,* 32, 3:10f.
Potok, C. (1954), "A Hope for the Future: The Leaders Training Fellowship," *The Torch,* 13, 1:20-21, 46.
Resnikoff, B. (1962), "On Producing Healthy Rebels," *The Synagogue School,* 21, 1:26-27f.
Response Editors (1968), "Religious Community in Cambridge," *Response* 2,2:36-37.
Schoem, D. (1979), *Ethnic Survival in America: An Ethnography of Jewish Afternoon School,* doctoral dissertation, University of California, Berkeley. Ann Arbor: University Microfilms.
_____ (1980), "Inside the Classroom: Reflections of a Troubled People,"

Jewish Education, 48, 1:35-41.

Schoolman, A. P. (1946), "The Jewish Educational Summer Camp: A Survey of Its Development and Implications," *Jewish Education,* 17, 3:6-15.

Schulweis, H. (1980), "Surveys, Statistics, and Secular Salvation," *Conservative Judaism,* 34, 2:65-69.

Schwartz, S. R. (1976), "Ramah—The Early Years, 1947-52," masters thesis, The Jewish Theological Seminary of America.

―――― (1978), "Ramah Camps—Then and Now" (Hebrew), in *Kovetz Massad: Essays in Hebrew Literature and Thought,* M. Havazelet (ed.). New York: Massad Camps.

―――― (1984), "Ramah Philosophy and the Newman Revolution," in *Studies in Jewish Education and Judaica in Honor of Louis Newman,* A. M. Shapiro and B. I. Cohen (eds.). New York: Ktav.

Shulsinger, S. (1946), "Hebrew Camping: Five Years of Massad," *Jewish Education,* 17, 3:16-21.

Silverman, H. (1950), "Preparation for Jewish Leadership," *The Torch,* 9, 4:21-26.

Sklare, M. (January 1972), "Recent Developments in Conservative Judaism, *Midstream,* 18, 1:13-19.

"To the Heights" (1963). New York: The Jewish Theological Seminary of America.

From Camper to National Director: A Personal View of the Seminary and Ramah

Burton I. Cohen

Origins of the Seminary's Involvement in Ramah Camping

As the Seminary celebrates the one hundredth anniversary of its founding, the Ramah camping movement celebrates the fortieth anniversary of its establishment. For people who have grown up within the Conservative movement over the past forty years it is difficult to conceive of the Seminary's program without Ramah. But how did this very staid scholarly institution give birth to a children's camping movement?

Were one to personify the Seminary one can imagine it saying as it neared maturity at age 60, in 1946, "Now that I have established myself as a premier academic institution, the time has come for me to see what steps I ought to take to educate the broad community of Conservative Jews, to introduce its youth to intensive Jewish living and serious study, and to encourage some of them to study for the rabbinate and assume roles of leadership in the North American Jewish community." While one hesitates to attribute rationality to the actions of institutions and movements, subject as they are at times to irrational and arbitrary forces, in the case of Camp Ramah, the above suggested fanciful personification seems to be not so remote from the facts of what actually occurred.

Shuly Rubin Schwartz has cogently suggested how the founding of the Ramah Camps resulted from the convergence of several independent factors, each making a vital contribution to the success of the innovative project.[1] One factor had its locus in Chicago where Rabbi Ralph Simon was initiating and coordinating an effort to establish an educational summer camp for the children who attended the Conservative synagogues' Hebrew schools in that city. A second factor was the presence in key positions at the Seminary of individuals (notably Moshe Davis and Sylvia Ettenberg) who had been involved in the Massad Camps and Cejwin Camps, both important efforts at offering a Hebraic/Judaic camp experience. These same individuals had also been leaders in the Hebrew youth movements in New York City. In the spring of 1948, Davis gave an address at the second Rabbinical Assembly Conference on Education, in which he called for the creation of a network of summer camps with an intensive Jewish educational program, which he regarded as vital to the achievement of the goals of the Conservative movement.

> We have much to learn, but he who has seen camp in action (i.e. the initial 1947 season of Camp Ramah in Wisconsin) can testify that an educational miracle has been wrought. This one single, as yet, baby institution has already raised the standards of all congregational work in the Chicago area, and has set off creative sparks in other parts of the country. Every aspect of our educational objectives can be taught in the twenty-four hour day, nine-week summer program. If the experience is repeated over a period of four or five years the results reproduce geometrically.[2]

Rubin calls attention to a third important factor which contributed to the readiness of the Seminary to get involved in the Ramah enterprise—the stark realization that the recent Holocaust had depleted a primary source of religious leadership for American Jewry. Davis' speech also makes reference to this concern.

Early in the fall of 1946, an historic agreement was reached between the representatives of the Chicago Council, United Synagogue of America and the Seminary: the Chicago Council took responsibility for purchasing a suitable site and accepted fiscal responsibility for the camp operation; the Seminary would be responsible for designing the camp program and recruiting the staff, and was given the authority to set educational and religious policy. At least initially, recruitment of campers would be done jointly by the rabbis, educators, and laymen affiliated with the Chicago Council, and the Seminary. The list of 98 campers enrolled that first summer attests to the effort made by the Seminary to create a national camp and not simply one which was local or regional. While the largest bloc of campers, myself among them, was recruited from Chicago, those recruited from across the country included Alice Aaronson (Zlatnick), Tulsa, Oklahoma; (Rabbi) Everett Gendler, Des Moines, Iowa; and (Professor) Yochanan Muffs, New York City.[3] The local initiative in Chicago had led (or perhaps compelled) the Seminary to embark on a national program.[4]

The Seminary's readiness to become involved in the education of the youth of the Conservative movement through its sponsorship and guidance of the Ramah Camps was already presaged in the founding of the Leaders Training Fellowship (LTF) in the year immediately preceding the opening of Camp Ramah. In creating LTF, the Seminary proposed to join Hebrew high school students from throughout the Conservative movement together in a national fellowship dedicated to study and community service, under the tutelage of the local Conservative rabbis. It was to some of those first LTFers that the Seminary turned as it recruited campers for the first Ramah season and, in fact, it applied the designation Leaders Training Fellowship (Hebrew: *Machon*) to the 14-17 year old campers at Ramah. Following that first Ramah season the Seminary encouraged the creation of a city-wide LTF unit in Chicago under the leadership of Rabbi Jacob Milgrom, then an assistant rabbi at the Anshe Emet Synagogue. For the other Chicago-area Ramah campers and myself, the monthly Chicago LTF meetings and the annual December Midwest LTF Kinnus provided a year-round support system. While open to all Hebrew high school students, LTF offered us the opportunity to maintain contact with Ramahniks throughout the year and even to participate once a month in the kind of stimulating religious and educational experiences that we had first experienced at Ramah.

The Seminary and Me

Camp Ramah has served as an unusually successful public relations medium for the Seminary, bringing the Seminary to the attention of tens of thousands of Jewish families throughout North America who otherwise would not have been aware of nor influenced by its existence. I am quite sure that my own family was not atypical of the vast majority of Conservative-affiliated families in the 1940s in the following regard: prior to my own involvement in Ramah they had never been solicited for a gift to the Seminary nor were they in fact aware of the Seminary's existence.

Prior to the establishment of Ramah, such field offices of the

Seminary as existed throughout North America existed chiefly, if not solely, to coordinate fund-raising efforts for the Seminary in the region where they were located. The presence of Ramah in a community, and at times in the same suite of offices, helped to shape the image of Seminary as an institution which was reaching out to create a new model of Jewish life and was not simply a collector of funds for a remote academic institution. The lay leadership in communities served by Ramah often understood this better than the Seminary's field staff. As the Ramah movement grew, lay leaders of the Ramah Camps often tended to be those same individuals who headed up the Seminary campaign in a given community.[5]

It should come as no surprise then, that when I was recruited by our rabbi in Chicago, at age fourteen, to be a Ramah camper, I had never heard of the Seminary. Though I (and other prospective campers) were interviewed by Sylvia Ettenberg (then registrar of the Seminary's Teachers Institute) prior to acceptance, I had no concept of the institution which she represented, or in fact that she represented any institution beyond Camp Ramah. In later years I learned that my synagogue rabbi, Rabbi Benjamin H. Birnbaum, who served on the Ramah committee which Ralph Simon had organized, and was a Seminary graduate, valued the Ramah-Seminary connection, but at the time I had no notion of this relationship.

Like many hundreds of young people who came through Ramah during the past four decades, I began to learn about the Seminary through the Seminary-affiliated people who served at the camp. That I might study for the rabbinate was far from my mind when I arrived at Ramah in 1947; yet, when I began to meet rabbinical students and recently ordained rabbis, I began to consider this possibility. From those earliest years I have fond memories of meeting David Lieber, Hillel Silverman, Kassel Abelson and Alexander Shapiro, and many others, all having been just ordained or soon to be ordained at the Seminary. My interest in pursuing a Jewish vocation was heightened by the presence in the Wisconsin camp each summer of a Seminary appointed scholar-in-residence beginning with Dr. Abraham Halkin, and including professors Ernst Simon, Shalom Spiegel, Seymour Siegel, David Weiss Halivni, Shraga Abramson and Dr. Michael Higger. I also recall listening to an informal though sharp debate between Hillel Silverman and Norman Podhoretz, both Seminary alumni, in the Wisconsin kitchen one Friday night, on the relative merits of Bialik and Mendele.[6] In my youthful mind I identified this intellectual ferment with what must take place constantly at the Seminary. Similarly, I was introduced to the new and fascinating world of modern Biblical scholarship by a brilliant college student by the name of Moshe Greenberg. Over recent years as I spoke with other Ramah alumni, I have confirmed that many of us were influenced at Ramah not simply toward enrolling at the Seminary, but perhaps more importantly, toward entering Jewish scholarly fields and embracing the approaches favored by the Seminary's faculty.

The Seminary and Ramah Religious Policy

In 1946, when then president of the Jewish Theological Seminary of America, Dr. Louis Finkelstein, agreed to accept responsibility for the setting of educational and religious policy for Camp Ramah in Wisconsin, prior to the initial 1947 season, the Seminary was for the first time undertaking to set religious policy for an institution and programs that lay beyond its own walls. It was a new role for the Seminary.

Right from the start, the designated policy-making body for Ramah, the faculty of the Seminary's Teachers Institute, was required to make policy decisions far unlike any theretofore made by the Seminary's authorities. These initial steps resulted in the creation of a unique pattern of religious observance at Ramah, independent of the deliberations and decisions of the Rabbinical Assembly's Committee on Jewish Law and Standards and in certain ways independent of the practices at the Seminary itself. For example, until September 1984, separate seating for men and women was the practice at all religious services at the Seminary — at Ramah mixed seating was the practice from the very start.

Another very significant policy decision relating to participation of women in religious ritual at Ramah was the decision to allow female campers and staff to lead the Birkat Hamazon (grace after meals) in the camp dining room. No woman had ever done this at a public occasion at the Seminary, so again, it was not in agreement with, if not contrary to, Seminary practice.

We should note that we are not able to reproduce the arguments or discussions that led to these decisions. We have never seen transcripts of the meetings where these matters were discussed, but are simply describing the practice at camps as recalled by those who were present at the start. What is clear is that a new pattern of religious practice was established independent of the Rabbinical Assembly, the Seminary's own practices, or the variety of practices in the Conservative synagogues which were sending youngsters to Ramah.

It should be pointed out that it was not only in the area of religious policy relating to women that the Teachers Institute faculty broke new ground. It also had to set policy on the use of electricity on Shabbat, determine which waterfront activities were permissible on Shabbat, approve an abbreviated version of the Birkat Hamazon, and decide which services were compulsory and within each service which prayers needed to be recited. It is not clear to the writer if all these practices were initially decided by the faculty or whether some were affirmed by the faculty only after they were initiated in the camps.

Over the past forty years, additions to the Ramah religious code were made, if not by the entire faculty, then by the Seminary faculty members designated by the president/chancellor to be the *posek* for the Ramah movement. The Seminary appointed a scholar-in-residence for each camp, each summer, whose primary task was to establish a Seminary presence in the camp and to assist with the implementation of the educational and religious policy. If, for any reason, no professor was present in the camp, or there was need for further clarification or elaboration of some policy, then the *posek* could be reached by telephone.

During the early 1970s, in response to questions submitted to the *posek*, the area of participation of women in ritual at Ramah was broadened to include the following:

1. Women were allowed to recite the *Kiddush* and *Havdalah*.

2. Women were allowed to chant the *Kabbalat Shabbat* service (up to *Borkhu*) on Friday evening.

Preceding the summer of 1974, Seminary Chancellor Dr. Gerson Cohen ruled that women could receive aliyot and read from the Torah at Ramah. This decision was preceded by a year of study and discussion involving Ramah staff members, Seminary faculty, Conservative rabbis from the field, and Ramah lay committee members. It came in response to requests from members of the Ramah constituency that the policy be revised.

More recently, Chancellor Cohen's 1986 decision to establish a minyan at Ramah Camps which grants full equality to women followed the decision of the Seminary faculty to admit women to study for ordination in the Seminary's Rabbinical School. It also came after the Seminary had established a second morning minyan ("Schiff II"), in which women could fully participate in the service.

Ramah and the Seminary: A Symbiotic Relationship

If at the beginning the development of the Ramah camping movement was the result of the fortuitous confluence of the needs and concerns of a local Jewish community with those of a national institution, it was not long before the local-national relationship developed into a fruitful symbiotic relationship, each side drawing strength from the other. At the start, the Seminary recruited staff for Ramah from its student body, provided a scholar-in-residence from its faculty, and supervised the development and implementation of the camp program. From the very first group of high schoolers who attended Camp Ramah in Wisconsin in the summer of 1947, three, Everett Gendler, Yochanan Muffs, and I, enrolled in the Seminary's Rabbinical School and were subsequently ordained. From that time to the present there has been no entering class at the Seminary which did not have in it one or more alumni of Ramah. Not infrequently the Seminary sent to Ramah weak but promising Rabbinical School applicants so that they might experience intensive Jewish living and have an opportunity to learn Hebrew at Ramah. After forty years it is possible to say that every significant administrative position at the Seminary, not to mention many faculty posts, has, at times, been filled by Ramah alumni.

There are other ways in which Ramah has strengthened the Seminary's program. In the early years of the Seminary's Melton Research Center, there was need to find a controlled situation in which the Center's newly developed Bible materials might be tried out. During the 1960s, experimental programs were established in several Ramah Camps to provide the testing situations which the Center required. This experimentation, by exposing many students, teachers, and visiting educators to the new Melton approach, helped to encourage the use and diffusion of these materials throughout the United States.

Final Thoughts

The picture of Ramah and the Seminary presented in the preceding paragraphs is drawn from knowledge gained in my experience as a Ramah camper, camp staff member, camp director, National

Ramah Director, and as a parent of three Ramah campers. From all of these vantage points it is clear to me that the Seminary has performed a remarkable service to the Conservative movement not only by supporting and supervising the Ramah Camps and programs over a period of forty years, but by urging the camps to continue to adhere to the same worthy educational objectives set at the start, forty years ago.[7] It is interesting to note that while Ramah was initially designed to supplement what a student learned in the synagogue school, it has survived into the era of the Conservative Day School — in fact, some Ramah Camps now enroll over fifty percent of their population from day school students. Once again, the Ramah idea has been proven to possess a vitality beyond the ken of its founders. We can only hope that as the Seminary enters its second century, it will continue to persevere in its crucial role of maintaining the educational and religious emphases of the Ramah program.

NOTES

1. Shuly Rubin Schwartz, "Ramah—The Early Years, 1947-52" (unpublished Master's Essay, The Jewish Theological Seminary of America, 1976).

2. Moshe Davis, "The Ladder of Jewish Education: A Program for Jewish Education in Conservative Judaism", in *Tradition and Change,* ed. Mordecai Waxman (New York: The Burning Bush Press, 1958), p. 440.

3. These four names, among others, are picked from that first Ramah enrollment roster because, aside from their diverse origins, they attest to the degree to which, from the very start, Ramah campers later studied at the Seminary, served on its faculty, married its graduates and were otherwise intertwined with the growth of the Seminary over the past 40 years. A listing of members of the current Seminary administration and faculty who were active at Ramah would include Chancellor Ismar Schorsch, Provost Raymond Scheindlin and Dean Mayer Rabinowitz, as well as Professors Yochanan Muffs, Burton Cohen, Joseph Lukinsky, Joel Roth, David Kraemer, Burton Visotzky, and others.

4. The trans-continental scope of the Ramah movement would only come to fruition in the summer of 1956 with the founding of Camp Ramah in California and in 1961 with the opening of Camp Ramah in Canada.

5. In this regard we might cite individuals such as Maxwell Abbell and Louis Winer in Chicago, Abe Birenbaum in Philadelphia, and J. Barney Goldhar in Toronto.

6. I did not realize at the time that this vigorous defense of Mendele epitomized Podhoretz' general critique of the way belles lettres Jewish literature was taught at the Seminary. See *Doings and Undoings,* Norman

Podhoretz (New York: Farrar Strauss & Co., 1964), p. 119.

7. There is a growing body of literature which describes how the Ramah camp directors and their staffs fleshed out the policies set by the Seminary. Among the most recent examples of this literature are articles by Alexander Shapiro, Shuly Schwartz, Burton Cohen, Joseph Lukinsky, Arthur Elstein, and Louis Newman in *Studies in Jewish Education and Judaica in Honor of Louis Newman,* eds. Alexander M. Shapiro and Burton I. Cohen (New York, Ktav Publishing House, 1984).

View from the quadrangle of the entrance to the Seminary and the tower which once housed the library's books (1985).

The Impact of the Seminary on Israeli Religious Thought

Reuven Hammer

In assessing the Seminary's actual and potential contribution to the State of Israel, its twofold nature — that of an academic institution and that of a theological center which has crystallized into a version of Judaism known as Conservative Judaism — must be considered. As an academic institution, the Seminary prides itself upon its scholarship which is objective and truth-seeking. The great scholars who taught there have left their impact on Jewish scholarship in Israel no less than in America. The rabbinic studies of Schechter, Ginzberg, Lieberman, and, *yibadel l'hayyim arukim,* Finkelstein are studied and quoted everywhere. The same is true of the giants in other fields — Bible, History, medieval studies, etc. Without minimizing the importance of such scholarship, it must be admitted that the critical methodology which is characteristic of the Seminary is not unique to it and that this methodology is the common property of all scholarly institutions in Israel, which is one reason why so many outstanding Israeli scholars who clearly identify themselves as Orthodox nevertheless find the atmosphere of the Seminary congenial to them.

Seminary-trained scholars, men who received their rabbinical ordination, master's degrees, and sometimes Ph.D.s from JTS, are to be found on every major campus in Israel and continue the Seminary tradition of scholarly excellence in training their own students.

Unfortunately, in the realm of religious thought, the Seminary circle has made little impact. The two major theoretical figures associated directly with the Seminary, Kaplan and Heschel, are hardly recognized, either academically or popularly. Although a few of Kaplan's major writings have been translated into Hebrew, they are virtually unknown. It may be that Kaplan's thought, although based upon Ahad HaAm in many ways, is still too much of an American product to be relevant to Israel. Although he gave great attention to the question of a Jewish State and of Zionism, there has been little response to his ideas. Heschel, while somewhat better known in philosophical circles, has not appeared in Hebrew except for a few of his minor works. His major theological works have not been published and he is generally not included in courses on Jewish Philosophy in the way that Rosenzweig, for example, is. The same is true for other creative theological thinkers such as Steinberg and Gordis, so that the impact of the Seminary — that is, the Seminary faculty — on religious thought is virtually non-existent.

Of all of the Seminary-trained men living and teaching in Israel today, the one who most consciously writes and speaks on issues which are theological and contemporary in nature is Moshe Greenberg, whose numerous collected essays on Judaism go far beyond the usual scholarly article in order to deal with the issues in which the Seminary as a theological center has always been immersed; issues such as the relationship of a religious tradition to a modern world, the translation of that tradition into contemporary terms and the transformation of that tradition into ideas and actions appropriate for the time and place.

Interestingly enough, it is the intellectual elite of the kibbutz movement and its school Oranim, who have sought most consciously to study the Jewish tradition *not* academically but as a continual, living guide to action and who have turned to the writings of Seminary scholars for guidance. Through them, the Seminary has had an influence — limited though it may — on teachers and pupils in the kibbutzim. The influence has been salutary in widening horizons, in creating a positive orientation toward Jewish study, but it has not gone into the realm of belief and of God. It has helped to stimulate an interest in tradition and in holidays but always in a limited way.

As the fountainhead of a movement, the Seminary is connected to the efforts to found an Israeli version of this movement. The role of the Seminary as an institution is limited in this, but the Seminary has served and does serve as the founder of institutions which make possible this movement — the Foundation for Conservative Judaism in Israel and the Seminary of Judaic Studies which, as a sister institution, will serve the same role in Israel that JTS serves in America, i.e., being the spiritual and educational center of a movement.

To speak of what this movement has accomplished until now is of less importance than to envision what it can contribute to Israeli life. The obstacles which make it difficult for the movement to function and grow are all too well known: the political connection, the official role of the rabbinate, the intrusion of religious law into the life of the individual. Effecting a change in this—if such a change is possible—would be a major contribution to life in Israel. The idea that pluralism must be allowed to exist in religious life, that the power of the State should not be used coercively, that variety exists in Judaism, that individuals must freely choose to observe mitzvot, this constellation of liberality and individualism as part of a religious view which is committed to observance would be unique and would contribute a new outlook to religious thought in Israel. What is lacking now is a sophisticated theological/philosophical theory encompassing all of this which our movement is uniquely qualified to produce. It has not been produced in America because the conditions there do not require it. It is taken for granted because the American Constitution and way of life posit pluralism, individual freedom, minimal government interference and separation of religion and state.

It is precisely in the areas wherein Israel differs that Masorti Judaism must meet needs and challenges that American Conservative Judaism has not faced. These include:

— The relationship of halakhah to state law and legislation
— Judaism and society
— The Jew as a majority figure, a ruler
— The definition of Judaism and the role of religion in a Jewish civilization
— The place of the synagogue in a society where Jewish identity is not a principal reason for affiliation
— The Jewishness of the street, of a community, of a kibbutz

In addition, the Seminary approach both academically and theologically, is vital to the task of combating the simplistic religious thinking and teaching which is taken for granted in Israel and which is identified with Judaism in the public consciousness, not only among the uneducated but among general circles including political leaders, who may not accept it for themselves but do accept it as normative. This is not to deny the existence of authentic Orthodox approaches that rise above notions differing little if at all from superstition. Unfortunately, because of the domination of official religion, and now even of the Chief Rabbinate, by the unsophisticated, any Orthodox approach of value is confined to an elite which has little if any effect upon the popular mind. Should these thinkers, for the most part academics, succeed in establishing ways of influencing the public, they will only strengthen our efforts in that direction. The major advantage of the theological thinking of the Seminary approach is its complete candor and lack of apologetics. Without meaning to condescend to our Orthodox colleagues, I must admit that all too frequently I have the feeling that they do not make the complete distinction between homiletic interpretation of Jewish sources and the scholarly, historical understanding of them. In dialogue with them, we serve to keep them from too easily passing beyond the border of acceptable hermeneutics.

On the other end of the spectrum, our concern with the authority of the tradition, its continuity and application to the present situation, contrasts both with the academic study of Judaism and with the secular vision of Judaism as old-fashioned and outlived. The value of our approach and its authenticity lie exactly in this: that we — like Israel — are the wrestlers with Jewish tradition. We neither accept everything nor we do not ignore what does not please, simplify it, falsify or reject it. We attempt to include, to clarify and to knowledgeably reinterpret. We question with respect, honor honest doubt, and leave a place for creative skepticism, all of which is difficult for the Israeli to understand, yet profoundly needed within the context of Israeli religiosity.

In the Diaspora, our approach to Jewish life has been to build strong Jewish identity through urging firm institutional loyalties. The synagogue, the synagogue school and the day school have been the foci around which being a Jew has revolved. Characteristically, it has taken a century for our circles to produce a *siddur* which includes material for the home and individual rather than being totally synagogue-centered. Our movement will have to deal with the fact that in Israel the synagogue is *but one* institution working for the Jewish community, but *it is not the* Jewish community. The individual Jew on the one hand and the larger community on the other are more important than the synagogue and our approach will succeed or fail on the basis of what it means to be a Jew both as an individual and within the context of the community.

We must also deal with the role of the rabbi within the community. The American perception of the rabbi as virtually identical with the congregational rabbi who is a spiritual leader, a personal counselor and a community leader is virtually unknown in Israel. I am not certain what the Israeli believes the role of a rabbi to be. I suspect that it is closer to that of *posek, dayyan, mashgiaḥ** or — in some cases — the "rebbe." The possible roles of the Masorti rabbi have yet to be determined.

What is clear is that our rabbis in Israel are faced with the most difficult challenges and tasks imaginable. The scope of Jewish involvement in Israel is enlarged so that it includes everything which is part of life and part of society. It is an illusion to think that life in Israel can be divided into areas, some of which are vital and of concern to Judaism, others of which are not. Living in the Jewish state and the state of the Jews, there is nothing foreign to the concerns of Judaism. The return to Zion was not a mere exercise in assuring the physical survival of the Jewish people, crucial as this may be. It was a return to the early vision of Judaism as a total way of life. This is an integral part of the history of Zionism. So-called secular approaches to Judaism, if they were Jewish and not assimilatory, also viewed the Zionist experiment as an opportunity to actualize what they saw as the reality of Judaism. In many ways, they felt that they were returning to the true Judaism which had been somehow perverted through centuries of exile and persecution. They were concerned to create not the new man but the new Jew and they were not loath to look into the Jewish past, especially the biblical heritage, in order to do so. What they were not ready to do was to recognize the rabbinic, halakhically-centered tradition as being authoritative. Thus there emerged a revisionist attitude toward Jewish history in which everything rabbinic was labeled *galut* and thereby deprecated. Historically, one can understand the feeling of these early leaders having to contend with the pressures of rabbinic leadership and, considering the way in which halakhah is interpreted today, one can even sympathize with it. Our approach, however, cannot be to confine Judaism to the traditional four *amot* of halakhah, but to seek to Judaize all of life. This is not a simple goal.

It is no accident that Second Temple Judaism developed a rabbinic tradition which was different from the earlier biblical one. Those two periods of Jewish sovereignty were not identical to one another. Our era is not the same as either of them. I suspect, however, that the Second Temple period had one thing in common with ours and that is that there was no overall agreement as to the nature of or

---

*In order: legal decisor, judge, kashrut supervisor.

the demands of Judaism, but that competing ideologies and groups existed side by side. What their relationship to the government was is not clear.

We, too, are going to have to learn to live in a situation in which differing versions of Judaism live side by side. They already do. Our movement is going to have to be an active participant in the creation of the total Jewish life of the nation. Each rabbi must feel that he* has a stake in everything that happens here, but at the same time we must contend with the fact that we are one voice among many, that Jews are the majority but not the sole participants in the State, that halakhah has many faces, not one, and that we have a deep respect for the rights of the individual and of various groups, even for those with whom we disagree.

In addition, we face a challenge not only from groups who, at worst, consider us dangerous, but also from those who, at best, consider us unnecessary. A secular Jew, for example, may be willing to defend our right to exist, but does not feel that we have anything to say to him. Unlike the case in America where secularism is not respected as a philosophy (even though it may indeed underlie the lives of most people), in Israel the contention that one can be a Jew and live a Jewish life without "religion" is prevalent and may even be true. There is some serious doubt as to the quality of that life and its power to endure, but the argument which is so popular in America — that if you want to be a Jew and you want your children and grandchildren to be Jewish you had better affiliate with a synagogue — carries little, if any, weight here. If we want to induce people to affiliate or to be concerned with our view of Judaism, we are going to have to show them that our version of Judaism is meaningful to them.

Our movement's approach toward the incorporation of halakhah — or, better, of Jewish values — into all aspects of Jewish life can serve as a major contribution. The civil legislation of halakhah has resulted in governmental enforcement of certain aspects of religious ritual and personal law. This includes aspects of medical practices: abortion, transplants and autopsies. Our voice in these areas needs to be heard. (It is important to note that the religious establishment as well as the overwhelming majority of Orthodox Israelis are convinced

---

*The Seminary of Judaic Studies in Israel does not admit women rabbinical students, although the subject is currently under discussion, nor are there any Conservative rabbis who are women presently residing in Israel.

that it is obvious that halakhah — as determined by whatever authorities the speaker recognizes — *must* be the law of the state. Therefore, if some matters are not insisted upon, it is taken as a sign of the willingness of Orthodoxy to compromise.)

On the other hand, most areas of halakhah and Jewish values are ignored. Despite the efforts of Alon and others, the influence of Jewish Law (*Mishpat Ivry*) is very limited. In civil matters, in criminal law, economic policy, and political situations, Jewish values play no role. In view of current political realities, this is a blessing, but from the long view of Judaism as a way of life and source of values, it is a disaster.

In light of this opportunity and this vacuum, we must develop an approach to the understanding of tradition which would aim *not* at enforcement of halakhah, a goal modern conditions make impossible and even undesirable, but toward an understanding of the basis and ideals of Judaism and an attempt to develop appropriate avenues of actualizing it today.

Within the realm of halakhic decision-making, the Conservative movement's method can become influential as well. *Teshuvot* issued by the Rabbinical Assembly of Israel's *Va'ad Halakhah* deal with topics which are specifically relevant to Israel. These include questions concerning the sanctity of the Temple Mount, the observance of *Tisha B'Av* and the *Sh'mittah* year. In each case, the methodology utilized has included a solid historical understanding of the development of the halakhah, as well as religious and ethical considerations reflecting modern needs and beliefs. These documents, once becoming known to the public, may well have an effect upon religious thinking and practice which could be far-reaching.

By planting the seeds of *methods of thinking* which deal honestly with Judaism, historically and intellectually, and which attempt to expound and expand Judaism to meet today's needs, the Seminary has the potential to profoundly influence Jewish life in the place which will be the most central of all in determining Judaism's future: The State of Israel.

Alexander Marx, Librarian and Professor of History, 1903–1953.

Louis Ginzberg, Professor of Talmud, 1903–1953.

Seeing the Future Through the Light of the Past: The Art of the Jewish Museum

Emily D. Bilski

"Great nations write their autobiographies in three manuscripts: the book of their deeds, the book of their words, and the book of their art. Not one of these books can be understood unless we read the two others, but of the three the only trustworthy one is the last."

John Ruskin

In 1904, Judge Mayer Sulzberger included twenty-six objects as part of a gift of books and manuscripts to The Jewish Theological Seminary of America. These works of ceremonial and fine art were donated "to serve as a suggestion for the establishment of a Jewish Museum."[1] It is tempting to see in Judge Sulzberger's desire to establish such a museum and in the great efforts on the part of the Seminary's professional and lay leadership to successfully realize this wish, a reflection of the insight articulated by Ruskin: a belief in the power of the physical object to communicate not only aesthetic values, but also the experiences, beliefs, aspirations and identity of a people. It is this extraordinary power of the art object that has fueled the Jewish Museum since its founding eighty-two years ago and continues to inform its collecting, exhibition and educational activities to this day. The Museum's original goals—the collection, preservation and research of material Jewish culture, coupled with presenting this material to the larger community in a compelling interpretive context in order to educate and stimulate—remain the priorities of the Jewish Museum today. And yet the unprecedented changes the world has witnessed during the last eighty-two years have altered the significance and application of many of these goals. The history of the Museum can be seen as a reflection of the ever-shifting values and concerns of the world Jewish community, the American Jewish community and the art world, as the Museum has continued to evolve and adapt over the years.

The founders of the Jewish Museum recognized the opportunities a museum would provide to enhance the Seminary as a center for research and teaching, as well as to facilitate the communication of Jewish culture and history to the general public.

In their aims, the founders of the Museum were part of the general *Zeitgeist*. Many of the major Judaica collections and Jewish Museums in Europe had their beginnings around the turn of the century. There was a new consciousness in the air concerning the importance of artifacts used in Jewish ritual observances as well as objects which in some way related to Jewish history or personalities. The first great exhibition of Judaica took place at the Exposition Universelle in Paris in 1878 with the showing of the Joseph Strauss Collection.[2] It was followed by the Anglo-Jewish Historical Exhibition at Albert Hall in London in 1887. Jewish museums were established in Vienna (1897), Danzig (1904), Prague (1906) and Warsaw (1910). In Frankfurt, a museum was founded with the collection amassed by the *Gesellschaft zur Erforschung jüdischer Kunstdenkmäler* (Society for the Research of Jewish Art Monuments), an organization begun in 1900 by Heinrich Frauberger, the (non-Jewish) director of the art museum in Düsseldorf.

A number of factors contributed to this flowering of interest in the collection, preservation, and research of Jewish material culture. Jewish emancipation, and the assimilation which followed, created an environment ripe for this development. In the first place, the departure from a strict adherence to traditional Judaism provided the psychological distance that enabled Jews to view ritual appurtenances as objects *per se*, apart from their religious functions. While retaining their ceremonial significance, the objects could also be seen as works of art, incorporating aesthetic as well as religious values. This objectivity was the essential prerequisite to moving a Torah shield or an eternal light from the synagogue into a museum.

Assimilation brought with it a decline in the use of many ceremonial objects for religious purposes. As synagogues fell into disuse, their rich holdings of artifacts were in danger of being damaged or altogether destroyed. People with foresight realized the necessity of taking quick action to save this aspect of their Jewish heritage, as was the case, for example, with Salomon Hugo Lieben who founded the Jewish Museum in Prague.

Yet another factor was the developing attitude within certain Jewish intellectual circles favoring a scientific approach to the study of Jewish history, philosophy and religion. The material manifestations of Jewish life could supply important data in the scientific investigations of Judaism, and the same stringent standards of inquiry could also be applied to a direct study of the objects themselves. It was hoped that collecting, exhibiting and studying Jewish artifacts in this way would serve a dual purpose: educate Jews about their culture and help them nurture a respect for their traditions, while at the same time enhance the non-Jews' appreciation and understanding of the Jewish heritage.

Such was the position of Cyrus Adler, one of the most passionate advocates in America for the scientific study of Judaism, who played a key role in the establishment of the Seminary, eventually serving as its president. Adler "believed that Judaism, studied and taught according to the canons of modern scholarship, would enhance its respectability and that of its adherents . . . Not only would the non-Jew be prompted to give due accord to the heritage that had nurtured Western religion, but the Jews themselves would understand the relevance of their 2000-year-old tradition."[3]

Adler, a founder of the Jewish Publication Society in 1888, the American Jewish Historical Society in 1892, and the Harvard Semitic Museum in 1903, also was active in the field of secular exhibitions and museums. In 1890, he worked on the preparations for the 1893 Chicago Exposition, and in 1893 he joined the Smithsonian Institution as librarian, rising to the position of assistant secretary in 1905. Adler's commitment to the study of Jewish culture and its dissemination to a wide public, coupled with his vast experience in the collection and exhibition of objects, uniquely qualified him to supervise the growth of the fledgling Jewish Museum. He provided the critical link between the museum world and the Seminary, between a consciousness keenly attuned to the aesthetic and one devoted to the written word. Without Adler's crucial leadership, the Museum might never have been more than a small group of objects tucked away in a corner of the Seminary Library.

Fortunately, there were philanthropists who shared Adler's vision of a Jewish Museum and provided the financial support required to begin to build an important collection. Jacob H. Schiff, a director of the Seminary from 1902 until his death in 1920, had been a founder (with Adler) of the Harvard Semitic Museum. Schiff's son-in-law, Felix M. Warburg, another great supporter of the Seminary, was for many years a director of the American Museum of Natural History.

Both men were art collectors, as well as patrons of Jewish scholarship. It was Warburg who actually supplied the first exhibition cases which were placed in the Reading Room of the old Seminary building on West 123rd Street. (Years later, it was Schiff's daughter and Warburg's widow, Frieda Schiff Warburg, who gave the museum its own home when she donated her family's Fifth Avenue mansion in 1944.)

Building the Collections

Any discussion of the Jewish Museum and its contribution to American Jewish life must begin with its collection, the core of all its activities and its chief *raison d'être*. The first major acquisition by the Seminary was the Benguiat Collection, purchased in 1925. This distinguished private collection was primarily assembled during the nineteenth century by Hadji Ephraim Benguiat, an art dealer from Smyrna (Izmir), Turkey, who had undertaken a "self-imposed family task to preserve . . . Jewish memorials of interest." Benguiat's diverse collection, which included outstanding examples of Ashkenazi and Sephardi art, had been catalogued by Adler with I. M. Casanowicz in 1901.[4] Adler described the acquisition of the Benguiat collection in his remarks on the occasion of the Seminary's fiftieth anniversary:

> In the building on 123rd Street, in a small way, there commenced to be brought together a few Jewish ceremonial objects. I think there were two or three cases. Before the present buildings were even projected, an opportunity came to secure a really notable collection. It was founded by the family of Benguiat, who spread over the larger cities in Europe and America. These men were collectors and dealers. They mostly sold what they collected with the exception of Jewish objects. In 1893, Ephraim Benguiat had a large shop in Boston, and I was looking for collections for the World's Fair in Chicago. When that exposition closed he transferred this loan to the Smithsonian Institution and later at his death, when it became necessary for his family to dispose of the collection, it was purchased by Felix M. Warburg with the assistance of a few friends, and placed in storage until such time as the Seminary could exhibit it. This is the origin of our present charming little Museum.[5]

As Adler made clear in his remarks, with the acquisition of the Benguiat collection, the museum needed a new physical space commensurate with its increasingly significant holdings. Thus, in January 1931, the Museum of Jewish Ceremonial Objects opened in the new Jacob H. Schiff Library Building on Broadway and 122nd Street as an annex to the Library.

The crisis in Europe in the two ensuing decades dramatically shifted the activities of collection and study of Jewish artifacts from the Continent to America and invested these efforts with a new urgency and a terrible new significance. Three important components of the Jewish Museum's present collection are the direct result of the events of World War II and the destruction of European Jewry at the hands of the Nazis: the Mintz Collection, the Danzig Collection, and the items presented to the Museum by the Jewish Cultural Reconstruction.

Benjamin Mintz began his collection as a professional art and antiques dealer in Warsaw, Poland. He was thus in a fortunate position to encounter and purchase some of the finest cultural artifacts of Polish Jewry. Judge Max N. Korshak, a friend, noted that "it was quite easy for him to buy Jewish antiques and ceremonial objects but he did not have the heart to sell them and so over the years he gathered together a most amazing collection which, when he gave up his business, he stored in one of the large rooms of his apartment in Warsaw."

Through the assistance of Korshak and others, Mintz and his wife Rose were able to bring the collection to New York for exhibition at the 1939 World's Fair. Although it was never exhibited, the Mintz Collection was safely in New York when Hitler invaded Poland in September 1939, and was thus spared the fate of so many other pre-World War II Judaica collections. In 1947, Rose Mintz, then a widow, sold the entire collection to the Seminary for a relatively small sum in order to keep it intact.

Danzig had boasted one of Europe's earliest Jewish Museums. Lesser Gieldzinski, a wealthy grain merchant, art collector and connoisseur and friend to Kaiser Wilhelm II, donated his collection of Judaica to the Jewish community of Danzig on the occasion of his seventy-fifth birthday in 1904 (the same year as the founding of the Jewish Museum in New York), where it was housed in a special room in the Great Synagogue. By the autumn of 1938, conditions under the Nazis had deteriorated to such an extent that the officials of the Jewish community thought it best for all Jews to evacuate Danzig. The large sums of money needed to finance this emigration were raised by the sale of Jewish communal property. The American Joint Distribution

Committee arranged for the community's entire collection of Judaica to be "sold" in America to raise some of these funds and, more importantly, to save it from imminent destruction. This collection consisted of Gieldzinski's donation, ceremonial objects from Danzig's five synagogues, and those belonging to private individuals.

On July 16, 1939, these objects, filling ten huge crates, arrived at the Seminary. Among the conditions of the shipment was the stipulation that if a Jewish community were to be reestablished in Danzig within fifteen years, the collection would be returned. If not, it would remain in New York "for the education and inspiration of the rest of the world." Today there is no Jewish community in Danzig — Gdansk, Poland since 1945 — but something of the vibrant community which thrived there has been preserved in the collection of ceremonial objects now housed in the Jewish Museum. The Jews in Danzig occupy a unique position in the history of the Holocaust — theirs was the only community with the foresight to save its treasures of ceremonial art.

At the conclusion of World War II, the disposition of Jewish cultural and religious property that had been looted by the Nazis and subsequently recovered by the United States Military Government was undertaken by the Jewish Cultural Reconstruction, Inc. (JCR). Founded in New York in 1947 as part of the larger Jewish Restitution Successor Organization, the JCR was headed by the prominent historian Salo Baron and managed by a distinguished committee. Whenever possible, materials were returned to the original owners, with the remaining items distributed to Jewish institutions worldwide. Along with looted books, Torah scrolls and archival materials were more than 5,000 ritual objects stolen from Jewish museums and synagogues. One hundred and twenty of these ceremonial objects, selected by the Museum's research associate, Dr. Guido Schoenberger, entered the Jewish Museum collection in 1952.

The individual who left the greatest mark on the Jewish Museum's collection was Dr. Harry G. Friedman. A prominent and philanthropic Jewish communal leader, Dr. Friedman was a nonpracticing rabbi who had a brilliant financial career on Wall Street. His passion as a collector was to salvage the artistic creations of the Jewish past for the benefit of future generations. From 1941 until his death in 1965, Friedman had acquired over 6,000 works of ceremonial and fine art, as well as archeological material, which he donated to the Jewish Museum. Many items were purchased at the time of the

Holocaust as great European private collections were being disassembled and sold.

Dr. Friedman's gifts to the Museum encompass objects from every place Jews have lived and range from examples of folk art produced by anonymous Jewish artisans to elaborate ceremonial works executed by some of Europe's finest silversmiths. Understanding that aesthetic judgments are often conditioned by one's culture, Friedman did not allow his selection of objects to be determined solely by contemporary taste or current value. He was concerned with the long-range and comprehensive preservation of Judaica.

This remains the Museum's primary collecting goal. Many individuals have donated objects or provided funds to enable the Museum to constantly upgrade and expand its holdings. Some of these donors are well-known philanthropists who have been ongoing supporters, for example Felix and Frieda Warburg and Albert and Vera List. Some have donated entire collections concentrating on one aspect of the Museum's holdings: The Museum's collection of 3,000 coins and medals, the most distinguished of its kind, is the result of the expertise and generosity of the late Samuel Friedenberg and his son Daniel. There are also many objects—discovered in a basement or thrift shop, or even treasured family heirlooms—that are donated to the Jewish Museum by people who are neither extremely wealthy nor knowledgeable about Judaica, but who realize the vitality of the Museum and the importance of its collection for the preservation and dissemination of the Jewish artistic legacy.

Part of that vitality must come from an involvement with the actual making of art. As important collectors of contemporary art, Albert and Vera List have for many years commissioned prominent American artists to execute an original graphic for the Jewish Museum on the occasion of the Jewish New Year. Dr. Abram Kanof and his wife, the late Dr. Frances Pascher, enabled the Museum not only to guard the treasures of the past, but have assured the continuous creation of Jewish ceremonial art. In 1956 they established the Tobe Pascher Workshop at the Jewish Museum, providing office, classroom, and studio space for resident artists and their students. Founding director Ludwig Wolpert was joined in 1961 by his colleague and former student, Moshe Zabari, who has directed the Workshop since Wolpert's death in 1982. Kanof recalls that the Workshop "was founded to apply the principles of contemporary design to Judaica . . . [It] continues to produce objects of quality and excellence, according to the newest design philosophies but always in the service of the most ancient rituals and traditions."[6] Through the generosity of the Lists, funds were made available for Zabari's works to enter the Museum's collection.

A new dimension to the Museum's collecting and programming was added in March 1984, with the opening of the National Jewish Archive of Broadcasting. Created with a major grant from the Charles H. Revson Foundation, the Archive collects radio and television material that documents or dramatizes Jewish history, culture, current events, and personalities. It provides a unique lens through which to view the Jewish experience as it is seen and interpreted through popular culture by both Jews and non-Jews.

The Museum's collections are a resource for other Jewish museums, Jewish communities, scholars and artists. Because of the impeccable provenance of so much of the collection, it provides a secure basis for evaluating the authenticity of other works of Judaica, especially today when forgery is rampant. The Museum has provided guidance for Jewish communities starting museums, loans for Jewish and secular museums, and has circulated exhibitions internationally. Some of these have been seen in non-Jewish museums and have created an awareness in secular circles of the beauty and significance of Judaica. Artists have turned to the collection for information or inspiration for their own work.

A Place to Show

The Museum's ability to present exhibitions and programs was greatly enhanced with the donation in 1944 of the Warburg mansion on Fifth Avenue at 92nd Street and the opening of the Museum in its new home in 1947. In 1963, a three-story addition was constructed to accommodate the Museum's growing programs, made possible by the generosity of the Lists.

In assessing the Museum's impact on the American scene, one still looks with pride and wonder at the dazzling array of exhibitions of contemporary art held at the Jewish Museum in the 1950s and 1960s. An exhibition in 1957, marking the tenth anniversary at the Fifth Avenue location—*Artists of the New York School: Second Generation*—presented the work of twenty-three young painters, including Helen Frankenthaler, Jasper Johns, Robert Rauschenberg and George Segal. In his introductory essay to the exhibition catalogue, Leo Steinberg noted that though this constituted "a departure from established practice," there was a "certain aptness" to the exhibition of modern art at the Jewish Museum:

> Both Jewry and modern art are masters of renunciation, having at one time renounced all props on which existence as nation, or art, once seemed to depend. Jewry survived as an abstract nation, proving, as did modern art, how much was dispensable. I would also add that, like modern painting, Jewish religious practices are remarkably free of representational content, the ritual being largely self-fulfilling, rather than the bearer of a detachable meaning. Lastly, both Judaism and contemporary art established themselves by uncompromising exclusiveness. And if I said before that it is hard to be a modern painter, there is an old Jewish proverb to match that sentiment. Which possibly explains why many young Jews find it easy to become modern painters.

Artists of the New York School proved to be only the beginning of an exciting and ambitious exhibition program developed under subsequent directors Alan Solomon and Sam Hunter, showcasing the best avant-garde talent. Much has been said criticizing the Museum's leadership during those years for concentrating on contemporary art that had no demonstrable Jewish content and "abandoning" the Museum's original goals. In retrospect, these criticisms seem unfounded. Not only did the Museum continue to present exhibitions on Jewish themes, but it added to its permanent collection of Judaica. The Museum's role in the discovery and promotion of artists who are now recognized as the greatest of their generation was a significant contribution to the development of postwar American art, and is but one example of a long and distinguished history of Jewish art patronage.[7]

Changes in both the art world and the Jewish world since the late 1960s have influenced the Museum's evolution and the way it sought to implement its goals. With the proliferation of museums, alternative spaces and galleries devoted to the exhibition of contemporary art in New York and, indeed, all across America, the Museum's role in this area lost much of its urgency. At the same time a new need was felt within the Jewish community, a need to explore the myriad components of Jewish identity. In the wake of the civil rights movement,

Americans from many different ethnic backgrounds began to question the desirability of the "melting pot" ethic. Pride in the unique cultural legacies of parents and grandparents and the wish to keep those legacies alive for the benefit of future generations supplanted the earlier desire to blend inconspicuously into the general fabric of American life. For Jews, this trend was further enhanced by pride in the accomplishments of Israel and developments in Holocaust education. The necessity of coming to terms with the enormity of what had been lost lent new urgency to understanding and preserving what remained. For affiliated Jews, culture became another arena for the expression of the revitalization of their communities. For those Jews who had rejected religious traditions, Jewish culture and history became a medium through which Jewish identity could be reaffirmed. Clearly, the Jewish Museum had a new and important role to play as a resource for Jews from all points on the religious spectrum. The decision was made to focus once again on exhibitions which relate to the Jewish experience.

In our exhibitions, programs, and publications, we continue to question the relationship between art and Jewish culture covering 4,000 years, embracing Canaanite antiquities and the constructions of Frank Stella inspired by Polish wooden synagogues. Some exhibitions focus on particular Jewish communities, their history, art and communal life. For example, recent exhibitions have delved into these themes relating to the Jews of Danzig, Frankfurt and Istanbul, Kaifeng, and India, and this past winter the Museum devoted an exhibition to the Jews of Ethiopia. We also present the work of individual artists, examine the state of Israeli or current American art dealing with Jewish themes, and document single historical events and their repercussions—for example, the Eichmann Trial. Often a whole new perspective can be gleaned by looking at a well-known subject through a different lens, as for example in the Museum's upcoming exhibition examining the role of the visual arts in the Dreyfus Affair. The Education Department uses these exhibitions to teach Jewish history and culture to 22,000 children annually, 60% of whom come from public schools. Our location on Fifth Avenue— New York's "Museum Mile"—attracts many tourists and visitors who would probably never seek out a Jewish museum or a Jewish institution of any kind. Both non-Jews and unaffiliated Jews can come here and experience something unique: the direct confrontation with objects embodying Jewish culture and history. The empathy and understanding acquired by looking at paintings made by a Jewish artist in hiding from the Nazis or by a child in the Terezín concentration camp goes beyond that gained by reading an historical account. Public programs enrich the exhibitions by providing new windows through which to examine the themes and ideas raised in the galleries.

A revived interest in all things Jewish coupled with the tremendous current visibility and popularity of museums in America, has created a mood especially favorable for Jewish museums. This is reflected, to cite just one example, in the tremendous growth in membership at the Jewish Museum in recent years: from 4,879 in October of 1982 to 12,839 in October of 1986. It is a propitious moment for an institution such as ours, an institution committed to fusing past and present with an eye to a healthy and vibrant future.

The foreword to the catalog of the 1957 exhibition of young New York artists declared: "the present show intends to look forward instead of concerning itself with the past." The Jewish Museum's winter 1986-87 exhibition *Jewish Themes/Contemporary American Artists II* offered an alternative. In his review of this exhibition, *The New York Times* art critic Michael Brenson called the show "prophetic", observing: "It is significant . . . for what it has to say about the possibilities for art in the postmodern era . . . It is again possible to make art . . . that looks forward and backward at the same time. Only when both directions are present is there the possibility of a prophetic voice."[8]

In those words we hear an echo of Cyrus Adler who wrote in a letter dated March 4, 1894: "The true prophet has ever been the one who saw the future through the light of the past."[9] Brenson concluded his exhibition review, stating: "The relation of the past to the present and future is part of what this show — and the Jewish Museum — is all about."[10] Exploring these relations in all their diverse and complex ramifications and manifestations is a continuous process of discovery and growth to which the Jewish Museum has dedicated itself.

NOTES

I would like to express my deepest thanks to the following members of the Jewish Museum staff who graciously shared ideas, information, and reminiscences and who offered valuable counsel in the preparation of this article: Joan Rosenbaum, Director; Susan T. Goodman, Chief Curator; Susan Braunstein, Associate Curator; Moshe Zabari, Director of the Tobe Pascher Workshop; Judith Siegel, Director of Education; and Andrew Ackerman, former Assistant Director.

1. Letter dated January 20, 1904, from Judge Mayer Sulzberger to Dr. Cyrus Adler, then president of the Board of the Seminary.
2. The Strauss Collection was later acquired by Baron de Rothschild for the Cluny Museum in Paris.
3. Naomi W. Cohen, "Introduction," *Cyrus Adler: Selected Letters,* Ira Robinson, ed. (Philadelphia and New York: The Jewish Publication Society and the Jewish Theological Seminary, 1985), pp. xxviii and xxix.
4. Cyrus Adler and I. M. Casanowicz, *Descriptive Catalogue of a Collection of Objects of Jewish Ceremonial Art Deposited in the U.S. National Museum by Hadji Ephraim Benguiat* (Washington, D.C.: Government Printing Office, 1901).
5. Cyrus Adler, "Semi-Centennial Address," *The Jewish Theological Seminary of America: Semi-Centennial Volume,* C. Adler, (ed.), (New York: 1939), p. 14.
6. Abram Kanof, "The Tobe Pascher Workshop 1956–1986," *Moshe Zabari: A Twenty-Five Year Retrospective,* Nancy Berman, ed. (New York and Los Angeles: Jewish Museum and Hebrew Union College Skirball Museum, 1986), p. 6.
7. An examination of the role of Jewish patronage is long overdue. Among the future exhibitions being considered for the Museum is an investigation of the interaction between Jewish dealers, gallery owners, critics, artists and patrons in fostering the avant-garde in Berlin during the first three decades of this century. A similar study could be undertaken on the New York art scene during the years after the Second World War.
8. Michael Brenson, "Bringing Fresh Approaches to Age-Old Jewish Themes," *The New York Times,* August 3, 1986, "Arts and Leisure" section, p. 27.
9. *Adler, Selected Letters,* p. 62.
10. Brenson, "Jewish Themes," p. 32.

The Seminary and "Havurah Judaism": Some Thoughts

Robert Goldenberg

I came to the Seminary as a direct result of being sent to Camp Ramah. At the time this happened, I would have said that Ramah had uncovered for me the richness of Jewish living and Jewish study, that I could not bear the thought of abandoning either, that I was coming to rabbinical school in order to learn more about the treasures revealed to me at camp. I decided to apply to the Seminary before I even entered college, and I must already have suspected that my interest in rabbinic study had more to do with a continuing search for personal religious direction than with a career decision in the usual sense. Otherwise, I think, I would not have had so little desire from the very beginning to lead a congregation in the manner typical of people called "Rabbi." I knew only that I needed to study, and that I wanted to pursue my studies surrounded by Jews doing similar things; in other words, I wanted to keep up the kind of life I had discovered at Ramah.

I said "at the time this happened" because I did not realize until years later that the crucial element in my reaction to Camp Ramah was the community that had embraced me there from the moment of my arrival. I tended for years to perceive my turning in terms of intellectual quest or adolescent rebellion (I am sure it did include elements of both), and not in terms of the other people with whom I shared those critical experiences. But it seems to me now that the primary effect on me of Camp Ramah was neither intellectual nor psychological but rather communal: I was at home there in the midst of people like myself, and with those other people I was free for the first time to begin shaping my own life. That sense of freedom within community changed me forever.

I realize full well that the preceding remarks can be set aside as over-sentimental and self-absorbed. I realize too that my experiences at Ramah were probably characteristic experiences of a teenager away from home for the first time (my first and only experience as a camper came when I was fifteen years old, though I stayed on as a staff member for ten more seasons), that Jewish life and study, while apparently central to my experience, were only accidental features of the setting in which I underwent my liberation from home. Be all that as it may, I acquired at Camp Ramah a certain conception of authentic Jewish living, and I continue to believe that conception is basically sound.

Outside of the artificial, age-specific communities of summer camp and the Seminary dormitory, I have found that conception better embodied in havurot than in any other form of community that American Jewish life has to offer. It doesn't really matter whether my interpretation of the Ramah experience was "correct," or whether that experience is necessary for people to reach my conclusions; the path I discovered by attending the Conservative movement's most effective educational institution and the path I now follow through my involvement in the National Havurah Committee are one and the same.

The rise of havurot is a response to a new reality. Prior to the last several centuries, Jewish communities were endowed with a structure of governance that enabled them to enforce community policy on recalcitrant individuals, and for hundreds of years that structure was largely entrusted to rabbis. Since people who violated the Sabbath or the laws of marriage and inheritance might be placed under a ban or in some other way deprived of their good standing in the congregation of Israel, it comes as no surprise that most Jews followed rabbinic teaching during those earlier periods of Jewish history. Later, the Jews were "emancipated," and this meant among other things that those who wished to flout rabbinic authority could do so with relative impunity. The rabbis' loss of the power to coerce is one of the basic causes of the religious crisis of modern Jewish life.[1]

Another is that the rabbis themselves have lost the consensus that once united them. Nowadays even Jews who want to "follow rabbinic teaching" are essentially on their own in deciding what this means. In other words, the religious crisis confronting American Jews today (and it seems clear that such a crisis is underway) has arisen because Jews in the post-Emancipation world are responsible for shaping their own Jewish lives; no constituted authority any longer exists to determine the meaning or the content of Judaism for our communities at large. Jews now seek help in confronting pressing questions for themselves, but no longer willingly accept other people's answers to those questions. The new purpose of Jewish community is to provide a framework in which Jews can together press this confrontation.

In my experience, Ramah — which for me represented Conservative Judaism at its best — offered an opportunity to pursue under ideal conditions the kind of shared exploration that modern Jewish life imposes on us all. We had access to highly expert practitioners of Judaism, but we knew at the same time that we were developing a style of practicing Judaism that would be very much our own, that the way *we* were Jews would be suited to our own circumstances and needs. We also knew it would take more than one brief summer to develop such a way and suspected that once we left camp we would not likely find it anywhere else. It is not surprising that I moved on from such an environment to a style of Jewish living where such exploration was a full-time, lifelong activity.

When things are working at their best, a havurah is a community of Jews engaged in the common project of learning how to lead Jewish lives in the modern world. These people share Shabbat and holiday celebrations, they *daven* together, eat together, study Torah together. They work together toward the improvement of the world, and take part together in the private joys and sorrows of their companions' lives. What makes this community a havurah is the awareness that such sharing takes place among equals, that no Jew is "better" at being Jewish or has a more reliable way of being Jewish than another, that no Jew can relieve another Jew of deciding for himself or herself what kind of Jewish life to lead. Individuals with stronger backgrounds in traditional Jewish lore can make this background available to others in the group who wish to integrate such lore into their lives; they can point inquirers in the direction of the texts or ideas they are looking for and can help those engaged in the process of discovery to form an understanding of that which they find. In a havurah community, however — and this is the key — learning as such no longer confers authority: *those who learn, not those who teach, must now determine the value, meaning, and use of what is taught.* As Rosenzweig already knew, that is the reality of modern Jewish life everywhere, but only the havurah incorporates this reality into its very structure, into everything it does.

The letter inviting me to contribute this essay included several specific questions that I was asked to consider. I would like now to address those questions more directly against the background of these introductory remarks.

What was JTS' role in the spawning of the havurah movement?

I have tried to approach this question by examining the course of my own life, and I have tried to suggest that the vision I have pursued through my life in the havurah movement was one originally granted to me at (or thanks to) the Seminary. The Seminary's influence on me was indirect, however, through its sponsorship of the Ramah camps, and through the sense of community in the Brush dormitory that repeatedly grew and withered during the years I lived there. In general, it seems to me the Seminary's role in initiating the havurah movement was always indirect. Many Seminary students or former students have played important roles in havurah activities, but none of these activities has been sponsored or even co-sponsored by the Seminary itself. So far as I know, the Seminary has never in any official manner taken note of the havurah movement or done anything to encourage it.[2]

What positive legacies — spiritual, intellectual, observant — did Conservative Judaism and JTS contribute to the havurah movement?

This is hard to answer, because different individuals — both in the Seminary world and in the havurah world — will have different opinions on what constitutes a "positive legacy." Is it a positive legacy when people decide to observe kashrut? Is it more positive if they become vegetarian altogether? Is it a positive legacy if people organize prayer groups where men and women are equal? Is it more positive if they refuse to join prayer groups where men and women are not equal? Is it a positive legacy if prayers are rewritten so as to eliminate the presumption that those speaking them are male? What of the presumption that the Deity to whom these prayers are addressed is male as well? Neither the Board of Directors of the National Havurah Committee nor the Rabbinical Assembly nor the Seminary faculty could easily achieve consensus on questions like these; how shall we speak of legacies?

Let me therefore return to speaking of myself. One enormously positive intellectual legacy I acquired from my years in Seminary-based institutions is that I learned the Hebrew language and then learned how to read certain great texts of the Judaic tradition. To be sure, I did not learn to read all such texts; in my day no one at the Seminary taught kabbalistic or hasidic texts except on a very private basis—I feel unlettered in those fields even now—and havurah-style Judaism has tended to lay very heavy stress on precisely those texts. But modern Jewish life is a matter of constant search for ways of bringing an ancient tradition to bear on situations it did not anticipate, and the Seminary taught me to carry out that search in a serious way. I think as well that I picked up my basic attitude toward the classical texts—respectful attention combined with critical independence—while at JTS, though the balance in my own approach has probably shifted from the former toward the latter during the years since I was ordained.

With respect to observance, I have been committed since that first summer at camp to some degree of traditional observance; traditional Jewish rules of behavior will in some way always govern my life. On the other hand, the reasons for this commitment and the procedures for determining the fine points of my own set of rules (every modern Jew has his or her own) have never been clear to me, and I am tempted to say such reasons and such procedures have been the particular goals of my search ever since I embarked on it. Here I found my Seminary experiences much less helpful. I found the Seminary was giving me skills that would help me learn how to observe but not why to observe. I was on my own with that matter, and once I had gone out into a world where the desirability of observance was not taken for granted this was a hard question with which to be left alone.[3]

What could/should JTS and the Conservative movement learn from the havurah communities? Many faculty, staff, and students at JTS regularly participate in havurot. What effect might this have on JTS?

We have all heard so much about the anonymity and alienation of the large American synagogue that I see no need to go on about it here; the glory of the king may be found in large gatherings of the people, but the face of the *Shekhinah* is harder to see when the *bimah* is too far away; and the still small voice sounds terrible through a microphone.

This matter, needless to say, is more complicated than is usually acknowledged, but for many people the synagogue is a place to visit and watch other people perform traditional Jewish rituals, and the rabbi is a professional you occasionally bring into your life to perform certain functions you cannot do for yourself. The havurah style of organization is designed to eliminate the causes of that impression. The group is kept small enough that everyone knows everyone else, not only by name but also in terms of each person's strengths and weaknesses, interests, needs and skills. Since members of a havurah know one another, every member knows what he or she can learn from every other member, and those responsible for the group's activities try to make sure all this learning can take place. Services are arranged so that everyone occasionally leads; not just participates but leads. Leadership is shared or rotated; no one is a professional leader of the group, and no one is in a position to tell the group as a whole how something "ought" to be done.

All this, of course, has its price. Decisions sometimes take forever; those individuals who wish simply to disregard group policy cannot always be deterred from doing so; and people without the knowledge or skills to perform certain traditional tasks are sometimes entrusted with those tasks nevertheless. Still, the sense of intimate involvement with one's fellow Jews and of serious engagement with Jewish practice and Jewish learning is so exciting to those who have tasted it, the satisfaction of returning to a Jewish heritage that had seemed irretrievably lost is so deep to those who have discovered it, that it is hard to doubt the value of this new path.

These are not matters the Conservative movement "could" or "should" learn; it has begun to learn them already. All over the country synagogues — frequently with their rabbis' encouragement — have begun to enroll their members in smaller groups called havurot. These groups often meet in members' homes, where they study together, share Shabbat or other festive meals, and somewhat more rarely have their own services.

But these developments conflict with some long-standing commitments of Conservative thought and practice; that is why they have been met by some of our colleagues with resistance instead of acclaim. They turn the rabbi from *mara d'atra* into something else — facilitator, perhaps, or "resource person" — and modern rabbis can easily sense that the authors of the very texts they have been trained to love would not have approved of such a transformation. The way out of this difficulty lies through the time-honored idea of the rabbi as teacher, but even so we must keep in mind that in our time the teacher must work to gain and hold an audience; neither the obligation to learn, nor the proper curriculum of learning, nor the correct interpretation of the subject-matter are things that many modern Jews will accept any more on someone else's say-so.

Moreover, the attitude of the Jewish tradition toward real pluralism has always been ambivalent at best. Diversity of opinion has generally been accepted, but it has often been limited to the learned elite. The idea of ordinary Jews (*i.e., ammei ha-aretz*) rejecting a rabbi's teaching, of such people instead developing their own rules for Jewish life or their own interpretations of some sacred text, has usually been met by the rabbis themselves with a kind of horror. Yet the havurah model implies that no interpretation of a Jewish text, or of Jewish history, is privileged. It is always better, to be sure, that thinking people have respect for evidence, so members of the group who can quote more sources or cite more precedents presumably can make some claim at least to be heard. But the truth is, as we all say all the time, that even our most hallowed texts come to us from another place and time, from cultural and social environments quite alien to our own. Conservative rabbis have from the beginnings of our movement claimed the right to set aside those aspects of our tradition that seem too tainted by these social and cultural differences; the rise of the havurah implies that a similar right is vested in the Jews at large, and the Conservative movement must frame a response to this development.

Let me restate these last points in different language. In a havurah, as many people as possible are involved in as much of the life of the group as possible. As I have experienced these things, this innocuous generalization poses a challenge to accepted Conservative thinking or practice on two fronts:

Liturgy: Havurah-style *davenen,* with its emphasis on group singing and its tendency to seat people in a circle, redirects the worshippers' attention from the front of the room, from the Ark and from the relatively small number of dignitaries sitting near it, to the center of the room and the larger crowd found there. This has obvious architectural implications, but also theological implications in the strictest sense (to whom is such a group addressing its prayers?) and also implications for the proper role of the "leader" in the larger community. Rabbis often call their congregants' attention to the fact that neither Jewish prayer nor Jewish marriage technically requires the presence of a rabbi, but this observation is easier to repeat when you do not expect your audience to act on it.

Authority: Any community that understands itself as based on a Divinely-given law delivered and interpreted by Divinely-appointed leaders is going to have a strong tendency toward a hierarchical structure. In the rabbinic tradition this led to a strong resistance on the part of rabbis to sharing their power with the unlearned; in the Conservative movement we have emphasized the independent authority of rabbis "over" their own congregations, but this is just another side of the same coin. The havurah model, on the other hand, presumes that all decisions concerning group life (worship, food restrictions, etc.) will be decisions of the group as a whole, reached by procedures adopted by the same group as a whole. It remains to be seen how Seminary faculty, staff, and students who live their own lives in a havurah setting will integrate these experiences into their studies and their teaching.

The rise of the havurot has offered American Jews of our time an experience of communal intimacy and shared exploration of Judaism that many have evidently welcomed. As will always occur in the early stages of a new development there have been excesses and mistakes, but on balance it seems hard to deny that a desirable source of new vigor and creative energy has now appeared on the scene. It seems likely that growing numbers of Conservative Jews in general and Seminary people in particular will come to enjoy the benefits available in a havurah. This offers challenges to those who frame the policies of the Conservative movement and lead its institutions, but precedents for these new developments have existed at the heart of Conservative Judaism for years. The challenges should therefore be met with optimism and open hearts and minds; only our fellow Jews will be the losers if we fail at this task.

NOTES

1. This is not the place for an extended inquiry into the nature of rabbinic authority in the post-Emancipation Jewish world, but I think it is worth noting that many of us went on from Camp Ramah, from a world where an authoritative rabbinate was virtually invisible, to the Seminary and its assumption that the traditional authority of the *mara d'atra* remains the foundation of Jewish religious life. It would be interesting to examine the ways in which people who followed this path recognized and reacted to this incongruity of models, and to explore whether rabbis who "graduated" from Ramah to the Rabbinical School of JTS were less likely than others to pursue traditional congregational careers.

2. If I am wrong to speak in such negative terms, then even my error is an important piece of information. If I am unaware of important Seminary contributions to the havurah enterprise, they have not been publicized very

well. I do not mean by this observation to invite a barrage of publicity; I merely suggest that the Seminary's role in havurah activities has not been important enough to the Seminary itself to warrant greater attention. It can be hoped that this situation will change in the near future.

3. I am struck by the fact that of my Seminary friends who came with me into the world of havurah Judaism some have become less observant and some (fewer) have become more, but none has become less studious. If this means that the Seminary's message about the value of study was getting through to us more strongly than its message about the value of observance, the finding is worth some thought.

Abraham Joshua Heschel, Professor of Jewish Ethics and Mysticism at the Seminary, 1945–1973. (photo by John H. Popper)

Saul Lieberman (left), Rector of the Seminary and Professor of Talmud and Palestinean Institutions, 1940–1983, with H. L. Ginsberg, Professor of Biblical History and Literature since 1941.

The Jewish Theological Seminary and the Academic Study of Judaism

Michael Panitz

Until recent decades, the academic study of Judaism, both in Europe and in America, was characterized by either a Christian-theological or an Orientalist approach. The former, with roots in the medieval university, treated Judaica, for the most part "Old Testament" literature, largely as a "preparation for the Evangelium." The great chairs of Judaica at European universities, at which a distinguished line of Christian Hebraists practiced their craft, filled the Christian need to produce pastors and theologians who were well acquainted with the Hebrew dimension of their Christian heritage. Rabbinics were also on the curriculum, but again for theological reasons: the Christian study of the Talmud in the Early Modern Era continued the medieval goal of alternately exposing the purported blasphemies and absurdities of the Talmud and "proving" that Jews ought to believe that the Messiah has already come once.

The latter approach to Judaica, no less subjective than the former, grew out of the discipline of Orientalism, as practiced in the nineteenth century European university. The proponents of this school viewed their subject in proper Hegelian fashion—chauvinistically. For them, the non-western Arabs and the biblical Jews whose literature they combined into the field of Semitics were on the same continuum of bypassed civilizations.

Jewish academicians—those whose study of Judaica had embraced the critical sophistication of nineteenth century *Wissenschaft*—were thus denied, for the most part, the opportunity to contribute to the university. Barring a few great exceptions, such as Wolfson at Harvard and Baron at Columbia, those who rejected baptism as a prerequisite for a university appointment pursued their calling at Jewish academies such as Dropsie College and at the great denominational seminaries of Germany and America. While their influence on the academic study of Judaism remained slight in

Germany, in the later and more liberal American setting, Jewish academicians in parochial institutions have succeeded in playing a role in the mediation of Judaica onto the non-sectarian campus.

The Jewish Theological Seminary has been a major partner in this enterprise. From the time of its reorganization, it viewed itself as a midwife of critical scholarship. During the decades of the Finkelstein administration, the acquisition of a first-rate faculty of scholars, primarily in Rabbinics but also in Bible, Education, Jewish History, Philosophy and Literature, granted JTS a preeminent status. While this faculty was engaged to train rabbis (some of whom went on to pursue careers in scholarship), the publication of its own research, largely in English, contributed generally to the various disciplines of Judaica. More specifically, the intellectual as well as geographical proximity to Baron at Columbia gave JTS an avenue of discourse with a major American university.

In terms of its own scholarly resources, therefore, JTS had the potential to influence the academic presentation of Judaism. To actualize this potential, though, the college campus itself had to become a more hospitable place for work in Judaica. This change began around mid-century, and is still taking place. During the third quarter of our century there occurred a great upsurge of Judaica programs on the American campus. Several factors may be cited to account for this: the increasing acceptance of Judaism in post-war America, the rise of ethnic consciousness on the part of American minorities generally and the concomitant rise in pressure to legitimize their experience academically by sanctioning its study, and even the growing awareness on the part of university financial planners of the benefits of attracting minority (and in particular, Jewish) patrons. Whatever the constellation of causes, the process of transforming Judaica into a staple of the college curriculum gained momentum. Writing in 1976, a participant in this phenomenon noted that "several times each year the academic community witnesses an instance of a university seeking to establish a program or chair of Jewish Studies . . ."[1]

Fairly early in the course of this growth of academic offerings in Judaica, JTS faculty and graduates began to assume the new positions. Institutionally, the Seminary responded by creating a scholar-training program. At first, this program was part of a larger agendum. The great work of Louis Finkelstein was the legitimization of Judaism as a part of the American cultural and intellectual heritage. One aspect of this work, which included ecumenical projects and symposia demonstrating the congruity of Jewish and Gentile religious vision on problems of social policy and ethics, was his creation of the Herbert H. Lehman Institute of Talmudic Ethics in 1956. This Institute, while dedicated to demonstrating "the relevance of the Talmudic tradition and other fields of Jewish learning to everyday moral and ethical decisionmaking", included a special studies program for students training "to teach Judaica at institutions of higher learning." The program exempted academicians-in-training from the pastoral and homiletics courses required of the other rabbinical students and amplified their rabbinics training. Upon completion of this program, the students earned the degree of Doctor of Hebrew Literature.[2]

Over the next decade and a half, the institutional shape of the Seminary's doctoral training program continued to develop. After the 1964 visit of the Middle States college accreditation team, and at that body's urging, JTS implemented a Ph.D. training program.[3] This would give JTS graduates the appropriate degree with which to pursue positions within academia. True, graduates with the degree of Doctor of Hebrew Literature had successfully entered academic teaching, but the Ph.D. was the recognized coin of the university realm. The adoption, on the Seminary's part, of the Middle States Team's recommendation reflects its growing commitment to create a cadre of scholars who would teach on campus.

But as yet, JTS itself offered the Ph.D. only in Rabbinics. In 1970, after the appointment of Gerson D. Cohen as the Jacob Schiff Professor of Jewish History, it added a doctoral training program in History. There being as yet no comprehensive graduate school, this program used the administrative framework of the Seminary's Institute for the Advanced Study of the Humanities, which had originally been created with other purposes in mind and which in 1970 enjoyed only a nominal existence.

Professor — by now Chancellor — Cohen's interest in building the graduate dimension of the Seminary came to fruition in 1974, with the creation of the Graduate School. The creation of a separate school allowed for the training of scholars outside the rabbinical department. The Graduate School, in the first dozen years of its existence, has grown to be the largest Judaica Ph.D. program in the world.[4]

This growth of concern with, and institutionalization of, the training of academicians has yielded a significant fraction of the Judaica faculty at American universities. In its 1974 Self-Study, JTS listed over 150 graduates of its various schools who were serving in college and university teaching positions. While this list included graduates serving on the JTS and University of Judaism faculties, teachers at other denominational institutions and those engaged in fields other than Judaica, there remained nearly 100 JTS alumni staffing Judaica programs in North America as well as Israel. It would not be excessive to claim that JTS played a major, if not the leading, role in training college-level Judaica teachers up through the last decade.

The JTS School

While it is a purely statistical question to determine the quantitative role JTS has played in the staffing of college Judaica teaching positions, it is more difficult to gauge the nature of the Seminary's influence on its graduates, and therefore, its indirect effect upon the way in which those trainees conceptualize and present Judaica in the colleges where they work. Several obstacles prevent the hasty generalization that all graduates of JTS form one school:

JTS training means different things for different scholars. The scope of its doctoral training program was at first limited to rabbinics. In other academic disciplines, the school functioned as a "sending district." It recommended that its doctoral-level students, having completed their rabbinic education, pursue their Ph.D.s at other institutions; hence the generations of JTS students of Baron in history, of Speiser in Bible, and so on. To some extent, JTS influence on these scholars is only propaedeutic — all the more so when students did no graduate work at JTS. For example, Robert Alter took his BHL at the Seminary, but did his doctorate in comparative literature at Harvard. The methodologies of the latter program are very much in evidence in his seminal literary criticism of the Bible.

This leads to a second factor preventing hasty generalizations about "the JTS approach." Even though the Seminary's doctoral programs are only decades old, changes in scholarly assumptions and methodologies already dampen the continuity of academic training at this school, as at any other. The literary approach to Bible criticism practiced by younger members of the Seminary's Bible department, to take an example already cited, differs markedly from the older scholarly emphasis on text reconstruction and source analysis.

Perhaps most fundamentally, JTS, in its commitment to pluralism, has itself been a home to diverse approaches. For example, Heschel and Kaplan, while lecturing in the same institution, could hardly be said to constitute one unified approach.

So it is not possible to delineate "the JTS approach" to Judaica simplistically in such a way as to define the work of a given scholar completely. Nevertheless, without attempting to reduce the real complexity of the phenomenon, it may be claimed that many JTS graduates share certain characteristic emphases:

The "typical" JTS-trained scholar places high priority on textual competence and stresses engagement with the text in his teaching and his scholarship. This is not simply a case of having mastered the tools; insofar as there is a JTS ideology, it includes a commitment to excellent scholarship as a *form* of religious expression. In this context, textual mastery is a form of piety. (Indeed, it is a more characteristic form of piety within the JTS milieu than is, say, social activism.)

Second, and as a consequence of this religious commitment to scholarship, the scholar of this type continues to practice a conservative form of *Wissenschaft*.[5] Scholarly objectivity is not the enemy of religious commitment, JTS has insisted in the face of challenges from both neo-Orthodox and academic circles. Study and *lernen* coexist in a creative tension. "A great Seminary can have both the genuine piety of a Yeshivah and the scholarly rigor of a University."[6] It is no accident that the Seminary recently elected as its Chancellor Dr. Ismar Schorsch, an expert on the *Wissenschaft* movement, who has forcefully argued that the nineteenth century scholars of that camp were engaged in the revivification, not the burial, of Judaism. This conclusion about scholars whom the JTS hierarchy has regarded as its own intellectual forebears is a key to the school's self-understanding. Scholarship may be technically disinterested, but the entire enterprise is quite passionate, as it entails personal involvement with Jewish destiny.

The JTS view that the critical study of Judaism and religiosity are ultimately reconcilable has facilitated an openness to the categories of academic study, both those that had been imported into Judaica by the Seminary's early years and those that were developed in recent decades. As an example of the latter, the newer social science disciplines have influenced the way contemporary Seminary scholars investigate problems of Jewish history and thought. For example, the field of sociology of religion has provided a conceptual vocabulary for the understanding of Jewish sectarian groups such as the Qumran community, the Ashkenazi Pietists of the High Middle Ages, and the contemporary Neturei Karta.

Implicit in this adoption of insights and methods developed within other disciplines is the conceptualization of Judaica as a branch of the humanities. The experience of other people is relevant to the study of both the sacred and the particularistic. At a lower-critical level, the life-work of Lieberman involved the comprehensive application of information about the Rabbis' Greco-Roman environment to their literature. Hence, also, the great affinity of JTS historiography to the Baron school, alluded to above, for that master has consistently stressed Jewish receptivity to environmental factors.

These emphases help explain the twin focus of this school on history and halakhah, and more — the insistence upon their interrelatedness. The claim that halakhah has a developmental history is, for JTS, a constitutional assertion resonating both pedagogically and in scholarship.[7]

These factors are not necessarily unique to JTS, but, in sum, they do characterize it; they are so much a part of the JTS perspective on Judaica that they are the constant, even when the changing factors already cited are taken into account. Therefore, one may justifiably speak of overarching similarities among the perspectives of JTS products, and hence of a discernible quality in the approach these scholars take, even when working in their university settings.

The Challenge of Success

The academic programs in Judaica that JTS has helped to fill for a quarter-century are reaching maturity. They now produce their own scholars. Today, the doctoral graduates in Judaica of many schools compete with Seminary Ph.D.s for openings in the field. Indeed, they have begun to teach at JTS itself. In its role as exporter of scholars, JTS repeated — albeit more quickly — the experience of the medieval Babylonian academies: its success at providing the personnel to mediate Judaica to a university audience led to the creation of competitors.

Will JTS be able to continue to play its historic role in staffing positions in Judaica at American campuses? One major problem is finances. If JTS is unable to compete financially with secular institutions, it will ultimately fail to attract the scholars it wishes to continue its tradition of academic excellence. That, in turn, would foreshadow the decline of its own graduate programs. On the other hand, if it meets this challenge, there is an added benefit to JTS in the existence of a large number of Judaica programs. It may be able to draw upon products of other schools to avoid the intellectual inbreeding that can be so stultifying to a premier academic institution—particularly in Rabbinics, where there have not been many institutions combining JTS' high standards of textual competence synthesized with source-critical perspectives. This school stands to gain intellectually from its loss of monopoly. But this leaves the topic of the past and present influence of JTS on the presentation of Judaica in the American university, and raises a question for the historian of the JTS second centennial: the influence that a new generation of American Jewish intellectual centers will exert upon JTS itself.

NOTES

In addition to the sources cited below, I am grateful to Dr. Raymond Scheindlin, Mrs. Renee Gutman and especially Rabbi David H. Panitz for their valuable insights on the history of the Seminary and on its nature, both past and present.

1. David Blumenthal, "Where does 'Jewish Studies' Belong?" *Journal of the American Academy of Religion* 44:3 (September, 1976), p. 535.
2. JTS Register, 1966-1969, pp. 97-99.
3. I am grateful to Rabbi David Kogen for this otherwise unrecorded datum concerning the development of doctoral training programs at JTS.
4. Interview, Dr. Mayer Rabinowitz, Dean, JTS Graduate School, August 18, 1986.
5. On the various types and aims of *Wissenschaft,* see Ismar Schorsch, "Introduction to Heinrich Graetz," *The Structure of Jewish History,* pp. 19-62.
6. David Halivni, Memorial Address: "Professor Saul Lieberman *zal*," *Conservative Judaism* 38:3 (Spring, 1986), p. 7.

It is not too farfetched to discern this combination of religious and scholarly concerns in individual works. Jacob Milgrom's trenchant investigation of the sacrificial terminology of Leviticus would be valid on purely scholarly grounds; yet the conclusion to his *Cult and Conscience,* in which he defends the Priestly stratum of the Pentateuch from charges of religious formalism, seems to be motivated by a religious agendum as well as by intellectual honesty. Again, while the elucidation of any linguistic obscurity in the Bible is philologically commendable, Jeffrey Tigay's attention to the clarification of the term *totafot* (*Journal of Biblical Literature,* vol. 101, September 1982), pp. 321-331, reflects the awareness that *this* obscurity has special significance in the religious life of Israel.

7. In this regard, it is noteworthy to compare the ways in which Joel Roth and Jacob Neusner utilize the famous aggadah of Moses and Akiba re-

ported in *Menaḥot* 29b. In Roth's presentation, the aggadah is a proof text for the developmental nature of halakhah. In Neusner's interpretation, the salient feature of the aggadah is its demand for scholarly humility in the face of an unintelligible reality. [Neusner, " 'Being Jewish' and Studying about Judaism," Emory University, 1977] Incidentally, in view of the lack of attention on the part of the JTS Rabbinics faculty to form criticism during the early 1960s, it would seem that Neusner's characteristic scholarly methodology was imbibed from another source, and that JTS can only claim a propaedeutic role in his scholarly formation.

Section Two

SYMPOSIUM ON SCHOLARSHIP AND BELIEF

Bible
Education
History
Literature
Philosophy
Practical Rabbinics
Talmud

Introduction to the Second Section

Raymond Scheindlin

The problem that was posed to the participants in this symposium was "How do you reconcile *Wissenschaft* and the *Kadosh Barukh Hu?*" In posing this question there is an assumption that science and God stand in opposition to each other and need to be reconciled, for *Wissenschaft des Judentums* — the science of Judaism — is simply the application of scientific thinking to the study of Jewish texts and the Jewish past. The problem of reconciling scientific thinking and religious thinking is not a new one; in fact it is not even a modern one, having, in an earlier form, been the main challenge and stimulus to our medieval philosophers. In modern times, the enlightenment and the rapid scientific advances of the last two centuries have created a climate in which scientific thinking overwhelmingly prevails in the Western intellectual world. The problem posed to contemporary religious Jewish intellectuals by the science of Judaism is not very different in principle from the problem posed by the theory of evolution or Bible criticism to Jewish and Christian intellectuals of the last century. Some liberal church denominations have allowed themselves to sidestep problems of faith by turning their attention away from the classic texts and doctrines of their tradition and concentrating instead on religion's social mission. The product has been a nearly secular religion centered on man and morality rather than on God and the commandments. Some Jewish groups have also taken this route. But in a peculiarly Jewish development, the powerful Jewish religious value of textual learning has likewise been secularized, so that Talmud Torah is assimilated to academic scholarship. It is now possible to spend a lifetime working with materials documenting the spiritual heritage of our tradition without ever personally confronting the religious challenges it poses.

The thirst for religious guidance that has unexpectedly emerged in this decade has led to discontentment with this particular variety of Jewish experience. At the Seminary we are conscious of the problem because of the challenge of students who come to us often lacking concrete grounding in classical texts but eager to find nourishment in the tradition; they are amazed and disappointed to find the Bible being taught in the same way as Shakespeare is taught at the university. Can academic study be a vehicle of religious experience?

The papers written for this symposium deal with two different aspects of the question. The theoretical problem of whether scientific thinking undermines religious belief is taken up by Marcus, Halivni, Roth, Tucker, Rembaum, Muffs and Greenstein. In the tradition of our movement, all seven affirm in varying ways the validity of critical scholarship while upholding the religious authority of the traditional texts, no matter what the effect of scientific study on them. For we cannot wish away scientific thinking, even if we would. It is the natural mode of our twentieth-century minds. But neither can we reason away our religious impulses and our reverence for our texts and our history, for they are the collective memory that makes us who we are. We must never allow our yearning for a simpler religious faith to reduce us to being intellectually less than ourselves; nor may we so favor the cultivation of our scientific minds as to suppress the religious instincts that are an authentic part of our humanity. "The honest religionist can no more deny his religious feelings than he can the logic of science," is Muffs' concise formulation of a dialectic that lies at the bottom of most modern religious thinking, including Conservative Judaism.

The papers of Rosenthal, Lukinsky, Roskies, B. Holtz, Rosenberg and Lerner focus on the pedagogical consequences of this dialectic for Jewish education, and specifically for Seminary training. Far from rejecting the claims of the scientific approach to Judaism, these papers embrace it; they are concerned with the balancing of scientific and inspirational approaches in our teaching. Particularly instructive is the testimony of Rabbi Rosenthal, deriving from a career in the pulpit, where the theoretical foundations of a Seminary education are daily put to the test by the Jewish public. Here the integration of the rabbi's spiritual mission and his scientific training is attested out of experience. While it is clear to many of the contributors to the symposium and to many of its readers that not every Seminary class has always made explicit the possibility of such integration, the intellectual challenge of a curriculum based on a dialectic of value-systems has in fact proved fruitful.

Introduction

It is our duty at the Seminary to remember that the ultimate purpose of the study of Jewish texts and history—or of any text or history—is to help us discover our spiritual selves. And in truth, this goal is not suitable only for seminaries: it would be pointless to teach Shakespeare merely for the sake of exploring influences, parallels, textual history, historical background, and the like. We cannot understand Shakespeare without knowing about quartos and folios, but we certainly have not understood him if we stop there. We study Shakespeare to understand ourselves and to satisfy our need to find ways to express eternal human dilemmas. The best university teachers know this and use their mastery of specialized knowledge gently to help their students find in the classics both a spiritual mirror and a spiritual window.

Many preparations are necessary along the way to making this use of our texts. Some of these preparations involve the disciplined mastery of complex skills and subject matters. The thread that connects these studies with our hearts and our hearts with God is sometimes hard to see, and the satisfaction is frustratingly delayed. Sometimes both teacher and student become so passionately attached to the preparatory studies that they forget to look beyond them. But skimping on the preparations will not solve either problem. The student must be helped to learn how to read the texts to find himself. This cannot be done honestly in our century without making full use of the discoveries of history, philosophy, comparative religion, and other secular disciplines. Nor can it be done with integrity unless the rudiments are fully mastered. But both secular disciplines and the textual rudiments are sterile if they do not contribute, however indirectly, to inner growth.

The old Library Reading Room in the Schiff Building at 122nd Street.

History and Religion: A Reflection on Ralbag's Torah Commentary[1]

Edward L. Greenstein

We are accustomed to regard the Torah from two sides, the Written and the Oral. The Written Torah had traditionally been understood to have been transmitted in immutable form since its revelation on Mt. Sinai. The Oral Torah has been viewed more diversely. By virtually all accounts it is the interpretation by which the Written Torah is applied to contemporary life and thought. But what is its origin?

The introduction to *Pirkei Avot,* the so-called "Ethics of the Fathers" in the Mishnah, says that "Moses received the Torah at Sinai and handed it down to Joshua," who continued to pass it on until it reached the earliest Pharisees, the founders of Rabbinic Judaism. Clearly what is spoken of here is not the Written but the Oral Torah. The ancient rabbis believed that they were in possession of the authoritative reading of the Written Torah, which reading came down to them side by side with the written text. Similarly, the contemporary Dead Sea sect believed that it possessed the correct interpretation of the Torah, which it had received alongside the Written Torah. According to one of their own official texts, the so-called Manual of Discipline (column 1, lines 3-4), God told Moses "Explain (*i.e.,* interpret) to the elders, to the Levites, and to all the priests, and command to the Israelites the words of the Torah."

In later rabbinic texts one finds the notion that all future interpretation of the Torah had already been revealed to Moses together with the Written Torah: "What the prophets will prophesy in the future in every generation they received from Mt. Sinai. . . . And not only did all the prophets receive their prophecy from Sinai, but even the sages who will arise in every generation, each one received his [teaching] from Sinai" (*Exodus Rabbah, Yitro,* 28). This has for centuries remained the Jewish myth of Torah.

History has changed—some would say spoiled—all that. This

view of Torah as a timeless, unalterable body of understanding assumes that it does not in any way respond to history, to shifting circumstances or different ideas. Like myth, it sees the world frozen in time. That which was, is, and will be takes place in an eternal Godlike perspective. Myth presents things in their paradigmatic relation to each other, as a model that exists in a forever fixed state. As Mircea Eliade puts it in *The Sacred and the Profane,* "religious man lives in two kinds of time, of which the more important, sacred time, appears under the paradoxical aspect of a circular time, reversible and recoverable, a sort of eternal mythical present" (p. 70). In the traditional religious Jewish view, then, Torah in all its ramifications exists in all times in an unchanging state of being-present.

Placing the Torah against the backdrop of history or, more precisely, within the ever-changing development of history, leads to a different view. In this view, the Oral Torah represents the progressive, or on-going, adaptation of what the Written Torah means within a changing world. Modern biblical scholarship would contend that the Written Torah underwent a similar historical development.[2] By definition, once one looks for the historical conditions in which the Torah (Written or Oral, it doesn't matter) developed, one will find them. If there is such a thing as history, or even time, then one can find the Torah within it. One can choose whether to view the Torah only mythically, or only historically, or in both ways for different purposes — with bifocals so to speak. But the historical perspective on Torah must by its very nature examine the Torah within history.

Contrary to what many think, the historical view of the Torah did not begin after the Renaissance. Without claiming that he was the first, Rabbi Levi ben Gershon, Ralbag, or Gersonides, the southern French Jewish philosopher of the early fourteenth century, displayed a historical approach to the contents of the *Written* Torah in his brilliant and barely studied commentary on the Torah. Ralbag did not have the benefit of ancient Near Eastern texts, archeological finds, and other materials that serve the modern historian. But he did have the Bible, and the Bible includes within it literature that spans many centuries. In addition, he displayed a sharply rationalistic and independent mind.

In contrast to the sages of the Talmud, who sought to connect the Oral Torah to the written text by the hermeneutical methods of classical midrash, Ralbag was determined "to explain the words of the Torah according to their own meanings," as he says in his Introduction to his Torah commentary. He eschewed the midrashic procedures of his rabbinic predecessors. On the other hand, he did not attempt to read the Bible in a naively literal manner. He looked for the message and often, in his eyes, the message was encoded in symbolic terms. He did not, for example, take the six days of Creation as six actual days. Rather, he interpreted them as a symbolic expression of the absolute orderliness of Creation, moving from causes to effects and from the lower forms of creation to the higher.

In his commentary on the building of God's sacred home in the midst of the Israelite camp, the *mishkan* (Exodus chap. 25 and following), Ralbag demonstrates that the *mishkan* and its appurtenances reveal the rootedness of the Written Torah in time and place, that is, in history. In Ralbag's view, the *mishkan* was constructed as it was because the Israelites happened to be living in the Sinai wilderness.

Most biblical interpreters, both in medieval and modern times, recognize a similarity between the description of the *mishkan* in the Torah (the Pentateuch), and the description of the Temple that Solomon built, related in the First Book of Kings. Despite differences in the sequence of construction and the fact that the *mishkan* was small and humble beside the monumental and ornate Temple of Solomon, the descriptions resemble each other in both substance and style.

The two passages are framed by a similar formula. In outlining the blueprint of the *mishkan*, God tells Moses: "they will make a holyplace for me so that I may dwell in their midst" (Exodus 25:8); likewise: "I shall dwell in the midst of the Israelites and I shall be God to them" (Exodus 29:45). The description of the Temple in I Kings opens with the Lord saying, "I shall dwell in the midst of the Israelites and I shall not forsake my people Israel" (6:13). At the conclusion of building the *mishkan* and at the completion of the Temple, the Presence of the Lord, the *kavod* radiating light through its cover of cloud, enters the holy site. "The cloud covered the Tent of Meeting, and the Aura of the Lord filled the Dwelling-Place. Now Moses was unable to enter the Tent of Meeting for there dwelled upon it the cloud; and the Aura of the Lord filled the Dwelling-Place." So it is written in Exodus 40:34-35. I Kings 8:11 is striking in its resemblance: "The priests were unable to stand to minister because of the cloud, for the Aura of the Lord had filled the Lord's Temple."

Modern scholars and Ralbag both attach great significance to these similarities. Moderns, who happen to follow the views of the important nineteenth century biblicist Julius Wellhausen, have surmised that in a later period Israelite or Jewish priests invented the description of the *mishkan,* imagining it as a small-scale precursor of the Solomonic Temple. The moderns can adduce evidence for their theory from the fact that Exodus 20:24-25 enjoins the Israelites to build an altar from earth or from unhewn stone. The section about the *mishkan,* however, tells the Israelites to make an altar of wood overlaid with bronze (Exodus 27:1-2). We encounter a bronze altar explicitly in descriptions of the later Temple (Ezek. 9:2; II Chron. 4:1; and cf. I Kings. 8:64). It seems to many modern scholars that the authentic pre-Temple altar was of the rougher type mentioned in Exodus 20 and that the altar in the *mishkan* constitutes a reading back of the Temple's design into an earlier period.

Ralbag would agree that the *mishkan* and Temple bore a direct relation to one another; but he saw the relation in the opposite chronological order. He explains that both the *mishkan* and Temple were constructed according to the same plan, only the Temple would be built permanently in Jerusalem, as Deuteronomy often states: "in the place in which the Lord chooses to have his name dwell." The Israelites, obviously, were in no position to construct the Temple until they had conquered the Land of Israel and Jerusalem in particular. Accordingly, only in the time of David and Solomon did the Lord command the Israelites to build the Temple on Mount Zion, as Solomon said in his prayer, dedicating the new sanctuary:

> Of blessing is the Lord, God of Israel, who spoke by mouth to David my father and charged him, saying: "From the day I had my people, that is, Israel, go out from Egypt I had not chosen any town from all the tribes of Israel in which to build a house for my name to be there; then I chose David to be over my people Israel." My father David's heart was to build a house for the name of the Lord, God of Israel (I Kings 8:15-17).

David and Solomon believed that by building the Temple they were fulfilling the command of God.

Yet, between the exodus from Egypt and the settlement of the tribes in the Land of Israel there was a need for a holy place in which the Israelites could properly worship the Lord. For this purpose the Lord commanded Israel to set up a temporary sanctuary in the Wilderness according to the design of the Temple that would be constructed later—only smaller. Ralbag explains:

> Now the *mishkan* that was in the Wilderness was only temporary, [designed in order] to educate Israel in the worship of God, may he be exalted, so that they would become God's people and he would allocate the Land to them; so that they would not stray for lack of a *mishkan* or temple until the site of the eternal Temple was revealed to them. For this reason the commandment [to build a permanent Temple to God] could only be fulfilled on the site where the Holy Temple would be, on Mount Moriah.

The command to erect the *mishkan*, then, was given for only a limited period. It was rooted in a specific time, while Israel was in a specific place.

With respect to the size of the *mishkan* one can readily understand that a temporary, portable sanctuary in the wilderness would differ in size from the permanent Temple to be built in Jerusalem. It makes sense that the *mishkan* would be smaller. But, much more interestingly, the *mishkan* and the Temple differ in the materials out of which they are made. The *mishkan* was made with hangings of leather and fabric (Exodus 26), while the Temple was constructed of cedar wood and stone. Why should the substances be so different?

Ralbag goes into this question. He realizes that the Torah takes into account the historical conditions of the Israelites in the wilderness. Where did they find the materials with which to build the *mishkan*? Ralbag answers:

> It is likely that each man cut them down in one of the places through which they passed, to make of them tables and the like; and those who were in possession of them donated them, as it is related in *Parashat Vayyakhel* (Exodus 35).

It is clear, then, that it is not the materials out of which the *mishkan* is made but the structure of it, its overall pattern, that is crucial. The materials are rooted in a specific place. The Sinai wilderness, and the Negev as well, happen to grow acacia wood and not cedars. But during the kingship of David and Solomon, when a treaty was made between Israel and Phoenicia, cedar could be imported from Lebanon for building the Temple.

Ralbag paid heed to what is written in Exodus 25:9: "According to all that I show you, the structure (*tavnit*) of the *mishkan* and the structure of all its appurtenances, so shall you make." From this

Ralbag learned that God commanded only the structure, the design, and the Israelites provided the materials depending upon their particular historical circumstances. Ralbag adds: And so it was not obligatory that the appurtenances of the Holy Place be of the metals mentioned here, for (God) only commanded that they make them according to the design that he mentioned, not from the metals that he mentioned."

Ralbag's comment, which penetrates to the core of the Bible's historical meaning, has far-reaching implications. God delineated the overall design of the *mishkan*, adapting its size to the historical conditions of the Israelites and the materials that were available to the people in a specific place and time. God provided the structure, and Israel would fill out that structure with what it had. He understood that the Written Torah embodies not an immutable word of God but an outline that the people of the Covenant must complete with regard to its own special circumstances.

For Ralbag, then, the Written Torah represents the revealed religion of the People Israel in a given time and place. In a later time and a different place, the Torah might be different, as it was when the Temple of Solomon replaced the *mishkan*. The Oral Torah, the mitzvot as interpreted and formulated in classical rabbinic literature and embodied in the Talmud, represent for Ralbag a later understanding of the Covenant. While Ralbag himself accepted the authority of the Oral Torah as it had been transmitted from ancient to medieval times, he did not adhere to the argumentation his predecessors had used for grounding the Oral Torah in the Written (as was said above). The midrashic explanations of Scripture in the Talmud were, Ralbag says in the Introduction to his Torah commentary, "very good statements in and of themselves, but they are not expositions of the verses in the Torah to which they [the talmudic rabbis] attached them." In other words, the Oral Torah has an independent basis apart from serving as a spelling out of the Written Torah. Ralbag, who believed in the revealed authority of the Oral Torah, gave his own principles of logic on which to found the Oral Torah in the Written. For example, the Torah presents us with specific instances, but we are meant to take them as paradigms for innumerable cases. The commandment in Deuteronomy 22:10 that forbids plowing with an ox and an ass together refers, says Ralbag, to any two animals performing any type of labor. Or, according to Ralbag's fourth principle of logic, a commandment should be interpreted in order to maximize its application and effect. Thus, *tefillin* should be worn near the mind and the heart, not simply on the forehead and arm. That the Torah as written was meaningful for Ralbag through his own reading stands out most clearly in what follows his summary or paraphrase of each section of the Torah. He lists and illustrates the various values that one should find in that section of the Torah. He finds theological, ethical, legal, and philosophical lessons in the Written Torah. His commentary amounts to his own Oral Torah, intended not to supplant but to supplement the Talmud.

In this way Ralbag overcame the potential obstacle that a historical perspective can pose to faith. He did not relegate the Written Torah to the historical past, even though it was clear to him that later revelation spelled out the Torah differently in later times. Rather, the Written Torah and the Oral Torah existed for him in the living present, the only time that true religion lives. The Torah meant for Ralbag that which he understood it to say according to the logic in which he grounded it and teaching the lessons that he derived from it. Religion collapses time and interprets history as the present. It mythologizes history. Historical perspective need not spoil religious faith. It does, however, inform it and compel it to seek out meaning in a manner that is now convincing to us. If we share Ralbag's commitment to struggle with, and in, the Torah—both written Written and written Oral—we, too, may be able to express our faith and nourish it through our effort.

NOTES

1. This essay was adapted from a *devar torah* that I presented, in Hebrew, at the annual meeting of the Jewish Educators Assembly in 1979. I want to thank Rabbi David Wolf Silverman, who first introduced me to Ralbag's Torah commentary. I deal with the broader implications of this essay in "Understanding the Sinai Revelation," published as a separate pamphlet by the Melton Research Center and as an appendix to the Melton *Teacher's Guide to Exodus* by Ruth Zielenziger (1984).

2. The historical connection between Written and Oral Torah has been discussed by Louis Ginzberg in "The Codification of Jewish Law," *On Jewish Law and Lore* (New York: Atheneum, 1970) pp. 153–184.

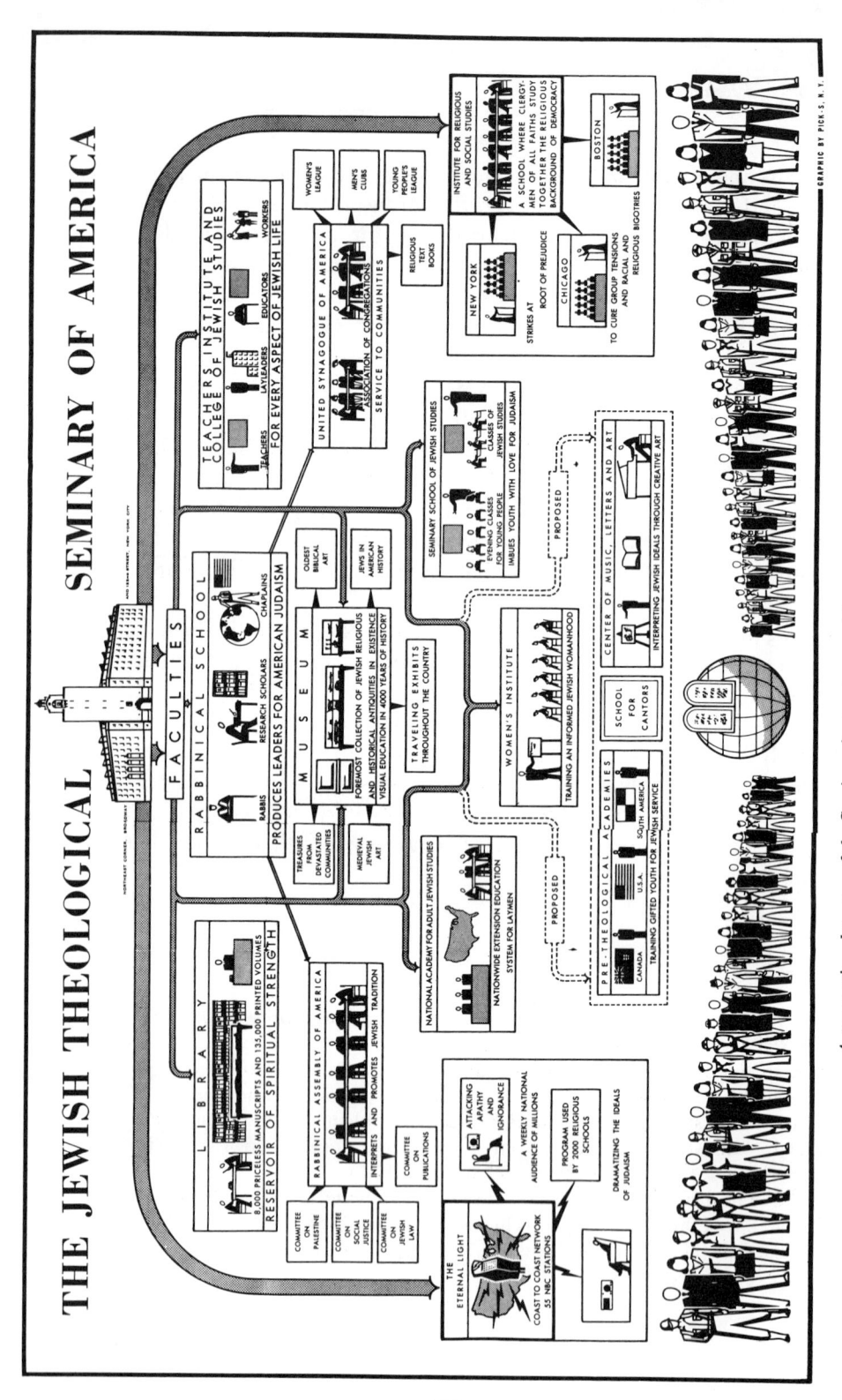

A promotional poster of the Seminary's structure and programs from the early 1940's.

Religion and Secular Culture

Yochanan Muffs

The relationship between monotheism and secular culture has always been problematic. On the one hand, secular culture was the world from which monotheism was born; hence it was part of it. On the other hand, it was the world with which monotheism fought; hence it was "the enemy." Finally, it was the world monotheism helped to reshape by contributing to it from its own and unique fund of ideas.

This complex of relationships is clearly reflected in the history of biblical religion. No matter how unique the idea of biblical monotheism may be, how inexplicable in terms of preceding religious developments, yet the actual forms in which the idea became a historical reality — law, cult, kingship, prophecy, etc. — all have clear Near Eastern antecedents. Furthermore, this dependence is more than a receptivity to forms. The very ethos of the Bible — its relative sophistication, and especially its highly developed legal structures and concern for social justice — all bear an unmistakably Mesopotamian stamp (so even Kaufmann). Yet, in spite of the Bible's debt to Mesopotamia, it was against this very environment that monotheism was to declare an uncompromising war — one which was to affect the very shape of Western culture.

All subsequent periods of Jewish history reflect this dialectic of receptivity, rejection, and influence. Thus, without the threat and stimulus of the Hellenistic experience, post-exilic Judaism might never have recovered from its century-long slumber, might never have produced the religious culture reflected in the Talmud and Midrash, in the speculations of its mystics and the history-making activities of its sectarians. Yet, instead of succumbing to the Greek presence, as did so many other peoples (with the notable exception of the Romans), the Jews creatively assimilated the Greek factor to their own national talents, illumining their law with its dialectic, stimulating their literature — the *Aggadah* — with its aesthetic, and ultimately creating a new synthesis which not only influenced the Greek world, but also helped to bring about its very collapse.

The experience of the Middle Ages is no less instructive. Under the influence of the Greek-Arabic synthesis, Jews were able to develop, for the first time in their history, an indigenous secular culture which complemented — and often conflicted with — the religious culture they had received from the past. As part of culture and illumined by its canons, religion now lost some of its old intransigence: even in its own eyes, it was no longer the only source of truth. Under the influence of the general culture, religion became self-reflective and attempted to explain to itself, in the language of culture, the logic of its own being.

Not everyone, however, saw in culture the necessary complement of religion — that which purified religion of its naivete and curbed some of its excesses. For some, culture was simply more real than religion. For others, culture represented the threat of moral and intellectual nihilism. Even these people, however, could not escape its power and charm: even their attacks against culture were informed by its logic and influenced by its style. The most, however, that culture contributed to the sympathetic man of faith was the sophistication that came with self-reflection; what secular culture did not — and could not — do was to add significantly to the basic ideas and structures of religion. Just such a religious enrichment of the tradition took place in the less cultured environment of Christian Europe.

It was in Provence that rabbinic Judaism experienced one of the most profound transformations of its entire history. Here, under the influence of local Gnostic currents, the interpersonal Midrash of the Talmud was converted into the cosmological myth of the Kabbalah, a myth in which man was not merely the partner of God in the creation of the moral world, but the redeemer of a God somehow held captive in the ruins of his miscarried creation. The *halakhah* — that commonsense discipline for the education of man — was now converted into a magic theurgy for the redemption of God.

And yet, Jewish mysticism represents more than an accommodation of tradition to its environment. In the Zohar, we witness the profound — and often hopeless — struggle to synthesize two deeply-felt religious truths: (a) the truth of a personal God, the model of man's humanity, reflected in the somewhat naive stories of the Bible and the Talmud; and (b) the truth of a spiritual reality beyond all personal attributes, the ineffable Ground of Being, the mysterious object of man's religious contemplation. Instead of declaring the personal creator of the world to be the enemy of the Spirit—as Gnosticism usually did—the Zohar proclaimed that the Spirit, the ineffable Ground of Being, was somehow the very source of creation and personhood. The God of myth and the God beyond the myth are One. Thus, as mysticism freed traditional religion from its literal attachment to the anthropomorphic model, anthropomorphic monotheism helped mysticism free itself from its anti-world and anti-personalistic bias.

It must be remembered that the impact of secular culture on the Jewish tradition was as subtle and unconscious as it was profound. Few of those influenced were actually aware of the process and, if they had been, many would have seriously objected to it. Many—but not all. In every generation there have been a few religious thinkers, quite aware of the influence of secular culture, who did not necessarily condemn it. The Torah was certainly their primary concern, but culture did have its legitimate function in their life. For them, the exercise of the intellect—and even the cultivation of the aesthetic sensibility—did have its place, however ancillary, within the divine economy. Furthermore, it should be stressed that these pre-modern religious evaluations of the secular are not merely of historical interest. For the modern thinker concerned with the role of the secular within the religious life, these traditional evaluations—however sporadic—provide precious guidelines for a modern, yet Judaic, approach to a theology of culture, an area of ever-growing concern to all modern theologians. In the following section, therefore, we will concern ourselves with the *conscious* attitudes of tradition to secular culture, specifically with the exercise of the intellect and the cultivation of the aesthetic—two activities usually associated with the person of culture.

Unfortunately, traditional sources—especially the more ancient ones—are rarely as self-reflective and as articulate in these matters as modern theologians would like. Nevertheless, the sources are not as silent as might seem at first glance. A traditional consensus concerning the uses of the mind will be something like this: any intellectual skill or discipline that (a) is not inherently associated with paganism, (b) that is not cultivated as an end in itself, but (c) is directed to the constructive solution of practical problems—is highly valued. Although revelation (Torah) is a superior form of knowledge, wisdom (*hokhmah*) is still considered as one of God's blessings to man, not merely Jewish man. This attitude is articulated in many statements of the rabbis, and is implicit in many biblical passages. Thus, although men of *hokhmah* like Solomon (who knew the languages of the animals) and Bezalel (who had the skill to build the Tabernacle) were not numbered among the saints of the tradition, they did merit a place among its cultural heroes. The *B'nei Kedem* (Moabites, Edomites, Amonites, etc.) are praised for their *hokhmah* in the poetic arts and some of their compositions were even quoted in the Pentateuch (cf. Numbers 21:27). The Bible even seems to have a grudging respect for the efficacy of pagan magic and soothsaying, even though it forbids their use. Man is supposed to rely on God, not on human science, for the guidance of his life. In magic, *hokhmah* became idolatrous.

However, when not idolatrous, *hokhmah* — whatever its source — was welcomed. Thus, Greek techniques used in editing the classics were creatively applied by the rabbis to the editing of the Bible; Greek science and medicine were used to solve halakhic problems; Greek rhetoric was used to sharpen the minds of rabbinic legalists. Even a rapid perusal of Lieberman's now famous books — *Hellenism in Jewish Palestine* and *Greek in Jewish Palestine* — gives the impression that the reception of the Greek factor was not merely an unconscious sociological trend, but a process that was consciously cultivated by the rabbis as well.

Finally, it should be noted that the rabbis were not unaware that much of their law, especially the law of their legal documents, was of a common Near Eastern source. The expression *leshon hedyot* or "layman's formulary" used by the Talmud to describe rabbinic legal documents, reflects the rabbis' awareness that the law of documents was of non-Jewish — or at least, non-rabbinic — origin. What was uniquely Jewish was not the law itself — this was more or less common to all Mesopotamians, Jews and gentiles alike — but rather the passionate concern to see God's demands for justice realized in their society. If the *hokhmah* of non-Jewish law was useful for this purpose, it too could be assimilated.

The Middle Ages are no exception to this trend. Arabic medicine and science were avidly pursued even by the most traditional. Jewish doctors and scientists are well known throughout the medieval world. Maimonides, the great master of Jewish law, was also the physician to the Sultan's court and the author of scientific treatises on rock-science and botany. The fact that many popes had Jewish doctors is well known. In our time, the affinity between Orthodox Jews and the sciences — especially physics, mathematics, and medicine — is also well known and is not simply a sociological coincidence. To sum up: The technical application of the mind to the solution of practical human problems was always looked on favorably by the tradition, if these activities did not seriously distract the man of faith from the central concerns of life — the study of the Torah and the observance of the *mitzvot*.

As long as human intelligence was applied to the useful solution of practical problems it posed little threat to religion. However, once the mind started to search for understanding — of its own workings, of nature, and especially of God — it confronted faith with a powerful adversary. The speculative intelligence questions everything; nothing escapes its probing. Is the God who exists a real force in the world? If so, is He a force for good? The question may be irrelevant: He may not exist at all.

The last question is the real enemy of all theistic religions. The first two, on the other hand, are dangerous only if faith is defined as the conquest of all rational barriers, as the belief in something that transcends the boundaries of logic, as "the absurd." According to this Kierkegaardian approach, typical of some types of Christianity and of certain trends in the Bible (cf. the *Akedah*), faith and doubt are in polar opposition. However, it should be noted that there is another type of faith represented in the Bible, one more "empirical" and almost tolerant of the frame of mind that insists that "seeing is believing." Instead of demanding affirmations of the mind that are rationally absurd, it calls for loyalty to the God who has manifested His power in the past, and for a sense of trust in His power to deliver in the future. The only "heresy" the Bible knows is disloyalty to God after having experienced His goodness (cf. Deut. 1:32 ff., Jeremiah 2:5 ff. among others).

Furthermore, God even allows Himself to be tested. Instead of being offended at Gideon's doubts that it may not have been God who was really speaking to him, God actually goes along with Gideon's almost scientific desire to authenticate the vision by sign — one that almost has the quality of an experiment. Gideon even has the audacity to request a second "experiment" — a type of "control" — lest the first sign merely be a coincidence! The extent to which God tolerates this skeptical frame of mind and the empirical methods by which He overcomes Gideon's doubts are truly remarkable (cf. Judges 6 end).

Paradoxically, at least in one case in the Bible, it is not the testing of the Lord that arouses divine ire, but the refusal of King Ahaz to test God's power when a choice of authenticating experiments ("signs") is actually offered the king by the prophet Isaiah (cf. Isaiah 7:10 ff.).

God does not want to outrage the mind by demanding affirmations of faith not grounded in experience. Furthermore, when actual experience conflicts with certain assumptions about God's justice, biblical religion does not seem to require the man of faith to repress his doubts in silent resignation. Abraham, Jeremiah, and Job — all men who questioned God's justice — are hardly numbered among the wicked. There is even some evidence that God even demands such criticism — at least from his prophets (cf. Ezekiel 22:30).

However, the doubt tolerated by the Bible was radically different from that created by philosophical speculation. Job's mind may have doubted God's justice, but his heart never for a moment doubted God's existence. It was just this that created Job's anguish — to feel that God exists, yet to know that He is unjust, was more than the mind could bear. (A capricious, or even wicked god, was not a problem for the Babylonian Job, who never assumed that the gods were, or had to be, just.)

Philosophical doubt is something entirely different. Philosophy has the power to declare religious feelings meaningless, and to deny not only God's justice, but his existence as well. Such radical doubt is something that few religions or political systems are prepared to accept without reservation. For theistic religion to allow room for atheism is to court suicide. Yet, religious and political establishments realize — usually after much bitter experience — that it is much wiser to contain free thinkers by allowing them carefully circumscribed areas of freedom, than to repress them altogether and thus unwittingly bring about an explosion of real heresy — a threat to the stability of church and state alike. This is the best any polity can do for its intellectuals.

Realistically speaking, no tradition can leave room for a free questioning of its own first principles. It is questionable whether even democracy *freely* allows those living under its aegis the right to question the validity of the democratic process. And yet, as long as those who have their doubts do not actively advocate the overthrow of the legal framework of democracy, the doubters are still allowed to voice their opinions. On occasion, these opinions may even help democracy to realize itself more adequately. The question facing us is: to what degree do the study of history, psychology, and philosophy — and the doubts they create in our minds — actually contribute to the deepening of our religious life?

In most cases, their contribution is not very constructive. On the surface, the probing of the historian into the genesis of religion, and the investigations of the psychologists into the nature of the psyche are rarely conducive to greater religiosity. A rigid historian tends to explain everything in terms of real and immanent causes, leaving little room for transcendental influences, and almost no room for divine intervention in the course of history. There is usually little room for God alongside of the id, ego, and superego.

Yet, the honest religionist can no more deny his religious feelings than he can the logic of science. Both make absolute claims on his loyalty. Instead of resolving this tension by eliminating one of the discordant poles, he bravely holds both poles simultaneously, having learned to live with this tension as a constituent element in his life. This dialectic is similar to that of the checks and balances built into political systems: no one branch of the government exercises absolute power. Similarly, no one mode of observation — whether it be history, religion, sociology, or aesthetics — can comprehend all of the reality. Yet, all of them make absolute — hence idolatrous — claims that they alone have the key to the truth. By setting the various modes of observation in dialectic tension with each other, the excessive claims of each mode are checked, their idolatry is broken, and a modicum of balance is hopefully achieved. Thus, for example, science challenges the myths of religion, but religion, in turn, challenges the moral nihilism of science.

The same holds true concerning the dialogue between religions. By comparing one religion with the other, not only are the implicit assumptions of one's own faith made clearer, but the inherent tendency of our own faith to make itself the measure of all things is checked. Historically speaking, religions are always aware of their limitations; otherwise, they would not have borrowed so freely from each other. These borrowings, however, did not signal the death of the religion but its basic spiritual health — its realization that the truth it needs, but does not possess, can be borrowed from the outside and assimilated to its own creative genius. What applied historically to the group is just as true for the individual.

The doubt stimulated by critical studies is healthy for yet another reason: it tests our faith and separates the man of real faith from the religious behaviorist. Faith is not a passive state, a status quo, but an inner struggle. It is an order superimposed on a chaos that constantly threatens to break forth. Doubt is that which stirs inert hearts from their complacency and sets the dialectic of faith-doubt in motion. Furthermore, the greater the faith, the greater the amount of doubt the man of faith will be able to digest without losing his equilibrium. If the man of faith has the good fortune to come out of this battle without having denied either religion or science, he will have unknowingly developed a new skill: the ability to hold life like a bird—hard enough that it doesn't fly away, gently enough that it isn't choked to death.

On the Training of Rabbis: Scholarship, Belief and the Problem of Education

Barry W. Holtz

Education is, at least in part, the enterprise of translation. In that sense all Jewish scholars are educators. For what scholars seek to do is find a way to mediate the literary, historical or cultural milieu of an "other" (be it in the past or even in the present) and make it intelligible to the "here." In other words, how can we, standing at this point in time, in this culture—America, 1987—make sense of the cultural and psychological context of Medieval Spain, the web of meanings imbedded in *Midrash Tanhuma*, the life of Rabbi Nahman of Bratslav, the events of the First Zionist Congress, the social structure of an old-age home in contemporary Los Angeles? All of these are topics alive in the world of Jewish scholarship today, and all involve different kinds of interpretation and methodology. But each is an exercise in translation, making the unintelligible understood, helping us see where we didn't see before.

But how do scholars themselves understand what they are doing? Oddly, we know very little about the self-perception, the concept of task, that the scholars bring to their work. Since the mid-1960s the explosion of interest in Jewish studies and the veritable creation of a field finds us with a cadre of over a thousand professors who do their work in the broadly defined world of "Jewish Studies." What are they doing there?

We do not know very much at all about why scholars do what they do and what they think about their work, even concerning issues of considerable import. The question, for example, of personal faith and its relationship to one's academic work deserves serious consideration, but the issue of scholarship and belief is one among many about which data are sadly lacking. Let us propose, however, one hypothesis: the academy by its very nature may offer some of those who become scholars an opportunity to avoid the big questions of belief and personal commitment that other tasks in Jewish life make unavoidable. It may in fact be that a generation of Jewish scholars found a way to solve profound dilemmas such as Torah as revelation vs. Torah as human document by simply saying that we are scientists, toiling like other objective researchers in the university. Personal belief simply is not relevant to the question on the table.

Or to put it another way: we are scholars, not rabbis. One way that rabbis differ from scholars is that rabbis have to defend Judaism. A rabbi has to deal with the way his or her teaching makes sense in the lives of the listeners. A scholar of, say, Dante does not have to justify Dante's views in the eyes of students. The scholar hopes that the students will appreciate the poet, perhaps even come to love reading the poet. But if not? There will be other students.

The Judaica professor can take the same position: "I am not here to defend *Genesis Rabbah*; I am here to look at it, to examine it with you, to understand it. If you happen not to like its views about miracles, or prayer, or gentiles, or women—well, that's your business." Now, obviously, there are few professors of *any* discipline who are so cavalier about their chosen area of study and teaching that they simply dismiss the reactions of students in the classroom. There is a kind of emotional defensiveness in all people about the things that they love. And teachers, who are forced to put themselves publicly on the line every day, are less exempt than others from the need to justify, even to apologize.

But there *is* a difference between the academic and the rabbi. The professorial robes offer a kind of protection that no rabbi can find. It may be, in fact, that the stress and loneliness that rabbis report about their professional lives comes as much from this factor as from anything else: a lot is on the line. Or at any rate this is the way the rabbi understands the job.

The phenomenon that I am describing, what we might call "the scholar's seclusion," did not begin with the movement of Judaic studies into the secular university. The world of *Wissenschaft* and the model of the "objective" scholar has an older pedigree and certainly has been the hallmark of the Jewish Theological Seminary through its history. The world of JTS (and Hebrew Union College) offers a different kind of problem, however: In an institution that trains rabbis, what is the role of the scholar? Is the scientific learning which is the goal of scholarship the kind that rabbis need in their training? And when rabbis go out into the field, what kind of teachers do we expect them to be? Like their professors? And if not, why do we train them the way that we do?

Research in education has long pointed out that people tend to teach in the way that they themselves have been taught. Thus we might expect that graduates of our rabbinical institutions, trained in the style of *Wissenschaft* scholarship, would teach their congregants in a fashion very similar to the education that they had received while in seminary. Now, of course, we can ask: What's so bad about teaching laypeople as if they were scholars or scholars-to-be? Perhaps what scholars do is, in fact, *precisely* what we'd like laypeople to do! Perhaps the ideal Jew out in our congregations would be a kind of Judaica scholar.

Obviously, most laypeople are not going to turn into Jewish studies scholars and it may be important to ask an educator's question and to start considering the kind of ideal "product" we'd like to see coming out of the educational institution called the synagogue. What, we can ask, is the relationship of the Seminary's *Wissenschaft* tradition to our congregational life?

To begin with, let us not forget that scholarship is or can be interesting in and of itself. It is quite possible to take any piece of scholarship and find a way of translating it for laypeople so that they will at any rate find it intellectually interesting. Israel Scheffler has pointed out a fact that we have all experienced: do not underestimate the emotional effect of an intellectual enterprise.[1] I often recommend to education students that they try curricularizing works of scholarship for their students—in other words, turn a scholar's article into a set of lessons by using the primary sources as used by the scholar and unpacking the scholar's argument. Scholarly works can be feats of intellectual exhilaration and one can help an adult student penetrate into that world by using the fruits of scholarly labor in a pedagogically sophisticated way.[2] In this way, you capture the issue, the importance, and the sense of excitement in the scholar's discussion, much to the benefit of the lay audience.

And yet: is that what we really want to be doing with laypeople—showing them the excitement of scholarship? My sense is we want to be doing something else—namely, trying to help people see that Torah can mean something in their own lives. Scholarship is not irrelevant here, but we have to remember what scholarship is really all about anyway: *the illumination of the meaning of the text we study.* The historical explorations, the Akkadian roots, the parallels to Islamic philosophy, the classification of literary genres — whatever — are there, after all, for the purpose of illuminating the core of meaning of the texts we study. And the insights of modern scholarship must come into play when we try to explicate those texts. But, as I've said, that is not the whole story.

Let us consider for a moment one important subject area as an example: in what way does an academic approach to the study of *liturgy* respond to the need of laypeople in congregations? If one looks at the approach of *Wissenschaft* scholarship (Elbogen or Joseph Heinemann or Lawrence Hoffman),[3] in general we find a historical approach to the development of liturgy: How did the prayerbook evolve? What is the influence of poetry on liturgy? What are the differences between the various liturgical rites? Now these central scholarly questions are all of important academic and historical interest, but I suspect that teaching the prayerbook in this fashion to a lay audience — interesting though the historical approach may be — will not in any way answer the central problems that Jews feel about prayer or about the prayerbook. *Those* questions are more on the order of: why pray? is prayer answered? how can these prayers in our liturgy speak to *me*? and why should I bother?

The question we must consider is how a rabbinic community trained in dealing with the first set of questions, the academic issues, can find a way to approach the second set of issues, the issues of personal significance. If our training institutions cannot deal with that dilemma, the rabbis going out into the community today — when issues of prayer are anything but clear — will have very little help in facing the situations of greatest moment in the lives of Jews.

My own sense is that the only way to make the sources of Judaism come alive for most Jews today is through a reading of those sources which is at once literary, personal and theological. This approach does not ignore the contributions of *Wissenschaft* scholarship — as I've said above, scholarship is an important tool in the illumination of meaning — but it does not make that scholarship an end in itself. Moreover, it should be clear that the approach I am suggesting is not limited to situations of the rabbi teaching laypeople. Indeed, because of the factor of "modeling" that I have mentioned above, it is obvious that rabbis themselves must be trained at the Seminary in a way that closely approximates the way that they themselves will later teach their congregants.

So how might we go about teaching in this fashion—both at the Seminary and in the congregations? I think this might be done in three ways. To begin with, we must take the text we are studying seriously in its own context and ask: how does this text address and deal with an issue that its writer felt was so important that he wrote[4] what we have before us? And this goes beyond the personal concerns of the writer at hand. We can also see that the great Jewish texts go beyond one individual's life to answer or address the great questions at the heart of all Western culture. When we teach the text to laypeople we ought to place it within that framework, and, here certainly with the help of scholarship, see its larger cultural context and meaning. Because the rabbinical student will in the future be the teacher of the text at hand, he or she should have the benefit of knowing in depth the contribution of *Wissenschaft* scholarship, if relevant, to the text being studied.

In addition, the rabbinical school course might also discuss what aspects of that scholarship are appropriate to teaching the material to a lay audience. It would be instructive, in other words, if rabbinical school classes dealt both with the text and the transmission of that text when the rabbi approaches the laity. The Seminary instructor need not be an expert in pedagogy for such a discussion to occur. Merely opening up the question for the class to consider may be sufficient, although, as I argue below, I believe the faculty as a whole should begin to address these issues.

Secondly, we have to go beyond the concerns of academic scholarship by then helping people try to see how that text might speak to them in their lives—as the text stands or with a new interpretation. That's the part that scholars often leave out. But that's the part that matters most to adults. This means that when we teach Bible or the prayerbook, we are obligated to address the significance of the Bible for the concerns of an adult today. And we must not dodge the questions about prayer that studying the liturgy inevitably brings up.

Finally, perhaps the best way to accomplish the task of relating to the lives of people is through a means that we as scholars must accustom ourselves to use: the teacher has to speak out of his or her own life and try to show the layperson why the *teacher* finds the subject matter important, interesting or moving. And one must do this with honesty: it is by expressing one's own ambivalence or difficulties, that one can become a kind of appropriate role model for other adults. The scholar has to put him- or herself on the line.

I do not believe that the teacher of rabbis need be an ordained rabbi. But such teachers must be sensitive to the nature of the rabbinic occupation in a way that scholars in other kinds of institutions may, as I suggested above, be able to ignore. Of course, the *teaching* competence of the professor is a controversial issue in all academic settings, but for a rabbinic training institution, even more significant is the professor's awareness of the pedagogical role that the graduated rabbi will come to play. In other words, more important than the professor being a good teacher is the professor's concern for developing teaching competence in the student. Matters of pedagogy, of translating the material studied in class in the future, are questions that should be seen as appropriate, indeed desirable, in a rabbinical school classroom.

In a way much of what I have been suggesting is another way of saying we need both *peshat* and *derash*. Scholarship provides the *peshat* (and you have to have the first before you have the second). But *peshat* alone is simply not enough. The rabbi or teacher has to help the layperson do both.

Obviously, what I have been saying has implications for the training of rabbis and other professionals within Jewish life. If people are going to work with others in contexts outside of the world of the academy, the preparation reserved for scholars is not sufficient. This is not to say that I would like to see rabbis and teachers uneducated in the skills of *Wissenschaft* scholarship, but it is crucial nonetheless that they be able to go beyond what these skills offer. And of course this presents challenges for those scholars who train the rabbis. If we continue to expect our rabbis and teachers to pick up these skills on their own, many will not. They are going to need help.

One solution to this difficulty might lie in adding courses to the Rabbinical School curriculum in the "translation" of scholarship. But my own sense is that disconnecting "content" from "method" does not make for good education. Indeed many philosophers of education have argued that method *cannot* be separated from content.[5] There is an inherent connection between the two. What I would propose is something considerably more difficult than relegating (and hence ignoring) these matters to the artifice of catch-all methods courses. What the Seminary needs to do is to engage in an examination of the issue of teaching Jewish texts to laypeople and to rabbis-in-training in the context of a serious, well-designed faculty seminar supported by the institution at its highest level.

The analogy I have in mind is the very influential seminar at JTS in the early 1960s led by Seymour Fox and philosopher of education Joseph Schwab. The goal of the seminar was to create the approach to education, the "blueprint," underlying the Seminary's then newly-created Melton Research Center. The impact of that experience has been profound both for Melton's work and for the thinking of scholars such as Gerson Cohen and Yochanan Muffs who participated in those sessions. Such a seminar would need to look at the philosophical issues associated with the structure of disciplines (see footnote number 5 for references) as well as contemporary historical and literary approaches (such as deconstructionism) and their implications for teaching. With the appropriate leadership and commitment, a seminar today on teaching Jewish sources could have a similar effect on the Seminary as a whole — perhaps on policy, but even more importantly on the thinking and approach of individual faculty members.

I have raised a number of issues about the training of rabbis in our rabbinical schools today and have focused here primarily on the teaching of texts in the classroom environment. Obviously, to be a rabbi involves a good deal more than being learned or even being a competent teacher and translator of traditional materials. My colleague Eduardo Rauch and I have in recent years been trying to address the question of Western models of training in the so-called "helping professions" and the implications of such training for working with Jewish teachers.[6] We have argued that the Western notion of competence, as demonstrated by fulfilling curricular requirements and passing examinations, may appropriately be only one part of a larger picture of "competence," but unfortunately this external mode of evaluation has become the whole story of legitimization in those professions.[7] The reasons why this has happened are complex and perhaps unavoidable, but we should recognize the shortcomings of the present system and see if there might be ways of adjusting them.

Is a person competent to be called rabbi merely because he or she has taken a certain number of courses and passed exams? Does our tradition not suggest that deeper qualities of character should mark the true Jewish leader? And if so, is the classroom the place where such aspects of *character* can be acquired? I suspect not. It is clear that the Seminary is going to have to think more carefully about the ways that people do become religious leaders. What are the ways that such leadership can be built and encouraged, at the same time respecting the privacy of individuals and the democratic traditions that we value and should not give up? One way certainly is to give students opportunities outside of the classroom to express their own religious dilemmas and to develop the spiritual dimensions that are at the core of religious leadership. Another way is to think more carefully about the need of students for the self-reflection that leads to religious growth and to find ways that such time and space can be found in the overly hectic schedule of rabbinical students. Unless we consider these questions we are doing future generations of rabbis and laypeople a disservice.

Sometimes I think about the Jewish world today as one divided by a kind of imaginary line. Picture if you will a large group of people assembled around a swimming pool. On one side of the line are those—by far the majority—for whom Jewish symbols, rituals and literary sources mean very little. Perhaps out of a kind of nostalgia they may attend a Seder or even light candles for Shabbat, but aside from that, Judaism does not speak to them in a meaningful way. They are standing around the swimming pool, fully dressed; they never really take the plunge.

The other group, considerably smaller, is already in the pool. Sometimes as they splash around in the ambiance of Jewish content that is their world, they are aware of that larger group, sitting by the sidelines occasionally peeking in but by and large taking little notice of the swimmers. Once in a while the two environments may collide. The non-swimmers might appear at a wedding or a Bar Mitzvah celebration. It is a moment to reach across the divide. But mostly it doesn't happen.

I think that one reason is connected to the enormous difficulty that those in the pool—the professional Jews in particular—have in realizing just what is involved in diving into the water: issues of commitment, the barriers of language and learning, cultural impediments. Once you are in the water the Hebrew phrase, the rabbinic allusion, the shared knowledge all seem so easy, so natural. And one forgets how difficult it really is.

I have found over the past few years, to take a very small example, that one of the greatest difficulties a person experiences in first trying to read Midrash is the way that midrashic texts use proof texts. Why, I am asked, is this text quoting another one? What's the point in bringing in this succession of biblical verses? What does a *proof* text really *prove*? These questions are completely legitimate, but for the experienced reader of rabbinic sources they are surprising and for the teacher, they can be downright frustrating. To get from outside the pool — where quoting biblical sources in good rabbinic style seems like a bizarre artifice — to inside the pool where it seems like the most natural thing in the world is no mean leap. The question for us today is not so much the conflict of scholarship and belief, but finding the ways of moving that large group of Jews without a world of Jewish symbols into a place where the questions that scholars raise will even begin to be interesting.

NOTES

1. Israel Scheffler, "In Praise of the Cognitive Emotions," *Teachers College Record,* Vol. 79, No. 2 (December, 1977), pp. 171–186.

2. In recent years, for example, I have based classes on Joseph Heinemann's work on the *petihta* or Scholem's essay "The Neutralization of the Messianic Element in Early Hasidism," (in his *The Messianic Idea in Judaism* [Schocken, 1971]) with groups of adults. Note that I am not talking about using these essays as *readings* in a class, but of the teacher using the essay as a curricular underpinning.

3. Ismar Elbogen, *HaTefillah B'Yisrael* [Hebrew] (Tel-Aviv: Dvir, 1972); Joseph Heinemann, *Prayer in the Period of the Tanna'im and Amora'im* [Hebrew] (Jerusalem: Magnes, 1978); Lawrence Hoffman *The Cannonization of the Synagogue Service* (South Bend, Indiana: Notre Dame, 1979).

4. And, of course, in many of the great Jewish texts of the past "spoke" is a more accurate word than "wrote."

5. See, for example, Lee S. Schulman, "Those Who Understand: Knowledge Growth in Teaching," *Educational Researcher,* Vol. 15, no. 2 (February, 1986), pp. 4-14. For a more theoretical exploration of the issues, see Joseph Schwab, "Problems, Topics and Issues," in *Education and the Structure of Knowledge,* ed. by Stanley Elam (Chicago: Rand McNally, 1964), pp. 4-47.

6. See, for example, "Jewish Teacher Education: New Answers to Tough Old Problems," in *The Melton Journal,* No. 18 (Summer, 1984) and the more theoretical discussion "Education for Change: Toward a Model of Jewish Teacher Education," in *Studies in Jewish Education,* Vol. 3, edited by Janet Aviad (Jerusalem: Magnes Press, forthcoming).

7. For contrast one can think about the training of "healers" in traditional societies, such as described by the anthropologist Richard Katz in *Boiling Energy* (Cambridge, Mass.: Harvard University Press, 1982).

A promotional guide to Seminary activities from the late 1960's. (photo by Kas Hebtner)

Jewish Education and Jewish Scholarship: Maybe the Lies We Tell Are Really True?

Joseph Lukinsky

"Behind the tangled thorns the princess sleeps. Enter a prince. It little matters whether he comes by chance or in deliberate quest. Under his gaze the princess warms, the courtiers stir, the palace comes alive, a world long dead awakens."

Eugen Weber
New York Times Book Review, July 22, 1984

A living community confronts its heritage, challenges it, is challenged by it, and, in the dialectic, creates something new. It does not merely transmit this heritage from generation to generation intact. It transforms it.

This is the rhetoric, if not the reality, of the Conservative movement. The purpose of this article is to address this dialectic by examining how Education can serve as a bridge between scholarship and personal meaning.

Jewish education at all levels is primarily concerned with the issue of meaning and significance. It deals with the connections, albeit in potential, between the domains of tradition and action. Tradition is explored by "critical" scholarship. Critical scholarship makes available to us a systemic picture of other worlds and other minds, their perspectives on life, their modes of thinking and behavior. It does not explicitly make normative claims for today. I shall claim here that we need access to these other worlds that scholars create in order to aid our search for meaning.

The Historical School

The primary scholarly discipline of the Conservative movement is history (the "Historical School"), whatever the substantive content that is studied. The goal is the illumination of an historical perspective held by the people described in the material or by those who authored it. A way of life and a way of thinking are recreated. A presupposition of the Historical School, in touching contrast to modern scholars' innocence about applying it to themselves, is the discovery that writers, editors, and redactors often selectively present early sources in terms of the concerns of their own time and place. In the long run, this point about the "deep structure" of scholarship may be its most relevant contribution to the search for meaning. As important as this may be in potential, it is not sufficient as I will try to show.

Despite the spread of a more sophisticated view of what historians do, it is still widely assumed that critical scholars look for the objective truth to the extent that it can be discovered. Like explorers or anthropologists who come to a strange land without ulterior motives, they reveal the available truth about the source, the period, the place, the text and the context in question.

In recent years we have become aware of how scholars, including anthropologists, work, and have a different concept of scholarly "detachment" and "objective" inquiry. The very questions asked, the choice of sources, the multitude of choice points, the processes of generating, choosing and rejecting hypotheses, the criteria for judging relevant facts, the organization of findings, and the drawing of implications are tied in a great many ways to the interests, values, and conceptual presuppositions that scholars bring to their research. This is unavoidable. Awareness of the process allows it to be taken account of, but it cannot be eliminated, nor should it. It is what makes possible scholarly inquiry in the first place and enables it to continue.

If scholarship is thereby bound to the *Zeitgeist* and to the subjective, then we are faced with the prospect that history will always need rewriting. This is the human condition that we must accept. Historians have long known this, but if they admit it in their hearts, it is not always reflected in the way they write their works. Still, since the seminal work of Thomas Kuhn,[1] it has become a self-perception of every major field, including the physical and natural sciences. There is no going back now.

If each age, then, finds its own truths, scholarly differences might be seen as contradictory, or as reflections of the multi-faceted nature of reality, or simply as different points on the continuum between these extremes. Juxtaposed, even without reconciliation, they may show us the texture of a more sophisticated truth. Whether there is an objective truth out there is another matter. It seems helpful sometimes to imagine the real story as some kind of mathematical limit like the concept of infinity. I am not saying that one work of scholarship is as good as another, just that there are many roads. The determination of validity addresses as much what the scholar brings *to* the work as the product itself.

Whatever the subjective element in critical scholarship, the cumulative effect of the latter has been to minimize the overt tendency for apologetics. Apologetics is defined here as the need to reconcile differences, to see certain materials of Jewish history as normative, essentially reflecting a linear and consistent viewpoint. *Wissenschaft* takes for granted that what came to be normative was a result of choices as well as historical forces, that it could have been otherwise. It is not threatened by the knowledge that different times and places had their singular historical responses. *This is the crux.* We claim that this is somehow of ultimate significance, but here the rhetoric tends to fail. We stop short, without an acceptable replacement for the old monolithic apologetic of the Orthodox or of those scholars in our own ranks who are able to split their lives from their work. Nevertheless, the *claim* that critical scholarship is ultimately central to the pursuit of Jewish meaning is the great divide.

Traditional experience with its traditional meaning were both carried forward in time by the community. Modern scholarship cannot be blamed for the breakdown of this process, but it does make us aware of worlds different from those brought to us by tradition. To the extent that it does this, it separates us from the constructive myths of tradition and the way of life which they constructed. Modern scholarship may provide fascinating pictures of different worlds, but those pictures may cease to relate to our own lives. We feel the gap, a distance between us and them, and, sometimes, the more we know, the greater the distance feels.[2]

Historians are sensitive to the genetic fallacy. They know, at least among themselves, that the origin of something does not determine its meaning for us.* Understanding the meaning of prayers created in different ages, or the difference between the *peshat* and the

---

*We should also avoid, I believe, what I have termed the "genetic fallacy *fallacy*." Origins may not be everything, but they are *something*. The overstress on origins in the historical approach sometimes is vulgarized as crude debunking. On the other hand, must we accept the view that origins are irrelevant if they conflict with

derash of a biblical verse, or the difference between biblical anthropomorphisms and Maimonides' philosophical explanation of them, is just the beginning of the problem for us. The fact that this knowledge is fascinating and intricate may be misleading if it is thereby assumed to be meaningful. The scholar's fascination with intricacy and immersion in the worlds studied leads us astray in this regard. In the PR of our movement there is a great deal of rhetoric on this point: honest scholarship automatically (or close to it) produces meaning! If we could only see in which senses this is so, it might help us to move beyond the reign of apologetic at the popular level where the translation of the PR never really reaches.

We usually fudge things here. The meaning for today of scholarly truths is not at all obvious. (Is the biblical concept of God the concept we are promoting today? How is it relevant to later developments? How do we make the connections clear?) Either we award scholarship a medal while we refuse to take it seriously, or we take the debunking stance that has so often been the fruit of historical studies. (The past is a museum. "We" don't think like that anymore, however proud we are of our ancestors' contributions to "Western Civilization.")

Something important *has* been discovered by modern critical studies, but is is not clear what we are to *do* about it. The scholar leaves it on our doorstep, a gift, a foundling; we are not sure how to proceed. If only we could accept scholarship as necessary for the development of meaning but not sufficient. Synthesis, the normative, may not be the scholar's mission *qua* scholar. A further step is necessary; reflections on that step follow.

Jewish Education: The Princess Sleeps

For Jewish education to take scholars seriously and build upon what they do as essential to the construction of meaning, some new directions are in order.

Assume then that Judaism is an enterprise about which we care deeply, a struggle to find our paths as Jews in each generation. Assume further that this enterprise will create new structures alongside those we legitimately maintain from the past, that it entails risks and

---

tradition? Even if not *l'maaseh*, are there not some relevant educational implications for us other than mere historical interest?

mistakes in combination with successful community building.

In this broad view, Jewish education means working with people to help them enter this total Jewish effort. It means sustaining ourselves and them, acknowledging different entry points and different tasks that need to be accomplished in different settings. The Jewish educational setting (and here we need to extend our horizons beyond schools to informal settings, communal organizations, congregational programs, camps, libraries, museums, Israel trips and the like) would ideally be a learning, acting community where people join to construct meaning and change their world.

A professional Jewish educator focuses upon the tasks, but all Jews share them, including scholars who may, as committed Jews, go beyond scholarship and become Jewish educators by definition.

Enter A Prince

How then might education serve as a bridge between scholarship and meaning?

The first level is curricular, the working-up of the scholar's product, so that the student may get at both its content and its "form." By the latter I refer to the philosophical framework embedded in it and the methodological processes which were followed to arrive at the results. This means gaining access to the scholar's "wastebasket," and this is difficult. Scholars present their research to other scholars, and they strive for a smooth presentation, speak in code with unspoken assumptions, and tend to bury their methodology in the footnotes. Oral presentations, too, reflect the phenomenon that Schwab has called a "rhetoric of conclusions" rather than a "narrative of enquiry."

Unpacking works of scholarship reveals the choices the scholar has made, the rejected alternatives, the roads not taken, the original reasons for undertaking the research, the underlying presuppositions and values that led to these questions and answers and not to others. Many scholars work so intuitively, however, that much of this texture and richness, all that makes their work educationally interesting, is thoroughly internalized. The impression is given that the final product *had* to turn out the way that it did. What the scholar sees as a superstructure to be dismantled once the final product is completed is, for the educator trying to build curriculum, *everything*.

Education means uncovering the apparatus and enabling the student to participate in the scholar's inquiry.[3] To learn is not only to gain a content but also to be socialized into a language and a culture, to enter into the scholar's consciousness and to experience from the inside what the scholar thinks and cares about. This is the first step on the path from knowledge to meaning. The exposure to the philosophy and values buried in the work of scholars is initiation into a corner of the contemporary universe of Jewish value deliberations.

A caveat: Scholars' popular writings, for the general public, or for children, are not necessarily to be trusted as authentic representations of their own best thought. The curriculum field of the past few decades has demonstrated many times the inability of scholars to transform their own advanced thinking into valid forms at the popular level.[4]

The Princess Warms

After participatory inquiry into scholars' works, *i.e.*, initiation into their consciousness and implicit ideologies, the next level is the *experiencing* of the world that has been represented, which may not be the same as the world seen through the eyes of tradition. Instead of springing quickly to the implications of scholarship for us, we need to go slowly, to immerse ourselves in depth in what has been discovered. The scholar's presentation is the key to the re-creation of worlds for students, but that *product* is ultimately reductionist; hence the need for the wastebasket. Students must be guided back to an earlier stage behind the lines of the final version, to the world itself. What scholars do for us is a control for authenticity that makes curricularization possible. Curricularization includes the traditional study of text and more. The challenge to education, therefore, is to find ways to enable participation in the inquiries of scholars and in the worlds that these inquiries create. This suggestion flies in the face of much that has been claimed about the need for relevance in education. What is required at first is training in the suspension of that very need. Much as we suspend reality considerations in accepting the conventions of attending the theatre or reading a novel, we also need to open ourselves to the experience of a historical world not our own.

The Palace Comes Alive

Construing modern critical scholarship as a resource for the search for personal meaning is an effort still in its formative stage. I will address some of the issues at this stage and suggest some lines of development. There is a subtle transition point where we move from being *learners* of tradition to becoming *creators* of tradition for future generations.

The most prevalent approach to using scholarship for curriculum has been that of simplification: taking the scholar's ideas from the forefront of a field and adapting them to the level of the students. A variant would have students "discover" in a simplified form a field's main concepts as determined by the scholar. This was the popular translation of Bruner's famous hypothesis that anything worth knowing can be taught in some valid form to anyone at any age.[5] I am suggesting something else: instead of making it simpler, make it more complex. The scholar's work is a window onto a world, but we need the world itself in all its richness, texture and difference; the territory itself, not the map. We need ways to use the paradigms generated by authentic scholarship as access instruments for the educator, but without reductionism and manipulation to learn *those* paradigms. Experience of the worlds underlying the paradigms is the key.[6]

Huston Smith has coined the term "Modern Western Mindset"[7] for the deeply entrenched (and significant) empirical, scientific, quantitative way of thinking of the modern era which predisposes us to assume that people in all ages thought the same as we do, only more primitively. This enables us to distance ourselves and justifies our feelings of superiority to them. This is another of the dangers inherent in moving from modern western-type scholarship to worlds it describes, worlds in which other forms of consciousness may prevail. Paradoxically, it is modern critical scholarship at its sophisticated best that can enable us to hurdle this barrier.

Success at the task of using rationalistic scholarship to enter worlds that have a different mind-set is liberating. It enables us to transcend the cliché of "choosing from the past that which meets the needs of our time." I am suggesting something else. The "I" doing the choosing is already a product of culture. The language we speak and the values we share come from the culture into which we were born. In a pluralistic society, we are the products of many sources; the Jewish is less explicitly weighty for most of us. The challenge to Jewish education is to enhance the functioning of the Jewish element in the teaching of language and history in a manner that replicates normal socialization to a native culture.

The ways of thinking and feeling, often different from our own, that characterize the different ages and places of the Jewish past are made accessible to us by scholarship. To experience them again is to be challenged by them, analogously to the way they challenged people in their own time. It is to recapture components of our own Jewishness screened out by the modern western mind-set which address something in us that we have lost touch with, as they addressed something in our ancestors. This indeed is what makes them classic, and even when we cannot fully articulate what they "mean," they help us understand who we are. With respect to choosing from the past that which is meaningful to "us," they create and inform the Jewish "us" that does the choosing!

The tradition is not just learned "about." It is something that is already in us; learning becomes self-discovery or, better, an attachment of a growing self to the different modes of consciousness created by centuries of our people's creative struggle. In an assimilated society, education would be, in part, a focused *simulation* of a lost historical socialization process.

Jewish tradition is, for the most part, a narrative tradition, not a propositional one, and the task of Jewish education, is I submit, to facilitate the joining of that narrative. *Wissenschaft* provides the authentic possibilities for this, but the realization of those possibilities requires education to join with the arts, humanities, and psychology so that we can enter worlds and world-views that seem to be not our own. I have found illuminating, in addition to the resources of the broad fields of literature, music, and art, pursuits such as games and simulations, story-telling, synectics, journal-writing, psychodrama, and mythic drama.[8] In a time of rootlessness, these, among others, have the potential for re-creating the past differently from the standard cognitive learning models that characterize our schools and other centers of learning.

From History to Our Story

After participating in the scholar's inquiries and experiencing vicariously the worlds that these inquiries open up to us, we move to the use of our critical and deliberative powers to the creation of meaning for ourselves. The understanding of tradition shades into the creation of tradition. This latter stage moves ahead of scholars' efforts at reconstructing the past for us and beyond educators' efforts at entering it. Synthesis is the most difficult task of all; it integrates what we have experienced at the first two levels with our other knowledge and values.

Synthesis is emergent, not a "given" imposed from the outside, not entailed. The confrontation with the worlds whose seeds are in scholarship and which are dramatized through education is fraught with the likelihood of paradox and conflict. Contradictory perspectives make demands upon us, each speaking to some part of our psyches. We begin to understand why certain perspectives became normative in history, and we may regret that others dropped by the wayside for historical reasons which we now may understand better. We can weigh whether our own situation calls for a renewal of possibilities long thought ended, of roads that can still be reopened.

Halakhah and the halakhic process in this perspective would necessarily relate to the claims that our enriched perceptions of Jewish experience have upon us in the situations which face us now. These claims would be formulated differently for different Jews in different contexts. The synthesis would be local, personal, and the result of serious individual and communal deliberation.[9] The past would speak not only to "religious" Jews in the standard sense but to all Jews who seek to be addressed by it. In many cases, for now at least, it would require the ability to live with contradictory demands for different segments of our people; the resulting pluralism would be a challenge to our best educational and democratic efforts. Good-will and *ahavat Yisrael* (the love for fellow Jews) would be indispensable. There would be those who could not accept the resultant turmoil, but how different would that be from the unprincipled pluralism that we now have?

Conclusion

The diversity of scholarly efforts to explore the diversities of Jewish experience is overwhelming. Synthesis and meaning are long-range goals, and meaning "for now" may mean living with contradiction. It may indeed not be possible to find a unified point of view that applies to all Jews anymore. Such smoothed-out versions of Judaism seem somehow, *davka* because of *Wissenschaft,* to be superficial. I have tried to suggest how we could respond to a scholarship that more truly renders the human and Jewish experience. We take pride in a scholarship and an education that enable us to join the ranks of cultivated and honest people at the same time that we take our place in the chain of Jewish tradition and peoplehood. Perhaps the deep structural meaning of modern scholarship is not in specific teachings but in the models it provides of Jews drawing upon their traditions and experience to find significance in the labyrinth of their own lives and times.

NOTES

Earlier versions of parts of this paper were presented at the International Conference on Research in Jewish Education at the Hebrew University, Jerusalem, July 1984 and at the Conference of the Association for Jewish Studies, Boston, December, 1985.

1. Thomas Kuhn, *The Structure of Scientific Revolutions,* Second Edition (Chicago: University of Chicago Press, 1970). See also Joseph J. Schwab, *Science, Curriculum and Liberal Education: Selected Essays* (Chicago: University of Chicago Press, 1978).

2. I am relating here to issues raised by Yosef Yerushalmi in *Zakhor: Jewish History and Jewish Memory* (University of Washington Press and Jewish Publication Society of America, 1982). See responses by David Roskies, *Against the Apocalypse* (Cambridge, MA: Harvard University Press, 1984); Ivan Marcus, "Beyond the Sephardic Mystique," (*Orim,* Vol. I, No.1, Fall 1985); and the Symposium: "Responses to Yerushalmi's *Zakhor*" in *Association for Jewish Studies Newsletter* (No.36, Fall 1986), among many others.

3. The most important treatment of participatory inquiry is Joseph J. Schwab's "Enquiry and the Reading Process" in Schwab, *Selected Essays, op. cit.*

4. I have dealt with this issue in my article, "Structure in Educational Theory," in *Educational Philosophy and Theory,* November 1970, and April 1971.

5. Jerome Bruner, *The Process of Education* (New York: Vintage Books, 1960).

6. See Joseph Lukinsky, "Myth, Fairy Tales, and Jewish Education," *The Melton Journal* (No.13, Winter 1982). I especially recommend Yochanan Muffs' concept of "remythologizing," which he has developed in a number of places. See, for example, his Introduction to the Tissot Exhibit (1982) catalog at the Jewish Museum.

7. Huston Smith, "Beyond the Modern Western Mind Set," *Teachers College Record,* (Vol. 82, No.3, Spring 1981).

8. I have tried in recent years to work in these areas in my courses at the Seminary and in workshops at conferences such as C.A.J.E. I am especially indebted to the work of Ira Progoff, James B. Sacks, W. J. J. Gordon, Richard Schechner, and Samuel Laeuchli. See also Sherry Werb, *Toward an Approach to Bible Teaching,* (Unpublished MA Thesis, Brandeis University, 1970), and Seymour Epstein, *Models of Jewish Education,* (Unpublished doctoral dissertation, Ontario Institute for Studies in Education, 1974).

9. See Lawrence Cremin, *Public Education* (New York: Basic Books, 1971).

An expanded bibliography of resources and practical applications by colleagues will appear in a forthcoming paper.

The Jewish Historian and the Believer

Ivan G. Marcus

The teaching of Judaism now takes place in two settings: academic, such as a secular university, and religious, such as the synagogue school. The Seminary is one of those mixed institutions that espouses a complex set of educational goals which appear at first glance to be both secular and religious and as such often seem to be self-contradictory and ultimately self-defeating. To explore why this need not—indeed, should not—be the case is the intention of these remarks.

I have been teaching at the Seminary for some fifteen years, and although I have taught part-time at an American university (Yale) and an Israeli one (Hebrew University), most of my teaching has been at a place that requires an instructor of Judaism to face up to the question not posed by either an American or Israeli university setting. That question is our question: How do I as an instructor in a religious and academic institution deal with personal religious values that I find in the sources and subjects I teach, and, at the same time, approach the subject in an academic manner?

Now, other instructors at American and Israeli universities, not just in Judaica or the history of religions, face the question of balancing commitment and detachment. They usually do not talk about it. But the issue is there just the same. A historian of homosexuality in Western culture who is himself an avowed gay person and speaks to gay constituencies also has the problem of balancing scholarship and commitment. A politically outspoken historian of the United States or of a European country or of the Soviet Union or of the Middle East faces this issue all the time.

In principle, then, the problem facing the scholar of a religious tradition who is also a practitioner or advocate of that tradition is on a par with other engaged or involved scholars in several other fields. We are not uniquely faced with this issue.

And what is the issue? It is nothing less than the reality of dealing with two sets of value systems that coincide in the same data, one academic, the other religious. The field of Jewish history, for example, contains data: records in written, as well as pictorial and other nonverbal forms. The academic historian is trained to apply a set of questions to the data to verify if they can answer a question posed to them. Suppose I want to know what Maimonides was like as a political figure. I am told that there are letters preserved in the Cairo Geniza that indicate that he was a self-promoter when the job of Head of the Jews in twelfth-century Egypt was open (there are such documents). I must then try to verify the authenticity of such letters. Were they forged? Did Maimonides write them but keep them in his desk drawer? Do we know how anyone reacted to them? And so on. Historians have a variety of methods that can be used, no, must be used, when seeking the truth about the past; that is, the historical truth, the truth about what happened and what causes led up to it, or about what it was like to live at a certain time and place.

But at the same time, many of the sources the historian of Judaism studies make truth claims of a different order. The Hebrew Bible obviously claims to be more than a historical record of "what happened." It claims to be the divinely revealed will of God. Similarly, rabbinic writings and the writings of the Jewish mystics, pietists and philosophers speak not about "what happened" but about the ultimate meaning of living as viewed from different perspectives of Jewish wisdom and tradition. How does the historian of Judaism who is also a committed Jew sort out these two types of meanings, the historical truth and the religious truth, both derived from the same data he or she studies and interprets?

I think that the first approach to this question is a confession about limits. Historical truth is not the only kind of truth. Indeed, it is limited in scope and limited by method and the survival of data. When confronted by claims about divine revelation, the historian cannot say, "That is not true" but only "I cannot accept that as historical truth." There is a difference. In the first formulation, the historian says that historical method permits one to disconfirm the truth claim; the second statement means that the historian's method is limited and cannot pass judgment either way. It is neutral.

But what about the claims religious sources make not about God but about human historical events that are alleged to have taken place: the Exodus, Sinai, the rapid Conquest by force? Does not the historical method have to deal with these matters and ask "what happened"? Yes, and here there are different possibilities. If there is no contradictory evidence, the historian has nothing to say except, "There is a biblical tradition that such and such occurred." If there is empirical evidence that contradicts the Bible's claims about historical human events, then the historian who is committed to both the values of academic discipline and religious truth claims of the Jewish tradition has a problem, but only as an historian, not as a committed Jew.

What I mean by that is this. The historian must evaluate all of the data impartially and decide which is more reliable *as evidence* and draw the more probable conclusion. To do this, the historian must treat the biblical (or rabbinic) evidence in a way that respects its literary style and genre. Historians confront many types of sources. Some are literary, others documentary. The documentary sources are the lists, records of transactions, letters, and so on, that derive from immediate life situations. They are not processed through the literary imagination, standard literary types from the past, and the like. Now, fundamentalists are bad historians when they treat the Bible as though it were a documentary record, take it at face value, and do not properly analyze it as a complex literary work. A good historian must know the type of source he or she confronts and ask the questions that such a source can answer. We do not ask Homer to tell us what happened on a particular day. We do not ask a shopping list from the Geniza to disclose to us a rabbinic master's expression of mystical union with God. These sources are totally different, and the historian's method is designed to deal with different types of sources.

When hard factual claims about the past are found in religious sources, like the Hebrew Bible, and they contradict extra-biblical data (say, the Joshua account of Jericho and archeological evidence that does not jibe with the data of the destruction of Jericho), the believing historian has a basic strategy. The historian's method applies to all data, biblical and extra-biblical. If the Bible claims Jericho was destroyed in the period of the Conquest but archeological evidence contradicts that historical claim, then historically Jericho was not destroyed in the period of the Conquest. Period. (At least for now.)

There cannot be two *historical* truths, one for the academic historian and one for the religious academic historian. But the religious meaning of the biblical or other religious account in which claims about historical truth are disconfirmed by the historian's method is not reduced. That is because the historian's method, as I said earlier, is limited to working out historical knowledge, not religious truth. And religious truth depends on criteria other than historical verifiability, even in an historical religion like Judaism. It is here that the historian bows to the criteria employed by theologians and religious philosophers.

The historian of religion is not alone in being limited when it comes to dealing directly with religious truth claims of the tradition he or she studies. The literary critic of religious literature is bound by similar methodological limits. I once asked the great New Critic, Cleanth Brooks, a deacon in his church, why studying the values in great literature was not as important as religion. (I may have been a sophomore at the time.) He answered immediately, "Literature cannot provide salvation." A literary reading of a biblical narrative, or of a philosophical parable, or a mystical poem is not to be equated with stating, let along confronting, its religious meaning. Like the historian, the literary critic applies a set (or sets) of questions and criteria when reading the complex webs of form and signification (a fashionable word for "meaning") in a text. The literary critic cannot assess the religious truth claims of the text. These transcend the methods of the literary critic as much as they do the historian's.

And so we are left with differences of method that can be applied to the same sources. As an historian of Judaism, I find the religious claims about the Bible, for example, to be grounded not so much in the Bible itself, but in the midrashic legacy which has applied and adapted the biblical word to living Jewish situations. In and of itself, the Hebrew Bible is not a Jewish book. It is a pre-Jewish, as much as a pre-Christian book, as Moshe Greenberg has put it. The Rabbis made the Hebrew Bible a Jewish book. But the biblical account, for me, has transcendent meaning as an elaboration of the terms of the covenantal condition on which the Jewish religion is premised. Because of the salvation experience of the Exodus, Israel (later, all Jews) is to observe God's will as it is revealed and interpreted. Do I believe that the Exodus experience was real in the sense that something was collectively experienced and recorded? Yes. As an historian, I have precious little to confirm it outside of the biblical narrative, but nothing to disconfirm it either. But even if there were ample documentary evidence to disconfirm or raise doubts that there ever was an Exodus, I would believe that an Exodus experience underlies Israelite religion and ultimately is the central early experience that led to the covenantal obligation at Sinai and the binding power, such as it is, of rabbinic Judaism to represent to me the will of God. The actual events as described in the Bible may not have taken place (discounting the miracles, that historians cannot assess), but some Exodus experience triggered a collective memory of group birth as a act of divine salvation. It led to Sinai and the public covenant, and that mythic truth encapsulates for me ultimate truth. Judaism as an historical religion is inexplicable without this basic mythic truth, but that statement is the historian speaking again. Apart from any evidence in later Jewish history, the paradigm of Exodus-Sinai is so powerful that it still moves me.

Exploring Religious Meaning at School

Here, then, the question must again be asked: "How do I as an instructor at a religious and academic institution deal with personal religious values that I find in the sources and subjects I teach and, at the same time, approach the subject in an academic manner?" The key here is to reject the implicit notion of synthesis, of trying to teach history *simultaneously* as a source of both religious and academic meaning. I do not think such an approach is possible. There are other ways, however, in which one can explore the religious meaning of Jewish history without compromising the academic integrity of the historian's enterprise.

At a secular university, the distinction should be made between the classroom and the extracurricular forum. In some respects, a Jewish historian who finds personal religious significance in Jewish history faces a similar challenge at a secular university. There, the lectures or seminars can be inspired with the instructor's belief in the centrality of the subject; the emotional level of personal enthusiasm can rise to ever greater heights of passion. But it is inappropriate for a committed Jew (or anyone else) to deal with the personal religious or existential significance of Jewish history (or any subject) in a private or public non-religious university setting. (At Yeshiva University in the U.S. or at Bar Ilan University in Israel, the situation would be different.)

This is so because the institution itself is committed to being an open academic forum that serves a diversified student body. There is a contractual assumption between faculty and students that an instructor's expertise does not carry over to expressing private religious (or political) insights, but rather is limited to academically controlled formulations — however enthusiastically pronounced — of truths that are based on a disciplinary foundation. The secular university is a forum for academic truths, not for personal ideologies posing as academic truths.

But outside the classroom, an engaged Jewish historian, like any other academic, is free even at a secular university to teach and discuss his or her religious (or political) views with students and others without restraint. In the '50s, some of the first academic scholars of Judaica in American universities tended not to be so engaged outside the classroom. They bent over backwards to play the role of detached university scholars, often distancing themselves from Hillel Foundations sorely in need of their guidance and Jewish intellectual and religious stimulation.

Today, that has changed. Many academic scholars of Judaica are involved with their university students, and with the larger Jewish community that supports chairs of Jewish studies at the universities, as models of Jewish commitment. These scholars are not threatened by their dual roles as religious or intellectually seeking Jews and as university scholar-teachers.

If an instructor's involvement in religious activities is appropriate at a secular university only outside the classroom, should that also be the case at the Seminary, a "mixed institution" that espouses both religious and academic values and goals? In the List College and the Graduate School, the same basic rules should apply as at a secular university. Academic competence and enthusiasm belong inside the classroom; religious discussion, outside. But in the Rabbinical School which is designed to stimulate and educate religious leaders, I think that it is unethical for a Jewish historian not to deal explicitly in the classroom with the religious meaning of the Jewish historical experience.

The question is: How? The two activities cannot be done "at the same time." They must be kept separate if either is to be genuine and honest. The distinction between the academic-intellectual, on the one hand, and the spiritual-personal, on the other, must be seen as being different experiences before either can be treated properly. The discipline of historical reconstruction cannot be "synthesized" with religious questions and issues into a single intellectual-religious experience. That kind of "synthesis" is a false trail. Not to see them as separate activities risks viewing the academic approach as the only one, as claiming a monopoly on The Truth. Not distinguishing clearly between these two strategies for finding meaning in the past also risks fudging the hard historical questions and reducing historical reconstruction to ideological uses of past facts to support present causes. The true and unbiased reconstruction of the past is an intellectual obligation of the Jewish historian qua historian.

But for the Conservative Jewish historian it is also a potential religious experience, and in the Rabbinical School some time should be devoted to exploring why this is so. Sessions, or parts of sessions, should be set aside and devoted to a religious agenda. I do not necessarily mean by this that courses on Jewish history should take data and conclusions about Jewish history and explicitly translate them into sermons for the student. That is a legitimate activity, but it is not necessary for Jewish historians or rabbinical students to do this in the history classroom. Nor do I mean that Jewish history courses should focus only on studying the background of contemporary issues such as egalitarianism and Jewish law. I support both research and instruction in issues of public Jewish affairs, religious and secular, but an instructor need not feel an obligation to make Jewish history "relevant" in that way either.

Rather, I think that an instructor should take some special time in the classroom and discuss the religious meaning of the study of Jewish history and do so apart from the activity of historical study itself. By distinguishing between the discipline of historical reconstruction and the discussion of its meaning as a personal religious quest, by not trying artificially to "synthesize" them, there is a chance of promoting an awareness of the religious meaning of Jewish history.

I would put my understanding of the two types of legitimate classroom study and discussion of Jewish history this way. To the Conservative Jewish historian, loyalty to the historical truth is also a sacred obligation because we believe that religious truth is congruent with historical truth and is enhanced, not threatened, by its discovery. More, I think that reconstructing the true Jewish past is a form of midrash in a theological sense. This is so because I believe that God continues to reveal Himself to the entirety of the Jewish people — to *klal Yisrael,* Schechter's Catholic Israel — and that this revelation takes place, by definition, in the continuing Jewish historical experience. For this reason, to understand the historical record — as it happened — is a religious activity. It is a form of midrash, of penetrating the revealing presence of God by studying the past experience of the Jewish people.

Good Jewish historical reconstruction, then, is as much midrash as is the careful philological study of Scripture or Rabbinics or Kabbalah or Jewish Philosophy. In every Geniza fragment, every charter, every Jewish inscription, the presence of God is potentially found. When a Conservative Jewish historian studies the historical experience of the Jewish people, and does so as an academic historian, he or she is also writing a midrash, glossing not the sacred text but the lived experience in time and space of the sacred people of Israel and our collective and ongoing reception of God's revelation.

These issues should be addressed in the classroom by a Conservative Jewish historian who teaches a Jewish history course in the Seminary Rabbinical School. They should not replace the course itself, but complement it. The course could be a survey of patterns of Jewish-Christian, Jewish-Muslim relations; a focus on the Jewish community's social agencies; a course on the variety of expressions of Jewish spirituality. The selection of courses and topics within courses also reflects the historian's values. But this is not unique to teaching Jewish history at the Seminary Rabbinical School. All scholar-teachers select their teaching emphases as well as their research topics.

What is unique at the Seminary is the opportunity to develop a consciousness of a Conservative theory of studying and teaching Jewish history as a religious activity analogous to, but different from, prayer and the study of sacred texts, other forms of Jewish spirituality.

I cannot develop this theme here, but I think that these assumptions would benefit from the advice and counsel of the future religious leaders who pass through the Seminary Rabbinical School in search of religious as well as historical truth. Such religious truth transcends the narrow parish of the historian and his or her craft. It probes one's deepest life stance. When the religious historian confronts the ultimate question posed of Adam: "Where are you?" (Gen. 3:9), the answer must be Abraham's, "I am here" (Gen. 22:1).*

---

*For other thoughts on the general subject of the Jewish historian and the Jewish community, see my essays "Bringing Judaica to the Liberal Arts," *Yale Alumni Magazine* 45:2 (November, 1981), pp. 25–28; "The Three Academic Cultures of Graduate Education in Jewish Studies," in Jacob Neusner, ed., *New Humanities and Academic Disciplines* (Madison: University of Wisconsin Press, 1984), pp. 153–164; and especially "Beyond the Sephardic Mystique," *Orim: A Jewish Journal at Yale* 1:1 (Autumn 1985), pp. 35–53.

Reflections of a Jewish Historian

Joel E. Rembaum

I am trained to be an historian, specializing in medieval Jewish history. As such I am heir to the *Wissenschaft des Judentums* tradition of Zunz, Geiger, Graetz, *et al.* The scientific quality of the "Science of Judaism" is something about which I may be less sanguine than my noble predecessors. My commitment to the truth of the historical interpretation of Judaism and the Jewish experience is relative and not absolute. If there is a truth in the process of historical inquiry it is to be found in the observation that the historian has difficulty in overcoming the intervention of the self into historical research. History is, after all, the evaluation of human events by a process that is by its very nature human. The data of history cannot be tested with the same empirical accuracy as those of the natural sciences, let alone the precision of mathematical models. The historian, therefore, must be satisfied with relative truths and reasonable conclusions that best reflect the data at hand.

Nevertheless, in assuming the role of historian one accepts the underlying operating principle of the historical method, which is to attempt to let the data speak for themselves and to interpret them without preconceptions. For the student of history who is also a believing Jew, the acceptance of this principle poses a problem: How can a unique, divine influence be perceived in the unfolding of the historical experience of the Jewish people? If the Jewish historian examines Jewish history with the same tools and methodological premises one would use to analyze American history, the results of the inquiry would present a humanistic picture of Jewish history categorically similar to that of American history. Where, then, is the role of God in the historical equation? Given the centrality in Jewish covenant theology of the notion of divine involvement in history, this issue looms large for the historian who finds meaning in the *brit*. If, however, a Jewish interpreter of Jewish history allows personal beliefs to color historical analysis, is that interpreter entitled to be called an "historian"? Would not "ideologue" or "theologian" be more fitting? Thus, one who seeks to maintain the double designation, "Jewish historian," faces a dilemma.

For me, the fact that I am confronted by these two issues—the relative truth of history and the tension that inheres in my attempt to be a "Jewish historian"—has moved me toward a resolution of my dilemma in which the first problem, ironically, helps me cope with the second. I have become very much aware of the limits of human intellect. Even as it relentlessly pursues knowledge, the human mind must be satisfied with finite data. Maimonides' humility in recognizing this reality is a legitimate response. While much of what we know remains valid, there is an evanescent quality to our knowledge. In history, as in all realms of science, what is accepted today as a "given" may be rejected tomorrow as false.

Consider these questions that indicate how historical "truths" change with the passage of time. How many nineteenth-century Jewish historians comprehended the integral part played by mystical thought and tradition in the development of Judaism? Should Josephus be viewed as the "Jewish Benedict Arnold" worthy of eternal condemnation or as an egotist with delusions of prophetic grandeur who, nevertheless, did have the best interests of the Jewish people at heart? Is 1096 really the date that symbolically marks the change in fortunes of medieval European Jewry, or would 1240 be a better choice? Were the Jews led "like lambs to the slaughter" in the Holocaust, or was resistance a more prevalent factor than heretofore realized, albeit in forms that we only now are beginning to appreciate?

The discovery of new evidence and the emergence of new insights into how that evidence ought to be handled make history a discipline that becomes a humbling experience for those who work in it. The study of history places the human being at the center of its focus, thereby clarifying the limits of human activity and potentiality, and opening the door for an affirmation of *faith* in an infinite reality that transcends the bounds that circumscribe the human realm.

Ironically, this limiting anthropocentricity helps me deal with my "Jewish historian" dilemma because it frees me from the necessity to understand the events of human history in theological terms. I can now say to myself: as an historian, it is my job to recognize and work within the limits of my human capacity to comprehend the limits of my discipline's methodology. I separate the role of the historian from that of the theologian. The historian, operating in the realm of a finite, contingent truth, seeks to present and analyze the data of *human* experience. History, as a circumscribed and limiting discipline that is the by-product of a limited human mind, is *not* intended to yield up evidence regarding infinite truths and divine activity. This does not deny the possibility of such activity, but merely suggests that the matter of history need not be viewed *a priori* as having been informed by the imprint of God's presence. Historical analysis can proceed unencumbered by the predisposition of viewing the Jewish experience as *Heilsgeschichte,* as punishment for sin, as the emergence of the "absolute spirit" present within the Jewish people, or as shaped by any other theological construct. Theodicy or apologetics need not enter into the discussion. Any theories that are offered can be allowed to rise or fall depending upon the degree to which they conform to the data. My job as an historian is completed when I have succeeded in clarifying the *peshat* or plain meaning of a slice of human experience.

A compartmentalizing of belief does take place when I take off my historian's hat, put on my *kippah* and seek out the *derash,* the interpretive theological meaning of history. Now my faith as a Jew emerges and I ask myself: Granted that human activity comprises the substance of history, if I survey the Jewish historical experience through theological glasses, might I not catch some glimpses of divine activity? Might I not find an affirmation of my belief in the *brit* and in the power of Judaism to move the world into the messianic era? Since as an historian I suggested a relative truth, as a Jew I can believe that there remains room for further theological reflection that may represent a higher or more absolute level of truth.

But am I not begging the question: What do I do if the *peshat* and the *derash* contradict each other? I struggle, the way a devout Jew struggles with the reality of the Holocaust. I attempt to maintain my integrity as an historian while at the same time maintaining the integrity of my belief as a Jew. There are moments when my belief in the evidence of historical research is stronger than the certainty of my belief in a theological principle and the latter gives way to the former. Thus, I believe that Judaism has evolved over a period of time as have other religious systems. I do not believe that the Torah in its fullness was revealed at Sinai. I have reached these conclusions through my study of history. This process has reinforced my commitments as a Conservative Jew.

There are other moments, however, when my religious belief

overwhelms what appear to be the logical conclusions of historical research. The fact that the Jewish people survives and remains a factor in human history is a datum that can be analyzed and rationally explained. I believe there is a point, however, at which the rationalizations fade into inadequacy, and I sense that I am a witness to an inexplicable incursion of the will of God into human experience. The *brit* remains a reality in spite of reasonable indications that could lead to a Spinoza-like skepticism.

As noted above, there is a significant area in my thinking where the historical has affected the theological. As an historian, I cannot avoid the conclusion that change is as integral a part of the Jewish experience as it is in the history of any great tradition. The problem in recognizing what appears to some to be so obvious (myself included) is that the tendency within traditions is to emphasize continuity and to de-emphasize innovation. So it is that in the Bible the belief in one God, which the authors knew to be a unique feature of Israelite religion, is traced back to the first humans and, hence, presented as the original universal religious principle and not a subsequent *novum*. Indeed, it can be argued that the biblical view of history is cyclical, with later events prefigured by antecedents. Novelty is thus relativized, and constancy rather than change is emphasized.

In a similar vein, the Rabbis often read history with the principle of *ma'assei avot siman le-vanim,* "the acts of the ancestors prefigure those of the children." Historical continuity is also dominant in the thinking of post-talmudic sages. As Jacob Katz has noted, the pre-modern writers continue in the footsteps of their predecessors in their conception of post 70 C.E. history as unfolding on a single historical tapestry. The period from the Destruction to the Messianic Era is one continuum. In this *Weltanschauung,* an awareness of change is discouraged and a *status quo* consciousness dominates. To be sure, there is an opposing aggadic tradition that views history as progressing through epochs that are essentially different from each other. Still, the pre-modern authors tend to see themselves and the generations that preceded them as living in the same pre-redemption era, facing the same trials and tribulations and maintaining the same traditions as they await the arrival of the Messiah. If radical change will be manifest at the onset of the Messianic Age (except in the Maimonidean concept), little or no change is perceived in the centuries that precede it. The influence of the halakhic process on this outlook, given the former's constant search for precedents, ought not to be minimized. In sum, Jewish tradition does not foster an historical outlook with a sensitivity to change.

And yet when the historian strips away the halakhic, aggadic, philosophical and theosophical preconceptions, he or she is left with clear evidence that change inheres within Jewish life and tradition. A series of examples will elucidate this point.

When Hillel the Elder instituted his *prozbul* edict, it represented a change in economic legislation that responded to a changed socioeconomic situation in Palestine. The biblical system of canceling debts in the *shmittah* year was not working. The very problem anticipated in Deuteronomy (15:9-11) — lenders not granting loans late in the sixth year — appears to have overwhelmed an economy in which the availability of liquid capital became an issue. Hillel's bold step responded to the need, but also effectively abrogated Torah law. Its controversial nature can be appreciated if one considers that in spite of its wide acceptance the great *amora*, Samuel, expressed strong reservations regarding the *prozbul*, and later sages went to great lengths to justify Hillel's *takkanah* (See *Gittin* 36a-b).

Another controversial change in Jewish tradition is Rabbi Yohanan ben Zakkai's *takkanah* (legislation) calling for the sounding of the shofar in the Great Court when Rosh Hashanah falls on the Sabbath. The opposition of B'nei B'teirah to this attempt to orient the people's spiritual attention away from the fallen Temple and toward a new center of religious authority was swift and unambiguous. Only through a bit of shrewd political maneuvering did Rabbi Yohanan succeed in pushing through this reform (See *Rosh Hashanah* 29b).

When talmudic sages in medieval Europe expanded the scope of rabbinic legal control of Jewish communal affairs, they often realized that socioeconomic necessity had to take precedence over the letter of Torah law. So it was that French rabbis had to deal with the reality that Jews were trading with their gentile neighbors before, after and during Christian holidays — this in spite of a clear talmudic prohibition. An accommodation was reached by determining that the gentiles of the twelfth century had abandoned idolatrous beliefs, maintaining only the "customs of their ancestors" and, hence, were not subject to the prohibition. In fact, the rabbis realized that the Jews' economic dependency on the Christians rendered the prohibition untenable. A modification in the legal tradition had taken place (see *Tosafot* on *Avodah Zarah* 2a).

Similarly, Rabbi Moses Isserles permitted the Jews of Moravia to drink gentile wine (*stam yeinam*). This radical enactment, flying in the face of talmudic halakhah to the contrary, was necessitated by these Jews' involvement in wine trading. To pursue their occupation, on which the economy of their community was built, the Moravian Jews had to be able to sit with gentiles to drink and taste wine so they could conclude their business transactions. Confronted by this situation, Isserles had no choice but to issue a lenient decree. In spite of seemingly valid reasons for such a judgment, Isserles came under fire for his enactment. (See H. H. Ben-Sasson, *Hagut VeHanhagah*, Jerusalem: Mosad Bialik, 1959, pp. 22–24)

As an historian who has examined these and other similar examples of change in Judaism, I have reached the conclusion that this evolutionary process is not an intrusion into Jewish life. It is, rather, an inherent component of Judaism. In each generation, authorized communal leaders, learned in the traditions of their people, introduced changes they deemed necessary to maintain the strength of their communities. Unanimity was not always present, but, dissent notwithstanding, the adaptation of Judaism to changing realities continued. To me this is a valid presentation of the *peshat* of Jewish history. It does represent a view of Judaism in which historical method has superseded theology. It is also consistent with the understanding of Judaism that flowed out of the Positive Historical School of German Jewish thinkers into the ideology of the American Conservative movement.

I have a problem with Conservative ideology, however. Because it is so closely linked to an historical-critical method of study, an academic and dispassionate attitude has, for too long, dominated the Conservative presentation of Judaism. We suffer from an "identity crisis" in which we struggle to determine if we should disseminate objective information about Judaism, the *peshat*, or motivate people to develop religious fervor and seek spiritual meaning in Judaism, the *derash*. Conservative Jews and Conservative Judaism have been adversely affected by this confusion because it has made it difficult for our movement's leadership to espouse a passionate approach to Jewish living.

If we believe what our historical research tells us, then ours is *the most authentic* form of Judaism. More Jews ought to be encouraged to adopt Conservative Jewish beliefs and practices for their own spiritual well-being and for the welfare of the Jewish community. I join with others who have called for the creation of a Conservative Jewish *mission to the Jews.* We should begin with our own constituents, our clergy, our educators, our lay leaders, the students in our schools and the members of our congregations. Outreach efforts should follow, and programs and institutions should be created and personnel trained to generate enthusiasm and commitment to Conservative Judaism. Young rabbis should be encouraged to spend the years immediately after ordination working in Conservative movement-sponsored outreach activities. These could include Conservative yeshivot for *ba'alei teshuvah* (those newly seeking their Jewish heritage), campus study and spirituality programs, "marketplace" study for business people, scholar-in-residence teaching in synagogues, spirituality sessions for youth groups, havurot and the like, crisis intervention for Jews who are being attracted by cults and missionaries, etc. The presentation of Judaism in all these settings would be passionate and motivational. The goal would be to help Jews find ways that Judaism — Conservative Judaism — can have a real impact on their lives.

Jews long ago realized that it was through midrash that Judaism continuously kept in touch with the real needs of the people. The *derash* allowed the tradition to respond. If it is to be meaningful, Conservative Judaism must rediscover the *derash* and actively promulgate it among the Jewish masses. This is not to say that the *peshat*, the scientific study of Judaism, must cease being pursued in halls of Conservative institutions of learning. A foundation of accurate historical information is necessary so that the subtleties of the Jewish experience can be understood and *peshat* interpretation can be made with that information in mind. If the *peshat* is, however, relative truth and the *derash* moves us closer to absolute truth, then let the *peshat* serve the purposes of the *derash*. For us Conservatives, the *derash* must be moved to center stage. If this sounds similar to the medieval "philosophy as handmaiden of religion" approach, so be it. We are not seeking converts to philosophy; we are seeking converts to *religion*.

This historian's reading of history leads him to conclude that now is *eit la'asot,* the time to act; *la'asot nefashot,* to make new souls who are committed to the truth that inheres within Conservative Judaism. Let Ezra the Scribe serve as our role model, as it is written: "For Ezra had dedicated himself — *li-drosh* — to interpret the Teaching of the Lord — *ve-la'asot* — and to act, and to teach laws and rules to Israel (Ezra 7:10)."

end

The ashes of books consumed on their shelves in the devastating library fire of April 1966.

Massive efforts were undertaken to salvage the books damaged by water in the library fire. Here, books stand upright and open to promote drying.

"My God, Who Is Without Ending"[1]: Modern Hebrew Literature as a Mode of Religious Quest

Anne Lapidus Lerner

"God, the Lord of those who conquered Canaan in a storm, — / And they bound Him in tefillin straps . . ."[2] In these words Saul Tchernichowsky, a leading poet of the modern period in Hebrew literature rails against the Hebrew God as reimaged by the Jewish tradition. The God Tchernichowsky is seeking in this poem "Facing the Statue of Apollo" is a young and virile one, the God of the ancient Hebrews, rather than the God of the Jews. What is striking about this poem by one of the most rebellious of modern Hebrew writers is that in his paean to Apollo, Tchernichowsky not only describes the merits of the Greek god and his followers, but also tries to make his peace with the Jewish God. While his approach is unsatisfying to those of us who see ourselves as the heirs of rabbinic Judaism, his resurrection of the biblical God of conquest serves as a reminder of the need to grapple with God, even when dealing with ostensibly secular materials.

This is, of course, not the only image of God we confront in Hebrew literature. Bialik, who often is considered the counterpart of Tchernichowsky, was no less engaged in the struggle to define a God to whom he could relate. Bialik often refers to God in the feminine form of the *Shekhinah* and metaphorically portrays Her as a broken-winged bird, lonely and abandoned. In a magnificently complex poem entitled *"L'vadi"* [I Alone], Bialik describes the ambivalent feelings of a young Talmud scholar who finds himself alone in the House of Study with the *Shekhinah*.[3] Torn as the young man is between the contrasting pulls of his happy, enlightened peers and the battered, shadow-wrapped *Shekhinah,* he cannot decide whether to remain loyal to God, as embodied in Jewish tradition, or to join his friends in the world of light and freedom. The inner struggle of the poem's narrator is only one aspect of its theme. What is striking is the shift in focus from the loneliness of the narrator to the loneliness of God. The God whom Bialik portrays is far from omnipotent. This Being is one who cries out, "The wind has lifted them all [the youth], they have all flown off/ And I remain alone, alone . . ." It is the boiling tear of the *Shekhinah* which is the closing image of the poem.

Even this cursory excursus into the image of God in Tchernichowsky and Bialik underscores the fact that many of the masters of modern Hebrew literature, particularly the poets, indulge in a good deal of "God-talk." Theology, theodicy, the transmission and translation of tradition are but a few of the clearly religious elements in modern Hebrew literature. Discussing modern Hebrew literature in the context of belief is a paradoxical exercise which would have seemed ludicrous at many stages of literary development. After all, those who laid the groundwork for the endeavor, the *maskilim,* or enlightened, claimed to be "enlightened" about religious issues. Considering a break with accepted religious belief as the *sine qua non* of a literary career has continued. Early in this century, Uri Zvi Greenberg described his fellow Jewish literati as "blasphemers who smoke cigars on Shabbat nights in order to destroy the lungs of our Hebrew God."[4] The pitfalls of an interest in *belles lettres* had long been apparent to the upholders of traditional Judaism. *Belles lettres* interfered with a man's most important obligation—that of *Talmud Torah,* or Torah study.[5] The time spent reading or writing non-religious literature could better be invested in religious study. Universally, the themes of modern literature have focused more on humanity than on God. They have thus served, from a traditional perspective, to lead both its writers and its readers away from religion.

The incorporation of modern Hebrew literature within the canon of sacred study, as part of the required curriculum for rabbinical training, is an innovation bordering on the heretical. It mandates the inclusion of a corpus of materials which were, from the outset, intended as a rebellion against the accepted religious tradition. At this point the original rationale for this curricular innovation is no longer relevant. Clearly, like some of the literature itself, the Conservative movement speaks both to the religious and to the ethnic or nationalist strands within Jewry. The blurring of this line, and the importance of modern Hebrew literature as an indication of the continued viability of Jewish culture in Hebrew and its rebirth in the modern period, would have been adequate justification for its initial and continuing inclusion in the curriculum.

Modern Hebrew literature continues to speak to us in religious and in national terms. It grapples with the issues which beset us individually and collectively. More importantly, it grapples with them in a manner which often parallels the ways in which people commonly think about these issues. The very ambiguities in literature parallel the function of ordinary human thought which tends to think and rethink, to weigh different perspectives and to come to conclusions which are not rigorously fixed. The latitude of interpretation in literature, as well as its ability to say different things at the same time with the same words, also enable it to deal with religious problems in an accessible human mode. Finally, our ability to identify with literary personae enables us vicariously to share their experiences. For all these reasons, literature provides an opportune forum for working through religious issues.

There are also aspects of modern Hebrew literature, often lost in translation, which facilitate its functioning as a medium for religious discussion. Primary among these is the allusive quality of the Hebrew language. As the longest linguistic tradition in western literature, Hebrew literature embodies within it debates and discussions which ring out across the generations. Bialik's aforementioned poem *"L'vadi"* uses texts from the Bible, Talmud and liturgy in order to create an argument with traditional Judaism which is woven into the warp and woof of the poetic text. The medium is the message, albeit an ambiguous one. Although the texts cited are often stood on their heads in their new contexts, they draw us back to the original sacred content again and again. They have gone through a process Adi Tsemah refers to as "ironic secularization" and will never be the same.[6] In fact the texts are not only changed within the poem, but they carry with them a soupçon of their secularized meaning even when they return to their original context.

The poem "Isaac" by Amir Gilboa can be used to elucidate this phenomenon.[7] In this poem Gilboa retells the story of the Binding of Isaac as though it were a nightmare. While the biblical Abraham and Isaac "walked on together" (Genesis 22:8), Gilboa's Isaac has his right hand in his father's left. This ostensibly minor addition to the biblical text moves us to reconsider the scene. It implies that the relationship between the two men is not the classic one between a powerful, supportive father and a weak, vulnerable son. Despite the fact that Gilboa's Isaac is clearly a child in age, he is held in his father's weak, perhaps sinister, left hand. Gilboa seems to be forcing us to ask the hard questions about the *Akedah*. How can a responsible parent justify his readiness to sacrifice his son? Did Abraham pass the divine test or did he fail it, only to have God stay his hand before failure turned to tragedy? When we read the modern poem, the biblical story is before us; when we next read the biblical story, whether as part of the annual Torah cycle, or in its liturgical setting, we will also ask these modern questions of the biblical text.

While the foregoing example represents a retelling of the biblical text in the light of modern sensibilities and experience, the relationship between text and context may be more subtle. Bialik's *"L'vadi"* is the story of a young man's struggle with the competing pulls of the tradition and secularism. In this poem Bialik's *Shekhinah* trembles "over her son, over her only [son]," protecting him with her broken wing.[8] The reference is, of course, to the story of the Binding of Isaac, where God calls to Abraham, saying, "Take your son, your only one, Isaac, whom you love" (Genesis 22:2). Again, the context reverses the meaning of the text. The paradigmatic nature of Isaac's experience, its serving as a model for pious Jewish behavior, is undercut by the clear message that the narrator is uncomfortable under the inadequate protection of the *Shekhinah*. Here, the reference to the *Akedah* is a death-reference, paralleling the reference to the *"El malei rahamim"* at the end of the preceding stanza.[9] That reference argues with the value of seeking shelter under the wing of the *Shekhinah*. The narrator is separated from his peers who have found themselves a world full of light and song, a world of youth and freedom. Again, reading the context back into the text, one can question the appropriateness of the prayer seeking shelter under God's wing. That image loses a good deal of its attraction when it is made, by means of the contrast, so unappealing.

Modern Hebrew literature, despite its occasional midrashic quality, can be considered a "safe" field within Jewish studies. Coming as it does from an anti-traditional point of view, it can be seen as an entity outside the framework of religious issues. Unlike the scholarship in Bible and Rabbinics, it deals with texts the sources of which are indisputably not divine. In its ties to other literatures, in its use of standard western literary forms, modern Hebrew literature can be seen as another corpus of texts to which a psychological, structuralist or deconstructionist approach may be applied. Although the problems of Jewish nationalism or ethnicity, Zionism or assimilationism may make it particularly appealing to the Jewish reader or scholar, it is essentially *belles lettres* and therefore religiously neutral.

Coming to Hebrew literature from the perspective of comparative literature, I started my career with the premise that Hebrew literature was not very different from French, American or Latin. Indeed from many points of view it is not. It possesses the same characteristics and is subjected to the same tools of criticism. Increasingly, however, I have come to admit to myself that the reason that it has become my major focus is that it speaks to me in a way that French literature does not. The fascination for me is that it can, on occasion, resonate with all those layers of tradition which are important for me. Unraveling its relationship with that tradition is both a scholarly and a personal challenge.

When, fresh from the rigors of graduate school, I first started teaching at the Seminary, I knew that the only way to teach literature was in a dispassionate way which would reveal as little of my own beliefs as possible, while introducing students to the arcane intricacies of analysis I had recently acquired. Ultimate meaning was not important; what was important was to analyze what Ciardi calls "how a poem means," or what makes a story work. The self-confidence to try to work with different types of meaning was developed through years of personal struggle and input from students. The adjustment from graduate seminars to undergraduate classroom, always difficult for new professors, was compounded by teaching required courses the need for which was not immediately apparent to students who often came to the Seminary on an inchoate religious quest. Slowly, I came to realize that the stuff of modern Hebrew literature was of relevance to that quest.

Raised in an observant Conservative family, I did not have to develop my own *modus vivendi* with religious belief and observance. Prayer, Shabbat and kashrut have always been part of my life. In a sense, grappling with literature, particularly with poetry, has provided me a welcome forum for grappling with Judaism. What engages me most is the ultimate ambiguity of much modern literature. Reading Bialik or Agnon, Zach or Pagis, one realizes that much of their writing is multivalent, often using traditional sources to express some of their ambiguities. Analyzing their works, seeing how they grapple with religious issues has helped me in my own religious growth. Repeatedly pushed to plumb their depths, I have had an opportunity to explore my own. When used, but really not abused, this way, literature can be a force for great enrichment.

Again *"L'vadi"* offers a relevant example of poetic ambiguity. There we find that Bialik expresses the ambivalent nature of the *Shekhinah* relationship with the narrator of the poem in the line *"Ukhmo sakhah bikhnafah ha-sh'vurah ba'adi,* And she sort of protected me with her broken wing."[10] Is the relationship between the narrator and the divine presence positive or negative? What is the nature of this protection? One way of trying to define Hebrew words more precisely is to examine the nature of their use in traditional texts. The Bible offers us two contexts for that root. The first offers us the Adversary's retort to the God who asserts that Job has always remained loyal to Him: "Why is it you who have fenced him round [*sakhta ba'ado*] him and his household and all that he has? You have blessed his efforts so that his possessions spread out in the land" (Job 1:10). If, indeed, this is Bialik's meaning, the narrator is presenting us with an image of the *Shekhinah* who, while not omnipotent, is doing Her best to protect Her remaining adherent. Another possibility exists, however. It is at least equally possible that the *Shekhinah's* action is cruel and confining. This verb appears in the Hebrew Bible in one more place, where it describes the symbolic action of the prophet Hosea who is trying to prevent his wife's whoring. Hosea exclaims: "Assuredly, I will hedge up [*sakh*] her roads with thorns and raise walls against her, and she shall not find her paths" (Hosea 2:8). What is Bialik's intention here? The determination of which meaning is primary and which secondary depends upon one's reading of the entire poem. In a way, however, what the ambiguity inherent in literature here allows is the expression of two contrary views of God in the same words, at the same time.

To the logician, philosopher or theologian, the ability to say divergent things at the same time is rather a liability. It leads to the blurring of categories and distinctions and to fuzzy thinking. At the same time, however, it must be borne in mind that this aspect of literature mimics our own everyday thought processes. We do not always think in clear-cut categories, despite the best efforts of schooling over the years. Our personal theology or philosophy is most often thought out in bits and snatches, not all of which are completely consistent. For me, at least, the ability to say that my relationship with God is both confining and confirming at the same time with the very same word is a dazzling opportunity.

Literature can facilitate religious thinking. Human contact with literature begins with the lullabies and nursery rhymes of infancy. While the overwhelming majority of American Jews will never see a page of Gemara, even in translation, they all have had some exposure to literature. In adult education settings, literature is a particularly effective tool in allowing people to articulate some of their most deep-seated religious feelings and beliefs. Even dealing with a translated text in order to get at the issues is not enough of a strain to block the process. Agnon's "*Tallit Aḥeret,* An Other Tallit"[11], is necessarily no less complex in English than in Hebrew. Either way, it is possible to be led to a profound consideration of the purpose of Yom Kippur and every Jew's experience of it.

Literary scholarship has granted me the opportunity to try to come to an ever-deepening understanding of Judaism, and to an ambiguous, but profound belief in it. Modern Hebrew literature allows me to do this in many areas of religious, ethnic, national and even universal concern. For me, and to some extent for my students, in formal and informal settings, the issues of moment have tended to be those with religious overtones. In that way literature has been a constant source of strength and support in my religious quest, even when it argues against belief. It offers the impetus to turn to God and ask, in the words of Leah Goldberg:

> Teach me, God, to pray, to praise
> the splendor of ripe fruit, the wonder of a wrinkled leaf,
> the freedom to see, to feel, to breathe,
> to know, to hope, and even to know grief.
> Teach my lips blessing, song, and praise
> when You renew Your time each night, each dawn,
> so that my days will not repeat my yesterdays,
> to save my life from mere routine of all days gone.[12]

NOTES

1. Hannah Szenes, *"Halikhah Caesarea"* [Toward Caesarea], *L'Lo Saphah* [Without Language] (Kibbutz Me'uhad, 1978), p. 19.

2. Saul Tchernichowsky, *"L'Nokhaḥ Pessel Apollo"* [Facing the Statue of Apollo], *Shirim* [Poems] (Tel Aviv, D'vir, 1966), p. 88.

3. Hayyim Nahman Bialik, *"L'vadi"* [I Alone], *Shirim* [Poems] (Tel Aviv: D'vir, 1966), pp. 141–142. An excellent translation and explication of this poem may be found in *The Modern Hebrew Poem Itself,* ed. Stanley

Burnshaw, T. Carmi, Ezra Spicehandler (New York: Holt, Rinehart & Winston, 1965), pp. 25-27.

4. Uri Zvi Greenberg, *"Aḥai Yehudei Ha-Pei'ot"* [My Brethren, the Jews with Earlocks], *Ha-Gavrut ha-Olah* [Masculinity Ascendant] (Tel Aviv: S'dan, 1926), p. 25.

5. Women were excluded from an obligation to Torah study, but did not loom large in the development of modern Hebrew literature because they were usually ignorant of Hebrew.

6. Adi Tsemah, *Ha-Lavi ha-Mistater* [The Hidden Lion] (Jerusalem: Kiryat Sepher, 1969), pp. 170-171.

7. Amir Gilboa, *"Yitshak"* [Isaac], *The Penguin Book of Hebrew Verse,* ed. and trans. T. Carmi (New York: Penguin, 1981), p. 560.

8. Bialik, ibid.

9. Tsemah, pp. 168-170.

10. Tsemah, p. 167.

11. S[hmu'el] Y[osef] Agnon, *"Tallit Aheret"* [An Other Tallit], *Samukh v'Nireh* [Nearby and Seen] (Jerusalem and Tel Aviv: Schocken, 1960), pp. 202-204.

12. Leah Goldberg, *"Lamdeni Elohai"* [Teach me, God], *Siddur Sim Shalom,* edited with translations by Rabbi Jules Harlow (New York: Rabbinical Assembly, United Synagogue), p. 800.

On Account of Two Hats

David G. Roskies

Et ḥata'ai ani mazkir hayyom. (I do remember my faults this day.) I came to the Seminary, in the Fall of 1975, with a profound anti-rabbinic bias. Fresh out of Graduate School and armed with (what I imagined to be) the one-and-only method of reading literature, I saw my task as spreading the gospel to majors in the field. I had nothing but disdain for rabbinical students whose only interest (I further imagined) was for sermon material. And the best of them, I was finally convinced (based on my jaded experience in Havurat Shalom), would never go into the rabbinate anyway. If today you hear me singing a different tune, it is because teaching at the Seminary has changed: (1) me, (2) my approach to the classroom and (3) my methodology as a scholar.

The Seminary combines under its roof two distinctly different kinds of teaching environments: one that is scholarly and academic, and the other that is explicitly value-oriented. Unlike our loyal opposition, Prof. Jacob Neusner, I see this as a tremendous boon, not as a structural handicap, for it allows us to develop both sides of our brain — the emotional and the cerebral, the homiletic-engagé side of our personality, and the dispassionate analytic side as well. As long as we know what we're doing, I believe it perfectly legitimate for us to shape the material we teach in the light of these different agenda.

On a more practical level, we have been debating among ourselves, lo these past ten years, what a rabbinical school education should entail and how it is distinct. Since 1977, when our new curriculum went into effect, we've been grappling with Levels III and IV in particular, asking how these courses (in critical methodologies and in "synthesis") actually contribute to our students' professional training as rabbis.

This paper was adapted from a presentation given at the Faculty Assembly on November 11, 1985.

I should therefore like to add my voice to the choir by teaching a text in two different ways. By presenting a condensed version of how I go about teaching the same story in the Graduate and Rabbinical Schools of the Seminary, I hope to illustrate the advantages of doing double duty with the knowledge that we, the faculty, possess. Nothing here will be invented. Even the digressions are a deliberate part of the script.

For the first setting we come in on the opening class of my graduate course on Sholem Aleichem. The story in question, "On Account of a Hat," serves as my entrée into Sholem Aleichem's narrative art. The second lecture comes at the mid-point in my Level III course in the Rabbinical School on critical methodologies in Jewish literature. This semester is devoted to storytelling as a form of modern midrash and the Sholem Aleichem story is brought to illustrate the theme of identity crisis in the Yiddish and Hebrew modern storytelling corpus.

* * *

Like the Mishnah, let us jump into our subject *in medias res*. Dispensing with a lengthy introduction on the state of Sholem Aleichem scholarship, or on the author's biography, or on the textual variants of his work, I shall lead you through a close reading of a sample text. The story I have chosen is the one most often anthologized, at least in English, beginning with the now-classic Howe & Greenberg *Treasury of Yiddish Stories* (1954) up until the *Big Book of Jewish Humor* (1981). As we read it through, we'll look at the story from four angles: the multiple narrations and how they work; the structure of the story; the function of language and style; and finally, time permitting, the matter of interpretation.

The first clue we have that this is not a carbon copy of an actual folktale is that it is told through multiple narrators. In order of sophistication, we begin with the implied author who is none other than the famous "Sholem Aleichem"; so famous in fact, that the second narrator, "who deals in stationery and is surely no *litterateur*," has read the author's previous work (this telling reference to Tevye the Dairyman was unfortunately omitted from an otherwise brilliantly accurate translation). With fame, however, comes a special responsibility to one's readership, as witness "Sholem Aleichem's" disclaimer in paragraph three:

I must confess that this story, which he related to me, does indeed sound like a concocted one, and for a long time I couldn't make up my mind whether or not I should pass it on to you. But I thought it over and decided that if a respectable merchant and dignitary of Kasrilevke, who deals in stationery and is surely no *litterateur*—if he vouches for a story, it must be true.

From here on in, we don't hear from the implied author again, and the story is given over to the merchant whom he happened to meet on board a train as both men made their way home for Passover.

As an occupational type, the anonymous narrator is typical of the Jewish Pale of Settlement at the beginning of the century: he is a petty merchant and luftmensch; he chain-smokes; he straddles the Jewish and gentile worlds but is firmly rooted in the former; he knows Kasrilevke from the inside. More typical of Sholem Aleichem's oeuvre: he is a seasoned raconteur, one of many stand-ins for Sholem Aleichem himself. We know this from his syncopated speech rhythm, his verbal tag-line, "do you hear what I say," used at strategic points in the narration. Once we get deeper into the story, we notice how a few choice Russian words function as a comic refrain and as a way of undercutting Sholem Shachnah, the hero. The anonymous narrator's two digressions—on the slowness of the trains and on the tyranny of wives—illustrate both his ironic perspective on modern life and his folk humor. But he, too, gradually bows out of the story as Sholem Shachnah himself takes over (as reported by the anonymous merchant and as faithfully recorded by the famous author).

We hear our central character talking in three different settings: on neutral ground, on alien ground, and on native ground (the categories are taken from an essay by Ruth R. Wisse that I've assigned at a later point in the course). On neutral ground, somewhere in the Pale, Sholem Shachnah clinches the first real-estate deal of his life. On closer inspection, however, the conquest appears to be purely verbal: it was Drobkin, "a Jew from Minsk province, a great big fearsome rattler, a real estate broker from way back—he and his two brothers" who actually clinched the deal. But Sholem Shachnah raises such a ruckus that the two brothers give him a cut of the profits just to shut him up! So elated is our hero that he sends a telegram home . . . in Russian: "*Arriving home Passover without fail.*" Just as this telegram marks his only real achievement, so it foretells his ultimate undoing.

The Zlodievke train station, its walls covered with soot and its floor with spit, is the alien ground that Sholem Shachnah must negotiate in order to make it home on time for Passover. As we already know from the second narrator's digression, the train schedules in Russia conspire against the passengers. What's more, it is here, in the train station, that Sholem Shachnah confronts his great adversary — Buttons, a tsarist official who occupies the last available spot in the whole station:

> Who this Buttons was, whether he was coming or going, he hadn't the vaguest idea — Sholem Schachnah, that is. But he could tell that Buttons was no dime-a-dozen official. This was plain by his cap, a military cap with a red band and a visor. He could have been an officer or a police official.

As always in Sholem Aleichem's writings, whenever a confrontation takes place, its arena is speech; more often than not, a monologue. Indeed, Sholem Shachnah is able to overcome his fear of Buttons by means of penetrating existential questions which he poses to himself alone:

> It's not such a bad life to be a Gentile, and an official one at that, with buttons, thinks he — Sholem Schachnah, that is — and he wonders, dare he sit next to this Buttons, or hadn't he better keep his distance? Nowadays you never can tell whom you're sitting next to. If he's no more than a plain inspector, that's still all right. But what if he turns out to be a district inspector? Or a provincial commander? Or even higher than that, and supposing this is even Purishkevitch himself (may his name perish)? Let someone else deal with him, and Sholem Shachnah turns cold at the mere thought of falling into such a fellow's hands. But then he says to himself — now listen to this — Buttons, he says, who the hell is Buttons? And who gives a hang for Purishkevitch? Don't I pay my fare the same as Purishkevitch? So why should he have all the comforts of life and I none?

After this pep-talk, Sholem Shachnah still has one more gentile to deal with, the porter whom he speaks to in Low Goyish (Ukrainian) in a rude perfunctory manner. The same speech pattern also holds in the dream sequence that follows. Sholem Shachnah dreams that he is riding home for Passover in a wagon instead of a train, "driven by a thievish peasant, Ivan Zlodi," at whom he yells to hurry it up, lest they arrive home too late. The last stage of verbal negotiation is still to come. Awakened from his sleep in the dead of night by the porter, Sholem Shachnah mistakenly grabs the official's hat with the red band and the visor and, thus disguised, he is treated with deference by the crowd, the ticket agent and the conductor. Everyone addresses him in Russian as "Your Excellency" but the words make no sense at all; in fact they make him angry.

When he finally does make it home, on the third day of Passover, his wife heaps scorn upon him and the community treats him with mock respect. The words "Your Excellency! Your Excellency!" ring in his ears as a bitter reproach. On native ground, it's almost impossible to talk your way out of a bind.

The structure of the story follows the rise-and-fall pattern that Dan Miron has traced throughout Sholem Aleichem's entire oeuvre. That this is indeed an embedded, mythic pattern, as Miron argues, can be seen by translating the plot into the formula of the standard European folktale. First the hero leaves home and makes good. In order to return he must pass through enemy turf (the Zlodievke train station) where he encounters the giant (Buttons). The hero then steals the giant's weapon (his military cap with the red band and the visor) and is magically transformed. He fails, however, at the final test and is duly punished (by missing the train and by the verbal abuse he suffers at home). And so what we have here is a humorous but realistic story that borders on being a mock myth.

In his best work, as we shall see throughout the course, Sholem Aleichem took conventional plots and well-known anecdotes (remember his disclaimer in paragraph 3!) and turned them into a sophisticated modern narrative. Just look at how many levels of language he managed to introduce into such a skimpy shell of a story: the richly idiomatic speech of the anonymous narrator; the use of High Goyish (Russian) when sending a telegram or addressing officialdom and of Low Goyish (Ukrainian) when talking to a peasant; not to speak of the two "authorial" styles: that of a professional writer and that of his surrogate storyteller. Language is both medium and message in the work of Sholem Aleichem. Speech is a surrogate for action and a shield against the forces of destruction. Some stories are also self-reflexive: they are *about* the workings of language.

Since this is a very open-ended story with a lot of clues as to its deeper meaning, and since we're running out of time, I can only suggest some angles to think about. The story was written in 1913 and the reference to the notorious Jew-baiter Purishkevitch tells us that this was a time of reaction in the history of Russian Jews. Thus the story can be read as a parable on anti-Semitism. On a social-psychological plane, there is the central issue of identity: what happens to the Jew (or to the modern person) when his identity is reduced to a hat. Finally, there is the metaphysical level suggested by Sholem Shachnah's wife at the end of the story. How could he be so sure, she cries. How could he write "without fail" in his telegram when nothing in (modern) life happens without fail? For all of Sholem Aleichem's surface humor, there is a deep sense of fatalism running through his work, which is why the "laughter-through-tears" formula (borrowed from Gogol) is so appropriate.

* * *

(I would begin the class by asking someone to retell the story in a few sentences. Unlike the previous class, these students will have read the story beforehand, but will only have an English translation to work from.)

The reason this story can be retold so easily is that it's based on a well-known joke. I once heard a more ribald version in which the hero exchanges gaberdines with a Greek Orthodox priest lying next to him in a filthy inn! By looking at how Sholem Aleichem fleshed out this anecdote, how he turned a culturally time-specific story into a universal parable will tell us where it belongs in the corpus of modern Jewish storytelling.

First let's look at the hero. Sholem Shachnah is the typical hero of the modern Yiddish story. He is a normative type: not a rabbi, a rebbe, a zaddik or a scholar. (We've already seen a similar humanistic trend in Peretz.) Neither is he a young revolutionary or a *halutz* (these appear only in the novels or as a foil to a character like Tevye). Sholem Shachnah is your typical member of the Jewish middle class (or the petit bourgeoisie, as the Marxists would have it), which is to say: a down-and-out, unsuccessful middleman. His Jewish profile is similarly standard: like every good Jew, he's going home for Pesah and is afraid to enter town without a hat (*cf.* the dream sequence). But he also knows enough Russian to send a telegram and to talk to officials. His psychological profile is perhaps his most interesting feature in that he's a celebrated scatterbrain, easily excitable and a henpecked husband to boot.

Of the various settings for the modern stylized folktale, this is the first time we've come across a train. Though he got the idea from Mendele Moykher Sforim ("Shem and Japheth on the Train"), Sholem Aleichem was the first Jewish writer to exploit the train as both a traditional and modern vehicle: traditional because that is where Jewish men still meet to swap stories, and modern because it is a battleground between rich and poor, Jew and gentile. In such a world it is easy to lose one's footing. Then there's the matter of the train schedule. The wise men of Kasrilevke joke about it, as we hear in the anonymous narrator's digression, but the point of the joke is deadly serious: instead of the train making it easier for a Jew to make it home on time for Passover, the opposite is true; technology and progress conspire against him.

And so do the goyim. As your typical shtetl Jew, Sholem Shachnah is caught between two classes of gentiles: the Russian bureaucrat personified by Buttons and the Ukrainian peasant represented by Yeremei the porter (in reality) and Ivan Zlodi (in his dream). Each meeting, you will note, is fraught with anxiety. It requires a profound mental struggle just for our hero to build up enough courage to squeeze in next to Buttons on the bench. The porter has to be paid off and is not to be trusted. And Ivan, whose nickname means "scoundrel," drives the wagon out of control on its way home to Kasrilevke, foreshadowing exactly what will happen to our poor Jew in a world run by goyim and their trains: he will lose his hat, and something more.

The dream sequence, of course, is the storyteller's shorthand for the hero's psychic state. It is also the pivotal point in the story, where reality gives way to hallucination. For once Sholem Shachnah awakens, he no longer knows what world he's in. Which brings us to the central theme of the story—the crisis of identity.

At first it's a comedy of errors with everyone mistaking him for some high official. He himself gets progressively more befuddled, vacillating between anger and confusion. The climax comes as the conductor ushers him into the first-class compartment, though he only paid for a third-class ticket:

Left alone in the carriage, Sholem Shachnah looks around to get his bearings—you hear what I say? He has no idea why all these honors have suddenly been heaped on him—first class, salutes, Your Excellency. Can it be on account of the real-estate deal he has just closed? That's it! But wait a minute. If his own people, Jews, that is, honored him for this, it would be understandable. But Gentiles! The conductor! The ticket agent! What's it to them? Maybe he's dreaming. Sholem Shachnah rubs his forehead and while passing down the corridor glances in the mirror on the wall. It nearly knocks him over! He sees not himself but the official with the red band. That's who it is! "All my bad dreams on Yeremei's head and on his hands and feet, that lug! Twenty times I tell him to wake me and I even give him a tip, and what does he do, that dumb ox, may he catch cholera in his face, but wake the official instead! And me he leaves asleep on the bench! Tough luck, Sholem Shachnah old boy, but this year you'll spend Passover in Zlodievke, not at home."

Can you think of a more brilliant way to portray the modern crisis of identity? A Jew looks into a mirror and sees—the farthest image of himself he could ever imagine! So great is his shock that he jumps off the train to wake his "real" self up and all his plans go up in smoke. Why? Where did he go wrong?

The lack of any clear-cut answer is precisely what makes this story so modern as a parable of identity. After all, Sholem Shachnah wasn't trying to run away, to assimilate; all he wanted was to make it home in time for the seder. Yet the world conspires against him. Is it because of anti-Semitism (note that the story was written in 1913 against the backdrop of the Beilis Trial)? If so, can a Jew be treated with respect only if he's dreaming or if they have the wrong guy? Living under tyranny is grossly reductionist: since a man is known by his buttons or his hat alone, the rigid hierarchy can be toppled only with dangerous consequences. Or perhaps this story is a warning of what happens whenever a Jew leaves his native turf: his soul goes up for grabs and he must be put back in his place by the collective superego. Or perhaps in every modern(izing) society one's identity is reduced to mere externals, which makes it that much easier to lose, confuse or abuse one's hat/identity.

There may yet be another interpretation, that the blame is to be placed not on tsarist tyranny or on the anonymity of a secular world but on the human condition itself. Remember what his wife said to him on his return: How could you be so sure? How could any human being, in these troubled, tenuous times, enjoy total mastery of his fate?

The assumption of a story such as this, written in a semitraditional mold, is that Sholem Shachnah could never become Buttons. Hence the issue is not the barriers that prevent a Jew from becoming a gentile. But because the vagaries of modern life (the train, the presence of anti-Semites) are so carefully woven into the familiar fabric of the plot, we are made to see how precarious it is to live as a Jew or to maintain any fixed identity whatsoever.

Which reminds me of two episodes in my own life — here at the Seminary. I came here via Israel where I had spent two years finishing up my doctorate and vainly looking for an academic position. There, no one knew me from Adam. I had to fight every clerk just to spell my name the way I wanted. Suddenly, I arrive at 3080 Broadway where they roll out the red carpet: "So pleased to meet you, Prof. Roskies." "This is your office, Prof. Roskies." "Should you need any assistance, please feel free to call, Prof. Roskies." Who was this "Prof. Roskies?" They must have the wrong guy! Soon enough, when you get your first pulpit, you'll have the same experience. You'll be coming from Reb School where you feel like an overgrown child and suddenly they'll be calling you Rabbi This and Rabbi That. So remember Sholem Shachnah staring at Buttons in the mirror.

And the other episode happened a few months after I arrived. I was asked to lecture on my research at a faculty seminar as a way of introducing me to my colleagues. The talk went very well. At intermission the Chancellor, Gerson Cohen, turned to me and said: "You know, I got a lot of flack from the Board of Directors for hiring such a right-winger as Roskies." I thought he was joking. It was only the next day as I ran through everything that had happened that I realized the truth: Both the Chancellor and his Board considered me (me!) a right-winger and they feared I might tip the delicate religious balance at the Seminary. How in the world did they arrive at that? Why, it must be on account of my hat! In those days I used to go around in a kind of Eastern European cap. I had started wearing it in Israel so as to avoid wearing a knitted kippah (a *real* political symbol). In New York I kept it on as a form of ethnic identification. It made me feel more Yiddish. Needless to say, my whole cap collection has been gathering dust in the closet ever since. I don't wear hats anymore, except in the winter.

These, then, are the two approaches I take when teaching in the Graduate and Rabbinical Schools. The first approach focuses on what critic E. D. Hirsch calls "meaning," that is to say, the fixed, immutable aspects of a literary text: questions of narrative voice, structure and style. As graduate students these critical categories should be familiar to them even if my particular application is not. Because they have access to the Yiddish original (which the rabbinical students do not), much more can be done with such things as wordplay, speech rhythm, dialect, and the like. I deliberately skirt the issue of "significance" (according to Hirsch, that which is open to change in a literary text), because graduate training deals in a discipline that transcends all boundaries, be they religious or political, ethical or, to some extent, even cultural. On a subtler level, the first approach stresses Sholem Aleichem's modernity—the sophistication of his verbal art—whereas the second seeks to place him within the framework of traditional Jewish storytelling.

The whole first semester of my course on Critical Methodologies in Jewish Literature is designed to reinstate storytelling as a central means of communication and to integrate secular Jewish writing within the classical traditions of Midrash. The second semester makes the opposite case, that modern Jewish literature is totally discontinuous with the past, and can only be understood within a Western, secular context. Here, instead of short stories, we look at poetry and the novel. I arrived at both parts of the equation after several years of trial and error, in an attempt to streamline the teaching of literature for my students' future rabbinic needs. In both I try to isolate the larger units of the literary code: types of heroes, basic genres, central themes. Because I am not training them to be literary critics and because they will most likely be reading Yiddish (and I daresay Hebrew) literature in translation, I am concerned with showing my rabbinical students how all the pieces fit together (Yiddish, Hebrew, Anglo-Jewish; premodern and modern forms; Europe, America and Israel) so that the corpus of modern Jewish literature can be put to creative homiletic use.

This method of linking literary history to statements of belief is my way of adapting the ideology of the Conservative movement to the classroom. Here I take issue with an illustrious Seminary graduate, my friend and teacher Arthur Green, who recently argued that "It is in faith . . . not in history, where the core of our Judaism must reside" ("Jewish Studies and Jewish Faith," *Tikkun* 1:1 [Summer 1986],

p. 87). As opposed to Green who would dehistoricize the *Akedah,* the Exodus and the Revelation at Sinai for the sake of achieving contemporary religious relevance, I maintain that it is precisely the historical method that vivifies the biblical archetypes, that brings them home to us as human constructs. Seeing how the ancients operated within an historical field can aid us enormously in our own daily application of Scripture.

So, too, the use of Jewish literature as a source of revelation. By locating Sholem Aleichem somewhere between Mendele and Kafka; by identifying the storyteller's code; by suggesting some of the historical and social-psychological issues that the author might have been grappling with, the story comes alive as a modern parable which, in turn, can always be updated in response to ever-more contemporary dilemmas.

To succeed, this method must involve a different teaching style as well, which brings me back to those two sides of our brain. Since the purpose of this course in the Rabbinical School is to teach students how to personalize literature on their own, the teacher must take the lead by making him/herself vulnerable. This explains the comical digressions: I am making my self a commentary on the text. These personal anecdotes are also a wonderful mnemonic: one hat-story will recall another.

And so, teaching at the Seminary, we can have it all. We can wear both hats with impunity and not lose our heads in the process. Wearing both hats we can also sharpen our own methodological assumptions and, true to Sholem Aleichem, can subject the hierarchies of the mind to the dictates of the heart.

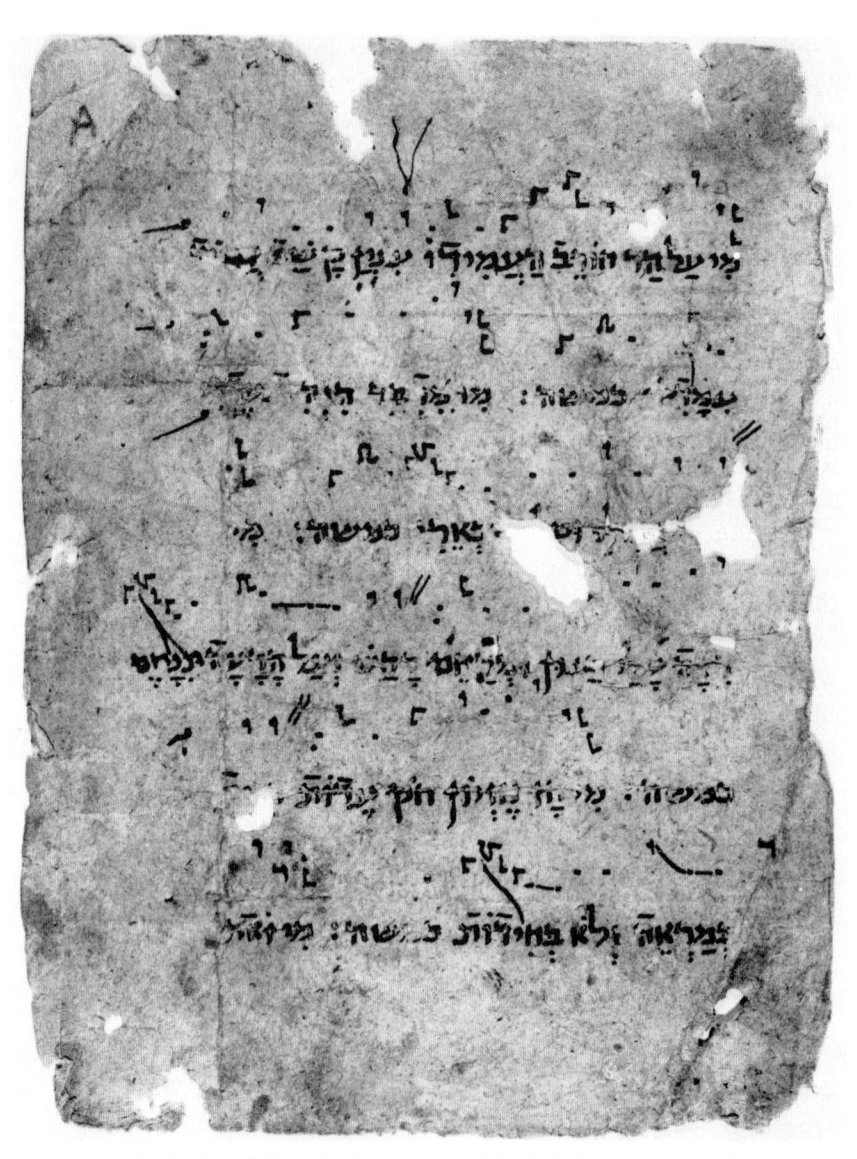

From the Seminary's Rare Book collection of Genizah fragments: the oldest surviving Hebrew manuscript with musical notation. The poem, written and composed by Ovadiah the Norman proselyte, a priest who converted to Judaism around 1102, is for Simḥat Torah or Shavuot.

A Philosopher's View on the Problem of Scholarship and Belief

Gordon Tucker

The career of Conservative Judaism is roughly coeval with the development of historical consciousness which began in the nineteenth century. That fact alone accounts for many significant characteristics of the Conservative movement, and for some of its nagging problems as well. Indeed, for much of the one hundred years that The Jewish Theological Seminary of America has existed, those who have studied and taught here have experienced a certain kind of dissonance which can be explained largely as a result of the parallel roots of the Seminary and the critical/historical method.

What is that method and what are its underlying premises? Van A. Harvey (*The Historian and the Believer,* NY: Macmillan, 1966) gives us as good a characterization as we could seek: "a sustained and critical attempt to recover the past by means of the patient analysis of evidence and the insistence on the impartiality and truthfulness of the historian." It was further marked by "the tendency to evaluate events in terms of their origins; the awareness of the relativity of one's own norms of thought and valuation; . . . the aim . . . to 'tell what really happened' " (p. 4). Harvey was speaking here of the research methods of Ernst Troeltsch; he could, however, just as well have been speaking of Leopold Zunz, Nahman Krochmal, or Zecharias Frankel. For these men, no less than for their counterparts in the gentile world, the "scientific" method that they embraced satisfied a powerful intellectual urge and intuition, but at the same time put them on a collision course with other factors of vital importance — to wit, their beliefs and religious commitments. That potential collision (or "dissonance," to use a less melodramatic term) arose in the following way: although the early adherents of the critical/historical method in Jewish learning studied and revered the classical texts of the Jewish tradition as a matter of *piety* (and in this respect were quite traditional

Jews), they also studied those very same texts (*e.g.*, Bible, Talmud, Jewish liturgy, etc.) as starting points of historical inquiry. Such inquiry must be, ideally, "dispassionate." Moreover, the consciousness that all that we know and receive has been refracted over and over again through an historically evolving human (in this case, Jewish) civilization—in short, the historical consciousness—is *not* the consciousness either that created the classic texts, or (more to the point) that made them into objects of piety in the first place. For part of what had, to all previous generations, made the Bible, the Mishnah, and the Talmudim pillars of religious life was the sense of *timelessness* with which those texts were studied, the sense that they conveyed an eternal message, and most of all, the conviction that the deep religious truths borne by those texts simply transcended all the contingencies of history.

Could we aim, when studying the Bible, to "tell what really happened"? Certainly we could; but an investigation of that sort makes sense only if we believe that there is some chance that we will conclude that the Bible's own account is not reliable. And once we entertain that possibility, the religious grip the Bible exerts on us is almost certainly loosened. Or, to adapt the excellently concise question formulated by Harvey (p. 18): can one and the same person hold a judgment only *tentatively* as an historian, yet believe it passionately as a Jew?

Thus arises the tension, the dissonance, which has marked the work of scholars in virtually every discipline that has been taught at the Seminary these hundred years. We have touched just now, for the sake of illustration, on the poignancy of the problem for biblical studies. Since the Seminary has always been so closely identified with Talmud, it will also be instructive to consider for a moment how the talmudists fared. The critical/historical approach to the Talmud presents to us a remarkably variegated text, one with many levels and intricacies, and above all with an extraordinarily complex *history*. All of these results are what make this kind of talmudic study so exciting and seductive. But the Talmud is, among other things, the basic text of Jewish law; and since observance of God's law, halakhah, has always been one of the pillars of Jewish piety, the Talmud plays a leading role in the religious life and identity of the believing Jew. If it is not a seamless whole, that is, if we cannot be sure that we can understand one part of the Talmud by referring to another part (because it may come from a very different school, or may be based on a later or erroneously transmitted tradition), then something quite radical has happened, and we may well have to revise our *religious* attitude to the text. Still, this point may not be so obvious at first, and perhaps this question should be asked: Why is it that *yir'at shamayim* (freely translated: a sense of God's presence) cannot flow automatically and naturally from a talmudic text that has been subjected to this kind of historical analysis?

I would suggest that the reason stems from some of the deepest psychological roots of Judaism, roots that it has by virtue of its being a monotheistic faith. Put most succinctly, what has been for Judaism the fundamental and unshakable belief in one God with a single, divine nature can lead, and has led, to other forms of "monisms" as well. It is, for example, not a great leap from the concept of there being one God to a predilection for thinking of the teachings of religion, or the record of revelation, as being simple and unitary. The process is already quite evident in the biblical book of Deuteronomy: One God means one form of worship, one place of worship, one kind of religious message (consider Deuteronomy's insistence on tight control of prophecy). Plurality in the expression of what religion demands of us, what God's will is, must, under the influence of this "religious monism," be explained away (and indeed, traditional Judaism always has attempted to do this, with notably little success, for the manifest and ubiquitous halakhic pluralism of the Talmud). The logic of radical monotheism, in other words, can lead to a conviction that there should be no change or differentiation in the sources of religious authority (which are, for Rabbinic Judaism, our texts).

It is no accident or coincidence that Moses Maimonides, one of the purest, most insistent of the philosophical monotheists, articulated this idea of simplicity and seamlessness in religious texts most explicitly and forcefully. In the eighth of the principles of Judaism which he rehearses in the introduction to his commentary on *Mishnah Sanhedrin*, chapter 10, Maimonides says that we are required to believe that the entire Torah is of divine origin, even those verses which simply give us genealogical data, or name the concubine of one of Esau's sons. One little lapse, such as suggesting that Moses might have written one of those little, inconsequential verses by himself, makes all the difference in the world, for it puts the deviant believer squarely on the slippery slope, sliding toward denying all divine authority. Why? Clearly, because the demands of the One, Infinite God cannot appropriately be housed in a complex, differentiated vessel.

What then does one do with the fact that there are many verses in the Torah that do in fact seem very inconsequential? Or with the fact that there appear to be contradictions galore among biblical verses? Maimonides' answer to that is quite direct: you must believe that there are "wisdom and wonders" without end in the text, that the surface meaning is just that, but the depths are infinite. In other words, the traditional point of view about our religious texts depended on an ahistorical exegesis, that saved the unity of the text by positing an infinity of layers of esoteric meaning. All this, I suggest, because of the underlying conviction that the nature of God is fixed, eternal and unchanging, and that there is no real change in the nature of people or the world except when God wills that change to take place, all of a sudden (such as at the creation, or at the Sinai revelation). Our texts, our piety, our liturgy, all must be interpreted as unchanging (and unchangeable) under this traditional view.

It should be quite apparent that this tendency of Jewish tradition is ahistorical at its core. It is only by understanding this that one can appreciate why the historical method of the nineteenth century was so jolting and so threatening. Overturning that traditional standpoint is extremely unsettling (and, to make matters worse, once historical consciousness enters the stage, there is no going back; even those who desperately fight it find themselves using historical arguments against it, for this mode of thought, like an opportunistic parasite, quickly latches on to *everyone's* consciousness). To focus on the history of the religious messages inherent in our religious texts is to concede a universal principle of change and non-permanence. It challenges the comfortable image of a steady-state, concinnate universe by asserting that even the truth about God and God's will is transmitted by, and is thus subject to, the contingencies of human history. That is the first challenge that the new historical method presented to the traditional, deeply rooted tendencies of Judaism.

There was a second challenge as well. For the method of the historian, which in the nineteenth century came to be patterned after a model of scientific method, stresses continuity, or at least analogy, over its universe of discourse. The historian looks for patterns and analogues in history; what makes history a *method* is that change is not assumed to be simply a randomly occurring phenomenon of human history. Rather, the historical method, like its analogue, the scientific method, posits that change is part of the nature of things, and that it therefore follows laws, or at least paradigmatic structures. There is no room in this method for accommodating what might be called "cosmic discontinuities"; the idea that one period of human history is radically and absolutely different in kind from another period would be unintelligible to the historian/critic who works on the scientific model. And both of these premises, i.e., that change is universal, and that it is a natural, lawlike event, profoundly challenge the orthodox view that was outlined above, and which was so forcefully articulated by Maimonides, among many others.

To return, then, to the critical talmudist: once the talmudic text has been demonstrated to be a creature of history, an artifact, its power to convey the voice of the One, Infinite God has been broken. The traditional view had it that there was a real halakhah, God's law, platonistically conceived, and that the talmudic text conveyed that law to us, in human language to be sure, but nevertheless as a totality. But the historical method of study takes seriously all the apparent "fault lines" and discontinuities in the text, and thus presents it as a record of God's law *becoming*. To insist on understanding every part of the Talmud in conjunction with, and by reference to, every other part, is to ignore the truth about the text that stares you in the face. Indeed, to insist that there is something unique about the talmudic period itself, that the editing of the Talmud somehow marks an end to a certain kind of legal authority and legitimacy, is to deny one of the basic premises of the historical method. And that is why the sense of the commanding presence of God no longer flows immediately and automatically from the text when it is studied in a critical way.

It does not follow, however, that *yir'at shamayim* can no longer flow at all. It merely means that, having adopted a critical standpoint, having embraced a certain scholarly method, we must also revise our *religious* attitude to the text. *Yir'at shamayim* has to be discovered, sought out, perhaps even argued for. When this is not done, the tension and dissonance take over. When the effort is made, and successfully made, harmony and a sense of religious wholeness can indeed be restored. It would be accurate to say that the supposed contradiction between piety and critical scholarship is much more psychological than logical. It appears as a contradiction not in the clarity of a logician's reduction to absurdity, but rather in stubborn patterns of thought about what religious authority is, and about what are proper objects of piety. Louis Jacobs has written some of the most accessible material on the subject of the dissonance we have been discussing, most notably in his book *We Have Reason to Believe*. In it he argues that in the face of the critical/historical method we have three options. The first might be called the "fundamentalist" option. It is simply the denial of the validity of the historical method, and a refusal to entertain any possibility, or embark on any investigation, that might contradict the traditional view about the religious texts. The second possible approach to the tension can be thought of as the iconoclastic response. It is, predictably, the polar opposite of the fundamentalist reaction. That is, it concludes from the fact that the religious text cannot be thought of as carrying authority *exactly as the tradition claimed it did,* that it cannot wield any authority at all. This response posits that it is unreasonable to accept the authority of a text that has been shown to be the product of different authors, redactors, and locales, and which may even be riddled with contradictions and ambiguities with respect to its basic tenets. Both of these responses share the same point of view about divine authority: it must be unitary and seamless. It's just that the former refuses to give up the belief in the text, and thus denies the method, and the latter accepts the method and thus denies the *religious* value of the text. All too often, these are presented as the only available options.

Jacobs pleads for a third alternative. It is a plea that we in this movement can scarcely ignore. But what could a third alternative be for our hypothetical (actually, not so hypothetical!) talmudist? What sort of synthesis is available to those who cannot discard the intellectual commitment to the historical method, but who are equally unwilling to, or incapable of, emptying their consciousness of the commanding presence of God? Answers to that question can get highly complex, and above all, quite personal. Yet a number of things can be said on this subject as general guides. At the very least, commitment to the historical method should mean a seriousness about its tenets and assumptions: that change, which is to say history itself, is a fundamental feature of the world, and that it can be organized and structured (by the *discipline* of history) into discernible and meaningful patterns. If we really believe that, and if we use the method to analyze and teach our sacred texts, then we must also appeal to our commitment to history when called upon to answer the question: "But *why* are these texts sacred?" It will not do simply to revert at that point to a pre-critical stance and reply, "Nevertheless they are sacred"; the word "sacred" desperately needs a gloss.

That gloss, however, need not be so difficult to formulate, if the historical consciousness we share is taken seriously. What is required is a religious conception that affirms that God's creation of a historically unfolding world necessarily carried with it a decision that the divine will shall unfold through the historical understanding and expression of human beings. Such a religious conception includes the conviction that humanity has a non-trivial role to play, not only as *discoverers* and *followers* of the truths about God and His commands, but as its *creators* as well. This would truly reflect our conviction that history is not a flaw in a unitary, unchanging world, but is rather important and irreducible. In the case before us, it would allow one (really, *force* one) to see the halakhic history and pluralism recorded in the texts as having real religious significance. In at least one sense, the practitioner of the historical method can actually be better off religiously. Having affirmed the divine preference for an historically developing world, the critical scholar need not find (or pretend to find) an event, a phenomenon, perhaps a text, which is immune to historical conditioning in order to find God. Evidence of God's presence can, in principle, be found everywhere, even (or especially) in the pluralistic literature of the Talmud. (Precisely how and where one finds that presence remains, of course, highly personal and individualistic.)

It seems to me that such an attempt at a synthesis, or third alternative, has another significance for Conservative Judaism. It evidently requires some skepticism about the idea that there are fundamental "jumps" or discontinuities in human history. For us, this would both affirm the naturalness of the change reflected in the talmudic text, and would have the consequence of denying any ultimate, privileged status to the jurists of a given era. Thus does a redefinition of what makes sacred texts sacred have important ramifications for religious *authority* as well. (It is perhaps worth pointing out that this kind of skepticism about what I have called "cosmic discontinuity" goes down much more easily for Jews than for Christians. Even interpreting Sinai in a evolutionary, naturalistic way is far less jolting to Jewish faith than is a skepticism about the difference in what human nature is before and after the life of Jesus. No doubt that accounts for the added poignancy of Harvey's book.)

This thumbnail sketch of an approach to resolving the dissonance between historical study of a text and religious devotion to that same text is no theoretical construct. Approaches such as these are already familiar; they have appeared, in various forms and stages of development, in the teaching and writings of many of the scholars and teachers who have been plagued by the tension, in a variety of fields. For it has affected not only Bible and Talmud, but Halakhah, Liturgy, History and Literature as well. Conservative Judaism has slowly produced some of the synthesis that is needed to sustain a community that values scholarship but also bases its sense of commitment, belonging, obligation, of being bound to a covenant and to mitzvot in the very texts that serve as the object of the critical scalpel. But though we may still await fuller articulations of this synthesis, we ought to understand and acknowledge that our views of biblical authority, and of the role of halakhah in Rabbinic times and in the contemporary world are not idiosyncratic by any means. They must be understood, and can be made persuasive, in the light of the philosophical and psychological elements of the historical consciousness on which we have here focused attention.

As a philosopher writing for this symposium, there is perhaps a bit more that I should say. It is relatively easy to analyze, using philosophical tools, the problem of critical scholarship and belief as it affected other fields, such as Bible or Talmud, for there the problem arose very dramatically and identifiably in the last two centuries. But what should be said about the field of philosophy itself? Does it, or did it, also suffer from the sort of dissonance of which we have spoken? In a way, the analogy clearly breaks down, because it is simply not true that philosophers at one time argued uncritically but now, as the result of some revolution of thought, they have changed. Uncritical philosophy is simply no philosophy at all. Indeed, to the extent that philosophers were ever really critical (e.g., Maimonides on creation, corporeality, and the afterlife, or Gersonides on divine omniscience, or Spinoza on nearly everything), they were greeted with a range of reactions from mild suspicion to excommunication. The need to subject religious texts and ideas to the same critical scrutiny one uses for religiously "neutral" topics is thus not new for philosophy. It is, rather, of its essence (and thus Judaism's perennial discomfiture with its philosophers).

Yet there is something that can and should be said about the field of Jewish religious philosophy and the historical/critical method. It is this: the consciousness of history, not surprisingly, is *itself* possessed of a history. It, too, developed and continues to develop, and that process has had an interesting and potentially profound effect on the way in which philosophers now see the significance of history for religion and belief. For example, in the Jewish world, one of the first to feel both the dissonance produced by the new scholarship, and to begin charting out a resolution, was Nahman Krochmal. He did indeed accept the assumptions of the historical method, and he ingeniously converted those assumptions from threats to tradition into supports. That is, he articulated a concept of human history in which the historical flow was essential for unfolding the reality of the universe. Krochmal dignified history, and made it non-threatening to the traditionalist, because he made it into the arena in which the divine Absolute Spirit manifests itself and reaches the consummation of self-consciousness. Like Maimonides, Krochmal believed that ultimate reality lay in the realm of ideas, or spirit, but he affirmed the creative, innovative role of history in a way that Maimonides never did, and which the eighth principle of faith discussed earlier suggests he never would have.

But at the core of Krochmal's thought was a particular way of viewing history. He was still very much tied to a conception of history which made it the stage on which events, assumed to have an objective, independent existence, get played out, revealed, and even developed. The revolution in historical consciousness in the eighteenth and nineteenth centuries brought us from the point of a conception of a timeless and eternal absolute reality to a sequential conception that affirmed the value of significance of the flow of events. An evolution has, however, taken place since then, and continues to take place; like the change in historical consciousness in the last century or two, this change also is parallel to changes in scientific views and methods. Briefly, it is this: because of the work of philosophers and theologians such as Rudolf Bultmann, R. G. Collingwood, Van A. Harvey, D. Z. Phillips, and Nelson Goodman, among many others, we now need no longer think of history simply as a stage for the succession of events. Indeed, the import of the work of these thinkers is that it may make no more sense to speak of discrete, objectively existing historical events than it apparently does to speak of objectively existing ultimate particles in the physical world. Just as physicists have come more and more to speak of relation between observer and event, of *participation* of the observer in the event, as being one of the primitive building blocks of our world, so have philosophers of history and theologians come to emphasize not the unfolding of discrete events, but rather the role of consciousness in *determining* history. As Collingwood argued in *The Idea of History,* we cannot simply discover an historical event, because the event depends ultimately on those experiencing and observing it. Human consciousness, in other words, may be an irreducible element in the understanding of history, and it may just be that we will have to get used to thinking of history as being *constructed* rather than being *discovered*.

This represents the next step beyond the profound change in historical conception which helped bring Conservative Judaism into the world. That is, the idea of one permanent, unchangeable reality impervious to history gave way to a notion that reality is diffuse and changing and that even the truth about God can only be understood as residing in history. This posed serious problems for traditional belief and required a new synthesis. Krochmal was an excellent example of this, indeed a paradigm for several generations of scholars who grappled with the tension. Now we find that the idea of an objective series of events residing in history is giving way to a conception of history as a product of *thought* and of *consciousness*, rather than as a static stage for the presentation of reality. This further augmentation of the human role in the "construction of the world," so to speak, is bound to have serious ramifications. Affected will be our views of what reality itself is, and thus, as believers, of what the relationship of the human and the divine is—indeed, what the divine itself is. All of this will, unlike the previous shift in historical thinking which vexed the textual scholars, affect *primarily* the philosophers. And it seems safe to predict that the second century of Conservative Judaism will be affected by it as well, though we have not yet clearly formulated the problem, let alone produced a proponent of a new resolution.

Scholarship and the Rabbinate: A Vital Symbiosis

Gilbert S. Rosenthal

The Nature of *Wissenschaft des Judentums*

Our late master and teacher, Professor Louis Ginzberg, described *Wissenschaft des Judentums* as "the most striking gift of the nineteenth century to Jews and Judaism." It was so terribly important, noted Ginzberg, because Emancipation, Reform and Zionism, the three greatest phenomena of that era, rested on its foundation. Moreover, *Wissenschaft des Judentums* is a genuinely Jewish creation and although outside influences have affected it, Ginzberg wrote that "its origins lay entirely within the fold."[1] What were the major characteristics of *Wissenschaft?* What were its goals and methods? What did it seek to do for Judaism and Jews? And are its goals and methods still meaningful for us today?

Wissenschaft des Judentums is the scientific and scholarly knowledge of Judaism. It uses the technique of criticism and shuns *pilpulistic* reasoning. It views Judaism as organismic growth, recognizing development and evolution. In the words of Professor Ginzberg, it sees Judaism as "historical process and not merely theological doctrine."[2] It is a combination of the old and new; it seeks to live in two worlds simultaneously—namely, the Jewish and the secular. It insists that we must rethink the nature of Judaism and, in the view of Chancellor Ismar Schorsch, it is the "primary vehicle for translating the ideas, institutions and values of an ancient and oriental religion into equivalent or related Western categories and beyond that serve[s] as arbiter of what is authentic Judaism and the source for new and diverse self-perception."[3] It seeks to conceptualize our thinking; it is problem-oriented, systematic, and ultimately synthetic.[4]

In its earlier phase, *Wissenschaft* posited the view that it held the key to gaining respect in the gentile world as well as the opportunities for civic and political emancipation and equality. Leopold Zunz put it succinctly: "The exclusion of Jews from citizenship and the neglect of *Wissenschaft des Judentums* go hand in hand."[5] The fathers of *Wissenschaft,* including Zunz, Abraham Geiger, Isaak Markus Jost, and others believed that "a meticulous and unprejudiced study of the past could become a force for revitalization" as well as a powerful social force.[6] These founding fathers were anti-obscurantists, hence, often anti-rabbinical because they viewed the rabbis of their day as medievalists and obstacles to the emancipation of Jewry in western Europe and the development of reason and modern thinking among Jews. In the case of Jost, he went so far as to denigrate the body of rabbinic literature and talmudic development.

Wissenschaft viewed religious reforms as essential to the emancipation of Jewry and its emergence from the cocoon of medievalism into the sunlight of the modern world. Some, such as Geiger, became radical reformers; others, such as Zunz and Zacharias Frankel were moderate reformers or conservatives. And a few, such as Samuel David Luzzatto, resisted religious changes, compartmentalized their critical views and scientific studies, and buried their doubts.

The Role of the Jewish Theological Seminary

These, then, are the basic characteristics of the *Wissenschaft des Judentums* which the Jewish Theological Seminary carried to the New World and planted in this soil. Solomon Schechter had been profoundly influenced by Isaac Hirsch Weiss, Meir Lector Friedmann, Heinrich Graetz, Zacharias Frankel and other luminaries of the European *Wissenschaft* school of thought. Moreover, Schechter sought to duplicate the ideals and techniques of the Jewish Theological Seminary of Breslau, the creation of Zacharias Frankel. Frankel had endeavored to translate his "positive-historical" approach to Judaism into the training of rabbis in his new rabbinical seminary. Breslau sought to balance traditional piety and modern scholarship; it attempted to train rabbis who would be at home in the old but also familiar with the new. Schechter was committed to free, critical, unfettered inquiry; his faculty would include men of disparate views and enjoy the fullest measure of academic freedom. Thus, he employed the peerless faculty that included Louis Ginzberg, Alexander Marx, Israel Friedlaender, Israel Davidson, and Mordecai M. Kaplan. He established the premier Jewish library and manuscript collection.

And he encouraged his colleagues and young alumni to produce critical and scholarly works of Jewish learning. His commitment to pluralistic viewpoints was singularly impressive:

> I would consider my work . . . a complete failure if this institution would not in the future produce such extremes as, on the one side, the raving mystic who would denounce me as a sober Philistine; on the other side, an advanced critic who would rail at me as a narrowminded fanatic; while a third devotee of strict orthodoxy would raise pretext against any critical view I may entertain.[8]

These words proved to be prophetic: The same Seminary that boasted of its naturalist-humanist philosopher, Mordecai M. Kaplan, also added to its faculty in later years the neo-Hasid and mystic, Abraham Joshua Heschel.[9]

To be sure, the old passions of European *Wissenschaft* had abated. There was no longer the need to utilize *Wissenschaft* for emancipation or civil rights: American Jews were already equal citizens by 1902 when Schechter arrived at these shores. Nor was it necessary to create "a historical consciousness that could serve as a base for a voluntaristic secular Jewish community" since such a community already existed here.[10] Still, some of the old *Wissenschaft* drives were needed. For example, *Wissenschaft* strove mightily to wrest the field of Judaic studies from the hands of gentiles and bestow scholarly respectability on Jewish scholarship, as Zunz put it. This was still very much a desideratum in American universities where courses in Judaica were nonexistent and where Bible and Hebrew were taught by none-too-sympathetic gentiles or apostates whose chief goals seemed often to be the denigration of Judaism and its categorization as a mere prelude to Christianity.

Additionally, there were lingering echoes of *Wissenschaft's* anti-rabbinical sentiments. Professor Ginzberg, for example, rarely concealed his disdain for the pulpit rabbinate even as he spoke sneeringly of the pants manufacturers who made up the lay leadership of the American synagogues. Also, the mood of scholarship at the Seminary was often one of pure wisdom, learning for its own sake, scholarship that was impeccable philologically, historically and critically, but devoid of *neshamah* — of heart and soul and passion. It was too often little more than desiccated scholastic exercises with little meaning for the American Jew.

With it all, the Seminary did succeed in holding aloft the banner of critical, historical, and analytical Jewish scholarship for all to admire and emulate. And if its alumni were inspired to scholarly pursuits either as full-time academicians or part-time scholars who served full-time congregations, it was due to the extraordinary achievements of Marx, Ginzberg, Davidson and their contemporaries as well as their heirs, Saul Lieberman, Boaz Cohen, Louis Finkelstein, Robert Gordis and a score of other worthies.

The Transmission of *Wissenschaft* to the Laity

May a rabbi accept the critical conclusions of *Wissenschaft* without undermining belief in God? Is it possible to transmit the enduring legacy of *Wissenschaft* to the laity? May a pulpit rabbi employ the findings of critical-historical scholarship and convey them to his congregants without undermining belief? Or is it fatuous to try to emancipate Jewish scholarship from the confinements of the four cubits of the academy or seminary or university and disseminate it to the broader Jewish world?

In the first place, I have experienced no conflict between the conclusions of the *Wissenschaft* school and my faith in God. I have been able, for example, to accept the main conclusions of the documentary view of the Bible and still believe that it reflects the Divine will. In my personal religious faith, I view historical development as the unfolding of the Divine purpose in human and national events even as I conceive of evolution as the unfolding of the Divine purpose in nature. Whether this world is 4 billion years old or 5,747 years old is irrelevant, in my opinion; whether the Bible was the work of one or a few or many God-intoxicated individuals is secondary, in my judgment. What matters is: behind it all there is a *Ribono shel Olam*. Hence, my understanding of halakhah as an evolving, developing organism which responded to social, political, economic, and ethical changes, and which is the masterly creation of thousands of sages in no way diminishes my reverence for the sacred kernel that is embedded within. I believe that halakhah is our authoritative guide in life for we are a *legal* religion. Unlike Pauline Christianity, we view the deed as more important than the creed; we believe that action is greater than faith alone.

But I do not believe that the Law is the Law and must be observed without carping or questioning. My critical studies of Jewish law and institutions have convinced me that there is a higher purpose to the Law so that I approach the mitzvot teleologically. I believe, with the Psalmist, that "the Torah of the Lord is perfect, it restores the soul." I accept the view of Proverbs, as interpreted by the sages, that "its ways are ways of pleasantness and all its paths are peace." And I endorse the view of Law that "the mitzvot were given to purify the creatures." It is, of course, not always easy to detect the sacred kernel within, and *Wissenschaft* may not be of great help in this area. *Wissenschaft* helps us to understand how a particular law or institution developed historically; it cannot uncover the sacred element within. That, I suspect, is dependent upon our leap of faith: we either perceive divinity within or we don't. For me, personally, the biblical core is sacred and that core is the revelation at Sinai and preeminently the Ten Commandments. The rest flows from that source and the halakhah and mitzvot are expansions on or crystallizations of those basic norms and tenets. The sacred kernel is the thrust of Judaism to engender justice, righteousness, compassion, mercy, truth, love, and peace; the mitzvot are attempts to concretize those norms and achieve those ideals. But the sacred kernel is there *not* because *Wissenschaft* scholars determine so; rather it is there because generations of saints, prophets, sages, and laypersons sanctified it with love, zeal, passion, devotion — yes, even blood!

I believe that the *Wissenschaft* approach is not only meaningful but also vital for the laity of the Conservative movement and three decades as a pulpit rabbi have reinforced that conclusion. To be sure, much of the *Wissenschaft* program is, as we have noted, obsolete and some is simply obnoxious. But its analysis of Judaism as organismic growth that has undergone historical development or evolution over the centuries; its stress on the need to blend the old and new, tradition and change, past and present; its commitment to truth objectively pursued and to reason rather than the irrational; its recognition that Judaism, like other institutions and establishments must be studied scientifically and historically — these elements of the *Wissenschaft* approach are still meaningful and especially for Conservative Judaism which, after all, is essentially the offspring of that school of thought.

In preaching, I often invoke the methods of *Wissenschaft* and I encourage my homiletics students to follow the same path. Recently, for example, I dealt with two controversial issues that agitated the Jewish community and caused much heated debate. The first concerned the

United States Supreme Court's ruling that an Orthodox Jew may not wear a yarmulke while on military duty. The second was the widely publicized visit of Pope John Paul II to the synagogue in Rome. The first issue was clearly halakhic: May a Jew go about his business without a head covering or is he required by law of the Torah or sages to cover up? The second issue seemed to have no clear-cut halakhic guidelines but was of historic interest, namely, were there historic precedents for a papal visit and what have been the relationships of the papacy vis-à-vis the Jewish people over the centuries?

I presume that in examining the first subject the Orthodox preacher would quote the relevant passages in the *Shulḥan Arukh, Orah Ḥayyim,* that "one may not walk four cubits without a head covering" and leave it at that. Since the Divine Law is crystal clear, an Orthodox Jew really has no business in the military if this ruling stands. As to the matter of the papal visit, most Orthodox rabbis would presumably snap, "*goyishe zakhn!* What business has a *shul* or rabbi hosting a priest anyway?"

My approach was quite different. I employed the *Wissenschaft* method of historical and critical analysis of the origin and development of the head covering in Judaism. I posed two basic questions: (1) What is the origin of the head covering? (2) Must a Jew wear a *kippah* at all times? Naturally I checked the normal halakhic sources, notably the *Shulḥan Arukh* and its classic commentaries. I sifted through hints in the Bible; I studied key passages in the Talmud (for example, *Kiddushin* 29b-31a). But I hardly stopped there. I turned to the *Jewish Encyclopedia* and *Encyclopedia Judaica* and checked out the many references and sources. I also dug into the *Encyclopedia Talmudit* for halakhic and legal references and responsa material. Some of the historical studies of *Wissenschaft* scholars such as Israel Abrahams and Jacob Z. Lauterbach were valuable to me in my research. Then I boiled down the bulky technical material into a semi-popular sermon lecture, the gist of which I subsequently published in my Temple bulletin. My conclusions were: (1) The origin of head coverings remains unclear; (2) There is a long-standing custom that head coverings are required, certainly at prayer; (3) Before the *Shulḥan Arukh* (sixteenth century) there were no clear-cut halakhic requirements.

Not surprisingly, in approaching the matter of the papal visit to the Roman synagogue, I turned to the history books and most particularly to the research of my teacher, Professor Salo W. Baron, as well as the studies of Solomon Grayzel, Edward Synan, James Parkes,

Cecil Roth, Attilio Milano, Herman Vogelstein, Paul Rieger, and other students of Italian Jewish history and the relationship of the papacy towards the Jews. Since there seemed to be no halakhic issue at stake here but rather a matter of historical precedent, I wanted to learn: (1) Was there indeed precedent for a pope visiting a synagogue or the Jewish community? (2) What were the relationships of the popes to the Jews over the centuries? (3) Would there be a positive value to such a visit today? The material proved to be rich and somewhat confusing, a reflection of the curiously ambivalent attitude of the popes towards Jews and Judaism, an attitude that can best be described as a mélange of love and hate, tolerance and contempt. The sermon-lecture I delivered distilled many hours of reading and research into perhaps 25 minutes of a didactic talk that included a dash of inspiration as befits a sermon. I then published it in my Temple bulletin and compressed its essence in a letter subsequently published in the *New York Times*. The point is clear: I utilized *Wissenschaft* techniques in dealing with vital and contemporary issues that cried out for interpretation and understanding. For those of us in the Conservative rabbinate, it is not only a historical imperative but a mitzvah to analyze, reflect critically and historically, and react appropriately.

Needless to say, the *Wissenschaft* methodology permeates my formal teaching both at the Seminary where I teach homiletics and in my congregation where I teach classes in Bible, Talmud, Jewish theology and Jewish history every year. In fact, I may teach as many as three courses a term. I believe that the search for truth is a great mitzvah and that, as Maimonides put it so beautifully, "We must accept the truth from whatever source." *Wissenschaft* helps clarify origins, roots, sources, the purposes of the mitzvot, the *telos* or goal of institutions. It shows us how we reacted to past challenges and how we searched for a greater sense of divinity and evolved by imbuing our institutions with an enhanced moral sensitivity. It really does not matter what the origins were and what pagan antecedents gave birth to Jewish laws and institutions. So what if our Shabbat was "borrowed" from the Babylonian-Assyrian *Shapattu*? We transmuted it and imbued it with an ethical motif; we stripped it of any pagan themes and thoroughly Judaized it, as Yehezkel Kaufmann, Umberto Cassuto, E. A. Speiser and other giants of *Wissenschaft* have proved. Here we see how critical scholarship enhances rather than undermines our appreciation of the genius of Judaism.

In my teaching, I approach each subject critically with an eye to the historical development of laws and institutions and with a dispassionate view of the personalities we study. I project a non-fundamentalist view of revelation and the Bible, preferring to consider Torah the work of many hands compiled in the course of many centuries as our ancestors groped their way to God and a moral code. I paint the biblical heroes as they were: warts and all—likewise with rabbinic sages. Thus, when teaching the Book of Samuel, I did not gloss over the embarrassing shortcomings of King David. Nor did I extenuate the character blemishes of Rabbi Eliezer ben Hyrcanus when we learned about him in *Pirkei Avot* or tractate *Berakhot*.

When I teach a law or a legal institution, I always view it developmentally. For example, when we studied chapter eight of *Bava Kama* and learned about the principle of *lex talionis* ("an eye for an eye"), I sought to demonstrate how the law progressed from a literal application of the rule (*mamash*) to five-fold compensation (*mamon*). Similarly, I spent many hours in teaching (and preaching to) my congregation about the role of women in Judaism, how it has changed, wherein women are seriously disadvantaged, and which way we must go to truly emancipate and protect Jewish women from exploitation and prejudice. All of these courses and sermons served as preparation for a greater ritual role for women in my Temple and I deliberately chose the *Wissenschaft* technique in order to demonstrate the validity of the longings of our female worshipers for a portion in synagogue life and communal leadership.

I try to convey this critical approach to my Seminary students because I believe that it is essential for the rabbi to be at home in both classical sources as well as critical studies so that he may teach his people the modern meaning of Judaism. The Orthodox content themselves with quotation; the Reform are generally more concerned about contemporary sources to the exclusion of the classics. Our cachet is reinterpretation of the classics in today's light. But *Wissenschaft* must be built on classical Jewish learning. As Ginzberg showed in his essay on Frankel to which I alluded previously, we must shape students of Torah and teachers who combine classical learning with modern, critical scholarship. Failing that, we end up either with yeshivah types or with savants or dilettantes. I am also convinced that we cannot inspire piety, love for Jewish learning, commitment to mitzvot, and genuine *kavvanah* (devotion) unless our *Wissenschaft* is grounded in knowledge of classical texts including the Bible and commentaries, Talmud, Midrash, etc.

The Ideology of Conservative Judaism

Does our laity *know* what Conservative Judaism stands for? Do our people read our great volumes? Therein lies the rub: for truth to tell, the average congregant is as ignorant of our theological position and halakhic norms as he is oblivious to the findings of astrophysics. And we are paying the price as more and more of our elders spurn our teachings and the younger generation of Conservative offspring hemorrhage into other movements, or simply drift away into limbo.

Hence, it is imperative that we formulate our ideological and philosophical position as quickly as possible and present it in a clear and unambiguous formulation and precise platform as a benchmark and goal: a benchmark to guide our people and a goal towards which they may aspire. I am convinced that our ideology is *not* too difficult or abstruse for the average layperson. Nor is it something to which the rabbis and scholars may adhere but not the people. It is true to the tradition while cognizant of the needs of today; it is a middle-of-the-road approach that eschews extremes and fanaticism. The platform of our movement is protean and kaleidoscopic enough to encompass the broadest spectrum of views and satisfy the neo-Hasid on the one hand and the ultra-rationalist on the other. Above all, it is a platform to which I personally can subscribe without doing violence to my conscience or sacrificing my commitment to reason and modernity. A preacher or teacher should never posit a position in which he does not believe: that is hypocrisy at its worst.

An Inspiring Thought

Many years ago, I remember hearing a particularly inspirational address at a Seminary ordination assembly delivered by my teacher, Professor Robert Gordis. He discussed two Hebrew terms: *talmid ḥakham* and *lamdan*. He noted that not all of us may become a *talmid ḥakham*, a scholar. Some have it; some don't. But he suggested that each of us can become a *lamdan*, a "learner." We can all devote some hours each day to learning Bible, Talmud, Midrash, Hebrew, Jewish philosophy, history, liturgy, etc. And that ought to be the goal of all alumni of our Seminary even as it must become the avocation of every Jewish layperson. Without such a national pastime for Jews, we degenerate into an archaeological artifact rather than a living, vibrant people. Pianist Artur Rubinstein once mused: "If I miss a day of practice, I know it. If I miss three days, the audience knows it. And if

I miss a week, the whole world knows it." So it is with our rabbis: sooner or later our laity recognizes our scholarship or lack thereof. It is the same with our people: If we miss out on Jewish learning, eventually the world knows it and we will have lost our *raison d'être* and forsaken our Divine mission. We are a people, insisted Saadia Gaon, by virtue of our Torah. I believe that holds just as true today as in the tenth century when he wrote it. Can we convey this idea to our people? Therein lies the challenge.

NOTES

1. Louis Ginzberg, *Students, Scholars and Saints* (Philadelphia: Jewish Publication Society, 1945), p. 195 in his essay on Zacharias Frankel. Incidentally, Professor Ginzberg suggested that Elijah Gaon of Vilna founded the scientific approach to texts.
2. *Ibid., p. 215.*
3. Ismar Schorsch, *"Historical Consciousness in Modern Judaism," Year Book* of the Leo Baeck Institute XXVIII (London, 1983), pp. 367-437. I am grateful to Professor Schorsch for providing me with this important reference.
4. *Ibid.,* p. 418. See Solomon Schechter's essay on Zunz in his *Studies in Judaism* (Philadelphia: Jewish Publication Society, 1945), III, pp. 88f. and 157. Cf. his *Seminary Addresses and Other Papers* (New York: Burning Bush Press, 1959), p. 2.
5. Cf. Leopold Zunz, *Haderashot B'Yisrael* (Jerusalem; Mossad Bialik, 1954), Introduction, p. 34.
6. See Schorsch, "From Wolfenbüttel to Wissenschaft—the Divergent Paths of Isaak Markus Jost and Leopold Zunz," *Year Book* of the Leo Baeck Institute XXII (London, 1977), pp. 109-128.
7. See Schorsch, "Zacharias Frankel and the European Origins of Conservative Judaism," *Judaism,* Vol. 30, No. 3 (Summer 1981), pp. 344-354. Cf. Ginzberg, *op. cit.,* p. 24.
8. Cf. Schechter, *Seminary Addresses, op. cit.,* p. 24.
9. See my *Contemporary Judaism: Patterns of Survival* (New York: Human Sciences Press, 1986), pp. 156-169 and *passim.*
10. Schorsch, "Historical Consciousness in Modern Judaism," *op. cit.,* p. 437.

Teaching Conservative Judaism

Yaakov G. Rosenberg

I have had the best of both worlds during the past thirty-seven years of my rabbinate. Twenty-nine of them were spent as a pulpit rabbi and the past eight as a member of the Seminary administration and faculty. My answers to the questions posed to me for this Symposium on Scholarship and Belief will be a reflection of both areas of my service.

1. How do you transpose/transmit the wisdom of *Wissenschaft* to the laity?

By and large most of our congregants and many, if not most, of our rabbinical students share a common lack of background, academically and experientially, in traditional Jewish living and Jewish learning. Both groups, however, do share a common intellectual and academic background in terms of an undergraduate collegiate experience.

As a result of the above, there is an openness to intellectual inquiry which refuses to recognize any realms as being forbidden to intelligent scholarly and critical investigation.

Wissenschaft des Judentums, meaning a scholarly, critical study of all classical Jewish religious texts, not only Rabbinics, has been extended now to include all biblical texts, including the Pentateuch. One of the best essays on *Wissenschaft* is the Introduction written by Chancellor Ismar Schorsch in *The Structure of Jewish History,* the Graetz volume he translated and edited. Up until fifteen or twenty years ago, all students were exposed to the critical study of all texts—rabbinic and biblical—except the Five Books of Moses. Now even the latter have been included. As a matter of fact, the Seminary's Melton Research Center has even published curricular material on Genesis and Exodus by Nahum Sarna and Moshe Greenberg, respectively.

It seems to me, therefore, that via the formal discourses delivered from the pulpit, the more informal — but serious — framework of the congregational Adult Education classes, the various havurah study groups, the increasing use of Torah Study Shabbatot/weekends with a Scholar-in-Residence — all of these and others are legitimate media through which the best and most authentic critical studies may be presented for absorption by non-scholarly but intelligent lay consumers. Parenthetically, may I suggest that it would be good to be able to make real a dream shared with us by our esteemed Chancellor Emeritus, Rabbi Gerson D. Cohen — that there be issued two to three times a year a journal that would bring to our laity the latest in the "World of Jewish *Wissenschaft*."

2. How can/do you use *Wissenschaft* to deepen the religious sentiments, commitments and understanding of Conservative congregants?

In his volume *Understanding Conservative Judaism*, Rabbi Robert Gordis quotes Franz Rosenzweig, " 'If all the Wellhausen Theories are correct and the Samaritans really had the better text, our faith would not be shaken.' " Then Rabbi Gordis adds, "That the Torah is Mosaic in essence is increasingly recognized among scholars, but the ultimate disposition of this issue does not affect the religious validity of the revelation which is the Torah's source" (p. 69).

Rabbi Simon Greenberg in *Foundations of a Faith* says, "The third camp consists of those who are equally insistent upon retaining the concept of a revealed Law, but would interpret the concept in the widest possible sense as to time and plan, and in the narrowest possible sense as to its provisions . . . They would scrutinize the provisions of the codes in the light of modern historical, psychological and philological studies" (p. 97).

Our colleague Professor Fritz Rothschild in a paper entitled "The Bible as Sacred Scripture" expresses a dominant view in our movement. "The Jew who is prepared to accept the Bible as Sacred Scripture does not have to sacrifice his intellectual freedom and the right and duty to scholarly research and scientific investigation." In an article published in *Conservative Judaism* (Vol. 31, No. 2) entitled "Revelation: The Embarrassment and the Necessity," Rothschild writes, "I suspect that despite our critical scholarly education many of us when tested in a lie detector would show that in our hearts we strongly believe that the Torah contains God's word and will."

From the days of Zacharias Frankel, through Schechter, Ginsberg, Finkelstein, Cohen and Schorsch in our own days—all of them represented, and the last three—may they live to be 120—still represent a commitment to religious ideas and practices as mitzvot, however differently they may conceive of the *Mitzaveh,* the Commanding One, and His relationship to the mitzvah and the *mitzuveh,* the commanded one. The commitment of all of the above to *Wissenschaft*—meaning a critical study of all texts—did not prevent them from retaining a genuine commitment to a religious lifestyle on a day-to-day basis that combined mitzvot between mensch and God and mensch to mensch.

Our revered teacher Rabbi Greenberg says, "I believe that my primary duty in life as a Rabbi is to preserve a knowledge of the Torah among Jews in particular and in the world generally, and to help people live in accordance with its precepts" (*Foundations of a Faith,* p. 83).

Although it is true that in the case of all of our teachers mentioned above, they all came from knowledgeable parents and varying degrees of religious commitment in their own homes, we are today blessed with a generation of Seminary graduates as rabbis and scholars who, despite the lack of parental and home models, in many if not most instances, nonetheless acquired knowledge of Torah and commitment to mitzvot on their own, with the help of rabbis, teachers, USY, Camps Ramah and Israeli experiences.

3. Do you ever present a theological or ideological view to your congregation which differs from your own for the purpose of making Jewish theology more palatable and more acceptable to your congregants?

I have always felt religiously obligated to accept all Jews at whatever level of sincere commitment they may have at a given time. While doing so, I have always urged continued study, investigation and inquiry that will enable the individual to grow from wherever he is to where we might like him to be, recognizing the pluralism represented in what we understand by Schechter's "Catholic Israel," as understood and interpreted by our masters and teachers since his day.

4. Do you feel Conservative ideology (however you define it) is too hard for many congregants to grasp? If so, should this be

considered a problem and what should be done about it? Specifically, how should rabbis be taught to handle It?

In dealing with Conservative ideology, I think the time has come for us to dare to put into print what the fundamental concepts of Conservative Judaism are in the twentieth and twenty-first centuries, based not only upon the writings of the founders and fathers of the movement, but also including the common denominators as found among the scholars and teachers of our day.

The Task Force on Conservative Ideology — comprised as it is of representatives of virtually all shades within our movement — will succeed in presenting us with a legitimate view of pluralism within Conservative Judaism. I trust that this will mean parameters of theology and mitzvot beyond which one may no longer be considered a Conservative Jew. Please note, I did not say "may no longer be considered a Jew." I do feel that we desperately need a clear understanding of what Conservative Judaism is and wherein it differs essentially from Reform, Orthodox and Reconstructionist Judaism. Hopefully, this process will not only highlight and explicate our legitimate differences but also the aspects and principles of Judaism that bind all of us. However, we must cease trying to be all things to all people.

Conservative Judaism in the twenty-first century must emerge with greater clarity, not bound to the point of view of one specific *gadol* (pre-eminent sage) of the past or present, but as a result of what is shared in common when you study the writings of all of our Seminary sages.

Let us not lightly and nonchalantly bandy about the rabbinic *eilu v'eilu*, "both these and those are the words of the living God." We know full well that *eilu v'eilu* assumed a specific framework of halakhic practice more than it did aggadic belief. Within a specific framework we, too, with the help of God, will be able to proclaim honestly and forthrightly "both these and those are the words of the living God."

An Unscientific Postscript

David Weiss Halivni

In a larger essay in *Midrash, Mishnah and Gemara,* we argued that the highest level of the study of Torah is *Torah lishmah,* the study of Torah purely for its own sake. To be sure, studying Torah for the sake of observance is a mitzvah, but it is a *derivative* mitzvah stemming from the fact that one cannot observe a mitzvah without knowing how to observe it. Such study shares, as it were, in the credit of observance, but it has no credit of its own. To fulfill maximally the mitzvah of Torah study as a commandment by itself (with its own full credit), it has to be undertaken for the sake of itself, for the sake of the mitzvah of Talmud Torah. If one eats maror for the sake of matzah, one detracts from the mitzvah of eating maror. Similarly, if one studies for the sake of observance, one detracts from the mitzvah of Talmud Torah. Each mitzvah must be performed for its own sake.

In the essay mentioned above, I singled out the commentary of the Rashbam on the Torah (and its ilk) as the highest genre of *Torah lishmah.* Rashbam, one of the greatest *poskim* (adjudicators) of his time, often explained the text against practical halakhah, to which he strictly adhered. He saw in this type of commentary, free of the restraints of practical halakhah, the epitome of the fulfillment of the study of Torah. He undoubtedly recited *birkat hatorah* every time he sat down to compose and write his commentary. It was Torah for Torah's sake, the highest level of fulfilling a mitzvah.

It follows then that one has a better chance to fulfill the mitzvah of Talmud Torah when one studies subjects that have no practical application. Rabbi Israel Salanter explained that, "When studying laws that have practical application, one is usually biased in favor of a particular conclusion . . . The value of learning is thereby diminished . . . But when one studies laws that have no practical application . . . the value of learning is complete and the reward is full."

Rabbi Salanter was referring to the laws regarding the rebellious son and the apostate city which according to the rabbis, as is well known, have no practical significance. Yet, the rabbis recommended studying these laws for the benefit of "receiving reward." When one studies these laws, according to Rabbi Salanter, one does so without favoring one particular resolution. The study of Torah is thereby raised to a higher level. Similarly, I would suggest that when one studies a biblical law critically, *i.e.*, according to *peshat*, with no intention of changing practical halakhah, one is fulfilling the mitzvah of Talmud Torah to a higher degree than when one is studying the same law according to traditional interpretation. This is especially true if the *peshat* proves to be in conflict with traditional interpretation (as, for instance, interpreting "an eye for an eye" literally, as opposed to meaning monetary compensation). This learning is fuller, purer, having no vested interest other than the welfare of learning.

In fact, it could be argued that critical study may indirectly sensitize religious observance by making it more voluntary, more autonomous, more volitional. It may help realize that it is not the law by itself that commanded observance, but the law interacting with (human) interpretation. When one observes a mitzvah, one is, as it were, a partner with God. They share a joint enterprise. That joint enterprise is more pronounced when done critically. As long as both are part of the divine communication of the larger revelatory moment, they will act unitarily rather than disruptively.

In a forthcoming work, the present writer makes the claim that the mode of interpreting a text is *evolutionarily* determined, that the criterion of what constitutes proper interpretation was innately different for the man of antiquity than it is for the modern man. A modern religious Jew must study the Bible in a dual manner, according to the perception fitting the evolutionary "rung" of his/her ancestors and according to the perception fitting the evolutionary rung of its own. (Remember, Jewish philosophers, since the time of Philo, have urged us to study the Torah dually according to the "open meaning" and according to the hidden—philosophical meaning.)

Pertaining to observance, the modern religious Jew has to follow the interpretation of those to whom the *initial* revelation was given. God spoke to them in their language, according to their mode of interpretation. Pertaining to exegesis, he or she remains a child of his or her age following the standards of his or her time.

God could have chosen another generation to whom to reveal Himself. In that case, a different mode of interpretation would have been followed, commensurate with that generation's evolutionary state of mind. The fact that He chose whom He chose is not an accident (believers in divine providence preclude accidents in matters divine), but an indication that He wanted us to follow in the footsteps of those to whom He first revealed Himself.

Of some relevance is the current debate with respect to "original intent." Advocates of original intent claim that the American Constitution ought to be interpreted according to the intention of its originators, even when the wording of the Constitution suggests to us otherwise. Opponents of original intent either ignore the intention of the originators or hold that the intention of its originators was that each generation should interpret the Constitution according to its mode of understanding. The former argument is inapplicable to a canonized text which claims divine authority. The latter would have been unacceptable to the rabbis.

The Rashbam's fear that an insistence on study for its own sake may lead to a weakening of accepted halakhah is not substantiated. Not enough observant people have applied his method to the study of the Talmud to allow us to learn whether or not it has an appreciably adverse effect on religious behavior. There is really no inherent connection between insistence on *peshat* and deviant religious behavior. Because the people who followed what is commonly called the critical textual method, where insistence on *peshat* is paramount, were mostly non-observant, the impression was created that insistence on *peshat* (*i.e.*, critical textual study) is incompatible with religion. It need not be so. Let more observant people enter the field and the impression will change.

Contrary to some, textual critical scholarship (which we equate with insistence on *peshat* wherever it may lead) can be quite exciting, adventurous, and, given the proper intellectual climate, popular. Like its subject matter (in this respect, it is different than most other textual critical studies), Talmud criticism is dialectically quite complex, often dealing with disparate, even contradictory, components, the integration and explanation of which requires great perspicacity. In the process, it yields enormous intellectual satisfaction.

Textual critical scholarship differs from *pilpul* primarily in that the former more scrupulously adheres to the text, whereas *pilpul* is loosely connected with the text. For *pilpul*, the text serves merely as a springboard from which to launch all kinds of logical contrivances after which the text gradually recedes in importance and may ultimately disappear altogether. It is possible that part of *pilpul*'s success lies precisely in its loose connection with the text. Like aggadah, it has a liberating effect. It frees one from slavishly following the text. It offers free rein to one's imagination. It is, however, not alone in that respect. Critical scholarship too contains liberating elements. Its encounter with tradition, its newness and above all, its freedom to explore any and all avenues or directions of inquiry, gives its students a sense of release, a feeling of having been mentally emancipated.

Another prevalent misconception is that Talmud criticism defined elsewhere as "always asking who said exactly what and to whom, and how much, if any, was subsequently altered either through transmission or redaction" is disrespectful of the Sages of the Talmud. By interpreting a text differently than the Gemara, so runs the argument, it portrays the Sages as faulty and unworthy of their high caliber. In fact, however, an opposite claim can be made. By often picking out instances where the Gemara rejects the opinion of a sage (concluding with such words as *kashya*—it remains difficult, or *tiyuvta*—it is refuted), or where the Gemara designates a statement of a sage as *beduta* (invented, without a justified base), or *beruta* (outside, not on par) and interpreting them in a manner that makes the opinion or the statement of the sage more acceptable—Talmud criticism can be said to have restored the dignity of the respective sage. Moreover, in purposefully seeking out and removing forced interpretations, whether they are stated as such or not, Talmud criticism is restoring the "dignity" of the text, which in turn transfers dignity to the authors of the text. Talmud criticism compares later interpretations with the original enunciations of the authors and finds the enunciations more in line with the plain meaning than later interpreters would have it. It is more laudatory of the ability of the sages to express themselves clearly and logically than is reflected by later interpretations. Were one to capsulate the methodological difference between traditional learning and Talmud criticism, one could say that traditional learning is content to say that the sages used "logic by association" while Talmud criticism demands tougher logic.

Critical textual study is not antithetical to the belief in the divine nature of Torah. It will even enhance it, providing it remains attached to the text, remains a commentary, paying, as it were, homage to the Author of the text. By leaving exegesis and turning to thematics, western Jewish Science has lost its religious base and become secular. Had it stayed within the purview of exegesis, its findings would have been absorbed into Torah. By turning to thematics it stepped out of the circle of Torah. The western founders of Jewish Science feared that continuation of the exegetical mode would enforce the barriers between them and the non-Jewish world in whose culture they so desperately sought to be integrated. They adopted the thematic model. In the process they lost some of the Torah world.

The early Mishnah, with its minimal Scriptural reference, came closest to becoming thematical of any classical Jewish book. It overcame that through its close contact with *Midreshei Halakhah* both as its offspring (the Mishnah was excerpted from *Midreshei Halakhah*) and through the use of midrashic methods as its source for new laws. The same tannaim labored in both vineyards and the exegetical need of the tannaim of the Mishnah was satisfied by their midrashic activity. Mishnah entirely divorced from Midrash probably wouldn't have survived. Exegesis is integral to Jewish learning.

Even Maimonides in his first few chapters of the *Guide of the Perplexed* engages in exegetical discussions to give the book an exegetical character in line with traditional Jewish learning. It was impossible to break with that mode without generating shock waves affecting the whole of Jewish spiritual existence. The western founders of Jewish Science ignored those waves and as a result, remained outside of the circle of Torah. Their activities were not considered specifically Jewish and their message did not penetrate to the Jewish masses. "Whatever comes out of the text"—we said elsewhere—"is Torah." That outcome must, however, accompany the text, and show its dependency and subordination to it. Otherwise, it is not Torah. To be Torah, the text has to be a part of the Divine, which in turn, lays claim on us to express His Supremacy at all times and at all occasions. Without that expression it is not Torah, but secular literature.

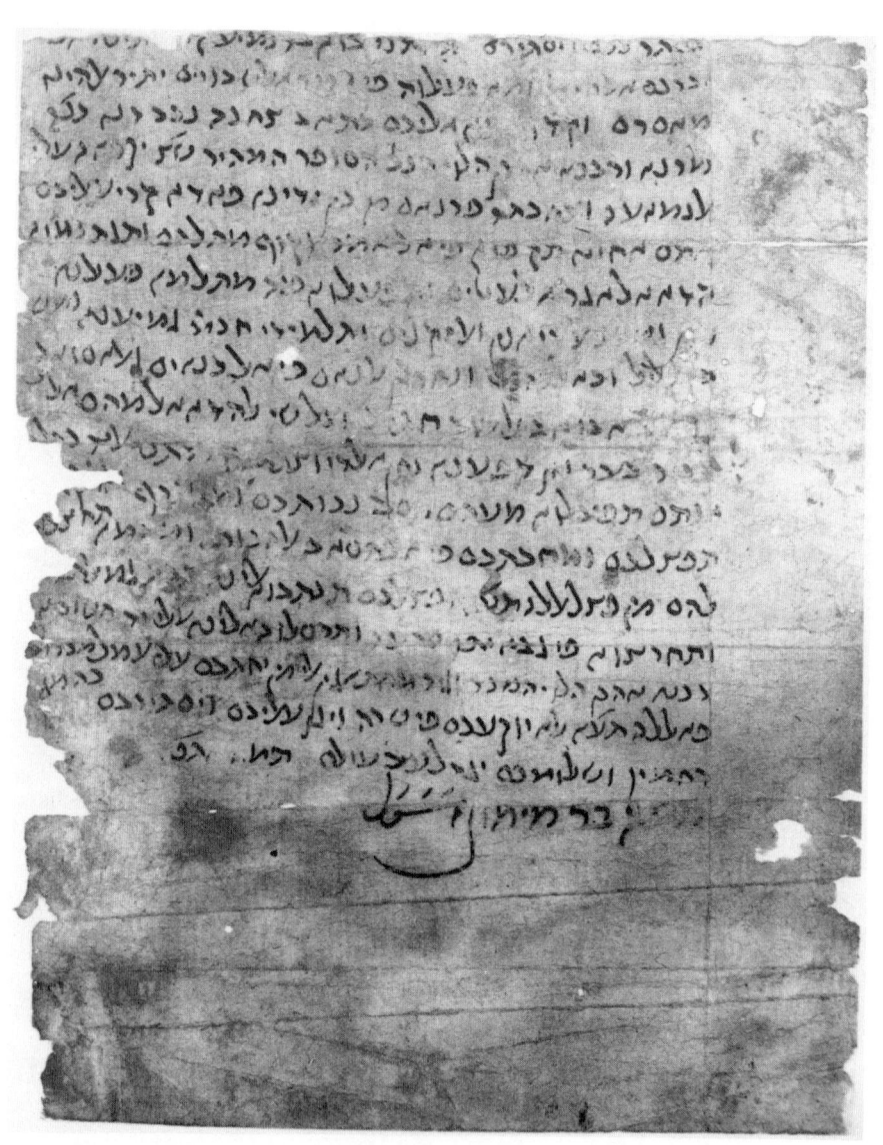

From the Seminary's Rare Book collection of Genizah fragments: an open letter, signed by Moses Maimonides and penned by his personal secretary, pleads for funds to ransom Jews taken captive in November 1168 in Bilbays, Egypt by Crusader King Amalric of Jerusalem.

Halakhah and History

Joel Roth

We tend to link the academic discipline of Rabbinics with halakhah, and for good reason. Halakhah is indisputably rabbinic. Its sources are embedded almost entirely in rabbinic literature, the authority of its decisors is predicated upon their expertise in that literature, and, for the most part, scholars of Rabbinics also served as *posekei halakhah* (arbiters). In the premodern period it was almost impossible to sever the bond between the study of Rabbinics and halakhah. They were virtually identical.

The post-*Wissenschaft* era marks a significant turning point. The linkage between rabbinic scholarship and halakhah is broken *in fact*, though the *perception* of the inextricable linkage remains. Rabbinic scholarship and halakhah become separate, though related, disciplines. The individual who served as both scholar and *posek halakhah* in the past can no longer *necessarily* be expected to serve as both today. It becomes possible to be a scholar of Rabbinics without being a halakhist, and to be a halakhist without being a scholar of Rabbinics in the modern sense. One can be both a scholar of Rabbinics and a *posek halakhah,* but if one is both, it is by virtue of his being expert in two fields and not because the two fields are one. Both rabbinic scholarship and halakhah continue to demand expertise in some shared bodies of literature which stand at their cores, but the ways in which those bodies of literature are studied and analyzed are no longer the same, nor is there any longer a *necessary* impingement of the disciplines upon each other. The dilemmas of scholarship and belief in the area of Rabbinics arise primarily, in my opinion, from the continued *perception* that Rabbinics and halakhah are virtually identical disciplines, and not just related ones. Those who are rabbinic scholars as well as those who are halakhists suffer the dilemma which arises from the very fact that each discipline is perceived by most within the Conservative movement as if it is, or ought to be, both.

Our rabbinists of European birth and background, raised in environments where *Wissenschaft* had made no inroads, must have suffered great internal anguish as a result of their own adoption of methods and ideas they had been raised to reject. Their constant adamance in finding hints and intimations of many of the various elements of critical scholarship in the writings of classical commentators must have had a purpose beyond the purely scholarly for them. The ability to link their own apparent departure from their roots to the roots themselves must have served them well psychologically, as well as academically. The chain of rabbinic scholarship remained unbroken as it entered into a new era. There was no break with tradition, for almost everything had already been anticipated by the *rishonim*. New and far-reaching conclusions that no *rishon* had ever stated became acceptable because of the conviction that the *rishonim* would have stated them if they had had access to all of the same data that could now be brought to bear. To state them now continues the process of tradition. Indeed, it is refusal to state them that constitutes the unacceptable break with tradition. *We* are the heirs of the *rishonim*, not those who refuse to follow where their footsteps lead.

These European-born giants slid adroitly into the world of *Wissenschaft*. They became its leading practitioners and contributed unparalleled works of scholarship to the field of Rabbinics. Since their scholarly work was the continuation of the tradition, the *Wissenschaft* approach itself was not a dilemma for them. But rabbinists are also halakhists traditionally, and therein lies the rub. Riding on the shoulders of the *rishonim* assuaged them psychologically as far as scholarship was concerned, but not as far as *pesak halakhah* was concerned. The hints of the *rishonim* which flow into *Wissenschaft* aid in understanding the *peshat* (the original meaning) of the Talmud. But for the purpose of *pesak halakhah*, hints are not enough. These rabbinists of ours, wise men that they were, recognized that while scholarship is best when it is dispassionate, *pesak halakhah* is not a dispassionate undertaking. One can study the *history of pesak halakhah* dispassionately, one can trace the evolution of halakhot dispassionately, but *pesak halakhah* is not either of these. Halakhically speaking, the results of critical scholarship are aggadic—non-normative, non-binding. Not so the results of *pesak halakhah,* which are normative and binding. *Pesak* itself is not a discipline to which the canons of *Wissenschaft* apply.

Because they understood these things, our early rabbinists often refrained entirely from engaging in *pesak* or, when they did engage in it, their *pesak* seemed to be entirely uninfluenced by the canons of critical scholarship. Regrettably, however, they did not explain why they refrained from *pesak* or why it seemed uninfluenced by their own critical work. This silence allowed their students to deduce that it was fear or psychological discomfort that motivated them to so refrain or to make their *pesak* sound so "Orthodox." Had they clarified that they acted as they did because *pesak* and critical scholarship are to be considered discrete disciplines, had they clarified why the canons of *Wissenschaft* are not directly applicable to *pesak,* had they themselves offered some guidance in the ways that the results of critical scholarship can be legitimately employed in *pesak halakhah,* they would have served us better. But, alas, they did not.

Significant misunderstandings of the nature of the halakhic process may have been caused by this silence of theirs. Their students, perceiving rabbinic scholarship and halakhah to be inextricably intertwined, and convinced that the silence of their teachers was caused by fear or psychological discomfort rather than the severing of the *necessary* connection between rabbinic scholarship and *pesak halakhah,* fell into several erroneous patterns—patterns that were not corrected by those who could have done so. To some of these we now turn our attention.

The greatest error, it seems to me, stems from the confusion of history with halakhah. If rabbinic scholarship and halakhah are inextricable, and if rabbinic scholarship demonstrates incontrovertibly that there are historical influences within and upon *piskei halakhah* (legal rulings), and if it demonstrates thereby that there is such a thing as the history *of* halakhah, the erring student can easily succumb to the trap of confusing history with halakhah. This error is widely reflected in *piskei halakhah* advocated by some within the Conservative movement, and usually takes one of two different guises. First, it occurs when some historical precedent is quoted with the intimation that the fact of its existence *ipso facto* validates its adoption or validates its being utilized as the grounds for the abrogation or modification of current practice. The fact, for example, that there is historical precedent for patrilineal descent no more justifies the adoption of the patrilineal principle today than would an historical precedent for mixing meat and milk justify the abrogation of the normative prohibition against mixing them. Can one imagine advocating rescinding the abolition of slavery or women's suffrage in America because there are historical precedents that allow slavery or that deny suffrage to women?

The ability to refer to an historical precedent may simplify the work of the *posek* just as the adoption of a previous *da'at yaḥid* (lone opinion), for example, is a simpler halakhic step than adopting a position for which there is no precedent whatsoever, but it is not the existence of that precedent which validates its adoption in the present. Valid, reasonable and defensible arguments in favor of adopting it must be offered. Careful analysis of the consequences of abrogating the current practice must be undertaken. Issues of the weight of precedent vs. modification of practice must be considered. To argue that the existence of an historical precedent allows or validates its adoption confuses history with halakhah. Indeed, it ignores the canon of *pesak* that halakhic decisions require halakhic defense in favor of the historical canon in which the conclusive demonstration of a fact is sufficient to establish it as fact. Historical fact alone cannot establish current halakhah.

A second error arising from the confusion of history with halakhah occurs when one seeks to argue in favor of a change in halakhic precedent from the fact that the history of halakhah demonstrates that halakhah has always evolved or accommodated to new realities. Translating this claim into a statement of purported *pesak* results in an argument that sounds like this: Since halakhah has always been able to evolve and to accommodate to new realities, and since X is a new reality, we declare that the halakhah is henceforth accommodated to that reality. This type of argument has become so widespread in some circles that those who question its halakhic validity are looked upon as having rejected one of the canons of Conservative halakhah!

This, too, reflects the confusion of history with halakhah. Halakhic evolution has never taken place on the simple basis of the assertion that it is able to evolve. I cannot conceive of evolution in any legal system taking place on the basis of the historically accurate contention that the norms of that system have always been able to evolve. Evolution takes place not by the assertion of the fact that it has always taken place, but rather, in exactly the way it has always taken place — namely, through the employment of those steps and procedures recognized as acceptable by the legal system itself. It is, ultimately, those steps and procedures that validate halakhic evolution, and not the historical claim that halakhah has always evolved. If the steps and procedures are ignored, the evolution is totally invalid. History can demonstrate that evolution has always taken place, but it cannot obviate the halakhic necessity for having it take place legitimately. The study of the history *of halakhah* suffices only to demonstrate that halakhah has a history. It does not suffice to determine halakhah. Historical study and *pesak halakhah* are simply not governed by the same canons.

Some, no doubt, will be quick to point out that *takkanot* and *gezeirot* (legislative as opposed to judicial acts) have a very legitimate place in halakhah, and can be easily utilized to "correct" every wrong that cannot be easily corrected by the more common methods of interpretation, comparison, and differentiation. Indeed, there are some among us who seem to view *takkanot* and *gezeirot* as the ultimate panacea and to have recourse to them for almost everything, including many things that could be easily done without recourse to them.

However, when we permit (or even encourage) *takkanot* and *gezeirot* to be promulgated without apparent regard for distinctions and conditions which are part and parcel of their legitimate use, we weaken respect for ourselves as halakhists and undermine the legitimacy of our *piskei halakhah* in general. Promulgating *takkanot* and *gezeirot* without regard for whether they are intended to fill in lacunae in the law or intended to supplant or abrogate precedented norms, fails to make a distinction that is extremely relevant halakhically. And if, when our *takkanot* and *gezeirot* are intended to "correct" laws that need correcting, we issue them without even noting the difference in halakhah between active and passive abrogation of earlier norms, or between temporary and permanent abrogation of earlier norms, or between abrogation of norms that are *de-oraita* ("biblical") and norms that are *de-rabbanan* (rabbinic), or between acts of legislation that forbid the permissible and those that permit the forbidden, we hold ourselves up to derision. There is a long history to the promulgation of *takkanot* and *gezeirot,* and there are universally accepted rules that govern their promulgation. We ignore those rules only at our own peril, and at the cost of the respectability of our halakhah. To claim that *takkanot* and *gezeirot* can be used to resolve difficult issues with ease on the basis of the fact that they have been used throughout history, but without taking into account the usual distinctions and strictures that have been applied to them, is not only bad halakhah, it is also bad history.

There is another type of error that often creeps into *piskei halakhah* of the Conservative movement as a result of the misperception that the results of critical rabbinic scholarship necessarily ought to impinge upon halakhah. Critical scholars of texts are attempting to establish the *peshat* of the texts they study: Bible scholars the *peshat* of the Bible, and Rabbinics scholars the *peshat* of rabbinic texts. *Peshat* is the primary preoccupation of critical text scholars, as, indeed, it no doubt ought to be. But, the *peshat* of biblical verses is far less important for halakhah than for biblical scholarship, and even the *peshat* of mishnayot, baraitot, and sugyot is far less important for halakhah than for rabbinic scholarship. In halakhic analysis it is as important to know whether the norm *purports* to be the *peshat* of a verse, or a mishnah, as it is to know the *peshat* of the verse or of the mishnah. In very many cases, non-*peshat* interpretations of sources are *knowingly* the basis for halakhic derivations. *Piskei halakhah* that elevate the *peshat* of sources to such halakhic significance *just because they are peshat,* miss the point of much halakhic interpretation. Scholars are interested in the *peshat* of a midrash, but the midrash itself is usually not concerned that its interpretation be the *peshat* of the text on which it is based. *Peshat* is, of course, one datum even in *pesak,* but only the confusion of critical scholarship with halakhah allows the conclusion that it is the *only* datum, or even the most important datum, in halakhah.

The most egregious error of all that results from confusing critical scholarship with halakhah and applying the canons of the former to the latter indiscriminately, however, has yet to be articulated clearly. The systematic and historical study of rabbinic and halakhic literature have demonstrated incontrovertibly that rabbinic literature and halakhah have a history. Law, even though it *appeared on the surface* to be ahistorical, objective, definitive, and stable, was demonstrated to be historical, subjective, indefinitive, and evolving. There was an actual *history* to halakhah in general, as well as to halakhot in particular. That history was now being traced and analyzed. Scholars could often point to a specific period of time during which certain changes in the law took place, and they could offer cogent and reasonable explanations to account for that change taking place at that time — explanations that often invoked not only historical events, but also economic, sociological, political, philosophical, and ideological factors. The view of halakhah that emerged from this global picture made possible by the *Wissenschaft* approach was one of a halakhah of almost limitless flexibility and evolutionary potential, in which *posekim* possessed the ultimate authority to interpret the law as they deemed appropriate. Each historical demonstration that halakhah was not objective and absolute, that it was subject to external influences, that it could be "bent" as needed, reinforced the feeling already incipient in those who were beginning to confuse halakhah as a living legal system with the history of halakhah. That incipient feeling, even among many who considered themselves committed to halakhah, was that what everyone had believed was a real *system,* was not a *system* at all! To talk of *the* halakhic system was to perpetuate a fiction. The historically analyzed power of halakhic authorities had demonstrated that halakhah was what the sages said it was, that *they* were in fact the system. History had demonstrated that the supposed system was so far from absolute, that halakhot flowed with so little objective inevitability, that it seemed to follow that there was probably no system whatsoever since its rules were not subject to precise definition.

Clearly, though, it does not follow from the limitless flexibility of halakhah and the ultimate authority of its *posekim* that there is no halakhic system. That conclusion, though very comforting to some, confuses history with halakhah. Roughly analogous, and patently unacceptable, would be the claim that since the history of Constitutional law in the United States clearly demonstrates that the Constitution means what the Supreme Court says it means, and since the authority of the Supreme Court to interpret the Constitution as it deems appropriate is virtually without limit, it follows that there is no system that governs Constitutional interpretation in the United States. The ultimate authority of the Supreme Court cannot be legitimately exercised in a limitless number of ways; it cannot be exercised in disregard of rules of procedure that themselves limit the justices of the Supreme Court in the exercise of their ultimate authority. These limitations define the parameters of the system, within which their authority is limitless.

So too the ultimate authority of *posekim* and the limitless flexibility of halakhah do not imply the absence of a system. The ultimate authority of *posekim* cannot be legitimately exercised in a limitless number of ways, and it cannot be exercised in disregard of rules of procedure that themselves limit *posekim* in the exercise of their ultimate authority. These types of limitations define the parameters of the halakhic system, within which their authority is ultimate. Viable legal systems are just that — *systems.* Even limitless power and authority do not imply the absence of a system.

The negative consequences of this error are most calamitous. Once talk of the absence of a system, or of *a* halakhic system rather than *the* halakhic system takes hold, and legalists begin to exercise their ultimate authority in limitless numbers of ways and in disregard of the rules of procedure that limit their exercise of that authority, those authorities have, in fact, stepped *outside* of the very system for which they purport to be authorities. When supposed halakhic authorities do so, they do violence to *the* halakhic system, and break the chain of authentic halakhic authority, all, ironically, in the name of halakhah.

Ours is not the first generation to be presented with challenges to our beliefs, nor is ours likely to be the last. It is probably no exaggeration to assert that every generation has had to confront challenges to its beliefs in some measure. There is, however, one very significant difference between the way our generation of Jews (with antecedents back to the mid-nineteenth century) confronts its challenges and the way normative Jews of the past have confronted theirs. For the generations of the past, the absolute primacy of halakhah was an ideological given. The thinkers who set their minds to meeting the challenges with which they were confronted did not consider the undermining of the primacy of halakhah as a possible outcome of meeting the challenges. There were certain things in Judaism that could be "tampered" with — given new and novel interpretations — in order to demonstrate that new ideas and philosophical approaches were compatible with Judaism. But there were also matters of belief that were so clearly central to normative Judaism that if it became necessary to "tamper" with them in order to make new ideas compatible with Judaism, the result would have been considered a *failure* to meet the challenges, not a successful meeting of the challenges. Meeting the challenge to belief by undermining the primacy of halakhah would not be meeting the challenge; it would be *failing* to meet the challenge. In attempting to meet the challenges of each generation we may have discovered that there were fewer things that could not be "tampered" with than we might earlier have thought, but belief in the primacy of halakhah and the inviolability of the halakhic process were always included on that list.

Since the rabbinic period, normative Judaism has been halakhic. And it can remain normative only insofar as it remains halakhic. If the "defenders of the faith" of our generation think that they meet the challenges of modernity when they advocate ideologies that undermine halakhah and the halakhic process, they are mistaken. Such ideological stances do not meet the challenges of modernity, they *fail* to meet its challenges. Among normative Jews of the past, the challenges of "modernity" were met by judaizing modernity. That process took place primarily through demonstration of the possibility of incorporating new ideas or ideologies into Judaism *without undermining the inviolable primacy of the halakhic system.*

The difference between Judaizing modernity and modernizing Judaism, however, is crucial. The former posits Judaism as inviolate, and the latter, modernity as inviolate. It is impossible to ignore the belief in the primacy of halakhah while Judaizing modernity, while the very process of modernizing Judaism tends to undermine that primacy. No generation of normative Jews has met or can meet the challenge of its modernity by modernizing Judaism. It can be met only by Judaizing modernity.

My non-philosopher's view of what led to the difference between the emphasis of the past on Judaizing modernity and the apparent emphasis of the present on modernizing Judaism brings me full circle to the beginning of this article, but now in a different discipline. Among Jewish thinkers of the past, philosophy and apologetics were virtually identical undertakings. One "did" philosophy in order to meet the challenges confronting normative Judaism. Jewish philosophy was not an objective, dispassionate undertaking at all. It was, almost in a very literal sense, a defense of one's own belief. It is in the post-*Wissenschaft* period primarily that philosophy and apologetics cease being one discipline among Jews. But, since we have historically viewed the functions to be the same (as we viewed the functions of rabbinic scholarship and *pesak halakhah* to be the same), we have failed to appreciate fully that the functions are no longer *necessarily* embodied in one person. Philosophy and apologetics share much common material (as do Rabbinics and halakhah), and it is possible to be both a philosopher and an apologist (as it is possible to be a scholar of Rabbinics and a *posek*), but they are not identical undertakings, and not governed by all of the same canons (just as Rabbinics and halakhah are not).

It is the duty of halakhists to Judaize modernity halakhically in a cogent and defensible way (that is, without allowing themselves to fall into the pitfalls that result from confusing history with halakhah). And it is the responsibility of apologists (in the very best sense of that word) to provide the ideological and philosophical underpinnings that will allow a modern Jew to meet the challenges of modernity by Judaizing modernity, without falling into the pitfalls that result from confusing Judaizing modernity with modernizing Judaism. But both halakhists and apologists must remember that *in those functions* they are not, *and ought not be,* dispassionate students of history. They are instead active and passionate participants in the ongoing and normative process of Judaizing modernity authentically, both legally and intellectually.*

---

*I am aware that I have offered hints throughout that critical scholarship and halakhah do have points of contact, and that the former influences the latter. I am also aware that I have not defined these points of contact or clarified how and when halakhah can be legitimately influenced by critical scholarship. Readers interested in my views on these subjects are directed to my book, *The Halakhic Process: A Systemic Analysis* (New York: JTS, 1986), particularly chapters nine through eleven.

Section Three

THE SELF DEFINED

How Others See Us
Questions of Definition
Responding to Feminism
The Next Fifty Years

Introduction to the Third Section

Kassel Abelson

Many of the contributors to this section are the thinkers and the doers within the Conservative community. Their essays are more than exercises in prophecy, for their thinking guides their activities which lay the foundation for the future of the Conservative movement.

Rabbi Howard Addison projects the future sociological profile of the American Jewish community fifty years hence in the year 2037. Rabbi Addison, currently serving as a rabbi in South Florida, projects the trends that are apparent in South Florida today as representative of the nature of the American Jewish community of tomorrow. The mass of second-generation East European Jews who were the mainstay of Conservative synagogues across the country will have passed from the scene. The prospective congregants of the year 2037, widely scattered, and living in smaller communities lacking rootedness and a sense of comfort in the synagogue and Jewish communal life, will be significantly different from the parishioners of yesterday and today.

Rabbi Addison sees the challenge that confronts the Conservative community as it looks to the future as being successfully met if we articulate and reinforce two of the basic principles of the Conservative movement: community and authenticity. By community he speaks of the transformation of the large "corporate" synagogue of the 1950's into the "department store" synagogue of the seventies and the eighties, which provides for small groups so that people can find the intimate, supportive relationships they may lack elsewhere. However, in the process something has been lost, a sense of the whole. Hence the work of the synagogue of the future will be not only to organize groups that will recreate primary relationships, but will provide a sense of belonging to the community as a whole. He calls for a redefinition of Jewish authenticity for the Conservative movement, by which he means regaining a sense of the Divine which underlies the unfolding of Jewish history.

Frank Kreutzer, President of the United Synagogue, echoes Rabbi Addison's call for authenticity, but an "authenticity without extremism." He calls for the setting of "outer limits both on the Left and on the Right" of what constitutes Conservative Judaism. The challenge of the future is the development by the leadership of our congregations of Conservative commitment to the Conservative forms of observance and discipline. Rabbi Benjamin Kreitman, the Executive Vice-President of the United Synagogue, sees a Conservative movement as "the most vulnerable and exposed of all the movements." He suggests that the future of American Judaism depends on the continued existence of Conservative Judaism for every community needs a "middle." He too expresses the need for "some exact definition" of Conservative Judaism. He bemoans the widening gap between rabbi and layman and sees the need for Conservative leaders to recognize that they must "fulfill their obligations as Jews as much as the rabbi."

Rabbi Elliot Gertel sees the future from the perspective of a rabbi of a once-large Conservative congregation which has experienced a decline in membership due to its urban location. His survey of adult graduates of the congregational Hebrew school is both comforting and disturbing. The good news is that our Conservative Hebrew schools are successful in implanting Jewish loyalties in many young people. The bad news is that these young people seem indifferent to Conservative Judaism. They will join synagogues, but they will do so for reasons of convenience, not conviction. He sees "the major function of the Seminary in concert with the national arms of the Conservative movement to provide an ideological footing for the Conservative congregant so that sociological and geographical factors do not do as much violence to loyalty to the Conservative synagogue, particularly in the next generation."

Rabbi Alan Silverstein deals with the changing image of the Conservative rabbi in the coming era. "An image of otherness, piety, maturity and paternalism is being replaced by a feeling of familiarity, comfort, accessibility and often less respect and awe." This reflects the fact that the children of Conservative families are becoming rabbis, and Conservative leaders recognize the need to deal with them and their wives and families in a more realistic fashion. However, the "demythologized" rabbi has become more a resource person, a teacher, and less an authority, a *mara d'atra*. Rabbi Schoenberg, speaking from his personal experience, calls for the Conservative community to free itself from dependence on the Orthodox community for the performance of many basic Jewish rituals. The movement needs to develop Conservative *mohalim,* Conservative kashrut supervisors, and to build Conservative *mikvaot* in each community. His essay repeats the theme so common in these essays of the need to develop Conservative congregants for our Conservative congregations.

Rabbi Benjamin Scolnic turns his attention to the role of ritual as a system of symbol in religion. He emphasizes the role of religion in transforming Conservative congregants into Conservative Jews. And he calls for a moratorium on change in the Conservative movement so that we can consolidate the gains of the past decades. Rabbi Neil Gillman approaches the question of ritual from a different perspective, but also stresses the need for commitment to ritual, "If this is an age of communal fragmentation, of growing anomie and isolation, of rootlessness and anxiety, of emotional aridity, then it is an age that demands more ritual, more theatrically performed than ever before."

Rabbi David Novak objects to the term Conservative ideology, or even Conservative philosophy. He prefers the term Conservative theology, and he begins to explore the implications of "covenantal theology" for the Conservative community.

Several of the essays look seriously at the impact that feminism has had on the Conservative movement. The ordination of women as rabbis and as cantors climaxes a century of the steadily developing role of women in the Conservative community. Selma Weintraub, Rabbi Amy Eilberg, Dr. Paula Hyman, Rabbi Leonard Gordon and to some extent Rabbis Elliot Schoenberg and Alan Silverstein examine the impact that feminism has had on the Conservative movement, and look with excitement and anticipation to future developments. They see women rabbis as bringing a unique perspective to the study of Judaism, and new dimensions to the Conservative rabbinate. Their essays are both thought-provoking and provocative.

Though most of the essays in this section are by insiders, outsiders too were invited to assess, from their perspective, the role and the future of the Conservative movement. Rabbi Eugene Borowitz in a polite but incisive way describes the ideological crisis confronting

Conservative Judaism as does Rabbi Jacob Staub. Both see the future of the Conservative movement as dependent on the ability to meet the challenge of developing a modern traditional approach which will be distinctive and provide another choice for traditional Jews who opt for modernity. They look forward to a partnership on behalf of the Jewish people, with each movement teaching its own approach, but working together on behalf of *klal yisrael*.

Rabbi Ronald Price grapples with the basic question that haunts the Conservative movement — "Can we remain united despite the diversity in approaches within the movement?" He asks, "How far does pluralism in the Conservative movement extend?" Rabbi Price raises questions as to what limits can and should be placed, and closes with the hope that we all share, "that tolerance will gain the upper hand: that we will be able to accept the differences which have developed amongst us, in practice and in belief, and that we will work together wherever possible. Where uniformity is not possible, may we compete in a healthy way for the hearts and souls of the Jewish people, not for the sake of our own victory, but rather for the sake of the continued strengthening of our people."

Reflections on the Conservative Movement

Jacob J. Staub

It is an honor to have been offered the opportunity to extend congratulations and best wishes at the centennial celebration of the Jewish Theological Seminary, clearly one of the pivotal institutions in the resurgence of Jewish life in twentieth-century America. At a time when "unity" is at the top of most Jewish agendas, I welcome the opportunity to reflect upon those things that unite us and divide us. The Reconstructionist movement was born in the environment of JTS and was nurtured there in its early years. It is thus an interesting and important challenge for me to consider Conservative Judaism on its own terms, without focusing on that which divides us. The directions that Conservative Jews pursue in the coming decades are very much of deep concern to *all* Jews who are concerned about our collective fate as a people.

Prognosis

Will the Conservative movement flourish in the next fifty years in ways comparable to its growth in the last fifty years? Prophecy ended with Malachi; when I represent the numerically tiny Reconstructionist movement, I often resort to proclaiming that we can't predict the future on the basis of the past. Nevertheless, in considering the future of Conservative Judaism, it is possible to note those factors that have contributed to its growth in the past and that are now changing.

By its own definition and the definition of others, the Conservative movement has always been and continues to be a movement in the middle, reacting belatedly rather than pursuing bold initiatives. Its dramatic growth after World War II reflected its appeal to the Americanized, successful children of Eastern European immigrants who sought a traditional but moderate Jewish atmosphere in their new suburban homes. The least ideological of contemporary Jewish movements, Conservative Judaism has served well large numbers of Jews nostalgically attached to tradition and interested in transmitting their heritage without too much commitment. The Conservative movement provided a way for them to pledge their allegiance to tradition, without the encumbrances of halakhic living or serious and painful confrontations with aspects of the tradition.

All this has been made possible through a pronounced gap between what others have called the elite and folk ideologies of the Conservative movement. In elite terms, the message has been that Conservative Jews accept the binding nature of halakhah, as long as halakhah is interpreted progressively, as it is by rabbinic authorities in the Rabbinical Assembly's Committee on Jewish Law and Standards. Despite the fact that only 5% of Conservative Jews live halakhic lives, the so-called folk ideology of the movement has enabled them to affirm nostalgically the authority of rabbinic standards that they have no need or desire to maintain themselves.

If this analysis of the movement's past growth is correct, then those who deal with its long-range planning ought to be concerned. It is unlikely that there will be a similar pool of Jews in the next generation who will be attracted for the same reasons. "Home" is no longer Eastern Europe, the Lower East Side, or even Brooklyn. For those whose earliest memories date back to the suburbs, nostalgia will be of a different order.

For those who are raised in prosperous homes where Jewish observance is pursued less than feverently and the issue of Americanization is a dim memory, connections to Judaism will not rise out of a subliminal but nonideological nostalgic longing for the flavor of the past. They will rather be either self-consciously and genuinely committed to halakhah as a way of life, or self-consciously and genuinely committed to struggling with the challenges of living Jewishly in a post-halakhic world. The former will find their needs met in Orthodox communities. The latter will not find Conservative Judaism a congenial home unless its approach to Jewish life is defined more clearly and its rightward drift halted. They will not sit for sermons about Shabbat observances that they have no intention of observing.

To its credit, the Conservative movement has done a wonderful job of creating a solid base of Solomon Schechter Day School and Camp Ramah graduates who are well educated. Some Conservative synagogues have begun to make room for havurot when members discover that they want to become more involved than is possible "upstairs" in the sanctuary. But if the movement is to maintain its current size, it will have to attract Jews in numbers that exceed by far this solid core.

Attracting Jews may prove difficult, given the movement's particular nonideological history. Through the decades, Conservative Jews have stood by the affirmation that halakhah is the authority and have built a consensus on that shared premise, using it to obviate the need for a consensus on ideological grounds. How does God act in history? What are the human elements in revelation? These and many other basic questions have never been addressed by Conservative Jews *as a movement*, because no consensus has ever been possible, even among its leaders.

This state of affairs has allowed the Conservative movement to include Jews with an extraordinary variety of beliefs and levels of Jewish practice. The inability to formulate clear statements of belief suited all those who joined synagogues for nostalgic rather than conceptual or confessional reasons. The use of the halakhic process as a substitute for ideology rather than as a system of practice allowed everyone in the movement—including the 95% who are nonhalakhic—to unite under its banner, without ever needing to address the question of how halakhah functions in a community where the overwhelming majority do not act as if they are commanded by its rulings.

It is difficult to imagine how such a coalition will survive current realities. As the Orthodox march to the right and the Reform and Reconstructionists become more bold in affirming post-halakhic positions, so too does it seem that the leadership of the Conservative movement has lost its consensus. Not long ago, everyone in the movement subscribed in principle to the belief that the halakhic system ought to be the bearer of normative Judaism. Today, many Conservative rabbis no longer regard halakhic precedent and process as a determinative voice, while others are using halakhah as a more powerful ideological tool. (Witness the recent R.A. debate and vote on patrilineal descent.) The establishment of the Union for Traditional Conservative Judaism and the current triumphalism of the movement's right wing seem to be pulling everyone rightward, for unity's sake, farther away from the positions of the vast majority of United Synagogue members.

Because of the immobilization caused by conflicting factions, it is difficult to determine whom the Conservative movement intends to attract. As it attempts to hold the center against both overly rapid change and growing halakhic inflexibility, it maintains official policies that exclude many of those whom one would expect that it would seek to attract. The new siddur does not come to grips with the conceptual challenge of feminism; certainly, prenuptial agreements do not touch the problem of the passive role of women in the *gittin* (divorce) ceremony. Rabbinical Assembly commissions are populated with appointees who seem insufficiently representative of the younger generation, the havurah world, and/or of women; by definition, laypeople are excluded from decision- and policy-making panels. Mixed married and conversionary married families seeking a way back into the Jewish world still find a great many United Synagogue congregations and Rabbinical Assembly members to be offputting, at best. Which portion of the Jewish population does the Conservative movement seek to address? While no one expects religious movements to tailor their convictions to the market, one hopes that those who plan for the future of the movement are measuring the likely effects of its current policies on its growth.

The slowness with which the movement moves has often been compensated for by individuals within its rabbinate and laity who act progressively in advance of official decisions. The danger of trying to maintain the middle position, however, is not only that you may move too slowly; it is also that you may lose a realistic grasp of where the middle is; it is, further, that the left and right may move so far apart that the center cannot hold. Dr. Gerson Cohen's recent call for an extensive survey of American Jews to determine the real rates of conversion, intermarriage, and affiliation is entirely appropriate for this reason.

Reconstructionists broke with the Conservative movement over halakhah and the process and rate of change. Our commitment to participatory involvement, in which rabbis no longer serve as halakhic decisors but instead teach laypeople enough to make their own informed decisions, demands a level of involvement that will not be matched by most Jews' commitments in the foreseeable future. Thus, the Conservative movement's willingness to hand down rabbinically-authored halakhic standards should serve many people well in their search for greater Jewish practice—but only if those standards are modified regularly so that they do not exclude most Jews.

Conservative Judaism's Projected Impact on Reconstructionism

The impact of the Conservative movement upon Reconstructionism will depend on how the Conservative movement's internal tensions are resolved. If the Conservative movement fragments, then it is possible to conceive of a basic restructuring of denominational lines in which we would be closely allied with the more liberal Conservative elements. Such a division in Conservative ranks, however, would have an impact on far more than the Reconstructionist movement, and its ramifications are difficult to imagine.

Should the Conservative movement unite in ways that would allow it renewed vibrancy, Reconstructionists would welcome that development. The Conservative and Reconstructionist approaches to Jewish living are sufficiently distinct that each appeals to a different audience. They are sufficiently close, however, so that it is easy to imagine a great deal of cross-fertilization and mutual nurturance—in educational programs, for example, or in camping. All of us need to avoid the sort of institutional competition and spitefulness to which it is so tempting to yield. We acknowledge and applaud a wide variety of approaches to Judaism; each of the alternatives stands to gain from the strength of the others.

Conservative Strengths and Weaknesses

The greatest accomplishment of the Conservative movement has been the Jewish Theological Seminary and its illustrious faculty. The faculty's scholarship has been extraordinary, and there is every reason to expect this to continue. Everyone in the Jewish world and in the field of Jewish studies remains indebted to the Seminary for its part in the renaissance of Jewish studies in the last decades. As mentioned above, both Camp Ramah and the Solomon Schechter Day Schools have done a remarkable job of transmitting the *shalshelet hakabbalah* (chain of tradition) to a new generation, and the Melton Center is a blessing to us all. Finally, I would call attention to the Conservative movement's success in its struggle to pass on a seriousness about Torah study that is manifest in the attitudes of current havurah movement leaders who emerged out of Camp Ramah. Indeed, the early leaders of the Reconstructionist movement also emerged out of the serious debate and study fostered at the Seminary.

As its greatest weakness, I would point to the wide gap, referred to above, between the mythic construct of Conservative Judaism as halakhic on the one hand, and, on the other hand, the non-ideological nature of the attachment of so many of its members, who simply don't care, or act as if they don't care, about halakhah. People who belong to Conservative synagogues because the Orthodox are "too old-fashioned" and the Reform are "not Jewish enough" do not constitute a solid, reliable constituency. On a list of weaknesses, I would also repeat the accepted Conservative role as moderate and non-initiating. For what does the Conservative movement stand? If the answers to that question were articulated more clearly and more often — despite the risks posed to the movement's coalition — the movement would be strengthened.

Joining in Common Cause

I would hope that in coming decades, the Conservative and the Reconstructionist movements will be able to join together in common cause on the following issues:

Pluralism in Israel

We need to work together to maintain Israel's pluralism. All non-Orthodox Jews have much to lose if the Orthodox Israeli establishment gains greater control over issues of personal status. Equally important is the need to open up liberal religious alternatives to the current *dati-ḥiloni* (religious-secular) dichotomies. The spiritual health of Israeli society depends on it.

Israeli Democracy

We need to work together to strengthen the forces for democracy in Israel. It is by no means axiomatic that Israel will be governed democratically in fifty years; the forces on the right are powerful, and receive much funding and support from foreign sources. It is our common duty to respond by supporting those Israeli institutions and individuals who are committed to the democratic nature of the Jewish state. For the sake of both pluralism and democracy in Israel, it is time that liberal Jews around the world unite in a single organization.

I would hope, therefore, that the Conservative movement would see fit to join the World Union for Progressive Judaism.

Outreach

Among American Jews, those who are affiliated with synagogues are already in the minority. Clearly, all Jewish movements must be concerned with reaching those who are not connected to Jewish life at all. While some are lost forever, there is good reason to believe that many are favorably disposed to their Jewish identification but have not yet found a comfortable corner of the Jewish world to call home. Jewish survival in North America may very well depend on cooperative ventures at outreach that overcome our competitive tendencies—because *none* of us has the one approach to Jewish living that will be most attractive to everyone.

If this is a wish list, I want to express the hope that, in coming years, we can cooperate on what is referred to as the patrilineal descent issue. As the number of Jewish children with non-Jewish mothers increases, there is every reason to expect that the Rabbinical Assembly will be moved to find humane solutions that do not exclude people who consider themselves, and are considered by what may be a majority of the Jewish people, active and committed Jews.

Spiritual Openness

Both of our movements share a common need to find more effective ways to make the spiritual treasures of our traditions more accessible to contemporary Jews. They need to learn to daven with uplifting *kavanah*, to sing with a full heart, to take responsibility for celebrating together the special moments of the life cycle and the Jewish calendar, and so they should be empowered to take risks in liturgical and ritual experimentation. They need to learn how to study the traditional and contemporary Jewish texts of Jewish practice and belief so that their Jewish identities are enriched by more than fear of anti-Semitism and love of the State of Israel. These are objectives that we all share, and our strategies to reach them overlap. It is up to all of us to transcend institutional allegiances and to be willing to learn from one another.

Jewish Unity

My experiences on panels addressing this issue do not lead me to be optimistic about the prospects for amelioration of Orthodox/non-Orthodox tensions. There is much room for optimism, however, about cooperation among non-Orthodox Jews. I hope that we are all committed to a unity based on diversity and mutual respect for divergent viewpoints. It is possible to imagine jointly sponsored symposia, publications, study groups, educators' conferences, and adult and youth programs. We are even within reach of establishing unified standards and mechanisms for personal status questions, since we would be dragged down neither by the issue of rabbinic legitimacy nor by the question of women's status. It is frightening to contemplate a Jewish world in which cooperation among non-Orthodox Jews would reflect our growing separation from the Orthodox. If growing separation proves to be an insurmountable fact, as well it might, I would hope that we will pursue unity where we can.

All Jews celebrate with the Jewish Theological Seminary on the occasion of its centennial. The Conservative movement deserves accolades for a century of profound accomplishments that have served us all. As we face ever new challenges in coming decades, let us hope that we all will be granted the courage and wisdom to pursue both separate and collaborative paths that will enable Jewish civilization to continue to flourish.

"His Majesty's Opposition,"*
As It Were

Eugene B. Borowitz

Since the Emancipation, most Jews have puzzled over how to integrate their cultural modernity and Jewish commitment so as to create a way of life newly relevant yet traditionally authentic. Except for the assimilated, happy to be rid of Jewishness, and the far right, resolutely set on self-ghettoization, we still puzzle.

The genius of the Conservative movement has been its lively, vibrant response to this problem. For a century, it has summoned modernized Jews to maintain and create rich Jewishness by giving their lives ethnic flavor, Hebraic tone and halakhic structure. Now that several Americanized generations have flourished under its guidance, the Jewish lives of countless American families as well as its great institutions and their impressive projects attest to the lasting power of its distinctive vision. All who care about the future of the Jewish people and Judaism join in the joyous celebration of The Jewish Theological Seminary of America's first century of service, not the least because we happily know we can look forward to equally remarkable achievement in the future.

In the broadest perspective, Reform Judaism and Conservatism share a common approach to the problem of fashioning a Jewish modernity. Both movements affirm that change is essential to a living Judaism, but instead of being made out of vulgar unconcern or willfulness it should stem from learning and devotion. Similarly, we see the university and its standards of scholarship not as threats, but as valuable instruments for understanding our heritage and the responsibilities that now devolve upon us as its happy continuers. Together, we especially esteem the modern study of history, which emphasizes the dynamic, evolving nature of social existence, providing telling in-

---

*Solomon Schechter's title when he spoke at the dedication of the new Hebrew Union College buildings, January 22, 1913.

sight into our Jewishly unprecedented opportunities and challenges. And we both rejoice in the spiritual courage it demands to create new forms of Jewish observance while bringing fresh vitality to old ones. The list could easily be extended.

Conservative Jewish spokesmen — as in Reform, women have not yet reached that status — have also served well the common aim of liberal Judaism in challenging Reform Jews about the Jewish component of their lives and thus, also, about the method and rate of their modernization. To begin with, their chiding has helped persuade Reform Jewish thinkers to reassess their movement's understanding of Jewish ethnicity and therefore its relation to Zionism, the Hebrew language and the luxuriantly variegated Jewish folk. They have also criticized it for seeking to give the prophets' categorically imperative style priority over the rabbis' legal realism and adaptiveness. Best of all, they have forced it to question its organizational concerns and priorities by educating and energizing notable numbers of highly concerned and motivated American Jews.

The theoretical focus of this discussion has been the place of halakhah in classic Judaism and in our contemporary development of it. Particularly as the issue in modernization has shifted from the right to change to the limits of change, they have urged Reform Jews to give the halakhic tradition greater weight in their decision-making, preferably by adopting a Conservative approach to tradition and change.

On these and other matters, Reform Judaism has benefited greatly from the different approach Conservative Judaism has taken in moving toward their common goal. To be sure, the evolution of Reform Judaism, so evident, say, in comparing the Pittsburgh Platform — now 101 years old — with the Reform Judaism of today, has been powered by many factors. Its internal dynamics, the shift of its Jewish ethnic base, the astounding developments in Jewish history, the loss of liberal self-confidence generally, all played a role in the refashioning of a group pledged to respond to its times. Yet, in the midst of these influences, one must not underestimate the effect of an attractive, thoughtful American competitor for the affiliation of those who cared to do something about their Jewishness.

To what extent the process worked in the other direction, that Reform Jewish experimentalism had a strong effect on Conservative Judaism — often after an effort to improve on the patterns — must be left for others to clarify. Today it is surely clear that there is considerable overlap in attitude, style and practice between traditionalists in Reform Judaism and liberals in Conservatism, certainly among the laity. Milton Steinberg's suggestion, some four decades ago, that Jews really are best understood as either traditionalists (in the strong sense of that term) or modernists, seems increasingly prophetic. Yet no one with an appreciation of the staying power of Jewish institutions or the love of human beings for their ideologies (independent of how faithful they are to them), would dare predict anything other than the continuation far into the future of the present movements. At the same time, to the extent that the area of practical concurrence grows, passage between the groups will become increasingly easy and frequent.

We cannot now tell whether western civilization's move to the social right will continue or, if it does, what its effects will be. In the past decade or so, all of Jewish life has benefited from the general return to ethnic roots and gained from the new seriousness about Jewishness, if only as a defense against a humanly corrosive social order. Yet the price of this shift has been the re-empowerment of orthodoxies, with group discipline radically subordinating the demands of the believing self. Should Christian and Moslem fundamentalism revert to fostering anti-Semitism, many Jews would surely re-ghettoize. But it seems more likely that the lessons of the Enlightenment, even if qualified, will continue to undergird modern culture and that liberal democracy — which vests such extraordinary dignity in each single self — will continue to flourish with continuing pendular adjustments. In some such neo-liberal environment, the future of the Conservative movement seems largely dependent upon its ability to redefine convincingly its present social role.

The task arises in no small measure from its successes in accomplishing its early goals. Consider first its great sociological triumph: it provided the chief means by which East European Jews could Americanize while maintaining their Jewishness. Against the European orientation and halakhic defensiveness of early American Orthodoxy, against the Germanic stiffness and churchified tone of early Reform and against the Europeanized philosophies of various Jewish secularisms, it proclaimed and demonstrated a way of living fully in two cultures — and it did so by creating upper-middle class institutional patterns to meet post-immigrant Jewry's social aspirations. With East

European Jews demographically dominant in American Jewry, Conservative Judaism could once reasonably lay claim to becoming our American Judaism.

Those triumphalistic days are now far behind us. The numbers of pre-World War II immigrants to America and their strong influences on American Jewish life continue to lessen. As the old stalwarts of Conservatism pass and their influence on their children becomes nostalgic rather than imperative, the balance they struck between modernity and Judaism no longer may seem desirable. They will not be replaced by the post-World War II immigration which, when religiously involved, has dramatically supported an inner-directed Orthodoxy. At the same time, the movement has been caught in an ideological squeeze. To the left, Reform Jews have shown that a healthy respect for tradition can coexist with an openness to change; and Reconstructionist Jews, few but increasing, by their continued separation from their parental home, give weight to the criticism that Conservatism has avoided rather than exercised leadership in responding to our historical transformations. To the right, Modern Orthodoxy, by exemplifying the fusion of American culture with the halakhic discipline claimed to be more authentic because less adaptive, has tellingly challenged Conservative Judaism's legal legitimacy. In recent years, as the body of those who study, teach and live by halakhah has grown more overwhelmingly Orthodox, that critique has intensified as even Modern Orthodoxy has been put on the defensive for its cultural flexibility. In sum, the old, easy victories that came with occupying the center are no longer possible. Many American Jews will surely always find themselves most comfortable in a movement that is "more Jewish" than the left and "not as fanatic" as the right, a basis for affiliation that bodes ill for the vitality and quality of the movement they will people.

The issue of redefinition intensifies as we look within. Consider the contrary criticisms of two youngish factions, both sufficiently educated and inspired that they aspire to a more serious and intensive Jewishness than most of their generation or, often, even of that of their parents. As to the first of these, one great success of American Judaism, largely due to Conservative influence, was the emergence in the 1970s of young adults seeking styles of being "more Jewish." Their first paradigmatic achievement was *The Jewish Catalog* and the impulse it celebrated soon took form as the havurah movement.

In their determination to fuse the ethics and involvement of the

'60s with the reclaiming of previously neglected Jewish practices, they seemed the fulfillment of Conservative Jewish teaching—but not for long. For one thing, they did not counsel tradition as discipline, that is as halakhah, but as invaluable resource, hence subject to autonomous choice. For another, the havurah movement has rejected the rabbi-centered, activity-filled, institutional synagogue which has been the mainstay of Conservative Jewish life. These developments evince creative dissatisfaction with Conservative Judaism. It seems willing to educate a lay elite but not to have its experts share significant power with them. Yet, paradoxically, its recognized authorities also do not demonstrate the efficacy of Conservative ideology either by reclaiming an increasingly usable past or creatively responding to social change, most notably feminism.

The havurah movement, as it has itself become institutionalized, has shown some staying power but has begun to fade as a major influence shaping American Jewish life. Yet its implicit critique of Conservatism has been partially substantiated by a later phenomenon, the emergence of a militant, often young cadre which demands a new halakhic seriousness from the Conservative movement. They seek to demonstrate its halakhic rigor and, while fulfilling Conservative ideology, end further questions about their halakhic legitimacy. They seek a Conservative decision-making process revitalized by intensified respect for the requirements of halakhah and a Conservative way of life effectively structured by halakhic discipline. Here, too, women's rights in Judaism has been a decisive issue. Stung by the movement's continuing equalization of women's role at synagogue services, they have organized as a caucus to reorient a movement they see as having lost a halakhic character it had classically retained for all its dynamic reading of Jewish law.

The social genius of the Conservative movement gave it the centrist advantage of claiming to combine the best of the left and the right. Today, however, with the failings of its organizational alternatives less apparent, it cannot long continue to enjoy the centrist privilege of refusing to define itself. Rather, the ideological problem now demands attention. Specifically, how does Conservative Judaism propose to integrate rightist tradition with leftist change without becoming either Orthodoxy or Reform Judaism?

This question raises the intriguing issue of the role of ideas in maintaining the vitality of social groups. We cannot say that communities never long or significantly continue without a reasonably clear and satisfying view of themselves and their world. Yet, considering our incomparably educated and cultured community, it is difficult to believe that a religious movement could flourish, though it survived, if it long remained powered essentially by social inertia, institutional loyalty and vested interest.

That brings us to the Seminary, that other great success of the movement, which itself now faces new challenges. To begin with, there are the issues created by the identification of the movement with this one institution—so great, that in celebrating the centennial of its opening, some of us have been invited to write, not about it, but about the Conservative movement. The ideological basis for the closeness of the two is plain: if Jewish law is to be read in a modern, historically dynamic fashion then only a faculty combining historians and halakhists can hope to muster the skills necessary to do so.

The academic accomplishments of the Jewish Theological Seminary faculty and students over the years, as well as its extraordinary library, have been a chief glory of Jewish life on this continent. But now, as the movement stands in critical need of philosophic clarity, the Seminary's great failure to fulfill the movement's expectations is glaringly evident. The Seminary faculty did produce memorable academic studies of Jewish legal documents, legists and laws, and notable research in Jewish history. But it did not, as enthusiasts had anticipated, fulfill the practical Conservative Jewish promise. That is, it did not demonstrate that a modern, historical hermeneutic of halakhah could provide practical rulings which are as halakhically authentic as they are adapted to post-Emancipation existence. Put otherwise, the faculty created no significant Conservative Jewish halakhic literature; it issued no paradigmatic *piskei din* (legal rulings) which, by their content and method, would provide future generations of Conservative halakhists with a basis upon which to build in their own way. It did not do the task Conservative spokesmen had claimed it uniquely qualified to do and eventually others, in their own way, have had to take it up.

An unhappy by-product of this reverence for "the Seminary" must also be noted. Over the years, so much emotion was vested in "the Seminary" and "the faculty," so powerful grew the myth of their unparalleled erudition, that young Conservative Jewish scholars knew they could never reach the expected level of Jewish scholarship. As a consequence, many found significant writing difficult and could not hope to move on to creative, independent work of their own devising. Happily, those days are largely behind us, but some traces of this undue image-making linger.

The Seminary must also now face an academic environment in which maintaining the scholarly preeminence the movement expects of it has become quite difficult. Once, it was the only institution with several faculty members investigating halakhah by modern methods and was one of the few institutions scrutinizing Jewish history. Again, substantially due to its accomplishment, it faces a new challenge. Today several institutions and many individual scholars compete for academic attention and respect in those fields. Our broadly scattered, highly demanding, institutionally sophisticated academic community cares far more about publication than about old institutional myths or self-image.

Organizationally, too, the decision by the Seminary faculty to admit women to the ordination program has exacerbated the issue of the Seminary's role, and that of its faculty, in the delineation of Conservative halakhah. Conservative ideology had prepared us to expect a decision of such magnitude to be grounded in halakhah, one that would not only be shared with the movement but with the community as a whole. The Seminary issued no such formal halakhic statement. Moreover, this apparently administrative decision by the faculty, itself raises new ideological questions if "the faculty" is still expected to have a role in determining Conservative halakhah. The faculty now properly includes experts in many diverse professional and academic disciplines. Are they all competent to render judgment on what constitutes an authentic if creative halakhic determination? And if not, who are the decisors of the Seminary's halakhic stands?

The latter question seems especially troublesome because of the contrary tendencies of the key disciplines Conservative ideology has counted on, history and law. Most historians emphasize change and development, to be sure, amid stability; most scholars of law look for continuity and precedent even as they note change. Perhaps we may say that the current struggle for the soul of Conservative Judaism is between these disciplines. The historians are convinced that their emphasis on evolution retains adequate respect for the centrality of law in Judaism. But older talmudists, at least, insist that halakhah must itself determine when history is relevant and how those who properly venerate the law may alone licitly employ it. Some such view allows the traditionalists in the movement to retain the old Conservative hope, that history might usefully combine with expertise in halakhah to give us a vital Jewish law. But those premises allow them to join the great body of those Jews who study and live by the halakhah in denying history a decisive role with regard to women's rights in Judaism. Their stand has placed the supporters of the Conservative ordination of women on the defensive to explain in essentially halakhic rather than historical terms, how a ruling that would have been considered Jewishly presumptuous before the rise of feminism, now can claim Jewish legal status.

The same theoretical issue may be provocatively posed in this fashion: why does not the same historical sense which legitimated the ordination of women not also validate patrilineality in Jewish identity? It is one thing to demonstrate one's continuing loyalty to halakhah by the political act of denying the practitioners of patrilineal Jewish identification a place in the Rabbinical Assembly. It is quite another to clarify when we are and when we are not to attend to historical change—in the case of patrilineality, so well documented for the rabbinic period by contemporary scholarship, and potentially well-justified in our own by the sociological evidence attesting that intermarriage as assimilation has given way to that which nonetheless seeks family Jewish identity.

Conservative Judaism appears to be facing an ideological crisis, one which will test whether the movement is a melange of refugee Orthodox *mekilim* (liberals) and slow-moving Reform Jews—or what it has always claimed to be: a substantively distinctive, Jewishly authentic response to modernity. As we move into the Seminary's next century, interested observers will be asking these questions to determine their answer: has the movement had the courage to make the decisions, whether for conservation or change, that show it to be concerned with the ongoing development of American Jewish life? Has it clarified the special lineaments of its halakhic approach in making these determinations and, in general, created a Conservative Jewish halakhic literature? Equally important, has it been able to move beyond elitist theory to create a community of Jews who live by the discipline imposed by its halakhah? And, at least for specialists in the field, can its theoreticians demonstrate not only that the notion of halakhah is important to them but that their systems themselves significantly grow out of halakhic sources?

In somewhat different form these weighty questions could be asked with equal cogency of Reform Judaism or Modern Orthodoxy. The fundamental problem that Emancipation has posed for Jews remains the same for all of us, despite the changes in our perception of modernity in the past four decades. All who admire the Seminary and Conservative Judaism know that we may continue to look to them to be in the forefront of those Jews determined to serve God in ways appropriate to this unusual time and yet in faithful continuity of our people's past.

The present campus of the University of Judaism in Los Angeles.

Toward a Conservative Theology

David Novak

The Need for Theology

Since "theology" is not a term found in classical Jewish nomenclature, it is often suspected by many Jewish thinkers as describing a basically Christian enterprise, not suited for a primary reflection on Judaism.[1] Nevertheless, despite its admittedly Christian connotation, it is preferable to two other terms with which many Jewish thinkers are more comfortable, namely, "ideology" and "philosophy."

Theology is preferable to ideology because ideology is essentially a rationalization of a political program. Ideology is not critical examination but rather elegant propaganda. It does not hold up a political program to a prior standard of truth and right to judge its validity or invalidity but, rather, it assumes that the political power of a group is its own justification. As such, ideology invents slogans and assumes that if they are repeated loudly and long enough, everyone will automatically accept the political program being promoted as true and right.[2] Ideology would, therefore, only be an appropriate denotation of a primary reflection on Judaism if Judaism were an invention of a particular group, answerable to no prior standard and part of no larger whole. Indeed, ideology is not reflective at all. It denies the very precondition of reflection, namely, that there is a background upon which one's own thoughts are reflected. Clearly, then, ideology is inadequate for our reflective purposes here. The term "Conservative" in "Conservative Judaism" surely should function as an adjective modifying the substantive noun "Judaism." Hence, a Conservative theology must not become an ideology, inasmuch as Judaism is always more than "Conservative" Judaism. Conservatism is answerable to Judaism, not vice-versa.[3] That is why Zacharias Frankel (d. 1875), the founder of our community, named his approach *Positive-Historical Judaism*. By "positive" he meant positive law, namely, that Jewish tradition is normative for all times. By "historical" he meant that the tradition was developed and that Jewish policies must be diachronic, that is, they must take the whole history of the tradition seriously.[4] Indeed, it was on these historical rather than strictly positive (that is halakhic) grounds that he disassociated himself from the program of the Reform rabbis in 1845. He refused to agree with their denigration of the role of the Hebrew language in Jewish worship. His intellectual successor in America, Solomon Schechter (d. 1915), regarded such departures from history as being contrary to the reality of what he called "Catholic Israel."

Nevertheless, much too much of what is being said today in the name of Conservative Judaism is ideology in the sense described above. It is simply the constant repetition of the policies of those in positions of political power, with no real debate on their truth and merit in the light of wider and deeper criteria.[5] For this reason, ideology and its whole approach is an intellectual dead-end for thoughtful Conservative Jews who are concerned with what truly characterizes our Jewish religious community and what can intelligently guide it into the future.

For this reason, also, one might wish to use the term "philosophy" rather than ideology to denote such a primary reflection on Judaism. For surely philosophy is a more exalted enterprise than ideology in that it is a critical attempt to discover truth.[6] This critical attempt accepts as its precondition the existence of an objective datum which functions as the background for its statements and against which they must be justified. As such, it is certainly worthier of respect and employment than ideology which has no criterion of truth.

However, most reflections on Judaism which have been designated as "philosophical" have another problem. Most of them are not really reflections on Judaism. Rather, they are reflections on general human experience within which they understand Judaism to be a part, albeit an important part. And this is a problem — indeed, an insuperable problem — because Judaism has been analyzed and judged by most Jewish philosophers on the basis of external criteria of truth and right. This is in direct contradiction of Judaism's own insistence on its own primacy in the very order of the cosmos.[7] Thus, the rabbis typically insisted that compared to the Torah all other discourse is at best "side-dishes for wisdom" and at worst "empty talk."[8] Jewish critics of philosophical reflections on Judaism have seen this enterprise as hopelessly reductionistic, whether it was Philo reducing Judaism to Platonism, Maimonides reducing it to Aristotelianism, or Hermann

Cohen reducing it to Kantianism. Jewish philosophy by its own project seems to be limited thereby to playing the role of apologist.

Moreover, most so-called philosophies of Judaism are not really philosophical at all, that is, reflections based on a cogent theory of truth. Rather, they have been based on an uncritical acceptance of the current *Zeitgeist* and a highly subjective and eclectic approach to the whole body of Judaism.[9] They have been ideologies rather than philosophies in any authentic sense. This has even been the case when an intellectually serious ideology has been put forth by as gifted a Jewish ideologue as Mordecai Kaplan (d. 1983). Thus, to cite an example of most intense current discussion in our community, namely, the attempt to reconstruct Jewish ritual practice based on criteria of egalitarianism, we see an ideological enterprise which many assume is philosophical. But a truly consistent egalitarianism would lead to the elimination of just about every distinction Jewish tradition has ever developed. Nevertheless, that the acceptance of egalitarianism by many Conservative Jews is nonphilosophical is clearly demonstrated by the fact that most of these very same persons who see the traditional emphasis of males over females in public ritual, at the same time reject the elimination of the traditional principle of matrilineal descent, a principle which emphasizes females over males in questions of fundamental Jewish identity.[10] Hence, Conservative egalitarianism is in fact the ideology of a group which wants to be both *au courant* yet not "Reform," a culture of taste if you will.

This ideological bent is succinctly expressed in what has become the unofficial slogan of the Conservative movement, namely, "tradition and change."[11] The slogan as it stands is clearly an oxymoron, that is, a statement combining two contradictory parts. If Conservative Judaism means by "tradition" the necessarily unchangeable past, and by "change" it means the future with its open possibilities, then there must be a third term invoked prior to both of these disjuncts, to decide intelligently between the inevitable conflicts which arise when these two disjuncts are not mediated. In other words, there must be a criterion to determine in specific conflicts just when there is to be change and when the tradition is to stand as is. The discovery and constitution of this third term minimally requires philosophical rigor; maximally it requires theological sufficiency to be authentically Jewish. Heretofore, I have seen neither condition met by those in our community who continually invoke this slogan.

The only kind of philosophy which is neither ideology nor

reductionism is a philosophy *of* Judaism, namely, an intelligent reflection on Judaism as a body transcending our own inventions and not regarded as a subordinate part of anything else. (Some might want to call it a "phenomenology of Judaism.") However, such a reflection presupposes that Judaism itself is of primary concern to the philosopher. And the only cogent designation of such an enterprise is "theology," that is, faith seeking self-understanding.[12] Indeed, those great Jewish thinkers whose works themselves have become part of the classical literature of Judaism (for example, Saadia Gaon, Nahmanides, Moses de Leon, Joseph Albo, Abarbanel, Isaac Luria, Abraham Isaac Kook) were surely theologians in this sense. They lived by their faith and attempted to explicate its inner truth as best they could. It seems to me that the Conservative community (a much more apt description of our shared history and vocabulary than "movement" with its connotation of a political party which one joins because of its explicit platform) at this point in time, when it is still very much engaged in the most passionate debate in its century-long history, requires the enterprise of theology as I have attempted to define it above.

A Covenantal Theology

A theologian is surely a man or woman who is totally committed to his or her faith tradition and assumes that "everything is in it,"[13] even though he or she can discover but a part of its truth due to human finitude and the specific concerns of his or her generation, which must be the focal point for the theological questions to be raised. One must humbly assert throughout any such theological enterprise that "as much as I have been rewarded for what I can explain I am rewarded for remaining silent in the face of what I cannot explain."[14] Since the theologian is an active participant in the life of his or her Jewish religious community, the theology which he or she will produce must be in essence responsa rather than a code or a *summa theologiae*.[15] Since no one generation can actively deal with all the factors in the tradition, the theologian will necessarily have to limit his or her scope to the deepest concerns of the generation at hand.

The aspect of the tradition which seems closest at hand to the concerns of this generation, especially in our own Conservative community, is the Covenant (*brit*). A covenant is a relationship, specifically a relationship between God and the Jewish people. It seems to many thoughtful persons in our community that an Orthodox insistence on the Covenant as being a divine monologue directed to passive recipients, and a Liberal insistence that the Covenant is nothing more than human insight into the divine factor in human existence, are both inadequate to explain Jewish tradition and the experience of religious Jews. Only a truly covenantal theology can adequately approach this divine-human relationship in a way that truly recognizes the reality and freedom of both participants.[16] Indeed, the two most gifted theologians that our community can claim (in the sense of its common theological agenda, not its formal political structure), Franz Rosenzweig (d. 1929) and Abraham Joshua Heschel (d. 1972), both engaged in their most creative and insightful theological work when reflecting on the meaning of the Covenant for contemporary Jews.[17]

Although the Covenant is a relationship between God and the Jewish people, it is clearly not a relationship based on equality. A relationship of equality must be based on some third factor prior to both of these partners to which they are both answerable. Jewish tradition consistently maintains about God that "I am the first and I am the last" (Isaiah 44:6) and that "God is not man" (Numbers 23:19). Therefore, God is always the ultimate authority of the Covenant and always transcends it.[18] As such, a covenantal theology must begin with the divine factor and continually emphasize its primacy.

If the Covenant is a relationship which is historical, it has a past, a present, and a future. At all three of these points in the relationship there is a primary divine factor and a secondary human factor.

Revelation — Covenant's Past

It asserts that the relationship between God and the Jewish people emerges from God's authority and that God did speak to the people in an unmistakable way. On the other hand, an affirmation of revelation does not entail the assertion that there was no human component in the very process of revelation. For Jews, revelation is mediated through texts transmitted through history. The Jewish people has not been a passive, silent, recipient as, indeed, the Scriptural and rabbinic accounts of the confirmations and reconfirmations of revelation indicate.[19] How much of revelation is uniquely divine, without human mediation, is a subject of much dispute in rabbinic theology and beyond.[20] Perhaps, one could offer as an analogy the rabbinic statement about the creation of tongs, namely, that the first set of tongs had to be created by God in order for all subsequent tongs to be made with them. Nevertheless, one can surely dispute precisely which is that first set.[21]

The human factor in revelation is the correlation of direct human reason and experience with the word of God in the Torah, as it has been transmitted to us from our past. "The Torah speaks in ordinary human language" is a point emphasized by many different Jewish theologians at many different times.[22] The Torah has a meaning and that meaning has been historically developed by the Jewish people in an evolutionary process. The development of that meaning which is concurrent with the divine truth of the Torah is the presupposition for the scientific approach to the classical texts of Judaism, that form of Jewish intelligence and learning in which our community has justly taken great pride. We have not been frightened by examining the whole tradition and discovering its multifarious human components, and we do not regard such inquiry as injurious to faith any more than Zecharias Frankel was cowed when the Orthodox theologian, Samson Raphael Hirsch (d. 1888), made that very charge when the Jewish Theological Seminary opened in Breslau in 1854.[23] (If anyone is looking for the starting date of our community, I recommend that one.)

Quite the contrary, such inquiry is actually a strengthening of faith because it rescues revelation from myth. By "myth" I mean that twilight zone where the divine is too human and the human too divine.[24] Scientific-historical critical method strengthens faith when it seeks to clarify the human component of the Torah in order that the transcendence of the divine origin be more greatly enhanced. Faith does not emerge from this method, however. Left to itself, this method quickly becomes relativistic if not skeptical and even nihilistic. But when this method operates with faith as its background, it becomes an important participant in faith.[25] What this method does eliminate is the elevation of the formulators of our tradition to the level of semi-divine *gedolim* ("great ones," or better, "infallible ones"), who like God are beyond the canons of truly human description and evaluation. Such an approach, which in contrast to the scientific-historical critical method we usually call "fundamentalism," as practiced by more and more of those traditionalists to the right of our community, not only flies in the face of what we have learned from history and the social sciences, but also blocks a more creative appropriation of the multifaceted tradition for the spiritual needs of contemporary

Jews. And it enables contemporary *gedolim* (whose opinions are considered to be infallibly *da'at Torah*, that is, "the Torah's opinion") to exercise basically unjustified authority. Fortunately, in our community we have had, and thankfully still have, great practitioners of scientific method as religious role models—Frankel, Lewy, Heinemann, Ginzberg, Boaz Cohen, Lieberman, and (may they be distinguished as living) Finkelstein and Weiss Halivni—who have shown us how critical study enhances piety and how piety stimulates critical study.

Authority — The Covenant's Present

Judaism has insisted, by making the *Shema* its liturgical centerpiece, that the kingship of God, necessarily followed by the acceptance of the yoke of the commandments, is the ground of all present action.[26] Ours is a religion of commandments, and these commandments in order to be commandments rather than "folkways" or even "sancta" must be based on the direct authority of the One "who has sanctified us by his commandments and commanded us." Human authority, which is required both for the interpretation and implementation of the commandments, is always to be regarded as subordinate. We see this in two closely related incidents told in Scripture about Abraham, our patriarchal progenitor. First, when God invites him to exercise the critical sense needed to be a subordinate authority in the divinely elected clan ("in order that he might command his children and household after him to keep the way of the Lord: to do what is right and just"—Genesis 18:19), he boldly ("Shall the judge of the whole earth not himself do justly?"—18:25) but reverently ("I am but dust and ashes"—18:27) seeks the intelligibility of God's judgment of Sodom and Gemorrah. However, the most important point to remember is that God has invited Abraham to so participate in the process of divine judgment ("Shall I conceal from Abraham that which I am doing?"—18:17).[27] When, on the other hand, he is commanded to act rather than inquire, namely, the commandment to offer his son Isaac as a sacrifice, he obeys without question. And his obedience has been taken by the tradition to be the paradigm for all subsequent Jewish obedience to the commandments of God.[28] That is one reason why the story of the *Akedah* is the Torah reading for Rosh Hashanah, the festival celebrating the Kingship of God.[29]

The human factor in this present aspect of the Covenant is the full process known as halakhah. Halakhah comprises the whole range of human interpretation, human implementation, and even human anticipation of the will of God.[30] In our community we have rightly emphasized the wide range of possibilities within this human side of the Torah. The times in which we live have called for such an affirmation of diversity and possibility inasmuch as we have seen such a variety of changes in the human condition itself. Any affirmation of a monolithic halakhah or a monolithic source of halakhic ruling can only limit the range of halakhah in a way that will not speak to the growing pluralism of our age. Here again, our emphasis on critical scholarship has an important role to play in the development of the Covenant, especially its normative development. All of this is of greatest importance and here we have just begun to make significant contributions for the benefit of the entire Jewish people in the modern world.

However, here too we have often confused the humanly structured halakhah with the divinely mandated mitzvot. By so emphasizing the dynamic, developing, character of halakhah, we have sent an incorrect and even dangerous message, especially to the unlearned, that all authority in Judaism is negotiable and that any Jewish norm can be changed if enough social and political pressure is exerted.[31] Such confusion undermines the Covenant itself. It undermines it by its clear assumption that this relationship with God is humanly determined. It blasphemously reduces God to the level of an equal with ourselves if not actually making Him our servant. As such, it destroys the only authentic reason for anyone to choose to live under the Covenant and the Law, namely, the human desire to participate with God in the work of creation which is begun and ended by God alone.[32] That which is permanent and is to remain permanent in the Covenant — "the word of our God which endures forever" (Isaiah 40:8) — is always primary. If its primacy is ever eclipsed, let alone denied, the Covenant would then become "a commandment of men, learned by rote" (Isaiah 29:13).

A Conservative theology must explicate these aspects of the Covenant as a practical imperative for the present.

Eschatology (Aḥarit Ha-Yamim) — The Covenant's Future

It asserts that "the kingdom will be the Lord's" (Obadiah 1:21), that the ultimate outcome of the relationship between God and the

Jewish people is in the hands of God. "No eye has seen but Yours, O God, what You will do for those who wait for You."[33] Eschatology is the theological antidote to Utopianism, which sees the full solution to the agonies in the human condition as being at hand and within foreseeable reach. Not only has history taught us the folly of all Utopianisms, but recent history has taught us how dangerous the practitioners of such Utopianisms can be, especially to the Jewish people. Extreme examples of this anthropocentric approach to the human future have been Fascism and Communism, both of which have been ferociously antagonistic to the Jewish people and to Judaism. The rabbis called such Utopians "calculators of the End."[34] Clearly, the classical Jewish eschatological doctrines of the days of the Messiah, the resurrection of the dead, and the world-to-come give the future the transcendence that we truly see in it. Our view of the future is mostly a view of a mysterious realm. (In our own day, these doctrines need to be readdressed to such pseudo-messianic groups as *Gush Emunim*.)

Unfortunately, our community, especially in its liturgical productions, has largely confused eschatology with Utopianism. Thus, if one looks at the latest liturgical product of our community, *Siddur Sim Shalom*, it continues the Utopianism of its predecessor, the *Sabbath and Festival Prayerbook* of 1946.[35] It confuses the transcendent doctrine of the resurrection of the dead with the altogether different immanent doctrine of human immortality. The doctrine of the resurrection of the dead asserts that God has the power to restore human life fully, if and when God so chooses. The doctrine of the immortality of the soul, on the other hand, implies that we already have immortality within ourselves. *Siddur Sim Shalom* confuses the idea of human progress with messianic redemption and thereby removes the main content of the anticipated redemption, the restoration of the Temple and its sacrificial cult in Jerusalem. And, it deemphasizes the whole supernatural doctrine of life after death. We need, therefore, a critical theological examination of the traditional eschatological Jewish doctrines in order to reemphasize the primary divine factor in them, and we need to do this before, not after, we rush to be innovative in liturgy. Liturgy, more than any other area of normative Jewish practice, requires a cogent theological foundation.

The human factor in eschatology is not Utopianism and its dangerous mythology but rather reflection on the aims and purposes of individual human life, the Jewish people and, indeed, the international world in which we are greater participants than ever before in history. The rabbinic doctrine of *tikkun olam* ("the mending of the broken world") is an important expression of this human side of eschatology for Jews.[36] It means the constitution of a Jewish *teleology,* that is, how Judaism makes policy decisions based not only on the inherent meaning of acts, but, also on their consequences in history. The human side of Jewish eschatology calls for the development in our community of the type of critical Jewish social and political thought which avoids the Utopianism we see from both the left and the right, without succumbing to the nihilism of those who have lost all hope for human society and civilization itself.

A Conservative theology must explicate these aspects of the Covenant as hope for the future.

All that I have stated above is merely the barest sketch which a fuller theology must fill in. It is, moreover, the view of but one theologian in our community. Nevertheless, it is a view which I believe is a Conservative option and not one which would be acceptable in any other Jewish religious community today. It is the result of my belief so far that our community will maintain enough piety and free inquiry to make such a theology a worthwhile project.

NOTES

1. Note, however, *Sifre Devarim,* no. 49. Finkelstein, ed., p. 115 (*viz., aggadah = theology, i.e.,* "God-talk"). Moreover, *Kabbalah,* by its own insistence, is essentially God-talk. See Gershom Scholem, *On the Kabbalah and Its Symbolism,* trans. by. R. Manheim (New York: Schocken, 1969), pp. 32f.

2. See Plato, *Crito,* 44C; *Republic,* 336Dff.

3. See *P. Pe'ah* 1.1/15b re: *Deuteronomy* 32:47; cf. *Sifre Devarim,* no. 336, pp. 385–386.

4. See Louis Ginzberg, "Zechariah Frankel" in *Students, Scholars and Saints* (Philadelphia: JPS, 1928), p. 202ff.

5. See, *e.g., Pe'ah* 4:1; *Nega'im* 9.3.

6. For analyses of the essential difference between philosophy and ideology, see Leo Strauss, *What is Political Philosophy?* (Westport, Conn.: Greenwood Press, 1973), p. 12; Yves R. Simon, *The Tradition of Natural Law,* V. Kuic, ed., (New York: 1965), pp. 16–27.

7. See D. Novak, *The Image of the Non-Jew in Judaism* (New York and Toronto: Fordham University Press, 1983), pp. 409ff.

8. See *Avot* 3:18; Maimonides, *Hilkhot Yesodei Ha-Torah,* 4:13 and Karo, *Kesef Mishneh* thereon; *Menahot* 65b.

9. See H. A. Wolfson, *Crescas' Critique of Aristotle* (Cambridge, Mass.: Harvard University Press, 1929), pp. 26-27.

10. See D. Novak, *Halakhah in a Theological Dimension* (Chico, Calif.: Scholars Press, 1985), pp. 64ff.

11. See *Tradition and Change,* M. Waxman, ed. (New York: Burning Bush Press, 1958), Introduction.

12. Thus, our late revered teacher, Prof. A. J. Heschel, subtitled the major statement of his own religious position (*God in Search of Man*) *A Philosophy of Judaism* (New York: Farrar, Strauss and Cudahy, 1955). However, he defines this "philosophy" as "depth theology" (see pp. 7-10). Also, see Isaiah 7:9 and note of R. Kittel, *Biblia Hebraica,* 11th ed. (Stuttgart: Privileg Wuertt. Bibelanstalt, 1959), p. 618; and D. Novak, "The Origin and Meaning of *Credere ut Intelligam* in Augustinian Theology," *Journal of Religious Studies,* 6:2-7:1 (Fall 1978/Spring 1979), pp. 38-39.

13. *Avot* 5:22.

14. *Bava Kamma* 41b.

15. Cf. A. J. Heschel, *The Quest for Certainty in Saadia's Philosophy* (New York: Feldheim, 1944), p. 1.

16. See Novak, *Halakhah in a Theological Dimension,* pp. 116ff.

17. See, *e.g.,* Franz Rosenzweig, *The Star of Redemption,* trans. W. W. Hallo (New York: Holt, Rinehart & Winston, 1970), pp. 154-155, 186; Heschel, *The Prophets* (Philadelphia: JPS, 1962), pp. 229-230.

18. That is why the kabbalists posited an aspect of the Godhead beyond any relationality (*sefirot*), *viz.,* the Limitless (*Ein Sof*). See Gershom Scholem, *On the Kabbalah and Its Symbolism,* p. 35.

19. See, *e.g.,* Exodus 20:15-16 and Mekhilta.

20. See A. J. Heschel, *Torah min Ha-Shamayim* (London: Soncino, 1965), 2:71ff.; also, Franz Rosenzweig, "Divine and Human" in *Franz Rosenzweig: His Life and Thought,* trans. N. N. Glatzer (New York: Schocken, 1961), pp. 242ff.

21. *Avot* 5:6; *Tosefta Eruvin* 8:23; *P. Eruvin,* end. However, since we cannot isolate this first set of tongs, we cannot evaluate the levels of the Torah. See, esp., *P. Berakhot* 1.8/3c and Louis Ginzberg, *Perushim ve-Hiddushim bi-Yerushalmi: Berakhot* (New York: Jewish Theological Seminary, 1941), 1:166-167.

22. See Heschel, *op. cit.,* pp. 3ff.

23. See N. H. Rosenbloom, *Tradition in an Age of Reform: The Religious Philosophy of Samson Raphael Hirsch* (Philadelphia: JPS, 1976), pp. 105-108.

24. See Hermann Cohen, *Religion of Reason Out of the Sources of Judaism,* trans. S. Kaplan (New York: Frederick Ungar, 1972), p. 61.

25. See David Weiss Halivni, *Midrash, Mishnah, and Gemara: The Jewish Predilection for Justified Law* (Cambridge, Ma.: Harvard University Press, 1986), esp. chap. 7.

26. *Berakhot* 2:2. See *Yevamot* 47a-b; *Sifre Devarim,* no. 33, p. 59.

27. Cf. Exodus 32:9-14; Numbers 13:11-20; Deuteronomy 3:23-29 (and *Sotah* 13b).

28. See Maimonides, *Guide of the Perplexed,* 3:24.

29. *Tosefta Megillah* 31a (cf. Rashi thereon and *Rosh Hashanah* 16a bot.). Cf. *Megillah* 3:6. See B. Mandelbaum, Introduction., *Pesikta de-Rav Kahana* (New York: Jewish Theological Seminary, 1962), 1:xiv (re Ms. Carmoli). Cf. J. Mann, *The Bible As Read and Preached in the Old Synagogue* (Cincinnati: Hebrew Union College Press, 1940), 1:178.

30. See, *e.g.*, *Shabbat* 23a, 87a (re *Aboth de-Rabbi Nathan A*, chap. 2, ed. Schechter, 5a [p. 9]).

31. See *Avot* 1:11 (and comment of Maimonides thereon, ed. Kappah, 271 re *Aboth de-Rabbi Nathan A*, chap. 5, 13b [p. 26]); *Tosefta Berakhot* 6:24; *Megillah* 25b re Exodus 32:24.

32. See *Niddah* 31b. Cf. *Tosefta Sanhedrin* 8:7 and *Sanhedrin* 38a. For the resolution of this conflict, see R. Jacob ibn Habib, *Iyyun Ya'akov* on *Niddah* 31b, who points out that humans are, in effect, the *junior* partners of God.

33. *Berakhot* 34b re Isaiah 64:3.

34. See *Sanhedrin* 97b; also, Will Herberg, *Judaism and Modern Man* (New York: Meridian Books, 1951), pp. 193ff.

35. See Alan J. Yuter, "*Siddur Sim Shalom*" in *Tomeikh keHalakhah: Responsa of the Panel of Halakhic Inquiry* (Mt. Vernon, NY: Union for Traditional Conservative Judaism, 1986), pp. 6ff. Cf. Ben Zion Bokser, *The Prayer Book: Weekday, Sabbath and Festivals* (New York: Hebrew Publishing Co., 1957), pp. x–xi; Robert Gordis, Introduction., *Sabbath and Festival Prayerbook* (New York: Rabbinical Assembly and United Synagogue of America, 1946), pp. ix–x.

36. See, *e.g.*, *Gittin* 4:2–7.

Rituals, Myths and Communities[1]

Neil Gillman

There is no precise Hebrew equivalent for the world "ritual." When classic Jewish texts refer to the body of observances such as the dietary laws, tefillin, Sabbath and Festival practices, immersion in a mikvah, or rites of passage such as circumcision, they use phrases such as *mitzvot shebein adam lamakom,* "commands [dealing with the relationship] between human beings and God" as opposed to *mitzvot shebein adam l'havero,* "commands [dealing with the relationship] between one human being and another." Or they use the terms coined by Rav Saadia Gaon (tenth century): *mitzvot shimiyot,* "revelational" (lit., "heavenly") commands as opposed to *mitzvot sikhliyot* or "rational" commands,[2] or, finally, the rabbinic interpretation of a biblical distinction between God's *hukkim* and *mishpatim.* The former, according to the rabbinic interpretation of passages such as Leviticus 18:4, are ordinances which idolaters (or the evil impulse) tempt us to flout precisely because they are totally arbitrary divine decrees.[3] The latter, had God not revealed them, would have been decreed by humanity itself, for they are the reasonable axioms of our social order.

These are practices, then, which have no clear interpersonal (read "ethical") impact but deal rather with our relationship to God; have no rational basis, but are arbitrary and hence more likely to be flouted; and are binding simply because of the weight of divine authority which lies behind them.

These characteristics account for the problems we face in making sense of these practices today. Obedience to arbitrary divine decrees does not come easily. In the scholarly arena, the absence of a precise Hebrew equivalent for "ritual" is often used to justify a vague discomfort with the entire issue. In many circles, the word ritual itself carries negative connotations. This entire dimension of religious life does not lend itself to the detached, critical or scientific approach which has been the hallmark of Jewish scholarship for the past century. With strikingly few exceptions — Gershom Scholem's work on Jewish mysticism being the most noteworthy — Jewish scholars have ignored the range of issues dealing with the phenomenology of religion — that is, the way in which Judaism, specifically as religion, functions in the lives of human beings in their communities. Ritual is central to this inquiry, which must be approached existentially and experientially, not simply objectively or cerebrally. Ritual touches the more primitive layers of our being, that part of us that cultivates fantasy or responds to a mytho-poetic reading of our experience. It can have a mysterious yet undeniably powerful impact at critical moments in our personal and communal lives — much more powerful than that of the more intelligible institutions of religious life. And, in fact, it is omnipresent, though often unnoticed precisely because of its omnipresence.

It should be added that "Ritual Studies" is an exciting and growing field of investigation, populated largely by social scientists and scholars in religious studies (largely of primitive religions and Christianity). What follows here is an inquiry into more specifically Jewish understandings of ritual.

Theoretical Options

In reviewing the more relevant theories on the function of ritual in religion, we need to remember that the distinctions are theoretical or functional, *not* institutional, and that any believer can fit into any one camp at any one moment.

Ritual As Magic

Ritual, if performed correctly, has an immediate, automatically coercive effect on the Force or forces that govern nature and history. Failure to perform the ritual or to perform it in the proper way can lead to disaster. Yehezkel Kaufmann's morphology of pagan ritual stresses its magical character but, as we know, magical residues can be found in the behavior of even the most sophisticated of believers. *Tefillat haderekh* for example, can be recited as a magical formula designed to "coerce" God to protect the traveler, or as a prayer that God freely intercede on his behalf, or as a simple acknowledgment of the traveler's vulnerability. The determining factor is more the inner state of mind than the theology (which is rarely explicit). The anxiety which results from *not* saying the prayer will serve as a reliable indicator of a more magical framework. Unique to this position is the automatic and coercive nature of the cause and effect relationship and the emphasis on the meticulous performance of the ritual itself as decisive. This position can also sometimes serve as the implicit mind-set behind the otherwise paradoxical juxtaposition of meticulous adherence to ritual and flagrant violation of the moral law. Jeremiah 7:3–15 records an early manifestation of that position and Jeremiah's appropriately monotheistic response. Finally, some formulations of the problem of theodicy actually signal the breakdown of a magical framework where the fulfillment of the *moral* law (sometimes along with the ritual) is intended to *coerce* the desired reward.

Ritual As Sacrament

Here, too, ritual effects a substantive change in the nature of things out there, beyond the believer, but in contrast with the magical approach, the sacramentalist insists that the efficacy of the ritual demands the proper state of inwardness, the correct belief structure. The magicalist, in contrast, ascribes inherent power to the performance of the ritual itself. The Roman Catholic understanding of the eucharist whereby the bread and wine *become* the flesh and blood of Jesus when the proper formulae are recited by the proper person within the proper belief structure, so that the one who partakes of them, again in the proper belief structure, is thereby saved, is sacramentalism at its purest. Mary Douglas captures that dimension:

> "The crux of the doctrine is that a real, invisible transformation has taken place at the priest's saying of the sacred words and that the eating of the consecrated host has saving efficacy for those who take it and for others . . . It assumes that humans can take an active part in the work of redemption, both to save themselves and others, through using the sacraments as channels of grace. Sacraments are not only signs, but essentially different from other signs, being instruments. This touches on the belief in *opus operatum*, the efficacious rite . . . "[5]

The more liberal wings of Protestant Christianity transformed the sacrament of the eucharist into a symbolic pageant or historical reenactment of Jesus' self-sacrifice. In Judaism, the Lurianic view of ritual as effecting a cosmic *tikkun* (repair) when performed with the proper *kavvanah* (intent) is sacramentalism in a Jewish vein. Here too, the mitzvot are efficaciously redemptive instruments.

Ritual As Obedience

Ritual does not effect a direct, substantive change in the nature of things but it is explicitly commanded by God. Performing a ritual, then, is nothing more than a concrete way of acknowledging God's authority and obeying His will. This *may* result in God's freely bestowed reward, but not automatically, inevitably or coercively. To ignore the ritual is to flout God. Again, this *may* result in God's freely bestowed punishment, but not automatically, inevitably or coercively. Ethical mitzvot can also serve to acknowledge God's authority but they can too easily be performed on rational or humanist grounds. Rituals are arbitrary. They serve, then, as the most complete expression of religious submission and therefore of authenticity within the believing community. Norman Lamm, for example, insists that we should perform even the ethical commands as if they were ritual, thereby transforming a "pale humanist act" into a "profound spiritual gesture."[7] Crucial to this position are a literalist understanding of revelation — God has made His will known unambiguously to His community — and a concept of God as totally free and non-coercible by any power outside His own will.

Ritual As Symbolic Action

This position will be developed in detail below.

Ritual As Anachronism

Ritual was a meaningful form of religious expression in the past, either in the earlier stages of civilization or in pre-modern times. It is now an anachronism. *Our* preferred forms are ethical behavior and/or spirituality (inwardness). This position identifies ritual behavior with "ritualism" which can be defined as ritual acts performed in a totally mechanical, routinized way, what Abraham Heschel so felicitously called "religious behaviorism." They have become purely outward forms of behavior, empty of any religious, spiritual or emotional content. Hence they should be abandoned.[8]

Some Problems

The problem with the magical position is that it denies the monotheistic God who is, above all, supremely free. It assumes that a human being can coerce natural processes or, in a monotheistic setting, God Himself. The position may meet deep-seated psychological needs in a human being but as an explicit theology of Jewish ritual, it is unacceptable.

The sacramental position runs into different problems. It can be accommodated to monotheism but, unless one is a Lurianic kabbalist, Jewish ritual simply has not exercised a sacramental function. There is no Jewish parallel to the Roman Catholic understanding of the eucharist. No Jew, for example, would find himself in the position of the adulterous policeman in Graham Greene's *The Heart of the Matter* who is torn between confessing his adultery and shattering his marriage, or taking the eucharist in a state of sin which means eternal damnation. No Jewish ritual carries that kind of power. In fact, there are rabbinic passages that explicitly deny this position. Note, for example, the claim of the third century amora, Rav, that God does not care if we (ritually) slaughter the animal by the nape or by the neck[9]; or that of the first century tanna, Rabban Yohanan ben Zakkai, that "neither does the corpse defile nor does the water (with the ashes of the red heifer) purify, but rather I (God) have issued a set of arbitrary decrees which you are simply not permitted to flout."[10]

More generally, there is not one single Jewish *ritual* that may not, on occasion, be suspended. Even circumcision which must be performed on the eighth day, even on the Sabbath *and* the Day of Atonement may be postponed indefinitely if the infant is ill or if two other children of the same mother died as a result of the ritual.[11] Similar conditions apply to tefillin (for the *onen* — a mourner before the funeral) or Sabbath observance, the Yom Kippur fast and the dietary laws (for *pikuah nefesh* — safeguarding a life.[12] Neither the magicalist nor the sacramentalist can tolerate the suspension of a central ritual act.

Which brings us to ritual as the paradigmatic act of obedience to God. Here we are on more familiar ground. Obedience to God's will is clearly the central model of spirituality both in the Bible and in rabbinic literature. But the problem with the position is its almost inevitable tendency to elevate ritual behavior to the pinnacle of religious expression. Prophetic literature, for one, insists on a different hierarchy of divine commands with ethical behavior taking priority. Justice, compassion, righteousness—these are inherently or absolutely divine, for they define God's relationship with us. God Himself is bound by these values and they then acquire absolute sanctity; that is why they must define our interpersonal relationships as well. But the non-ethical commands have a derivative sanctity. God is not bound by them; He does not participate in nor is He affected by the cult. If God were to choose, Hosea 6:6 tells us, God would want *hesed* over *zevah*, acts of lovingkindness over sacrifice. The first chapter of Isaiah, which we read liturgically prior to the fast of *Tishah B'Av*, has God denouncing Israel's sacrifices and festivals. What God demands of us is that we should cease to do evil, devote ourselves to justice, aid the wronged, uphold the rights of the orphan and defend the cause of the widow.

Finally, what more dramatic repudiation of the priority of ritual can there be than God's decision to destroy His Temple—the very site of the ritual cult in biblical religion—as punishment for Israel's moral shortcomings. God's destruction of His Temple would be inconceivable to the magicalist or the sacramentalist. It *could* be viewed as supporting the view of ritual as anachronistic but: (a) Ezekiel does prophesy about the rebuilding of the Temple; (b) what Isaiah 1, Jeremiah 7 and Amos 5 (21ff.) denounce is "your" ritual cult, *i.e.,* the one that is being practiced now, not the cult in general; and (c) the exiles did in fact rebuild the Temple with God's clear approval (Haggai 1:2ff). It does, however, challenge the claim that ritual has any kind of priority.

Finally, this position also assumes that all of the mitzvot are explicitly, *i.e.,* literally or verbally, revealed by God, a position that raises theological problems all its own.[13] If we prefer an alternative theology of revelation, we have to redefine what we mean by mitzvah in general and the ritual mitzvot in particular.

Finally, the reductionist dismissal of religious ritual as anachronistic cannot be evaluated from within any of the customary theological assumptions. Here, the inquiries of the social sciences and our common human experience take on heightened significance. From these sources, we learn this cardinal principle: the issue is never ritual or no ritual but rather *which* ritual—for significant portions of our lives are inherently ritualized.

Ritual As Language

A tennis club will prescribe certain rules of behavior which must be obeyed by all members. Some of these are perfectly reasonable: tennis shoes must be worn for traction and to preserve the playing surface. Others are completely arbitrary. Just try to appear on the court wearing a navy blue shirt and yellow bathing suit! A detailed code governs every moment of a meal in an expensive restaurant: the placement and use of cutlery, plates and goblets; the selection and presentation of wine and food; the correlation of wines and dishes; the juxtaposition of foods and even the choice of ingredients — all are subject to stringent and detailed regulation. Elaborate codes of behavior govern an appearance of and before the Queen of England or the President of the United States or, for that matter, the way in which a baseball team celebrates a home run, or the hierarchy of seating around the table in the boardroom of a large corporation. A violation of any of these regulations would have much the same effect as bringing a slice of bacon into the kitchen of a traditional Jew.

There is a tight nexus between ritual and community. Ritual is a language which, like other languages, creates community. Verbal language is a highly precise form of communication. There are other messages, however, that do not lend themselves to verbal communication. "Words fail me," we say, when we want to express powerful emotions. We hug our children and recognize that it would take many words to express what is in the hug. Or we resort to visual symbols such as showing the flag, or aural symbols such as singing *Hatikvah*, which communicate powerfully and directly the full weight of our national pride.

Language creates community. It unites those who share the language but it also excludes those who do not. By definition, communities also include and exclude; some people are in and others are out. Languages and communities are inherently separatist. It is no accident that Leviticus 11 which details the foods which the biblical community could or could not eat concludes with the repeated injunction that this community was to be *kadosh*. We normally translate *kadosh* as "sacred" or "holy" but a more technical definition would be "separated out" or "distinguished" (in the non-valuative sense of the word). The Sabbath day which is *kadosh* begins with *kiddush* and ends with *havdalah*, which are synonyms. The Sabbath is distinguished from the other days of the week as the Israelites are distinguished from other communities, the land of Israel from other lands or the Hebrew language from other languages.

To say that the issue is never ritual or no ritual but rather which ritual, is the same as saying that the issue is never community or no community but which community. One invariably belongs to a community and speaks its idiosyncratic languages.

From Language to Theatre

How do languages create community? I suggest we broaden the metaphor and see ritual as a form of theatre — a miniature, liturgical drama. Theatre, too, creates community. The proscenium collapses and players and audience are united in a shared experience. Take the Jewish rites of passage — circumcision, marriage, and the rites of burial and mourning. At each of these, all of Israel is present, symbolically, in the form of a minyan. Each celebrates a private moment in the life of an individual, yet each is also an event in the life of the community — so the community belongs. A script is read — the liturgy. There are the main actors: bride and groom, *mohel,* infant, mourner; and supporting actors: the *sandek,* witnesses, comforters. There are even off-stage, fantasy characters: Adam, Eve and Jeremiah at the wedding, Abraham, Phineas and Elijah at the circumcision, Job at the graveside. The *huppah,* Elijah's throne, and the low chairs in the *shiva* house serve as sets. Stage directions are provided: the ring on the right forefinger, the tearing of the garment, the cutting of the foreskin. The characters wear costumes: the groom, a white *kittel*; the mourner, a torn garment. The Passover seder is the pageant at its most elaborate where word, body language, set, script, stage directions and even costumes all come together to teach the founding story of a community to its next generation.

Rituals accomplish two purposes superbly well. First they define identity. They shape the social experiences of everyday life — eating, dressing, leisure — and the transitions in nature and life — from day to night, from season to season, from life stage to life stage — and garb them in the distinctive values of a particular community. In the process, *this* community takes on a distinctive identity. It becomes separated out from other communities.

Second, rituals are powerful pedagogic devices. They transmit identity from generation to generation. Effective education is always theatrical, particularly when it goes beyond the cognitive, when it is tinged with affect, when it speaks to the senses as much as to the mind, when it addresses the whole person. At the Passover seder, the table is both stage and classroom, the *haggadah,* both script and textbook. The rituals of reclining, eating and drinking, lifting and lowering, covering and uncovering are both stage directions and experiential learning. They are theatrical, also, because they depart from what is usually done "every other night of the year." It is this *mah nishtanah* quality which transforms a meal into a ritual experience. We don't usually dip our fingers into the wine, eat horseradish root, or, for that matter, wrap leather thongs around our arm, tear our garments, smell spices, wave palm branches or move into a sukkah. It is the unfamiliarity of the choreography that makes them educationally unforgettable experiences. But precisely because the choreography is unfamiliar, it is also threatening. Hence we are tempted to substitute a familiar choreography for the unfamiliar. The visit to the house of mourning becomes a social call; the tuxedo replaces the *kittel*; the black ribbon replaces the torn garment. The anachronist claims that we have done away with ritual. In fact we have substituted one set, costume, script and stage direction for another. There is no escaping ritual.

The trade-off for beginning our inquiry with our common human experience is that ritual behavior becomes generic. We flatten the differences between the rituals of religion and those of everyday life. In the short run we may gain pedagogically. But eventually we must deal with the distinctive qualities of the rituals of religion.

Rituals and Myth

The rituals of religion are dramatizations of religious myths. No term in contemporary religious scholarship is more misunderstood than "myth." A brief digression, then, is in order to indicate how we understand the term.[14]

In popular parlance, a myth is understood to be either a fiction (the myth of the invincibility of the New York Yankees) or a legendary tale (the myth of Oedipus). Technically, it is neither of these, but rather a structure of meaning through which we make sense of our experience. Experience does not come to us as brute fact laden with objective meaning. The very determination of what constitutes a "fact" in the first place, let alone how facts assume specific patterns that convey meaning, requires a complex transaction between the "out there" and the way we choose to "read" it. Myths are created by "reading communities," individuals joined in efforts to shape, order and make sense of what seems to be blooming confusion. Gradually, as the myth works to explain why things are as they are, it is refined, shared, and transmitted from generation to generation. It becomes embodied in official, canonical texts. In its final form, it becomes authoritative, even coercive, and quasi-invisible — so much has it become part of our intuitive stance toward the world.

Myths explain, account for, answer questions such as "why." In general, they explain overt data by referring to an invisible or elusive world "behind" the data. This accounts for the imaginative or apparently "fictional" character of many myths — even, it should be noted, the myths of science. Psychoanalytic theory, quantum mechanics and astronomy are notable examples of scientific myths; they too explain the overt data of observation by referring to a hidden world "behind" experience.[15]

Myths are intrinsic to communities. A living community acquires its identity through its myth. It explains how that community came to be, what distinguishes it from other communities, how it views its distinctive destiny, what constitutes its value scheme. From its myth, a community derives its raison d'être; when the myth dies, the community's death is not far behind.

Religious myths function in much the same way. They too explain, account for, confer identity, promote loyalty and motivate behavior on behalf of a religious community. They, too, reveal unsuspected or elusive depths that lie behind experience. But they differ from other mythic structures in their content. First, they convey the community's distinctive answers to the ultimate questions posed by human existence: Why am I here? What am I to accomplish? How should I live? Why do I suffer? Why must I die? How do I deal with my guilt? How do I achieve authenticity? fulfillment? salvation? In short, they convey a community's answers to the intuitive search for meaning. Second, they do all of this by viewing the panorama of nature and history as the work of a transcendent God.

To say that God is within the mythic structure is to say that all characterizations of God and His activity are colored by the fact of our humanness. This is not at all to say that He is a fiction. Our ancestors no more "invented" God than Freud "invented" the psyche or a physicist, the electron. They experienced God's presence in nature and history; that was the original, experiential source for the myth.[16] They simply could not account for their communal experience in any other way. The myth and the original experience fueled and continued to fuel each other. The (mythic) characterization of God shapes the experience. But at the same time, the ongoing experience of His presence has verified the myth over countless generations. Otherwise, it would have died long before our time.

Religious myths are canonized in Scriptures, sacred books that record the authoritative version of the myth and become textbooks for communicating it from generation to generation. Though the sacred books are sealed, the myth itself remains plastic enough so that succeeding generations can expand, contract, refine or revise the mythic structure in terms of their personal experience; we Jews call that process midrash. Religious myths also generate liturgies or dramatic recitations of the myth which celebrate significant moments in the life experience of the community or its members. Often, the sheer recounting of the narrative portion of the myth is itself an act of worship, a way of praising God who is the supreme actor in the story.[17] Finally, religious myths also generate rituals, equally dramatic renderings of the myth, this time in the language of the body.[18]

Ritual draws its power from the myth. A living myth has enormous power to generate emotion, loyalty and activity. People die for their myths. Ritual draws on that power. In fact, it is precisely through the ritual that the power inherent in the myth is channeled to a community.

Take the ritual of circumcision. Covenant is the linchpin of the Torah myth and the circumcision is the ritual expression of "covenantedness," the *ot* or visual, dramatic symbol of the Covenant. The indelibility of the act captures the indelibility of the Covenant itself. And the fantasy characters that are invoked—Abraham, Phineas and Elijah—are all models of undeviating loyalty to the Covenant through the most severe of tests. Note also the interplay between the two languages, the verbal and the behavioral, the liturgy and the ritual. Each does what it does best. The ritual lends drama and affect; it creates the almost palpable sense of awe that pervades the room. The liturgy lends specificity. It brings the event into the explicit framework of the myth and locates it within the broader vision of the community. Together they form a complex pageant which celebrates another link in the chain of "covenantedness."[19]

Conversely, the absence of a distinctive liturgy and ritual is invariably an indication that the myth has nothing distinctive to say, as yet, about the event or experience at hand. We are keenly aware of the lack of either liturgy or ritual to memorialize the Holocaust or to celebrate the founding of the State of Israel or, until recently, the birth of a daughter. The flood of new proposals for the last of these is the clearest indication that the impulse for the creation of new liturgical and ritual forms emerges out of a deeply felt, human and communal need. We may not teach our children to say *k'riat Sh'ma* at bedtime, but most children will then produce dramatic and equally coercive bedtime liturgies and rituals of their own.

Ritual and Ritualism

The position advocated here suggests that Jewish ritual be understood as a complex symbolic system. The term "symbol" as used in this context, has two implications. First a symbol "stands for," "represents," "reflects," or "captures" some other, more ultimate reality, usually an elusive or hidden reality, in highly dramatic form. It possesses no inherent meaning or power of its own but draws on the reality which it represents. That is what separates ritual-as-symbol from ritual-as-sacrament. On the other hand, a symbol is more than a "sign." A sign is a mere convention, easily established and just as easily abandoned. The red traffic light is a sign; a national flag is a symbol. Spitting on the flag is a very different matter than ignoring a red light. That's what separates rituals from "ritualism."[20]

A symbol can "die," that is, lose its power to represent or capture the reality for which it stands. It then becomes a "sign," outward behavior alone, empty of any genuine content. We have then fallen prey to "ritualism." But that condition is neither inevitable nor permanent. "The Star Spangled Banner" played before a hockey game at Madison Square Garden is ritualism; the crowd feels free to cheer throughout. But this does not destroy the hymn's power as an authentic national ritual when it is played at the funeral of John F. Kennedy. Sometimes we *daven* ritualistically; at other times, we can recite the same liturgy as an authentic ritual of prayer.

The danger of degenerating into ritualism applies less to the grand set pieces of Jewish ritual life than to those rituals such as the dietary laws which are part of the furniture of everyday life. What distinguishes the latter is their omnipresence as a structure imposed on the most ordinary aspects of living. These are so far from being theatrical that they become quasi-invisible. To take these common experiences and to classify, organize and structure them in a distinctive way is intrinsic to community building.

This entire discussion of the interrelationship of myth, ritual and community converges in the notion of the significance of distinctions. To have an identity is to be different from someone else. By definition, one community is distinct from another community. The community's myth lends content to that distinction and its rituals concretize and dramatize that content in the life experience of its members. This is the point of departure for the anthropological inquiry into the notions of sacred space and sacred time in religion.[21] Thus *parashat Kedoshim* (Leviticus 19:1–20:27), not incidentally ". . . the pentateuchal portion that was recited before the entire assembled community because most of the pillars of Torah are based on its contents",[22] pursues the making of distinctions of all kinds in meticulous detail. That's how a community becomes *kadosh*.

The confusion of ritual and ritualism is part of a more general contemporary tendency to disparage ritual. For Mary Douglas, this "contempt of external ritual forms" is followed by two successive stages, first "the private internalizing of religious experience" and then "the move to humanist philanthropy," that is, to ethics as substitute for ritual.[23] The process is hauntingly familiar to students of recent Jewish religious history. In effect, to disparage ritual is to disparage distinctions. But what really takes place is the substitution of one set of distinctions for another, one community and its ritual forms for another. There is no escaping community and ritual. The only question is: which community, and which ritual system?

Obedience to God or Symbolic Behavior

In the last analysis, my sense is that our choice lies between seeing ritual as obedience to God's will or as symbolic behavior. The two positions are not mutually exclusive, at least in theory. God *can* command us to act in symbolic ways. But in practice, the two positions will lead to widely divergent outcomes. The issues involved in making this choice are both theological and programmatic. The first position assumes God's explicit, *i.e.*, literal or verbal revelation of His will. The second assumes an active human and communal role in the formulation of the content of revelation. Where we stand on that issue will be decisive.

Programmatically, the symbolist position assumes that any ritual can "die" and that new rituals can be generated by the community. The first cannot abide that possibility. It also cannot abide the possibility that a ritual can become morally offensive to segments of the community; the symbolists will have much less difficulty with that eventuality. Having said this, we should be enormously cautious about abandoning any one ritual. We never know when it can be reinfused with meaning, and it is painfully clear that the process of creating new rituals is long and arduous. There is then one further difference between the two positions. The symbolist will be much more tolerant of pluralistic ritual patterns and extended periods of indecision as the process of eliminating, revising, retaining or creating works itself out. We are squarely in one of those periods today in regard to prayer rituals for Jewish women. Kippah, tallit, and tefillin are being worn or not worn in every possible combination. The process is exciting and not a little anxiety-filled.

But this period also affords us an opportunity to study the process of "ritualization," the development of new ritual forms. In regard to the Holocaust, for example, David Roskies' *Night Words* is a particularly creative proposal that unites verbal and body language in a highly theatrical way and is gradually winning communal acceptance as a *Yom Hashoah* ritual.[24] Presumably the Passover seder began this way as well.

Beyond this, much work remains to be done on sharpening the distinctions between convention, custom, ceremony and ritual. There are few universally accepted definitions as yet. Even more important is the attempt to catch in a more rigorous way what each of these symbolic forms in fact represents. Finally, totally obscure, as yet, is the relationship of Jewish ritual to our view of the human body which is the instrument for ritual behavior. We are still at the very beginning of the inquiry.

For the present, however, our problem is that we belong to multiple communities with multiple myths and ritual systems. To put the matter in another way, we accept the need and value of distinctions, but we are confused as to which ones we want to retain and which we want to abandon. Some of us have abandoned the distinction in gender roles in the synagogue, but we all maintain the distinction between meat and milk. Sometimes, our multiple communities and languages cohere; we can have a kosher wedding at the Plaza, even a kosher *nouvelle cuisine* wedding. Sometimes they don't cohere; we can't serve shrimp cocktail at a kosher wedding, even at the Plaza. We are then forced to choose. The ambiguities of those choices is one of the most difficult trade-offs of the symbolist position.[25] This is probably what impels some of our contemporaries to the obedience position.

Finally, it should be absolutely clear that the symbolist position in no way advocates a contraction in ritual behavior. If this is an age of communal fragmentation, of growing anomie and isolation, of rootlessness and anxiety, of emotional aridity, then it is an age that demands more ritual, more theatrically performed than ever before. We may or may not be prepared to believe that God explicitly commands us to act in these ways but we might more easily believe that our very humanness and our communal identity does—and that we should harken as obediently to these demands as our ancestors did to God's.

NOTES

1. The author acknowledges his debt to his colleagues, Dr. Aryeh Davidson, Dr. Elliot Dorff and Ms. Renée Gutman and to his students in classes in Jewish Philosophy at the Jewish Theological Seminary who read earlier drafts of this paper and helped clarify many of the issues it raises. Many of their criticisms are reflected in this version though the author alone is responsible for its content.

2. *Book of Doctrines and Beliefs*, chapter 3.

3. Rashi *ad. loc.* and on Numbers 19:2. *Yoma* 67b.

4. See, *e.g.*, his *The Religion of Israel*, translated and abridged by Moshe Greenberg, (Chicago: The University of Chicago Press, 1960), pp. 53–58.

5. *Natural Symbols*, (New York: Pantheon Books, 1970), pp. 47–48. Mary Douglas' work on ritual is enormously suggestive, though both my terminology and conceptualizations differ from hers. See, in particular, chapters 1 and 3 in this volume as well as her provocative "The Abominations of Leviticus" in *Purity and Danger*, (London: Routledge and Kegan Paul, 1966), pp. 41–57. Robert Alter's "A New Theory of Kashrut," *Commentary*, August 1979 (68:46), pp. 46–52, is an incisive critique of the latter piece.

6. *Major Trends in Jewish Mysticism*, (New York: Schocken Books, 1941), pp. 273–276.

7. See his contribution to *The Condition of Jewish Belief, A Symposium* compiled by the Editors of *Commentary*, (New York: The Macmillan Company, 1965), pp. 125–126.

8. A classic expression of this position is in American Reform Judaism's Pittsburgh Platform of 1886 and its European and American antecedents.

9. *Genesis Rabbah* 44:1.

10. *Numbers Rabbah* 19:8.

11. *Shabbat* 19:5; *Yevamot* 64b; *Shulḥan Arukh, Yoreh De'ah* 262:2, 263:2.

12. In contrast, we must accept martyrdom rather than commit incest, homicide or idolatry. *Sanhedrin* 74a; *Mishneh Torah, Yesodei HaTorah*, 5:1–3

and *Shulḥan Arukh, Yoreh De'ah* 157:1.

13. Norman Lamm's statement cited above (note 7) is an unapologetic defense of that theology of revelation. See my "Toward a Theology for Conservative Judaism," *Conservative Judaism,* 37:1, Fall 1983, pp. 4-22 for a critique of that position.

14. The literature on the problem of defining myth is abundant. The author continues to find Paul Tillich's *Dynamics of Faith* (New York: Harper and Row, 1957) absolutely indispensable. Also helpful are: Lauri Honko, "The Problem of Defining Myth," in Alan Dundes, ed., *Sacred Narrative: Readings in the Theory of Myth,* (Los Angeles: University of California Press, 1984), pp. 41-52; Ian G. Barbour, *Myths, Models and Paradigms,* (New York: Harper and Row, 1974), chs. 1-2; and Will Herberg's "Some Variant Meanings of the Word 'Myth' " in his *Faith Enacted as History,* (Philadelphia: The Westminster Press, 1976).

15. The three examples noted above share these qualities; they are elaborate, imaginative constructs. On the "mythical" quality of scientific theories, see Ian G. Barbour, *op. cit.,* chs. 3-5. See also Thomas S. Kuhn, *The Structure of Scientific Revolutions* (Chicago: The University of Chicago Press, 1970) for numerous suggestive parallels between the evolution of religious myths and scientific paradigms.

16. An impressive, phenomenological description of that experience is in Henri Frankfort *et al., Before Philosophy,* (Baltimore: Penguin Books, 1949), pp. 11-36. This description is helpful for an understanding of religious experience as described in the writings of theologians such as Martin Buber and Abraham Joshua Heschel.

17. Such as Nehemiah 9:6-12 followed by Exodus 14:30-31 in the daily *Shaharit* service; also Deuteronomy 26:1-11, Psalms 105, 106, and 136 as examples of historical narrative in liturgical form.

18. The literature on the relationship of myth and ritual is equally extensive. See, in particular, Theodor H. Gaster's "Myth and Story" in Alan Dundes, *op. cit.,* pp. 110-126; Mircea Eliade's "Methodological Remarks on the Study of Religious Symbolism" in Eliade and Joseph M. Kitagawa, eds., *The History of Religions: Essays in Methodology,* (Chicago: The University of Chicago Press, 1959) pp. 86-107; Edmund R. Leach, "Ritual," *International Encyclopedia of the Social Sciences* (New York: Macmillan Free Press, 1968) vol. 13, pp. 520-526; Victor Turner, "Myth and Symbol" in *ibid.,* vol. 10, 576-582; and Mary Douglas, *op. cit.* In general, the author has found the writings of Eliade, Douglas and Turner to be most suggestive on this entire complex of issues.

19. There is also, of course, a significant psychological component to the rituals of religion. Specifically in regard to the rites of passage, see our colleague Amy Eilberg's "Views of Human Development in Jewish Ritual: A Comparison with Eriksonian Theory" in *Smith College Studies in Social Work,* Nov. 1984.

20. On the distinction between "symbol" and "sign", see Tillich, *op. cit.,* pp. 41-43; also John Herman Randall Jr., *The Role of Knowledge in Western Religion,* (Lanham: University Press of America, 1986) pp. 109-116. The

latter, long out of print but now republished, is a masterpiece of scholarship. Tillich and Randall taught all of this material in seminars in philosophy of religion at Columbia University.

21. As in Mircea Eliade, *The Sacred and the Profane*, (New York: Harper, 1961) chs. 1 and 2. Heschel's characterization of Jewish ritual as "... *architecture of time*" in *The Sabbath*, (New York: Farrar, Straus and Giroux, 1951) p. 8 is a remarkably felicitous formulation of this position. In general, *The Sabbath* is a remarkable achievement not only for its poetic, meditative or pietistic style. Its thesis is that Jewish ritual has to be understood from an anthropological perspective, not only a theological one. In retrospect, that was a radical, ground-breaking proposal. Equally radical in its implications was "Judaism as a System of Symbols" by our teacher, Louis Finkelstein, printed in Bryson, Finkelstein, MacIver and McKeon, eds., *Symbols and Values: An Initial Study*, (New York: Conference on Science, Philosophy and Religion in Their Relation to the Democratic Way of Life, 1954), ch. 5. For a development of Heschel's view of ritual as "sanctification of time," see Arthur Green's "Sabbath as Temple; Some Thoughts on Space and Time in Judaism," in R. Jospe and S. Z. Fishman, eds., *Go and Study: Essays in Honor of Alfred Jospe*, (Washington: B'nai B'rith Hillel Foundations, 1980), pp. 287–305.

22. Rashi *ad. loc.*; *Sifra Kedoshim* on Leviticus 19:1. The two sets of structures—the mythic and the ritual—reflect and reinforce each other, one conceptually and the other experientially. The process is captured by Clifford Geertz in his seminal "Religion as a Cultural System" in his collection, *The Interpretation of Cultures* (New York: Basic Books, 1973).

23. *Natural Symbols*, p. 7.

24. Published and distributed by B'nai B'rith Hillel Foundations, Washington, D.C. In particular, the ritual of inscribing a number on the arm is a brilliant and classic use of symbolic behavior which has the added advantage of being Holocaust-specific.

25. This author, for example, has pleaded for the institution of an egalitarian *Birkat Kohanim* within the framework of an egalitarian synagogue service—an ambiguous position if there ever was one! My sense is that it is mandatory that we restore a heightened sense of drama to the synagogue service and *Birkat Kohanim* is one way to do that.

The Seminary Sukkah, which attracts hundreds of visitors every year, plays a central role in the institution's community relations and education programs.

Here, Simon Greenberg, Senior Vice Chancellor of the Seminary, leads the Birkat HaMazon, the blessing after the meal, in the Seminary's large Sukkah. Rabbi Greenberg, who graduated the Teachers Institute in 1919 and the Rabbinical School in 1925, has been actively associated with the Seminary for seventy years.

For over seventy years, Adele Ginzberg (right) coordinated the lavish decorations which adorned the Seminary Sukkah.

Pluralism in the Conservative Movement Today

Ronald D. Price

In an interview that appeared in the fall of 1986 in the *Bergen* (New Jersey) *Record,* a young rabbi was quoted as saying: "We should not saddle religion with traditions of previous centuries when the cultures were so different." These words were spoken neither by a Reform ideologue nor by a radical Reconstructionist thinker. They were expressed by a rabbi recently ordained by the Jewish Theological Seminary.

The question, "How far does pluralism in the Conservative movement extend?" is raging in our movement of late. We want to know how far our movement reaches to the left and to the right. Many would agree that the kind of thinking expressed in the preceding quotation belongs in the Conservative movement. The idea which our young rabbi voiced must certainly be considered liberal. It is radical as well. If taken to its logical end, such a notion could spell the demise of most of the Jewish tradition, since that tradition was formed under cultural realities very different from our North American experience. Yet this approach is tolerated within our movement and our Seminary.

On the liberal end of the spectrum, then, the boundary of the Conservative movement is hard to discern. Some would say that patrilineal descent marks that border. Yet even this issue is no longer the litmus test for the limits of Conservative practice and philosophy. In this centennial year of our Seminary, a petition has been circulated, signed by many prominent Conservative rabbis, suggesting that the acceptance of a patrilineal standard for determining Jewishness should not be considered inconsistent with membership in the Rabbinical Assembly.

At the other end of the spectrum, however, the boundaries between acceptable and unacceptable, between Conservative and "not-

Conservative," are being drawn. Spokesmen of our movement have pronounced egalitarianism a "moral imperative." They have thus implicitly categorized those Conservative Jews who see no such imperative as immoral. Disagreement with this position, albeit on traditional and halakhic grounds, has been treated as obstructionist. Complete redefinitions of such fundamental terms as halakhah and mitzvah have also begun to appear. These redefinitions have graver consequences than may at first appear. What begins as a redefinition of certain Jewish concepts easily leads to a reading out of those who see no need to redefine. Insisting on loyalty to original denotations and connotations is cast as primitive at best and "orthodox" and immoral at worst.

Within our midst today we are struggling with radically different approaches to the tradition and observance. There are those who feel that the mission of the Conservative movement and its rabbis is to create an observant community out of a non-observant body, and so to change the nature of our community. There are others who believe that the basic nature of observance must change. Both approaches are attempts at achieving Jewish survival. Both may even claim to be attempts at determining the nature of God's will for us. The question is whether both approaches can and should live together under the rubric of a *pluralistic* Conservative movement.

It is true that many rabbis and laymen are at neither end of the Conservative spectrum. There are those who believe in identical ritual roles for men and women and consider themselves halakhic. In their honest and earnest attempt to carve out a middle path between egalitarianism without halakhah and halakhah without egalitarianism, such individuals deserve respect. However, their position is not a middle way. It is simply inconsistent. It is only a matter of time before those who accept egalitarian ritual will ultimately be faced with the challenge of even more extreme change in halakhic practice. Despite sincere protestations to the contrary, patrilinealism follows logically. For the principle underlying patrilineal descent is precisely that of egalitarianism: identical roles for men and women in religious life.

In the end, those who have chosen to hold a position which is neither consistently traditional nor thoroughly liberal, will ultimately have to choose where their loyalty and belief lie. For one to whom halakhah is the essence of God's will for the Jewish people, with its roots going back to Sinai, continued radical change, no matter how popular it may be for the moment, must ultimately create a tremendous conflict. This conflict must result in the abandonment either of the traditional process of Jewish Law, or of the ideology of radical change. Consequently, the seeming middle position in our movement will not resolve the increasing divergence between the left and right.

We come back then, to the question of whether diametrically opposed approaches to the tradition can co-exist within the same movement. There are clear indications that there is a strong desire for this to happen. Many who have become increasingly disenfranchised ideologically by recent policies and trends within the Conservative movement have chosen to create groups *within* the movement which represent their approaches. The creation of these groups, such as the Union for Traditional Conservative Judaism, can prevent our pluralistic movement from becoming monolithic.

Our Conservative movement has long described itself as pluralistic. The belief system of a Kaplan lived alongside that of a Lieberman, albeit in tension. Today we are not sure whether such a situation is a desideratum. The increased urgency of ideological debate forces us to ask whether pluralism is still viable for us. Three alternatives present themselves through our responses to the following questions:

1. Do we believe that one Conservative ideology should be accepted by all members of the Conservative movement?

2. If not, do we believe that each ideology represented in Conservative Judaism today must recognize the correctness of every other?

3. Do we believe that several, diverse ideological groupings should be allowed to co-exist, each striving to show the virtue of its own position in an atmosphere of open and measured debate?

Answering affirmatively to the third approach, although difficult to achieve, promises the greatest reward for our movement. We must avoid the tyranny of orthodoxies on either end of the ideological spectrum inherent in the first approach, and the anarchy of relativism inherent in the second.

We must learn to tolerate each other's approach, in the grand tradition of America. We must also appreciate the passion of those who adhere to these ideologies and face one another with respect and love, without rejectionism, in the tradition of *ahavat Yisrael*. Only thus will we be able to achieve a creative tension in our troubled movement.

As a Conservative movement, we have changed greatly during the last hundred years. With God's help, we will grow, mature and evolve further during our next century. We must not become defensive when challenged by new developments in our midst. All approaches must be given equal access to our constituency. Nor must we fear the free market of ideas. We must be wary only of the attempt to silence proponents of a particular approach.

If we cannot sustain an open discussion of divergent viewpoints, there will be no pluralism in Conservative Judaism. The ideology of our movement will be determined through the manipulations of politics, rather than through creative discussion and inquiry. Such a situation would bode ill for a religious movement, and particularly for one, such as ours, whose hallmark has been open and disciplined discourse.

It is my hope that tolerance will gain the upper hand amongst us, that we will be able to accept the differences which have developed amongst us, in practice and in belief, and that we will work together wherever possible. Where uniformity is not possible, may we compete in a healthy way for the hearts and souls of the Jewish people, not for the sake of our own victory, but rather for the sake of the continued strengthening of our people.

Kol Isha: * A New Voice in Conservative Judaism

Amy Eilberg

The Conservative movement has always figured centrally in the history of Jewish feminism. In fact, the institutional birth of the Jewish feminist movement may well date to the appearance of Ezrat Nashim, a small but highly educated group of like-minded women, at the 1971 Convention of the Rabbinical Assembly. On that occasion, the women of Ezrat Nashim, most of them personally identified with the Conservative movement, presented to the rabbinic leadership of Conservative Judaism a revolutionary agenda for change in American Jewish life. They advocated a thoroughgoing investigation of the institutional disenfranchisement of women in Judaism, urging that women be granted equal access to all areas of scholarship and roles of ritual and communal leadership in the Jewish community. With this groundbreaking set of proposals, the struggle for the religious equality of women in Judaism was launched, paving the way for the decade-long pursuit of the civil libertarian agenda in Jewish feminism.

Fourteen years later, another turning point in Jewish feminist history was reached when, in response to the Jewish Theological Seminary's decision to ordain women as rabbis, the Rabbinical Assembly voted resoundingly to admit women rabbis to its ranks. With this step, it appeared to many that the Jewish feminist agenda had run its course, as the reality of rabbinic leadership by women in all non-Orthodox movements symbolically marked the empowerment and inclusion of women in all realms of Jewish life. Undoubtedly, the fourteen intervening years had seen a breathtakingly rapid period of change in attitudes toward Jewish feminist issues. By the mid-1980s, women were recognized *talmidot ḥakhamim,* if not scholars, in all fields

---

*Literally, a woman's voice. This term traditionally refers to the prohibition against a man hearing a woman singing.

of Jewish inquiry. The granting of ritual equality to women in Conservative congregations had become normative practice, and the symbolism of the ordination decision persuaded many that the exclusion and devaluation of women in Jewish life had come to an end. Yet, at the time of this writing, there is no doubt but that serious obstacles to the full equality of women in Conservative Judaism persist.

Today, resistance to the full inclusion of women in Jewish life is by no means limited to the outright rejection of the feminist revolution by the vocal right wing of the Conservative movement. It is expressed more subtly but just as powerfully in the failure of central arms of the movement, even those which have considered themselves bastions of egalitarianism, to deal meaningfully with continuing feminist concerns. In fact, sluggishness in putting egalitarian principles into action has been more rule than exception since the ordination decision, reflecting continuing latent resistance to the full enfranchisement of women, even denial of the underlying significance of the dramatic developments in policy that have already been made.

Most obvious in this area is the oft-stated charge that the movement has failed to deal adequately with the halakhic implications of the ordination decision. It must be noted that those who voice this objection betray a fundamental lack of understanding of the way in which halakhah develops in Conservative Judaism. The Committee on Jewish Law and Standards has been presented over the years with *teshuvot* (legal opinions) supporting both sides of each of the major halakhic issues in question, and all of these positions remain as acceptable standards among which local rabbis may choose. The Law Committee has quite rightly opposed the view of the many misguided Rabbinical Assembly members who have called for unanimous decisions on issues related to women. To require a criterion of unanimity on women-related issues is a fundamental violation of the Conservative view of halakhic pluralism. Hence, one must wonder how often the demand for unanimity is simply a tool wielded by Conservative Jews who prefer to express their deep-seated emotional resistance to women's equality in halakhic terms.

Nonetheless, the Law Committee's failure to address the women's issue throughout the tumultuous years of the ordination decision functions to support resistance to the basic equality of women in the movement. If the Committee's intent is, as I have suggested, to continue to rely on earlier rulings, this intent should at least have been clearly articulated to the movement. The Committee's years-long silence on the issue can scarcely be considered a cogent educational tool in reminding the rabbinic public of the decisions that have already been made, nor of the basic processes which govern the development of halakhah in the movement. Hence, the Committee's inactivity unwittingly but powerfully strengthens the position of those who continue to assert that halakhic process has been subverted.

Ironically, the Seminary, the author of the ordination decision, has itself allowed a number of administrative ambiguities to cloud its newly-declared position in favor of women's equality. One such issue is the still-unresolved question of the legal requirement (ḥiyyuv) of women rabbinical students to observe positive, time-bound mitzvot. Another is the policy of the Rabbinical School which happily continues to admit qualified candidates who oppose the equality of women, but without providing any guidance or education for students on this fundamental feature of Conservative Jewish life.

It might have been hoped that by the time the Seminary began to ordain women rabbis, the prerogatives of United Synagogue-affiliated congregations regarding women rabbinic candidates would have been articulated. An unspoken policy seems to be in place, affording congregations full autonomy in the decision of whether or not to consider the employment of a woman rabbi. While I personally question this view, I am most concerned about the failure of the movement to address the issue in any meaningful way.

Nor has any institutional arm of the movement to date made significant efforts to provide educational opportunities for congregations who have not grappled with the relevant issues. To allow this sort of autonomy is to tacitly encourage such communities in their evasion of the issue. The movement may, for the foreseeable future, permit congregations to dissent from the emerging pro-equality consensus. However, commitment to pluralism must not mean support for denial of a basic religious reality of our time. In this era, the leadership of the movement should not sanction a congregation's desire to simply close its eyes to the movement's new commitment to women's equality. It may be hoped that the newly-appointed Rabbinical Assembly Task Force on Women in the Rabbinate may prove instrumental in exploring these sorts of issues with United Synagogue and with congregations around the country.

In sum, great progress has been made in the quest to provide women with equal access to all realms of Conservative Jewish life, even if significant work remains to be done in this area. As the barriers to women's equality have begun to fall, however, a new agenda of feminist concerns has emerged, an agenda which will no doubt occupy the movement for years and decades to come.

Women's civil and religious liberties in Judaism are now nearly assured. But beneath the processes of halakhic and administrative decision-making lies a deeper challenge, an ultimately more debilitating impediment to the inclusion of women as fully equal members of Jewish society. Here the restrictions lie not in the arena of policy but of ideology, not in halakhah at all (as it is normally, narrowly defined) but in sociology and theology. The new area to which the movement must begin to direct its attention deals not only with equal access for women in Jewish society, but with equal value accorded to women in the life of our community.

In order to begin this new stage of the work, the Jewish community must once again exercise its ability to learn from its environment, to make creative use of insights and concepts developed outside the classical world of rabbinic wisdom. In this case, we must turn to the literature of the contemporary feminist movement, reading carefully and critically, prepared, as our heirs have always been, to absorb and adapt the best of other thought systems and literatures for the enhancement of Torah and Jewish life.

At this time, two central concepts developed in secular feminist writings demand the attention of every person concerned with the continued vitality of Jewish life. One is the basic feminist insight that all culture as we know it presumes that maleness is the norm by which all else is judged. This revolutionary notion of women as "the other" in human society was captured and immortalized in Simone de Beauvoir's image of woman as "the second sex." It suggests that in a plethora of ways, all of our thinking and life experience has been deeply influenced by the fundamental equation of humanness with maleness, relegating women's particular experiences and ways of being in the world as secondary to those of the male. Feminists, following the lead of de Beauvoir and other groundbreaking thinkers, have uncovered the evidence and effects of this view on wide-ranging dimensions of human experience.

In experiential terms, Cynthia Ozick poses the matter poignantly, giving voice to the pain of countless Jewish women when she writes, "In the world at large I call myself, and am called, a Jew. But when, on the Sabbath, I sit among women in my traditional shul and the rabbi speaks the word 'Jew,' I can be sure that he is not referring to me. For him, 'Jew' means 'male Jew.' "*

While the male-centeredness of classical Judaism can be understood as historically inevitable, the continued equation of humanness with maleness cannot be tolerated in contemporary Jewish society. To accede to the continued influence of Jewish institutional sexism is to repudiate *Am Yisrael's* most basic mission as an *or lagoyim,* as the guardian and disseminator of every generation's best understanding of social ethics. To quote Cynthia Ozick again, in this era a six hundred and fourteenth commandment must thunder out to us from the midst of the Torah's pages: "Thou shalt not lessen the humanity of women" (*ibid.,* p. 149).

For me, this means that every Jew today must respond to a new *ḥiyyuv,* a personal imperative, to grapple with the exclusion of women from Jewish texts and Jewish life. This means laboring for the fundamental enfranchisement of women in Jewish life, struggling to leave behind the notion of women as other, and working to comprehend women's experience in its own terms.

Feminist literature contributes a second, related axiom about society's view of women. This is that, in some fundamental ways, women are different from men. It is one of the ironies of feminist history that until very recently this was a concept with which few in society would disagree. But the years of struggle for women's equality in secular society brought with it a period during which the subtle evidence of women's psychosocial and spiritual differences from men was suppressed. At that time, it was felt by those concerned with women's equality that any notion of gender-linked traits was dangerous, a threat to women's struggle for basic civil liberties.

Today, with years of successful struggle for women's civil equality substantially behind us, it has become possible to reexamine the timeless truth about the differences between the sexes. This is best done, in my view, in Harvard social psychologist Carol Gilligan's central work, *In a Different Voice.* In a delightful and unwitting reversal of the notion of *kol isha,* a concept which encapsulated woman's status as "the other" in classical Jewish society, Gilligan advances a contemporary theory of women's unique developmental path. Be it primarily

---

*Cynthia Ozick, "Notes Toward Finding the Right Question," in Susannah Heschel, *On Being a Jewish Feminist* (Philadelphia: Schocken, 1983), p. 125.

for reasons of nature or nurture, an unanswerable and thus merely academic question, women, says Gilligan, speak "in a different voice" than do men. Women tend toward a different set of psychological values, most often favoring such traits as nurturance, interdependence, and facilitating the growth of others over the individualism and achievement orientation which tends to characterize men's lives in our society.

Surely, we have seen tremendous strides in the ability of individual men and women to break out of the traditional prison of sex-role stereotypes, and there is no doubt but that our society is more tolerant today than it was even fifteen years ago of the assertive woman and the gentle man. But equally clear is the fact that American society as a whole continues to value the male dimensions of life more highly, valuing professional achievement over family, abstract principles over devotion to cooperative relationship, individuality over nurturance. Just as undeniable is Jewish society's unchanged preference for intellect over emotion, personal power over relationship, knowledge over experience.

While it may be ultimately desirable to overcome all sex-linked dichotomies, the short-term goal which must engage us all at this juncture is to work for the day when society, Jewish and secular, will be able to value the feminine dimension along with the masculine, lest the quest for a sex-blind society simply result in a contemporary version of the equation of the feminine with otherness. It is for this reason that the civil libertarian agenda of Jewish feminism, albeit a mandatory beginning, is by no means the end of the matter. Many may yearn to utter *"baruch shepetarani"** on "the women's question." But to allow women into a man's world, grudgingly permitting women to function in it, is simply not enough. No creative, forward-looking society can continue to suppress its women and its feminine-associated values and continue to grow.

Recognition of the fact of women's noninvolvement in the formation of Judaism's sacred texts requires that active attempts now be made to incorporate women's particular life experience into our understanding of Judaism. Fundamentally, what is needed is the inclusion of women in a process which is at the core of Jewish creativity, the exegetical endeavor by which subsequent generations encounter

---

*A blessing stating one's release from responsibility, said in particular by a parent upon a child's coming of age.

received texts. More than any other, it is this process of midrash, the continuing dynamic of reading and rereading ancient texts in the light of new realities, new experiences, and new worlds of understanding, that has accounted for the dynamism of Jewish life throughout the ages. Today's demand of the hour is to see to it that women now join in the midrashic journey.

It is already clear that women will contribute to this midrashic encounter along three specific dimensions: the personal, the communal and the theological. Much meaningful work has already been done in this direction in the personal realm, particularly in terms of life cycle rituals for women. For example, nearly two generations have now passed since Mordechai Kaplan observed the lacuna in Jewish tradition's treatment of the female life cycle, and proposed the bat mitzvah ceremony, now a normative feature of Jewish life across the denominational spectrum.

Whatever the specific content of these rituals, it is the process which is most crucial, the way in which women lovingly engage in active dialogue with the siddur and the halakhah, both noting its many points of applicability to their own lives and courageously addressing the points at which gaps must be filled in. It is imperative that Jewish leaders respect and support these creative efforts. To object to such experiments simply because they have not previously been a part of Judaism is to invoke halakhah mindlessly, failing to recognize the deep Jewish motivation of women who labor in this direction. Such rituals have not existed before because women have never before been fully involved in the process of Jewish creativity. Rather than object that newness is a danger, every Conservative rabbi should celebrate the ways in which women are now embracing their role as partners in the midrashic process.

More broadly, urging women to join in the midrashic process means inviting them in a special way to encounter all of the classical texts of Judaism, applying their own particular insights and perspectives to the study of Torah. In some cases, women's inclusion in the process will simply mean, finally, the inclusion of all Jews as travelers on our people's timeless exegetical journey. At other times, women's voices will have a different timbre, and women's midrash will have a different character, reflecting the particular life experiences and world views which women bring to their encounter with the text.

Women have a particular contribution to make on the communal level as well. Gilligan and other feminist scholars have identified an attitude toward community and the nature of leadership which is particularly associated with women. Flowing from women's orientation toward nurturance and relationship, women's views of community tend to be egalitarian, cooperative, and interdependent. Experientially, those who have participated in women's organizations of various kinds typically identify an intimate style of sharing and a cooperative style of leadership that is associated with all-women's endeavors. It follows, then, that as women become more fully integrated in the lives and leadership of mixed communities—not simply in the adjunct role of Sisterhood groups, nor in token positions, but truly in partnership—that the woman's way of developing community is sure to express itself.

What is most exciting to me about this process is the way in which it dovetails with another deep concern about Jewish community which is shared equally by non-feminists today. I refer to the crisis in participation which afflicts so many of our congregations, a tendency for the laity to regard Judaism as a spectator sport in which Jewish professionals engage and which congregants occasionally observe. It is striking to me that the same generation which has witnessed the emergence of feminism is also the era that has given birth to more participatory forms of congregational life, including havurot and synagogue-affiliated mutual support networks.

There is every indication, then, that as women become more welcome in the inner circles of community activity and leadership, the style of community will become less hierarchical and theatrical, less distant and more familial—precisely the kinds of changes for which so many laypeople clamor in this era of anomie and depersonalization. While I wish by no means to suggest that women's full inclusion will be a panacea for the ills of synagogue life, there is no question but that feminine styles of nurturance and intimacy are precisely those qualities which many congregants have found lacking in the typical large urban synagogue today.

Surely, many talented men have always been drawn to the rabbinate precisely because of the ways in which it drew on their own feminine, nurturant dimension. Such rabbis have always considered it their mission to care for others in times of deep personal joy and sorrow, and to create Jewish community in a harried world. Still, the emergence of cadres of women rabbis who are primarily oriented toward this vision of the rabbinate rather than the aloof, hierarchical rabbinic figure of generations past will provide additional support to those male rabbis who have long striven to make the rabbinate responsive to congregants and respectful of their needs.

This kind of rabbi, whether male or female, is uniquely gifted in the art of engaging congregants in their own spiritual journeys. Such a rabbi is incapable of providing spectator sport or theater, for he or she respects the congregants' own spiritual questions, even if they are not framed in traditional rabbinic language. This type of leader clearly communicates respect for congregants' responsibility for their own religious lives and offers himself or herself as facilitator rather than as distant authority to aid in the quest. One can only dream of the results when generations of women rabbis, whose basic life experience has trained them to work in this facilitative mode, laboring alongside male rabbis who are especially talented in this area, will have had the chance to reshape concepts of community and of leadership in our movement.

Finally, the full integration of women into the workings of Jewish community is already demanding fundamental rethinking of Jewish theology. It is my feeling that, through years of discourse on the halakhic and sociological dimensions of the possible ordination of women, the theological issue lies beneath the surface. That is to say, many Conservative Jews have felt discomfort with the prospect of a woman on the pulpit because, on some level, the rabbi is regarded as a representative of God, and the God of Jewish imagination continues to be male. Of course, on the literal level, the equation of rabbi and deity is preposterous and offensive in a Jewish context. Yet, such emotional and spiritual associations are the stuff of religious experience, and there is no denying the fact that for many, the first encounter with a woman rabbi challenges very deeply held, often entirely unconscious, religious images.

In fact, as women — both rabbis and congregants — have begun to ascend to the *bimah,* consciously held theological beliefs have also begun to be challenged. It could not be otherwise, for the sheer incongruity of a woman rabbi speaking of God in exclusively male terms demands attention. Generally, the questioning process begins with a sense of cognitive dissonance, as congregants observe the woman rabbi calling out to God in anthropomorphic terms with which she, as a woman, can not personally identify. Women congregants have begun to experience the pain of exclusion as they become aware of the predominantly masculine language and imagery in which Jewish liturgy is couched. If humanity is created in the image of God, they muse, and God is so unmistakably male, then, unavoidably, I as a woman am less like my Creator than is a man. The logic is irrefutable, and immensely painful.

Those who dare to entertain these thoughts, despite the untouchable aura that still attends them in Conservative circles, soon find confirmation for these ideas from a number of sources. Sociologists have long observed that the language which a people chooses to describe its relationship with God both reflects and reinforces the ways in which life is lived here on earth. If it is thought to be in the natural order of things that a male Being rules the heavenly realms, how natural it is that males hold dominion on earth as well. Clearly, the choice of masculine imagery was a perfectly cogent one during millennia of patriarchal society, with religious imagery serving as a comfortable and sensible reflection of the human world. But as we have moved away from male domination of women in human society, exclusively male God-language has become less acceptable, and for some, intolerable.

Most importantly, this line of reasoning leads to the ultimate objection to the maleness of the traditional Jewish God-concept. Simply put, to imagine God as male is nothing less than idolatrous in Jewish terms. Surely, we have always permitted ourselves, out of the poverty of our human imaginations, to image God in anthropomorphic terms, knowing that we have no other cognitive framework from which to operate. But to confuse our flawed imaginings with the Creator of the world, to begin to worship the metaphors which should at best only aid us in our inchoate strivings for encounter with the ever-living God, is to confuse the product of our own minds with the One who created us. One need hardly be a feminist to be concerned about this development, one very deeply entrenched in the Jewish community.

This issue is one of deep Jewish concern, or so it should be for Jews who are not afraid that new questions will taint their image or somehow tarnish the Torah itself. Torah is not so frail that it will crumble at the first sign of a question that has not been voiced before. On the contrary, Conservative congregants and rabbis alike have long languished in theological lethargy, failing to devote much energy to the encounter with God for which our davening is a metaphor. If it is in the name of Jewish feminism that Jews begin to awaken from their spiritual slumber, I am proud to be a Jewish feminist. This is so even if, as if so often the case when I lecture in Conservative congregations around the country and come to the part of my talk devoted to theological issues, an older woman calls out from the congregation in great fear, "Oh, please don't talk about *that*!"

In sum, the Jewish feminist revolution has raised a series of issues of profound importance for the consideration of the Jewish community at large. The first stage of work has yielded impressive results, in terms of the relative success of our movement in providing its women with equal access to all roles and dimensions of Jewish life. But unquestionably, the more profound work is yet to come, as the underlying ideological and theological issues come to the fore. As the dynamics of fear and denial begin to abate, Conservative Judaism can take its rightful place as an ideological innovator on the American Jewish scene, leading the way in the exploration of previously uncharted territory of Jewish belief and practice.

But in another sense, the latest phase of the feminist challenge poses before Conservative Judaism a new version of its oldest, most basic question: How can traditional Judaism be lived and believed in the contemporary world? The specifics of the question are different, the agenda of concerns new and, to many, frightening. But the very wrestling with such questions is, after all, the raison d'être of Conservative Judaism.

At Camp Ramah, 1969.

In a study session at Camp Ramah, 1969.

A Woman in the Mirror: Conservative Judaism Faces Feminism

Leonard Gordon

> At a time when efforts are being made to eradicate discrimination between the sexes . . . the differences between the sexes are being rediscovered . . . it is difficult to say "different" without saying "better" or "worse" . . .
> Carol Gilligan, *In a Different Voice*

On the day when the Seminary faculty voted to admit women to the Rabbinical School, a handful of students and our wives gathered to celebrate this milestone in the history of our movement. The occasion was subdued. This long-awaited moment was dampened by the prevailing atmosphere of sadness and regret which pervaded the Seminary building that day. Teachers had declared a day of introspection and prayer, threats of walkouts circulated, and acrimonious charges were exchanged. In spite of the mood, those who had long championed egalitarianism in principle and who had argued for women's ordination on moral grounds felt that their ultimate objective had been achieved: women and men were now equal in Conservative Judaism, with equal rights and equal opportunities.

In these pages, I will suggest that our movement's steps towards egalitarianism do not represent the attainment of any final feminist goal. The Conservative movement is indeed in the slow but irreversible process of removing halakhic impediments to equality for women and men in Judaism.[1] Still, numbers of crucial questions remain unanswered and such steps towards equal rights and opportunities as have been taken, though substantial and important, do not indicate the acceptance of a feminist agenda. Such a development remains for the future and offers Conservative Judaism unprecedented opportunities for reevaluation and dynamic growth. This essay considers, therefore, what might be gained from embracing the feminist opportunity in the areas of synagogue life, halakhah, theology, prayer, ritual, and scholarship.

Feminism As Opportunity

> . . . (W)e believe that the most exciting and important development in contemporary Judaism has been the emergence of a movement for women's liberation . . . Our commitment to women's liberation means much more than a simple equality—it means reclaiming the parts of women's experiences that have been lost or repressed, learning from the insights of women . . . supporting the explorations of women as they develop new rituals and new ways of being Jewish and new forms of political and social actions, and understanding that women's liberation is not just about women but about a transformation in what it means to be a human being.
>
> Michael Lerner, "Why *Tikkun?*"

Feminism is a consciousness, a way of (re-)reading, (re-)acting and (re-)telling our tradition from perspectives that have been hidden because of the marginalization of Jewish women by the classical rabbinic tradition and its successors in the modern era. As the diversity of modern Jewish feminism indicates, feminism *per se* mandates no halakhic program, only an openness to women's experiences, women's voices, and women's active participation.[2] Presumably, even those who reject specific instances of equal ritual roles for women and men can find nothing objectionable in this fundamental feminist position.

While women have been admitted to both the Rabbinical and Cantorial Schools, these actions do not reflect a new attitude towards feminism. The summer 1984 issue of *Conservative Judaism,* for example, reveals the extent to which feminism is still seen as a foreign perspective. This issue, devoted to the subject of prayer, omits any contribution by women. More significantly, none of the articles addresses the problem of the male imagery which dominates the language of our prayers or of those life experiences specific to women which continue to be omitted from our liturgy. This gap is highlighted by contrast with a volume on prayer published in *Response* (1981). In this issue, fully half of the contributors are women and many of the male writers take notice of feminist concerns in their essays. The neglect, of course, is not peculiar to our movement. Even such dedicated egalitarians as the editors of *Back to the Sources* and of *Judaism* magazine's recent issue on contemporary readings of the Bible (Summer 1986) ignore both women writers and feminist responses to the Jewish tradition.

The Rabbinate

> Undoubtedly, many believed that I was studying [to become] a *rebbetzin* rather than a rabbi. . . .
> Rabbi Sally Priesand, *Judaism and the New Woman*

When the faculty voted to admit women to the Rabbinical School, students who had entered the Seminary under one set of rules and assumptions suddenly found themselves faced with a new situation that they were inadequately prepared to accept, let alone affirm. As late as 1983, students were being told that women would not be admitted to the Rabbinical School in the near future. Suddenly a new reality emerged. Without a *takkanah* (legislative ruling) to authorize the move, without a rethinking of the structure of learning or the nature of halakhic process, women would be entering an environment that had previously existed for men alone.

The outsider would become insider, but on what terms? The Seminary never answered the fundamental question that had been agitating feminist communities for years: would women enter previously male-dominated fields differently, as women, or as men? Would women be expected to wear tallit and tefillin? Would a woman who rejected the notion of equal obligation (either because she believed in separate ritual roles for women and men or because she did not theologically accept the idea of obligation) be refused admission to the school?[3] Would the presence of women in the classroom lead to new modes of learning and a reevaluation of the curriculum's traditional emphases? In a school with a deeply entrenched system of values and a status system based on the ability to manipulate rabbinic text and on halakhic observance, how would those women fare who entered with alternative sets of skills and interests? During the first transitional years these questions have barely been asked, let alone answered.

As congregations think about hiring women rabbis, a related set of issues emerges. The laity may value a woman rabbi more as social worker/psychologist than as teacher/*posek*. To some extent, this perception reflects the fact that a number of women rabbis and rabbinical students have training in social work. The danger of this situation is that a rigid set of expectations will be established according to which women rabbis are appreciated for a distinct set of interpersonal skills different from (and invariably valued less than) those of their male colleagues. Inasmuch as the tradition of the male rabbinate extends into antiquity and our movement has established a widely accepted model that dictates which skills make a rabbi a communal leader—how do we expand the current definition of rabbinic leadership without reinforcing prejudice? We might expect that, ultimately, what had been considered distinctions between female and male modes of rabbinic authority will dissolve into an enlarged and improved understanding of the rabbi's role in the community. In the interim, the presence of women in the Rabbinical School, on the Seminary faculty, and in the pulpit rabbinate must be allowed to alter the environment; for women to enter these previously male enclaves as second-class men would be demeaning (to say the least) and ultimately a loss for all concerned.

Halakhah

> What if Rosenzweig had been a woman? Would her experience upstairs behind a heavy curtain in that same Orthodox synagogue have inspired her with similar Jewish commitment? Would the talents and fervor that brought him to a position of religious leadership have brought her to a comparable position?
> Susannah Heschel, "Women Before the Law"

Conservative rabbis are fond of telling the (apocryphal?) story of Franz Rosenzweig's return to Judaism, a return inspired by a High Holiday visit to an Orthodox synagogue where he was impressed with the liturgy's full inner power. By conjuring up the image of a female Rosenzweig, Heschel calls upon us to realize that the halakhic system has not accommodated the talents of all Jews at all times. Instead, halakhah has a history and, like all human creations (even divinely inspired ones) it arises out of the life situation of those who translate divine command into human law.

Those who understand the halakhic distinction between women and men as something other than historically conditioned sexism have accordingly used the argument that Judaism, at its best, acknowledges and celebrates difference. According to this view, Judaism is a religious system that creates meaning by sanctifying separation: the dietary laws of Leviticus, the gentile as presented in tractate *Avodah Zarah,* the havdalah liturgy's separation of the Sabbath and the weekday. Women and men function in different realms because Judaism works by legally defining and ritualizing division in all aspects of life. I would point out, however, that each of Judaism's acts of separation is an act of evaluation: the holy Sabbath and the profane week, kosher and *treif,* pure and impure, insider and outsider, subject of the law and object of the law. To claim that women and men must be categorized within this system of oppositions inevitably locates women on the negative side of the balance as outsider, legal object, vehicle of impurity.

Throughout Jewish history, legal reasoning, the ability to develop refinements in the halakhic system in response to new situations, has necessarily been an important talent. Compromise, the blurring of boundaries, and radical change were regarded as potentially dangerous to the social order. The necessity for maintaining this posture has recently been questioned. Twentieth-century America is neither imperial Rome nor Czarist Russia. For the Jew, it has created a new set of problems. We are faced with the need to retain our identity in an open society.

Carol Gilligan has proposed that socialization has made it so that women "are more tolerant in their attitudes toward rules, more willing to make exceptions, and more easily reconciled to innovations" than men.[4] If Gilligan's observations are correct, then we can expect women to initiate new modes of halakhic decision-making, modes that may be more appropriate to current needs. We cannot expect a process that has been closed to women's voices for thousands of years to remain unaffected by the sudden enfranchisement of half of the Jewish world.

Alongside changes in process, changes may be expected in the content of the law as well. Rituals of integration and transition may replace or modify our tradition's nearly exclusive attention to division. New terms and appropriate ritual expressions will have to be developed. Feminists have written extensively about ways to achieve integration without loss of self, and about the unity that can often underlie diversity. Conservative Judaism needs to build on that experience and profit from that expertise as it designs new strategies for creative Jewish living in America.

Theology

> What if the subordination of women in Judaism is rooted in theology, in the very foundation of the Jewish tradition?
> Judith Plaskow, "The Right Question is Theological"

Classically, Conservative Judaism has embraced halakhic and avoided theological challenges. Our movement has failed to develop widely accepted understandings of God, revelation, theodicy, the meaning of prayer, and other basic theological questions. The work of numerous feminists is already providing the energy and intellectual resources for a creative rethinking of a full range of theological questions that we have eschewed in the past.

As outsiders to the textual tradition, women have noticed and responded to theological omissions that men have long since considered natural and unproblematic. Written with man as the norm and woman as the anomaly to be controlled, rabbinic legal texts cannot be viewed by women as timeless works. Women have had to place halakhot in their historical contexts in order to find them religiously plausible. Biblical texts which narrowly delimit women's activity to domestic space had to be reinterpreted through the re-discovery of Midrash as a technique for reading. The prayer book's language, with its unquestioned use of male imagery to describe a God whom our community increasingly imagines in non-anthropomorpic terms, had to be heard afresh. In each of these areas: law, midrash, and prayer, the questions asked by feminists—how are women imagined by the tradition? How can women's experience contribute to the tradition?—open up vast new areas for revitalizing our theological discourse. The fact that our movement is committed to struggling with problematic texts rather than expelling them from the canon or declaring ourselves to be "post-halakhic" creates an even greater need to learn from those who have been forced for generations to come to terms with such difficulties.

The textual tradition represents only part of our contemporary theological problem. Attending to the voices of women will allow us to develop new theological categories and raise fundamental questions about accepted ways of doing theology. The historical situation of women includes different experiences of evil in the world which demand explanation, experiences that include this-worldly oppression by Jewish men. Feminist theology, therefore, often bases itself on lived personal experience as a co-equal source for theological reflection beside texts and history. Recovery of this mode of theology may put contemporary (largely rationalist) Judaism in touch with the rich, partially hidden resources of Jewish mysticism. We can fruitfully *and authentically* draw upon mystical literature, which also focuses on lived experience and offers several female God images.

Prayer and Ritual

> So what is the rabbi afraid of? Surely inelegant language and "inauthentic" ritual are used by respectable Jews every day . . . Contemporary Jewish life cannot help but benefit from serious new thought about the nature of authority, spiritual practice, our own needs and natures as female and male *human* beings, and a reconsideration of the historical separation between elite and non-elite religion.
>
> Drorah Setel, "The Contribution Being Spurned"

As in no other area of Jewish life, the impact of feminism on Jewish prayer and ritual demonstrates the value of the feminist opportunity for Judaism. From the bat mitzvah to Rosh Hodesh celebrations to the *simḥat bat,* new rituals have been developed and assimilated by our communities. Within a few short years after its introduction into the Ashkenazic scene, for example, the *simḥat bat* ritual has increasingly been accepted as halakhically requisite. With no rabbinic rulings and only rare rabbinic assistance, families developed rituals to express their joy on the birth of a daughter and to welcome her into the community. The creation of new prayers, many in English, and the inclusion of personal statements at the *simḥat bat* have also led to a rethinking of the *brit milah* ceremony. Now that the ceremony for the entrance of a daughter into the community has become so rich and personal, families are adding new prayers to the older ceremony which had increasingly been taken out of their hands and made the exclusive responsibility of paid professionals.

As the female life-cycle and female experience are increasingly seen as bases for religious responses in our communities, there will be calls for new rituals and prayers. This appeal to Judaism from contemporary voices provides our movement with a rare opportunity for liturgical creativity in an halakhic framework. Rather than threaten existing structures, new prayers and rituals have the potential for bringing people closer to a tradition that can now be seen as relating more exactly to the experiences of all Jews. Women's ritual, women's prayer groups, and women's study groups can be the proving ground for the development of a renewed sense of closeness to prayer, a sense that has long been missing in our community. As long as we are prepared to acknowledge that the siddur is a collection of male-oriented prayers, that the *beit kenneset* has been a men's prayer center, and the *beit midrash* a male study group, we must welcome the creation by Jewish women of alternative institutions during this perioid of transition. An open Conservative community prepared to add and grow need not abandon the halakhic framework within which it has traditionally done its liturgical work.

Recovering Our Past

> It is no surprise that the back-to-the-roots variety of Jew of the present decade is not looking for problematic aspects of the tradition. Unfortunately, such is history, particularly when it is about human beings.
> Susan Einbinder, "Review of *Back to the Sources*"

One position long maintained by Conservative scholars which feminism *does* challenge is the myth of objectivity in scholarship. Noting that "objective" histories frequently omit the life-experience of half of the population, feminist Jewish scholars, like Jews in general academics, have been calling for the rewriting of standard texts. Blind spots can now be replaced by vision. Students of rabbinic Judaism have long claimed that the life of study followed by male Jews during the medieval period deserved attention alongside the history of political and military developments in the surrounding culture. In similar fashion, feminist historians recognize the limitations of what Jewish history has hitherto valorized. Nearly every standard work on the history of the Jews and the history of Judaism requires rethinking. Sources long forgotten or ignored need to be re-examined so that a history of women's lives can be made part of our teaching. While we need not criticize the rabbis of the Talmud for not having included women in their deliberations, we can not afford to ignore the significance of that exclusion. By directing our attention to the limitations of our textual tradition and the subjectivity of existing scholarship, this feminist approach frees us from the burden of apologetics while creating new opportunities for rethinking our past and applying history's lessons to our present.

Conclusion: Egalitarianism and Pluralism

> Egalitarianism is . . . a principle which we cannot yield in good conscience . . .
> Rabbi Albert Axelrad, "Principle Encounters Principle"

During the Seminary's second century, Conservative Judaism has the opportunity to avail itself of the wealth of feminist thinking and practice. The assimilation of feminist insights depends in the first place on the adoption of egalitarianism as the dominant position of the movement. If it is true, as the founders of our movement claimed, that Judaism's classic sources were created in communication with developments in the life of the people, then halakhic change towards the realization of egalitarianism in Judaism represents the workings of classical Judaism in the modern period. The decisions of the Rabbinical Assembly's Committee on Jewish Law and Standards which have moved toward facilitating the development of egalitarian Judaism represent such a development and should be recognized as expressions of a fully *authentic, halakhic, and traditional* Judaism. The perspective which implies that halakhah is monolithic and unchanging in its application represents a radical departure from our movement's teaching and should be named as such.

The Mishnah cites a number of cases limiting the principle of pluralism within the rabbinic movement (see, for example, *Eduyot* 5:6). In our present context, the question arises of how to deal with colleagues who reject the egalitarian perspective as defined by the decisions of the Law Committee and the Seminary admissions committee. I propose the following criterion: an applicant who disagrees with egalitarianism on halakhic principle may be admitted to the rabbinical school. One who denies, however, the legitimacy of our decision-making bodies and the legitimacy of their conclusions regarding the position of women and men in Judaism will not be able to function within our movement and should be directed elsewhere. The feminist opportunity is an opportunity for self-definition and growth. Pride in our great achievement in creating an halakhic framework for the adoption of egalitarianism and the incorporation of feminist perspectives is well earned. The brightness of our future depends upon our trusting Conservative Judaism to face itself in the woman in the mirror.[5]

NOTES

1. The next major step will come when the Law Committee reconsiders the question of women as witnesses.
2. See the appended bibliography for a representative selection of books and anthologies whose authors range from traditionalist to post-halakhic/non-halakhic in perspective.
3. While the recent JTS catalog includes the statement: "Women are expected to accept equality of [halakhic] obligation in the performance of *mitzvot*," this principle is not uniformly enforced.
4. Carol Gilligan, *In a Different Voice* (Cambridge: Harvard Univ. Press, 1982), p. 10.
5. The ideas developed here reflect the outcome of many years of study with my teacher, colleague and friend Lori Lefkovitz. Her guidance has been invaluable, even when conflicting perspectives have led us to different conclusions.

WORKS CITED AND SELECT BIBLIOGRAPHY ON FEMINISM (AND JUDAISM)

Many of the works on this list contain comprehensive topical bibliographies. Additional bibliographies and information may be obtained from: The Jewish Women's Resource Center, 9 East 69th St. New York, N.Y. 10021.

Adelman, Penina, *Miriam's Well: Rituals for Jewish Women Around the Year* (New York: Biblio Press, 1986)

Axelrod, Albert, "Principle Encounters Principle: The Havurah Movement and Religious Egalitarianism," *Havurah,* Vol. 2 (Summer, 1986)

Baum, Charlotte, Paula Hyman and Sonya Michel, *The Jewish Woman in America* (New York: New American Library, 1975)

Biale, Rachel, *Women and Jewish Law* (New York: Schocken Books, 1984)

Einbinder, Susan, "Review of *Back to the Sources,*" *Response* (Winter/Spring 1986)

Eisenstein, Hester and Alice Jardine, eds. *The Future of Difference* (New Brunswick: Rutgers University Press, 1980)

Gilligan, Carol, *In a Different Voice* (Cambridge: Harvard University Press, 1982)

Heschel, Susannah, ed. *On Being a Jewish Feminist: A Reader* (New York: Schocken Books, 1983)

Koltun, Liz, ed. *The Jewish Woman: New Perspectives* (New York: Schocken Books, 1976)

Lerner, Michael, "Why Tikkun?" *Tikkun* I:1 (1986)

Priesand, Sally, *Judaism and the New Woman* (New York: Behrman House, 1975)

Schneider, Susan Weidman, *Jewish and Female* (New York: Simon and Schuster, 1984)

Schneir, Miriam, *Feminism: The Essential Historical Writings* (New York: Vintage Books, 1972)

Setel, Drorah, "The Contribution Being Spurned," *Sh'ma* (January, 1986)

At Camp Ramah, 1986.

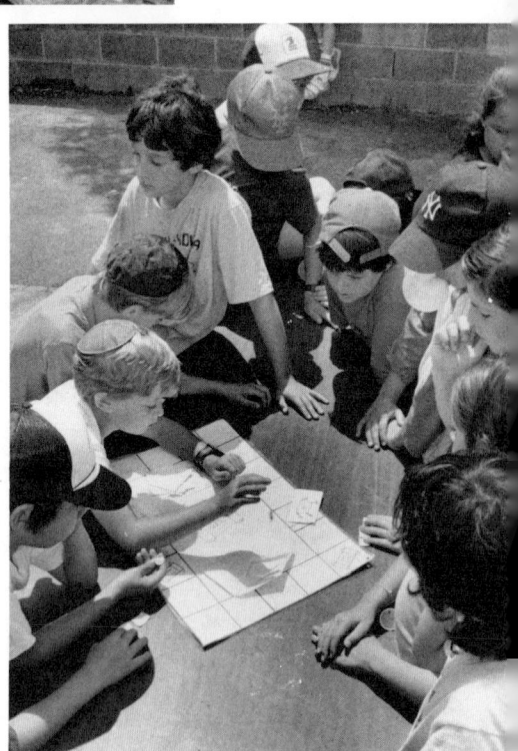

At Camp Ramah, 1986.

Feminism in the Conservative Movement

Paula E. Hyman

The most conspicuous change that has occurred within the Conservative movement in the past century is the entry of women into roles which were previously reserved solely for men. In our synagogues and at the Seminary women join men in prayer, in the study of Jewish texts, and in positions of spiritual and scholarly leadership. Most dramatically, the Seminary now ordains women as rabbis. While many of these changes reflect the impact of the feminist movement of the past two decades, others hark back to the earliest years of the Conservative movement. In fact, the "women's issue" has long provided the most pressing challenge to the Conservative claim that it is possible to reconcile the legacy of tradition with new social conditions and values. As we enter our second century, feminism will continue to challenge the movement, for the entry of women into the Conservative rabbinate by no means resolves all aspects of the "women's issue." Moreover, the practical implementation of Conservative policy on this issue raises with clarity the question of the meaning of pluralism within the Conservative context.

From its inception the Conservative movement chose to distinguish itself from Orthodoxy in its approach to the proper place of women. It called for primary education for girls equally with boys at a time when girls traditionally received little formal Jewish instruction. Although the Seminary admitted Henrietta Szold as a special student in 1902 only on the condition that she not demand rabbinic ordination, its Teachers Institute, founded in 1909, offered higher Jewish education to women and men on an equal basis. The Conservative movement also introduced mixed seating in most of its synagogues, thus enabling women to share more equitably in the "sacred space" of the synagogue even though it reserved the *bimah* and contact with the Torah for men. Mixed seating was a radical break with tradition and sealed the separation of Conservatism from Orthodoxy. Thus, when attempts were made to merge the Jewish Theological Seminary and

Yeshiva College in the 1920s, they foundered in part on the issue of mixed seating, for graduates of the Seminary were known to officiate in synagogues with such seating arrangements.[1] Responsive to the changing status of women in the larger society, the Rabbinical Assembly's Committee on Jewish Law and Standards issued opinions which permitted women to have *aliyot* (1955) and be counted in a minyan (1973).[2]

As is well-known, the feminist movement of the '70s and '80s penetrated deeply within the American Jewish community and stimulated grass-roots pressure for change. As early as 1972 Ezrat Nashim, a small group of young, well-educated women, most of whom had been shaped by the institutions of the Conservative movement, presented to the Rabbinical Assembly convention a call for the acceptance of women as rabbis and cantors, and for the public affirmation of women's equality in all aspects of Jewish life. Recognition of the moral claim of the feminist message and of the danger in the dissonance between women's role in contemporary society and in the Jewish community led both local and national leaders of the movement to wrestle with the "women's issue." The number of Conservative synagogues giving *aliyot* to women, for example, soared from 7% in 1972 to 50% in 1976. By 1986 those synagogues according partial or full equality to women have become the vast majority.[3] After six years of investigation and consideration, on October 24, 1983, the Seminary faculty voted to accept women as candidates for rabbinic ordination. By 1986 two women have completed their rabbinical studies at the Seminary, and two additional women, trained at other institutions, have been accepted for membership in the Rabbinical Assembly.[4]

The Conservative movement has proved responsive to the call for women's equality insofar as that message has been couched in terms of equal access—*i.e.*, the entry of women into positions formerly restricted to men. With the rabbinate open to women, and the cantorate sure to follow suit within a short time, many Conservative leaders presume that the "women's issue" has been resolved and the movement may proceed to deal with other important questions. They pay little attention to another aspect of feminism, which accords equal value to women's cultural concerns and particular experience. This second facet of feminism seeks not merely to adopt the values and behavior patterns of men, but to enable women's values and modes of behavior to become viable options for men and women alike.

What this means in practice is that women in the Conservative movement — both rabbis and laity — may raise issues of significance for the community as a whole. The work of Harvard psychologist Carol Gilligan, for example, shows that women place moral dilemmas in a relational context, while men tend to analyze such problems on the basis of the application of abstract rules. Similarly, women in general display a less hierarchical style of interpersonal behavior.[5] Whether such differences are innate or socially constructed matters little. As I hear from my colleagues, women raise different types of questions as they study traditional texts. Such questions must be attended to, rather than deflected with the comment that there is no time to explore the moral or psychological implications of the subject matter.[6] Moreover, women should be encouraged to participate freely in the ongoing interpretation of sacred Jewish texts, to contribute their insights to what I have called "women's midrash," which will complement the exclusively male-created midrash we now have and serve as a resource for the entire Jewish community.

With the entry of women into the rabbinate, it is likely that new styles of rabbinic leadership will emerge. While some women rabbis will feel comfortable with male models of rabbinic behavior, others will seek to develop different patterns tending to narrow the distance between the laity and the rabbinic professional. Such changes could reinforce trends towards a growing involvement of laity as partners in synagogue worship and in study rather than as passive consumers of a religious service produced by synagogue professionals. Congregants are likely to perceive the woman rabbi primarily as a caregiver and teacher (two traditional female functions), thus reinforcing the transformation of the rabbi in modern times from master of Jewish law to pastor of a congregation. Insofar as congregants subconsciously identify the rabbi as God's representation on the *bimah,* the visibility of women rabbis is bound to expand their recognition that God cannot be defined solely in terms of masculine attributes.

Feminists have begun also to question whether traditional Jewish liturgy gives full expression to the presence of women as equal members of the congregation as well as to our understanding of the nature of God.[7] We are concerned not only with non-sexist language in describing both ourselves and God but also with our ways of imaging God. The new Conservative prayerbook, *Siddur Sim Shalom,* has been sensitive to the issue of including women as members of the congregation and has even presented alternatives in the feminine gender for certain Hebrew formulations generally recited only in the masculine singular. Its supplementary readings and alternative versions of parts of the liturgy provide opportunities for non-sexist prayer. Yet, with all its stylistic grace and its attention to ways of enabling its users to compose individual prayers, it simply does not adequately address the more far-reaching linguistic and theological issues raised by feminist thinkers with regard to God-language. Here the Conservative movement must find a way to strike a balance between our real emotional commitment to the traditional liturgy and our need to find modes of expression that reflect what we truly believe. Certainly the halakhah allows us far more flexibility than we seem willing to utilize.

The inclusion of women as full partners in the Conservative movement also raises weighty theoretical and practical questions about the meaning of pluralism within the movement. The Conservative movement has recognized that the halakhah, since it is not monolithic, can accommodate divergent positions. The Committee on Jewish Law and Standards often issues more than one opinion for consideration by its rabbinic constituency. The local rabbi, as *mara d'atra*, then decides which opinion to implement within the community. Yet, on the issue of women's equality, this commitment to pluralism is both confusing and morally troubling.

The pluralistic approach of the movement is particularly confusing and morally troubling in this realm because women's equality is such a significant and all-encompassing issue, not merely a technical halakhic problem. Many who favor according full equality to women within the Jewish community believe it is *wrong* and therefore unacceptable to exclude them from any roles; those who oppose granting full equality to women feel that the changes already made and the way they have been determined do untold damage to the halakhic process which is at the heart of Conservative Judaism, and hence are wrong and unacceptable. It is difficult to see how one movement can assert both positions without appearing to lack integrity.

In practice, egalitarian and non-egalitarian positions can be accommodated by respecting the position of the *mara d'atra* on the local level and by establishing two religious services (fully egalitarian and non-egalitarian) in all national Conservative institutions. That is not yet the case in the United Synagogue Youth and in some Ramah camps, because of the failure of the movement's leadership to make it clear that the provision of a fully egalitarian minyan must now be standard Conservative practice. For some reason it is presumed that those who oppose women's equality have religious scruples which must be respected while those who support women's equality are thought to have personal preferences on the matter which can occasionally be set aside, rather than deeply held and equally valid religious scruples. Children who are graduates of Solomon Schechter Day Schools and have grown up in egalitarian Conservative congregations must not find themselves treated as Conservative Jews of the second rank when they attend the camps and the youth groups of the movement.

The official position of the Conservative movement is to endorse both egalitarian and non-egalitarian religious services. However, it is not at all clear to me whether the Conservative house can survive in the long run embracing both egalitarian and non-egalitarian positions. The status of one half of the community is a difficult subject on which to agree to disagree. Further, both sides deny the legitimacy of the opposing point of view, one on moral grounds, the other on halakhic grounds. Pluralism requires reciprocal respect. While most egalitarians have at least accepted the non-egalitarian position as valid though not preferable, that is not the case with the non-egalitarians, who continue to denounce the steps toward equality already taken.

I would not suggest that the Seminary reject candidates for Rabbinical School who oppose the notion of women rabbis, the inclusion of women in a minyan, the granting of aliyot to women, and the acceptance of women as *shliḥot tzibbur*. We have also accepted candidates who assert that the Torah is to be understood literally. However, I would expect that just as we challenge the fundamentalist through our Bible and Philosophy courses, so we must challenge the non-egalitarian by making explicit in our curriculum the values and the process of halakhic reasoning which have brought the Conservative movement to affirm the equality of women.

That process of education should extend beyond the walls of the Seminary. Our constituents in general have little idea of what we stand for and how we have developed as a movement. On the "women's issue" the leaders of the movement who support egalitarianism, perhaps in an effort to mute controversy, have not conducted the type of comprehensive educational campaign which should accompany any important social change. Instead, the opponents of egalitarianism, although a small minority of the movement, have taken the initiative and have determined the framework in which the issue has been discussed. Instead of using the "women's issue" as an opportunity to enlighten the laity on the Conservative approach to halakhah and to modernity and to encourage women through role modeling towards a greater commitment to religious observance, the movement has appeared to choose the path of evasion.

As far as the placement of rabbis is concerned, the question of popular education will become crucial. It is likely that women rabbis, like women who have entered other male-dominated professions, will find it difficult at first to be hired for positions of greatest authority and prestige but will be channeled into small or geographically isolated congregations and into Hillel or the chaplaincy. If we train women rabbis for unemployment in the field or for what are often considered the least desirable of rabbinical jobs alone, then we will have failed both them and the movement as a whole. While no congregation should be coerced into hiring a woman rabbi, every congregation should be exposed to the rationale for accepting women as rabbis and perhaps, too, to a flesh-and-blood visiting woman rabbi. A deep-seated psychological resistance to women in positions of authority, particularly in the religious realm, can hide behind halakhic objections and should be aired for discussion rather than accepted as an unchangeable factor.

The "women's issue" thus raises issues that transcend the acceptance of women as rabbis, issues that will require a generation or two to resolve. Yet we should not lose sight of the fact that much has been accomplished in response to the moral imperative of conferring equality upon women. We have created a new social reality in our synagogues and in our communities as a whole. I can remember my first *aliyah*, while I was in college; my daughters cannot remember a time when women did not receive *aliyot*. Indeed, they and their peers see the equality of women and men in the religious realm as normal. When the first baby-naming ceremonies for girls were instituted less than two decades ago, they were rare occurrences. Now such ceremonies are widely accepted throughout the entire Jewish community. Just a short time ago women were often completely disenfranchised in synagogue adminstration; now they serve at all levels on synagogue boards and as presidents of congregations. When I began my graduate work in Jewish history with Gerson Cohen and Ismar Schorsch, I had few female role models (less than a handful in the U.S. and Canada). Now women scholars in Jewish Studies are a recognized entity and have begun, however hesitantly, to introduce the experience of women into a male-defined curriculum.

The Conservative movement can take pride in what has been accomplished in its sphere in the past fifteen years but it should not be complacent. The thrust towards equality that began in the infancy of the movement with equal education for girls has culminated a century later in the ordination of women as rabbis. Yet, as I have tried to suggest, the story has not yet ended. Jewish women have much to contribute to the Jewish people not only in their traditional roles as wives, mothers, and communal volunteers but also as teachers, scholars, and spiritual leaders. Within the Conservative movement lay and rabbinic leaders alike must now actively seek ways to show girls and women the new possibilities for religious expression, education, and leadership available to them. It is our challenge to involve women in all aspects of Jewish public life and thereby to draw upon these newly unleashed energies for the enrichment of Judaism and the Jewish community.

NOTES

1. For a discussion of this episode, see Deborah Dash Moore, *At Home in America: Second Generation New York Jews* (New York: Columbia University Press, 1981), pp. 197-98.

2. For a history of these issues, see Robert Gordis, "The Ordination of Women—A History of the Question," *Judaism,* XXXIII, 1 (Winter 1984), pp. 6-12.

3. For these developments see Anne Lapidus Lerner, "Who Hast Not Made Me a Man," *American Jewish Yearbook* (1977), pp. 3-40; and Rela Geffen Monson, "The Impact of the Jewish Women's Movement on the American Synagogue: 1972-1985," unpublished paper. The latest figures, from a survey conducted by Dr. Anne Lapidus Lerner and Rabbi Stephen C. Lerner in 1983 indicate that 59% of Conservative congregations then counted women in the minyan and 76.6% granted them *aliyot* on at least some occasions. See *Rabbinical Assembly News,* Vol. I, No. 5 (February 1984), pp. 1, 8.

4. Faculty of the Seminary prepared position papers and responsa which were collected in an as yet unpublished volume entitled *On the Ordination of Women as Rabbis—Position Papers of the Faculty of the Jewish Theological Seminary of America.* For abbreviated versions of two of those papers, see Joel Roth, "Ordination of Women: an Halakhic Analysis," *Judaism,* 33:1 (Winter, 1984), pp. 70-78 and Mayer E. Rabinowitz, "An Advocate's Halakhic Responses on the Ordination of Women," *ibid.,* pp. 54-65.

5. Carol Gilligan, *In a Different Voice: Psychological Theory and Women's Development* (Cambridge: Harvard University Press, 1982).

6. This issue is not necessarily gender-related, but reflects a problem-

atic aspect of the curriculum of the Rabbinical School. The academic focus of that curriculum often neglects value-related concerns.

7. For the most trenchant feminist critique on these issues, see Judith Plaskow, "Language, God, and Liturgy: A Feminist Perspective," *Response*, 13:4 (Spring 1983), pp. 3–14 and her "The Right Question is Theological," in Susannah Heschel, ed., *On Being a Jewish Feminist: A Reader* (New York: Schocken Books, 1983).

Masorti Judaism:
Challenge, Vision and Program

Lee Levine

On one level, the story of the Masorti Movement in Israel is about the development of synagogues, a youth movement, adult education activities, day camps, a kibbutz and moshav, and a newly founded rabbinical school. On a more profound level, it is the saga of a small, but growing, cadre of Conservative olim and native-born Israelis attempting to create a religious alternative in a polarized society. They wish to offer a vision of a society which can be Jewish and pluralistic, committed and tolerant, nationalistic and morally sensitive. These people, who today number some 10,000 and are organized into almost 40 synagogues and communities, are deeply committed to the Zionist dream of building a Jewish society in our ancestral homeland, a society which has become in a few short decades the center of the Jewish people, and which by the middle of the next century will encompass well over half (some say ⅔) of the Jewish people world-over.

Challenge

There can be little doubt, as any astute observer of the Israeli scene will attest, that the major challenge facing Israeli society today is internal. The general feeling in the country is that the continued military, political and economic threats — for all their importance — are manageable. It is the internal dimension which poses a far greater challenge. The very social fabric of Israeli society is being sorely tested by the one component which ought to provide cohesion and unity — Judaism and the Jewish tradition.

This rift has become increasingly exacerbated during these past two decades. The emergence of a messianic nationalism, combined with the rising power of anti-Zionist, ultra-orthodox elements and the racist platform of a Kahane, each speaking in the name of religion, project Judaism as a major subject of controversy. Everything which these extremist groups oppose becomes *ipso facto* delegitimized: Arab rights, the Jewishness of Ethiopian immigrants, Conservative and Reform rabbis, and all non-Orthodox religious services. Once one embarks on the path of delegitimizing, there are no bounds. Even the legitimacy of the State of Israel itself is called into question. "Zionism is diametrically opposed to Judaism" reads a not uncommon slogan painted on the walls of Mea She'arim.

The issue, however, is more far-reaching than only political or religious intolerance. What is at stake here is nothing less than Judaism itself, or put differently, the Jewishness of the Jewish state. "If that is what Judaism means and says, then I want no part of it" is a refrain heard time and again. The religious establishment has succeeded in alienating a large portion of the public from any kind of meaningful association with the Jewish enterprise—history, tradition, Jewish peoplehood, the Diaspora.

This is the challenge confronting Israeli society which the Masorti movement is attempting to address. Our goal is to create a religious "center" in Israeli life. The polarization crystallized in recent years cries out for a strong middle position to stabilize the society religiously. Not merely a compromise between extremes, the centrist position should make positive ideological assertions, attempting to synthesize the best among the alternatives into new and meaningful models, while avoiding the negative elements and pitfalls of each. A responsible center in a democratic society should attempt to be inclusive, aiming to unite as many alternatives as possible, allowing for maximal freedom for individuals and groups while being careful not to jeopardize the integrity of the tradition.

Vision

What is this vision of an Israeli-Jewish society offered by Masorti Judaism, and wherein lies its uniqueness? Such a vision ought to combine three important spheres—Judaism, Zionism, and modernity—viewing them as interrelated and mutually reinforcing. Let us briefly note each component.

Judaism

Masorti Judaism emphasizes the two concepts basic to any Jewish religious approach: Torah and Mitzvot. In both of these areas, the

Masorti approach has a unique and important message, faithful to and informed by the historical approach of the Conservative movement.

The Masorti approach to Torah is far more encompassing than any other approach known in Israel. In Israeli universities, traditional texts and modes of inquiry (midrashic and medieval) are, for the most part, relegated to secondary importance, while in Israeli yeshivot modern approaches to the study of ancient texts, as well as the fruits of critical scientific inquiry, are unknown and considered anathema. In our approach, Torah is understood in its widest sense, including all Jewish culture and civilization with a focus on our religious tradition. An emphasis on Bible does not preclude knowledge of archeology, nor rabbinics Josephus, nor halakhah Jewish philosophy, nor Kabbala history. Not only is the scope of Torah greatly expanded, but so are the tools utilized for its study. Rashi, Ibn Ezra and Ramban are essential for an explication of the biblical text, and so are archeology, comparative religion and ancient Near Eastern history.

With regard to mitzvot, the Masorti approach also has a unique message. A thorough grasp of Jewish texts together with an awareness of the historical development within Judaism leads inexorably to two conclusions. No religious movement in Judaism can claim to be authentic without positing the centrality of halakhah and the indispensability of a serious commitment to its observance. However, a historical view of tradition also reveals a continuous process of development and evolution. Throughout the ages, Jewish religious tradition has never remained static, although the pace and extent of change were always subject to debate. Moreover, the fruits of modern research have demonstrated not only historical development, but the variety within Judaism and the significant amount of cultural and social interaction with the surrounding world at any given time. Rather than being a sign of weakness and uncertainty, variety and some degree of acculturation ought to be regarded as a natural, healthy and even desirable phenomenon in Jewish history.

Zionism

Within religious circles in Israel of late, Zionism has been subjected to severe strains. It is denied as a legitimate form of Jewish political expression, and it is vilified with the zealousness of a Sinaitic imperative for any position which does not rule out territorial compromise. Thus the Judaism which most Israelis encounter today either rejects the Jewish state entirely, or has adopted a messianic mode with extreme political implications.

What gets lost in all this political controversy are the burning moral and social issues facing Israeli society. No less important than the boundaries of the Jewish state or sovereignty over all of historic Eretz Israel are questions regarding social justice and ethical sensitivity within the Jewish state. The imperative of Zionism is no less strong in this realm than in that of settlement or sovereignty. Another, related issue involves the responsibilities of the Jewish state toward its minorities. What, indeed, are the powers and limitations of sovereignty? What ought to be the moral restraints and ethical concerns of a Jewish state? We have inherited many wonderful and inspiring moral insights in the pages of our traditional sources. These ideas, however, were enunciated when Jews were powerless, and it is always easy for those without power to be idealistic and moral. What, however, is to happen now that we Jews have power? Will it be used wisely and moderately? These and similar questions constitute part of the challenge facing Masorti Judaism. Can it offer a meaningful religious approach to the many social and moral issues confronting Israeli society? The voice of Judaism need not only be politically shrill, but can and should be morally calming and compassionate as well. The integrity of our tradition deserves more faithful representation, and so does Israeli society.

Modernity

Despite Israel's full participation in the Western world, many Israelis view Judaism as incompatible or, at least, uncomfortable with the culture and values of the larger society. Although many elements of the modern world are indeed antithetical to Judaism, there is clearly no basis to the claim that Judaism *per se* is opposed to contemporary culture. Just the opposite! Historical research has provided ample data illustrating the ongoing and positive interaction between Jewish and general culture. From biblical through talmudic, medieval, and modern times, Judaism has both influenced and been heavily influenced by regnant intellectual and cultural streams of the societies in which the Jews found themselves.

The above three foci can provide the framework for a vision of Israeli society. Each reinforces the other. Judaism without Zionism is a tradition without real roots or a sense of belonging; a soul without a body. Zionism without a viable and meaningful Jewish expression is just the opposite, a political framework without a full spiritual and cultural dimension. Zionism without regard for contemporary society would constitute a betrayal of its roots, for Zionism did indeed spring from western nationalistic revival. And Judaism, as noted, can and has flourished in a creative symbiosis with its surroundings in each and every generation.

Moreover, the vision described above allows for a certain degree of diversity and adaptability for the individual. However, within this diversity, the three elements — if common to all — will assure a significant degree of unity, allowing differences to be expressed without threatening the overall commonality. The major contribution of the Masorti approach in this regard is specifically bringing these three areas into a vibrant healthy synthesis, thus allowing for the continued growth of the Jewish tradition within nationalistic and universalistic frameworks in which the Jewish people in the late twentieth century participate.

Program

Given this vision, how does the Masorti movement propose to implement it? What institutions must be developed or created anew in order for these ideas to begin permeating society effectively and meaningfully? When speaking of such institutions, it might be well to divide them into two categories. First, there are those formally affiliated with the movement; secondly, there are institutions which, although independent, are closely associated with the movement's educational approach through the activity of its members. In the former category there are five important areas to nurture: the synagogue-centers; the Israeli rabbinical school; Hannaton educational center; an overnight Ramah camp for Israelis; and an extensive publication program.

Synagogue-Centers

These institutions have, until now, constituted the core of the Masorti movement, and probably will continue to do so for the foreseeable future. The synagogue-center provides a focus for activities geared to all ages: religious services, adult education classes, youth groups, pre-school nursery and kindergarten programs, as well as social functions. It must be remembered that the synagogue in Israel is a very narrowly defined institution providing only religious services, and a place of study for very limited circles in very specific areas of learning. In effect, the Masorti movement is reintroducing the model of the ancient synagogue as it functioned some 2000 years ago and as it has evolved over the past century in North America. Moreover, sociologically speaking, there is an acute need for such a community framework in Israel today, something which can stand between the modular family and the wider society.

Rabbinical School

With the opening of the Masorti movement's Seminary for Judaic Studies two years ago, Israel got its first modern rabbinical school. Previously, the notion of a modern rabbinical academy providing the education and training for future leaders who would then be charged with mediating between the Jewish past and contemporary society, was foreign to the Israeli scene. The Masorti movement thus continues the traditions of earlier generations of Jews, who felt a need for rabbinic academies to bridge two worlds — the Jewish and the general — and then proceeded to create suitable institutions.

Hannaton Educational Center

This first Conservative venture into the socialist-agricultural setting is an important event in and of itself. It makes an important statement of our desire to identify with Israeli society, and to participate in creating institutions associated with nation-building. However, what gives Hannaton even greater significance is the fact that the kibbutz intends to serve as a major educational center for the Masorti movement, for the Israeli public generally, and indeed for the world Conservative movement. Study sessions, seminars, retreats and tours focusing on the history of the Galilee, its peoples, traditions and archeology are envisioned. Additional programming units will be devoted to the study of the Jewish tradition, Zionism, Israel-Diaspora relations and Masorti Judaism. There is little doubt that once the education center is functioning, many other opportunities will present themselves to expand and develop its activities.

An Overnight Ramah Camp

Such an institution would constitute a major breakthrough in Israeli camping. Nothing comparable exists in the country. The current encampments within the context of Israeli youth movements are much less ambitious, time-wise and regarding their educational goals. There can be little doubt that Ramah constitutes one of the finest contributions of the Conservative movement to American Jewish education. Such a camp adapted to the Israeli scene would complement and strengthen existing youth activities which already include a youth movement (Noam) and a series of Masorti-related schools (see below). The educational potential of such a camp is even greater in Israel than elsewhere, since Israel's small size makes cooperation and coordination between winter and summer programs far more easily achievable.

Publications and Communications

Perhaps the most pressing issue facing the Masorti movement today is to raise its public profile. We must inform Israelis as to what it is and what it represents. On one level this means a more serious public relations effort. On a wider scale a serious effort is required to introduce the Israeli reading public to the extensive literature which explicates the Conservative approach to halakhah, theology, history, and contemporary issues. Important books and articles already exist and must be translated into Hebrew: Klein's *Guide*, responsa from the Rabbinical Assembly's Committee on Jewish Law and Standards, and the major works of Heschel, Kaplan, and Gordis, among others. Moreover, a publication program must also include current Hebrew writings which reflect our movement's approach, a Masorti siddur, and a journal devoted to modern Jewish thought, something perhaps in the order of the now-defunct *Petaḥim*. We would be performing a great service to Israeli society by undertaking such projects.

Educational Contributions

In addition to the above programs which are directly related to the Masorti movement, a number of other important areas in Israeli life are significantly influenced by the movement's ideology and educational approach. Two examples will suffice:

Jewish Education in the Israeli Army

Second to none, Zahal has an extensive educational program. Part of this effort is geared towards those soldiers who entered the army with a deficient general education. Additionally, everyone who serves in the army is exposed throughout the year to lectures and seminars on subjects relating to Judaism and Zionism. Among the most effective and popular lecturers in these fields are Masorti rabbis or graduates of North American Conservative institutions.

Masorti (Tali — Tigbur Limudei Yahadut — Enriched Jewish Studies) Public Schools

Ten years ago a major breakthrough took place in Israeli education with the founding of the first religious, non-Orthodox public school on French Hill in Jerusalem. Established within the general school system, the French Hill school intends to address a number of issues. First, it aims to provide an educational setting where children from different backgrounds (more observant, less observant, and largely secular) learn together, sharing their knowledge and experience, thus beginning to correct an unfortunate lack of communication and shared experience between these groups. Secondly, the school aims to deal with Jewish studies in a meaningful, comprehensive way, from the perspective of both tradition and modernity, and to provide an experiential dimension as well. The Masorti schools seek to combine the best of both the general and Orthodox systems, nurturing a deep commitment to Judaism and Zionism along with a high degree of tolerance, extensive knowledge of things Jewish, along with the capacity to appreciate and support pluralistic expression.

The success of the school on French Hill has been phenomenal. Ten years ago it began with three classes and 33 pupils, drawn from all over Jerusalem. Half of the youngsters were children of *olim* (immigrants), half were children of *sabras* (native born). Today almost 800 children attend its 10 grades, and within two years the school will go through grade 12. Moreover, in the lower classes some 90% of the pupils are the children of *sabras* who come from the immediate neighborhood. There simply is no room for children from other areas. By 8:30 A.M. on the first day of the two-week registration period for the first grade, the Masorti first grades are filled, often by parents who had moved into the neighborhood for the express purpose of sending their children to this school. Today seven other such institutions exist throughout the country, and many more parent-groups have expressed an interest in starting similar programs in their locales.

Such are the challenges and opportunities facing the Masorti movement in the eighties. The Conservative movement has developed institutions and an educational approach which can have an enormously positive effect on Israeli society. The time is ripe. Israel has benefited over the decades from the contributions of Jews from many and diverse lands: the Russian immigration of the turn of the century, the Polish of the twenties, the German of the forties and the Oriental of the early fifties. Now is the time for the American Jewish community to make its presence felt in areas that Israel so desperately needs. We in Israel have the ideas and institutions to contribute, and there exist the human resources to implement such programs. Hundreds, if not thousands, of Conservative rabbis, Ramah and USY alumni, Seminary graduates, products of Conservative synagogues, and Israelis who have been exposed to Conservative institutions are now in Israel, and many of them can be called upon to help implement this ambitious and formidable program.

The growth and impact on the Masorti movement have been limited by the meager resources available. This has happened precisely at a time when the need for such an approach has never been more sorely felt. As noted, religious extremism in Israel today knows no bounds, and polarization between the Orthodox minority (15%) and the non-Orthodox majority (85%) has become seriously exacerbated. The very soul of Israel is at stake. Will the social fabric be torn apart as the extreme elements push towards uncompromising theocracy governed by political fanatics? Or will it remain true to the vision of Jews the world over—a pluralistic, tolerant, democratic society with which all Jews can identify, and which they regard as theirs? We have something to offer, a vision and a program of action which has already been tested. The only question remaining is whether we can muster the commitment, the energy and the resources to do what can be done, what must be done, and what our colleagues in Israel are poised to accomplish.

Therein lies the challenge!

Studying at Neve Schechter (the American Student Center), in the Midreshet Yerushalayim program in Jerusalem, 1986.

Conservative Judaism in Israel: Problems and Prospects

Theodore Friedman

The problems facing Conservative Judaism in Israel are as numerous as they are diverse. To begin with, there is the towering fact that the preponderant majority of Israel's population today derives from backgrounds untouched by modern Jewish religious thinking or practice. Consider the old Yishuv. Its descendants overwhelmingly retain the spiritual horizons of their forebears and that with a militant zeal far beyond that practiced by the latter. (As recently as the 1920s there was no *meḥitzah* in front of the Western Wall.) The Second Aliyah represented, for the most part, a revolt against the Yiddishkeit of Eastern Europe and replaced it with socialism *cum* Jewish nationalism. Their descendants are either staunch secularists or spiritually adrift, some of whom are seeking a rapprochement with the Jewish religious tradition. Later waves of immigration from Eastern Europe brought Jews who held onto the image of Jewish religion familiar to them from their country of origin. Today, fifty-five percent of our population consists of Jews of the *Eidot Hamizraḥ* (Jews from Arab and eastern countries), communities in which any mode of Judaism other than the traditional was totally unknown. (But be it noted that many members of these communities would probably describe themselves as *masorti* — traditional, rather than *dati*.)

In sum then, for Israelis, aside from the relatively few who derive from Anglo-Saxon countries, Conservative Judaism is a novum. The differences between the latter and Reform Judaism are certainly beyond otherwise fairly well-informed Israelis. On more than one occasion, despite my informing the Chairman that I was a Conservative rabbi, I found myself introduced to an audience as a *Rav Reformi*.

Then, there is the oppressive fact that the only form of Judaism legally sanctioned and financially supported by the Israeli government is that of Orthodoxy. The latter, the religious establishment, in keeping with the growing religious extremism, has latterly grown increasingly hostile to Conservative Judaism. The hostility takes the form of pre-High Holiday advertisements in the press warning the public to avoid attending a Conservative synagogue on the Days of Awe. More recently, our Chief Rabbis signed a widely-distributed flyer warning parents not to enroll their children in the so-called Masorti schools. (These are schools in which twenty-five percent of the curriculum is devoted to the study of religious subject matter in the spirit and approach of Conservative Judaism.)

This hostility on the part of the religious establishment is as nothing compared with the repellent image of Jewish religion it presents to most Israelis. Its stand on various questions in the recent past (for example, on the status of Ethiopian Jews) must move many an Israeli to say, "If this is Jewish religion, I'll have none of it." The number of issues and situations in which the position of the Chief Rabbinate succeeds only in alienating Jews from Judaism can be readily multiplied. To mention but one more example, we cite a fairly recent letter by the Chief Rabbis (who, be it recalled, are government officials) in which they aver, "that it is preferable for young men to study Torah rather than join the army." Incidentally, one wonders what halakhic support they could muster for this position in light of the Mishnah's declaration (*Sotah* 8:7) that in a war of mitzvah (*i.e.*, in defense of the land and the people of Israel) a bridegroom must leave his chamber and a bride her huppah in order to join in the defense.

What are the prospects for changing the system in which Orthodoxy enjoys an official monopoly? This monopoly exists because the Orthodox political parties have been wielding the balance of power in the Israeli government ever since the latter's inception. That balance of power, in turn derives from the peculiar Israeli electoral process whereby minor parties can always manage to achieve such balance of power between the two almost equally divided major parties. For purposes of election, the country is not divided up into districts. All votes are tallied nationally. A candidate need receive but 21,000 votes nationally in order to be elected to the Knesset. If votes were counted according to district, the Orthodox Bloc in the Knesset would probably have its representation cut to less than half. As it is, the tail frequently wags the dog.

True, for some years now, there has been a movement afoot to change the system and give us a truly representative government. But any major party in power would soon find itself out of power if it were to attempt to reform the electoral system. Its coalition partner, the Orthodox Bloc, would withdraw from the government and thus bring it down. Hence, despite popular approval, the chances of a change in the electoral system are not bright.

This is the climate and system within which Conservative Judaism in Israel must operate. Despite the situation described, this close-up observer of the religious scene in Israel believes that the potential for the Masorti movement (the change in nomenclature from Mesorati is significant) is enormous. This estimate is based on a number of observable facts. The notion, frequently heard, that religiously, Israeli society is polarized between *datiim,* strictly observant Orthodox Jews, and out and out secularists is a myth. The truth is that religious observance and commitment run on a scale with the bulk of the population falling somewhere between the two extremes, people who would probably describe themselves as *Masortiim.* To be more specific, they are not regular shul-goers but, for the most part, maintain kosher homes, light candles on Friday night and on Chanukah, attend a Seder, have their sons celebrate their bar mitzvah in a synagogue, etc.

If one may be permitted to draw on direct personal experience, I recall that of my early years in Israel when I served as Rabbi for the *Yamim Noraim* (High Holidays) in a Conservative synagogue (not in Jerusalem). It was obvious from the size of the attendance that in good measure it consisted of people who, though they did not come to shul week after week, were not totally estranged from the synagogue either. Now, more than a decade later, that particular synagogue with a year-round rabbi has standing room only Shabbat after Shabbat.

Then there is the growing number of schools that may well be described as Masorti even though they have no official connection with the Masorti Movement. These schools in the past decade, have grown sevenfold and are to be found in various parts of the country. As indicated, twenty-five percent of the curriculum is devoted to Jewish religious subject matter including prayer and is in the spirit and approach of Conservative Judaism. It may be confidently predicted that the youngsters who emerge from these schools will carry with them a very positive attitude towards the Jewish religious tradition and practice. To this corps of potential Masorti Jews, one must add the hundreds of youngsters who attend the Summer Day Camps sponsored by Ramah. In all, the potential is there and growing.

However, if the potential is to be realized, there must be vision, conviction and personnel of the highest calibre. In down-to-earth Israeli terms, vision translates itself into a deep sense of *shlihut* (mission). The latter must be seen in the light of the religious situation in which we find ourselves in this hour. There is no mistaking the fact that we are in the midst of a *Kulturkampf,* initiated by the ultra-Orthodox who have succeeded in the past few years in dragooning the religious establishment into joining in their demonstrations, vigils and protest activities. How can the religious establishment afford to stand aside and show itself less zealous for "Judaism" than the ultra-Orthodox? The result of all these unending demonstrations, vigils and even occasional boycott activities is readily predictable — the alienation of scores of thousands of Jews, the silent majority — from Jewish religion. In fact, a recent public opinion poll revealed that for a very high percentage of the respondents, the term "dati" (religious) evoked a highly negative image. This could prove to be the final blow to the hope of building a truly Jewish society in the Jewish State.

It is against this potential spiritual disaster that those who labor in the camp of Conservative Judaism are called upon to see their task as a *shlihut* of the highest order. What must be made evident is that there is an alternative between the Orthodoxy that has forgotten nothing and learned nothing, and a Jewish spiritual vacuum powerless to shape our society in the light of both Jewish forms and Jewish moral purposes and ideals. The tears and the blood — whose end is not yet in sight — that have been spent in establishing and maintaining the State, were not spent that we might become *kekhol hagoyim* (like all other peoples), only more so. If that is indeed what will emerge, then we would have been best advised to remain *bekhol hagoyim* (amidst the other peoples).

The vision was and remains that delineated by our prophets and translated by the noblest insights of our sages. In this respect, we of a latter generation must perform, as the Talmud puts it, *shlihutaihu dekamai* (our age-old mission). And that is to fashion a society in which the prophetic ideals of truth, peace, justice and compassion find resonance in all aspects of life, individual and collective; all this, in a mode readily identifiable with such traditional Jewish sanctities as Shabbat, holidays, kashrut, etc. But these sanctities and their like must be so interpreted as to make their observance comportable with the functioning of a modern State and its essential services. The task is formidable but, for us, that is the vision. There is no other.

The enormity of the task can only be matched by a conviction no less large—that the essential idea of Conservative Judaism— continuity and change—contains the method, if not the blueprint, for the accomplishment of that task. Furthermore, this conviction must be firmly grounded and illustrated by the insight that this has ever been the authentic method of Judaism almost from its inception. The distinction between our conception of what Judaism should mean in our time and place and that of Orthodoxy, ultra and moderate, should in no wise be blurred. A watered-down version of Orthodoxy will not do when the genuine article is readily available on almost every block.

There is something else no less important, something to which we have already alluded, but which must be spelled out. Orthodoxy here believes in religion by legislation; thus its deep involvement in politics. At the moment there are three Orthodox political parties and all three accept the aforegoing proposition. After almost forty years of the operation of that proposition, experience has proven beyond debate that legislation on religious affairs has not added a whit to the attractiveness of Jewish religion for the average Israeli Jew. That, clearly, is not our way.

Should we then favor the separation of Church and State? But what happens then to the Jewish character of the State? There is another alternative—the *de jure* recognition by the State of the legitimacy of forms of Judaism other than Orthodoxy. These should be given the same legal status and financial support now exclusively enjoyed by Orthodoxy. A present precedent for such arrangement can be found in the *Haredi* community which maintains its own *beit din* since it does not recognize the official Rabbinical Courts nor the Chief Rabbinate. Despite that fact, it receives government financial support for its schools, etc. We too should be granted the right to establish our own *beit din* and deal with all those matters of personal status presently in the exclusive jurisdiction of the official Rabbinical Courts.

That, in my judgment, is the goal towards which we must struggle with all the means at our disposal. In the meantime, there is much to be done on another front.

Orthodoxy here is almost exclusively concerned with ritual punctiliousness. The moral and social blemishes that darken the Israeli landscape are beyond the purview of the Religious Establishment. To offer but one example: despite years of stoning passing vehicles on Shabbat by *Haredi* elements, the Chief Rabbinate has yet to raise its voice on the issue even though both *hillul Shabbat* (the desecration of Shabbat) and *pikuah nefesh* (human safety) are involved. One could readily make up a large register of moral and social matters that cry out for a forthright stand on the part of the spokesmen of Judaism.

In this connection one recalls the sentences delivered by Abraham Joshua Heschel before a Zionist Congress in Jerusalem some years back. "The Rabbinate sees to it that there are *mashgihim* (religious supervisers who ensure that proper performance and procedures are followed) in the butcher shops. Who will see to it that there are *mashgihim* in the banks?" He spoke prophetically. The banks for some years had been boosting the price of their shares beguiling their customers to invest in them. Then came the debacle of October 1983 when the market for those shares collapsed wiping out the life savings of thousands of people. Only the intervention of the government prevented a financial panic. That intervention will cost the Israeli taxpayer hundreds of millions of dollars. Here is a prime task awaiting an Israeli Masorti Rabbinate.

All of which brings us to the crucial question of personnel. Hopefully, the recently established Seminary for Judaic Studies, which includes a Rabbinical Department, under the aegis of the Seminary, will a few years hence begin to fill this need. Nevertheless, there remains an urgent need for high calibre rabbinical personnel, people who are impelled by the "vision" and the "conviction." In addition, such rabbis must possess total fluency in both spoken and written Hebrew, for here congregational rabbis have more than a pulpit at their disposal. If they have something original and cogent to say, their voices can be heard in the media. Such rabbis must also bring to their task a very broad grounding in the sources. A real desideratum in the latter regard is a volume of responsa that will take up among other questions of public concern, those dealt with by the Chief Rabbinate. The volume should indicate that a different reading of the halakhic sources is possible. Here, the official district Rabbi (*Rav Hashekhunah*) gives a *shiur* (Torah lesson), serves as a *posek* (answers legal questions), gives a *pilpul* on *Shabbat HaGadol* and a *derashah* on *Shabbat*

Teshuvah and that's that. (My district rabbi has an unlisted phone.) Certainly, the Masorti rabbi must view his task in quite other terms, terms borrowed in part from his American experience. The Masorti rabbi must become a public figure in the best sense of that term. If the requirements are high, so is the satisfaction — the knowledge that one is constructively participating in the greatest enterprise undertaken by the Jewish people in two thousand years.

Erica Lippitz (left) and Marla Rosenfeld Barugel, who in 1987 were the first women to receive the diploma of Hazzan from JTS.

The Next Step

Benjamin Z. Kreitman

Of recent date, observers of the contemporary Jewish scene have reported disquieting news about the Conservative movement and made dire predictions about its future.

The forebodings of these analysts and sociologists are shared by many of us in the leadership of the Conservative movement. On the basis of their data and by their interpretations, we who are the largest movement on this continent, we who have experienced the most extraordinary growth of any denomination since World War II, are now declining more rapidly than the general Jewish population. This was bound to take place since we are considered a "movement of the middle," one embracing a great diversity of ideologies. As time has gone by, the right is now moving towards the left and the left is moving towards the right, while we in the middle are being eroded and diminished. We are the most vulnerable and exposed of all the movements.

This fact which I have put almost in a simplistic form is alarming, not only because our numbers are being diminished, but because it reveals that we are unable to hold the loyalty of our constituency. To quote Professor Ruth Wisse in an article in *Commentary* magazine (October, 1979), "By choice and by necessity, Conservatism remains the proving ground of American Judaism, reflecting its patterns of change and its degree of stability" (p. 59). Hence, what will happen in the future of American Judaism is dependent upon how we face the challenge of Conservative Judaism.

Our worry is not a parochial one, but a concern for what will happen to American Judaism if Conservatism fails. In a deeper sense, as Ruth Wisse points out, the future of Reform and modern Orthodoxy is dependent on Conservative Judaism. Some have suggested that we shore up our ranks by becoming even more diverse. Thus we can gain both from the left and from the right. But how much more diverse can this Conservative movement become and yet remain a movement? After World War II we experienced unprecedented growth because of our diversity and because of our ideological fuzziness. We recited over and over again the cliché "unity within diversity," even encouraging unbearable contradictions. The momentum of this type of growth has ceased. It is time for clarification and consolidation. The contradictions borne so easily and readily in the past cannot continue into the future as we are pressed to articulate our distinctiveness. Women relegated to the balcony and women placed in the pulpit as cantors or rabbis are no longer matters of diversity, but of contradiction. Or women as rabbis, yet considered incompetent to be witnesses of the *ketubah* (marriage contract) and the marriage ceremony — how much more diverse can we get? This strategy I would have to call "escape to diversity." Conservatism by its very nature can and should be pluralistic, but it dare not be weighted down with a diversity rampant with contradictions. A new word in describing ourselves has come to fore of late, and this is "coalition." The idea of coalition is not compatible with the idea of a movement — distinctive, separate and apart from others. Such a concept would doom Conservatism to a one-generation span.

Heretofore, we have spoken of the need for a more exact definition of Conservative Judaism that would help extricate us from some of the dilemmas we face. Perhaps we thought we would thereby stem the tide of defections to the right or to the left, defections that result from our ambiguities. The Jewish Theological Seminary is now 100 years old; the Rabbinical Assembly, 86 years old. Solomon Schechter came to the reorganized Seminary about 84 years ago. The United Synagogue of America is now 74 years old. The Historical School out of which Conservatism emerged is at least 160 years old. It is about time we have some exact definition.

Conservatism, more than any other movement or denomination, is involved with the history of its ritual patterns. Conservatism emerged out of the Positive Historical School which concerned itself with the scientific study of the ongoing, developing dynamics of Jewish life. From its inception, Conservatism embraced Zionism which sought and succeeded in returning the Jewish people to the realm of history. Conservatism reflects the dynamics of Jewish history, hence eludes exact definition. For that matter, rabbinic Judaism — dealing with the marketplace, the courtroom, the thoroughfare, the Sanctuary, the ebb and flow of daily life, concerned with the meeting of the absolute and the temporal — was unable to define itself in exact terms.

Without wrangling and wrestling over terms of definition, we have a general concept of our directions, of our objectives and of our goals, quite similar to the general concept at the foundation of rabbinic Judaism. On the basis of this concept, we can delineate the parameters of our movement and avoid the contradictions that plague us at our every step.

It is particularly important that Conservative Judaism formulate its philosophy of revelation on the basis of rabbinic theology. From its perspective, revelation and the subsequent developing tradition, the absolute and the historical, are two dimensions of one whole and unbroken reality. Under the aspect of the Eternal, Sinai and the developing tradition are both parts of a totality; from the perspective of the human, Sinai is the divine starting point whence there emerged a constant and ongoing and, it is hoped, ascending traditional development. The talmudic fathers note, therefore, that every minor argument of a scholar in the academy has already been revealed at Mount Sinai. In an aggadic way, they project this same thought by saying that Moses came to study the Law, in its interpretations, from the Sage, Rabbi Akiba.

The general concept of Conservative Judaism has already been articulated in the phrases "tradition and change" or "tradition and adaptation." This implies that innovations or adaptations must be tested by examining their compatibility with the requirements of tradition or of halakhah. In turn, tradition and halakhah need be examined in how they meet the needs of their day. It is therefore understood that this testing is not to be accomplished through the application of hair-splitting exegetical methodologies, but rather by seeking out the spirit and the philosophy of our ongoing halakhic development. In sum, a definition in narrow terms, were it possible, would not help but hinder us at this juncture. We need to know, however, in what direction we are heading and what our goals and objectives are.

Withal, I believe the problem of Conservatism is not theological but psychological. Yes, we have to rethink some of our theological presuppositions, our halakhic methodologies, but we remain with a psychological problem, unique to the Conservative Jew. We desperately need to change our self-image which plagues and even paralyzes us. We view ourselves as being the minimalists in the spectrum of religious and halakhic observance. We see ourselves as minimalists because we compromise our religious observance to meet what we consider some of the exigencies of the day and we make concessions to the weakness of the flesh wherever possible. The maximalists are to be found elsewhere, not in the Conservative movement.

With ambivalent feelings, we believe minimalism gives us — for the moment — greater access to those in the Jewish population who want to be free from some of the heavy obligations that normative Jewish practice demands. But in these ambivalent feelings is embedded a terrible religious inferiority complex. Though we cannot follow them, the maximalists take on in our minds the aura of authenticity. These feelings of inferiority are inevitably conveyed to children and grandchildren, and when they start searching for the truth or for religious experience, it is not within their parental sanctuary.

Furthermore, when speculating about the future, we feel the more rigid we are the better chance there is for survival. The maximalist is the least likely to assimilate, while we cannot have that assurance for the future. This poor self-image of the Conservative Jew leads to a theological split-personality. The Conservative Jew yearns for a maximalist Judaism and yet is unable to accept it because it is impractical and beyond reach in daily life.

If the Conservative movement is to survive and progress, meeting the dangers on its various flanks, rabbis as well as laity must change their self-image. We must stop regarding ourselves as a minimalist denomination simply conceding to the weaknesses of the flesh and making compromises that are of a temporary nature. We must stop thinking of ourselves as a middle-of-the-road movement, looking to the right and to the left for approval and encouragement. We must insist that Conservative Judaism is rooted in rabbinic, talmudic Judaism and we must seek to embody its qualities and attributes.

Rabbinic Judaism expanded the law, related the halakhah to the needs of the day, oft abrogated and suspended even biblical laws, and radically reinterpreted others. Yet rabbinic Judaism never looked upon itself as a minimalist movement. The fathers of rabbinic Judaism demonstrated the belief in their authenticity by the sincerity of commitment to the regulations and practices they established. Within rabbinic Judaism, there were lenient schools and liberal constructionists, as well as literalists and strict constructionists. There were the schools of Hillel and Shammai, but no one would dare call Hillel or his school a minimalist position. Nor would anyone dare to compare their authenticity with the stricter school of Shammai.

There is a famous story, recorded in the Mishnah, of Rabbi Tarfon who sought to depart from a lenient majority ruling and instead to practice his own severities. He brought down upon himself the condemnation of his colleagues because he was putting into doubt the authenticity of their interpretations. His strictness, even with himself, was considered a flouting of rabbinic authority. On the other hand, the rabbinic fathers—whether strict or lenient—demonstrated the strength of their commitment to their interpretations by adding on *humrot,* special severities sometimes admittedly unnecessary. They did not want to be known as a convenient religion. We too need our *humrot.* The Committee on Jewish Law and Standards now has a large corpus of interpretations and opinions based on various approaches to the law. These decisions, whether they be considered on the side of leniency or severity, must be taken seriously by both laypeople and rabbis. They range from permission to ride to the synagogue on the Sabbath, adjustments of dietary laws, the unbinding of the *agunah,* annulment of a marriage in the face of a recalcitrant husband, to *aliyot* for women and counting women as part of a minyan.

The interpretations and decisions of the Committee have been looked upon by some as simply releasing from restrictions and disciplines those who are too weak in spirit to follow the normative ways. They are considered compromises, the corollary of which is that one who wants to practice a full, complete and authentic Jewish life must resist enabling opinions and decisions.

Responsibility for this defective self-image lies in part with the rabbis and teachers in the Conservative movement, who act as if they have bestowed special dispensations on the laity while they alone must preserve that which is "maximalist and authentic." They have become the disciples of Rabbi Tarfon.

There is a widening gap within our movement between the rabbi and the congregant—a kind of gap and separation that has not existed for hundreds of years. On the one hand is the rabbi, the surrogate pious Jew, the maximalist, and on the other hand the layperson who is spiritually weak and must be pampered with concessions. Either ours is an authentic tradition or not. If it is, then it applies to rabbis as well as laity. We need now to strengthen our commitment, insist that lay leaders of our congregations fulfill their obligations as Jews as much as the rabbi. There needs to be a series of *humrot* introduced into our Conservative ritual for their intrinsic worth and as a demonstration of our sincerity. Then our own developments of Jewish law and practice will be seen as the fulfillment of the spirit of rabbinic Judaism.

It has been argued increasingly of late, that Jewish life—if it is to be preserved in its integrity—cannot really follow along Conservative lines that seek to adjust traditions and religious behavior patterns to the needs of the day and to make our teachings and our observances relevant to contemporary society. A feeling of inauthenticity is bound to emerge from such a posture. There is bound to be a sacrifice of our basic precepts in the search for relevancy. That argument holds that the only way our tradition can be preserved is to compartmentalize our religious/ritual life, completely separating it from the influences of the workaday world. That philosophy has met with some success. This practice, however, requires a price of a terrible moral inconsistency. From its very inception Judaism has been and continues to be a religion that refuses to relegate to the Sanctuary that which is sacred. It insists on entering into the marketplace and suffusing the secular with a sense of the sacred.

The future of American Judaism lies in the hands of those who lead and sustain the Conservative movement. If our convictions are strong and our commitments are deep and if we see ourselves as a legitimate and authentic version of Judaism, then through our efforts American Judaism will survive and flourish.

Our task is far more difficult than that of the Patriarchs and that of Moses. We cannot command. We cannot order. We must persuade, argue, cajole, and then demonstrate by the example of our own lives and commitments—by the meaning, exaltation, and even joy being Jewish gives to our lives. We do so in an open environment that is hostile to many of the ideals we espouse—an environment and society that seek to entice our children and our grandchildren away from any sacrifices for idealism. Our task is indeed a formidable one. And yet it is a great summons of destiny comparable only to that of the first Jew, Abraham, and his summons to destiny.

To paraphrase a modern philosopher: A people of character seem to have the same experience recurring time and again. In the past, we have met the test of faith. With new skills, new strategies and new insights embodied in the Conservative movement, we pray we will be able to meet the tests of today and tomorrow.

Looking Toward the Next Century

Franklin D. Kreutzer

In an era of extremes, when the middle path is frequently considered cowardly, Conservative Judaism all too often finds itself in the position of being forced to re-authenticate its existence. The question being asked with increasing frequency is whether our movement, in some respects formless in ideology and structure, can be defined as truly authentic Judaism. The answer to this question may represent the most compelling challenge we face at this time in our history.

Conservative Judaism enjoyed its greatest growth in the years following World War II, an era of great economic expansion when the restrictions of definitions and of extremism were non-existent. Conservative Judaism was particularly suited to these prosperous times as a movement in the middle of an ideological spectrum. Therefore, it was able to incorporate within it a wide variety of versions and practices of Judaism. Conservative Judaism looked upon its diversity as the source of its strength, and its capacity to tolerate contradictions as evidence of its dynamism. In a time of growth and prosperity, it is easy to shrug off the challenge of authenticity, if anyone ever dares to raise it. From that period of expansion, we have now entered into a period of retrenchment, accompanied by an insistence on certainty and a search for authenticity. Young and old insist on an answer to the question, where do we stand? If they don't get a straightforward reply, they either embrace a form of extremism or drift off to aimless indifference.

The development of the Conservative movement is a clear example of authenticity without extremism. Conservative Judaism emerged out of the Historical School which represented the continuous and developing interactions between life and law. Evolutionary in concept, it was readily distinguishable from the Orthodox movement with its stationary stance and the Reform movement with its revolutionary direction. Setting aside the organizational diffusion and confusion that characterized Conservatism's growth in number and diversity, its major thrust has been the attempt to carry forth into the modern scene rabbinic Judaism's approach to halakhah, liturgy and theology. As we enter this new period, Conservative Judaism continues to be a powerful force in translating rabbinic Judaism into the contemporary scene.

It is one thing to engage in an academic examination of the roots of our movement in order to demonstrate its legitimacy. It is yet another to resolve those organizational, ideological and structural difficulties that generate the questions about its authenticity. It is my belief that at this juncture in the history of our movement, we can no longer afford to "muddle through." Some definitions must be fixed, at least setting the outer limits both on the left and on the right. Moreover, these definitions must be acted upon organizationally. How confusing it must be both for the rabbi and the layperson when the Committee on Jewish Law and Standards in a landmark opinion admits women to the minyan while some synagogues within the movement still segregate women at worship. Of what avail are our demonstrations of the validity of halakhah when synagogues and organizations on both the right and the left scorn it?

For much too long, Conservative Judaism has been viewed as a religion of compromise and convenience, an easy way to avoid the decision of remaining Orthodox or becoming Reform. All the proofs that Conservatism is legitimized by rabbinic Judaism will not remove from the heart of the congregant the suspicion that we are indulging in some form of compromise. We need men and women, particularly in the leadership of our congregations, who will demonstrate the sincerity of the Conservative commitment by some special forms of observance and discipline.

We need to build on the successes that have been unique to the Conservative movement in the past half-century, most particularly United Synagogue Youth, Kadima (the pre-teenagers), and the Camp Ramah network. Informal education, as has been proven by many of today's educators, is as successful as formal classroom education. In a short period of time basic ideals, principles, and precepts are imprinted upon the minds of the children in a meaningful way. We need to expand these programs by making them accessible to many more of our congregants. Regrettably, because of the excessive costs of USY Pilgrimage and Camps Ramah, these programs tend to be limited to a more affluent group within our community. Funds must be made available to offer scholarships to youngsters from all of our economic groups. In terms of formal education, the Solomon Schechter Day Schools have been most successful, given the short space of time for their development and growth. Day school education is without doubt the most effective means of formally educating the youth of our movement. An all-out effort for the funding of such schools must be on our agenda for the next century of the Conservative movement.

At the same time that we concentrate on youth programs and education, we must expend more of our energies on adult education. The synagogue of the Conservative movement must again become a *beit midrash*—a house of study for all ages. Renowned theologians Franz Rosenzweig and Martin Buber proved in Germany that Jewish adult education can sustain the Jewish community even in the midst of the worst adversity. It is in this way that our young people growing into adulthood will feel a commitment to Judaism and will make themselves available for leadership for the years ahead.

In recent years, new liturgical materials have been produced by the United Synagogue of America and the Rabbinical Assembly. Liturgy is the truest expression of our theology and of our hopes as a movement, and we can look with pride to our new prayerbook, *Sim Shalom,* and the Rabbinical Assembly *Mahzor,* both of which address the needs of the contemporary Jew in the modern world. We need to develop other liturgical materials, such as a volume of home prayers for distribution to every Conservative household, if we are to unify the movement meaningfully.

The synagogue today must also become a true *beit knesset,* a place where our people can gather to find Jewish answers to the plethora of problems besetting modern man. The United Synagogue has committed itself to respond to the changing times in which we live with its goal of providing relevance to the individual Conservative Jew as we approach the twenty-first century. All surveys indicate that there is a proliferation within our synagogues of individuals who are not married. For too long, our synagogues have been geared only to the family unit. In a time when singles of all ages, including the widowed, the divorced, and the never-married are seeking roots, we must open ourselves to them if they are to remain among the affiliated. How do we make them feel comfortable within the traditional framework which does not include them? How do we assist them in strengthening their ties to Judaism while accommodating their lifestyles? What do we offer to provide direction to the single parent who must fulfill the roles of both mother and father, in terms of Jewish observance? How do we make a place for them within the synagogue structure so that their single status and their working schedules are not obstacles to their involvement? The United Synagogue is presently in the process of evolving new programs and directives through our Commission on Singles to assist our congregations in reaching out to this ever-expanding segment of our population.

Another category of synagogue membership which mandates our attention is the aging population. Statistics indicate that the median age of the Conservative Jew is climbing rapidly and we must welcome those in this age bracket who still have much to give. In today's world, when the quality of life for many of our elderly has not diminished, we must utilize their age and experience to the benefit of our congregations. Are we properly involving them in synagogue life? Are we turning to them to aid us through their expertise and experience in committee deliberations, in ongoing projects, in religious services, in synagogue office work, on telephone squads, and in a myriad of activities which cry out for the resources they can offer?

Yet another area which demands our attention is the development of young leadership. Why are our young people not assuming positions of leadership in our congregations? How do we impress upon them the significance of synagogue service? Where do we turn to strengthen ourselves in the future if we have not communicated to them the value of giving of themselves to the cause of Judaism? Why does leadership in the synagogue not convey a sense of status to those who must follow after us, and how can we change that perception? Young leadership development has become a major agenda item for United Synagogue as we seek to insure the future and generate a greater continuity from generation to generation.

Perhaps the greatest challenge to the Jewish future in North America is the alarming increase in the rate of intermarriage, an area we can no longer ignore, and our leadership is now addressing this situation with the sense of immediacy it requires.

Within the definition of the Conservative movement, there are various expressions of halakhah, theology and even liturgy. We must learn to appreciate and respect these differences, recognizing that Judaism was never monolithic in nature. As we continue in our efforts to make Conservative Judaism relevant to each of our members, it is my hope and prayer that all of us together — laity and rabbis alike —

will go forward to the next hundred years with a sense of confidence in our movement and with a strength of commitment that will overcome the difficulties which may lie ahead.

View of the Seminary quandrangle and the new library building, 1985.

Dreams Are Realized in Accordance with Their Interpretation

Selma Weintraub

"We are living in a time of crisis," Adam is reported to have said to Eve. Whether our crises are more critical than those of the generations which have preceded us, only history will judge. But there is little doubt that how we meet them will determine the outcome.

I have been asked what I would like to see happen in our Conservative movement over the next fifty years. Here are my priorities, developed from the viewpoint of some forty years as an observer/participant of the Jewish communities in which I have lived, and most recently from where I have stood during the last four years, at the helm of the women's arm of our movement.

Women and Pluralism

In the forefront of developments in recent years with which the next half-century will inevitably be coping, is the women's movement. The drive for equality in the general community has translated into the quest by groups of women in the Conservative movement for halakhic revisions on some basic positions.

In the next generation, unless the backlash of right-wing conservatism in the general community affects the Jewish community strongly, support for the ordination of women, investing them as cantors, recognizing their eligibility to be counted as part of a minyan, to be called to the Torah, to serve as witnesses on legal documents, will continue to grow. With normative sociological development, as a generation grows up for whom "it was always this way," time will dissolve some of the tensions.

In our Conservative day schools and in our congregational schools, in the early years, at least, girls are receiving the same education as boys. How can we suddenly at the age of twelve or thirteen tell the girls — potentially motivated leaders — that what is acceptable in the school is not acceptable in the synagogue? What do we say about their role in the synagogue to those young women who have fought and are continuing to struggle for full recognition of women in the general community?

On the other end of the spectrum, how do we meet the needs of the more traditional members of our movement who ideologically do not fit into the Orthodox community and who, in practice, have not found a halakhically satisfactory answer to the changes which are occurring?

Some Conservative synagogues are experimenting with parallel services in the effort to embrace unity in diversity. In some places, the "downstairs" service is for the traditionalists; in some for the egalitarians. But to which service do the rabbi and cantor go? And who, thus, are designated as the second-class citizens? I fear such divisiveness and the separation — sometimes even of husband and wife — it invites. There must be room for all, and respect for each other's viewpoints, under a pluralistic umbrella — a formula which must be found speedily, before we fragment irreversibly.

I believe that if we are not to cut off our right arm or our left, we must strongly voice the need for our scholars to come up with a way to accommodate to contemporary societal changes within the framework of halakhah. Didn't they do it before, when the sage Hillel created the *prozbul* as an acceptable bridge to move from an agrarian to a mercantile society? When Rabbenu Gershom drew a line of demarcation between eastern and western mores by banning polygamy in the West, though it continued to be fully accepted in the East far into the 20th century?

The Jewish Birthrate

If we do not reverse our current minus zero birthrate and soaring assimilation rate, the statisticians are telling us, there will be no need for concern about the future of our American Jewish community — there will be none. A positive program to counteract the dire prediction is a very high priority. We have met and discussed and viewed with alarm. *Action* is the prescription!

Is there any good news? There are straws in the wind, at least. We are beginning to see such media headlines as one in a recent issue of a leading Anglo-Jewish weekly: "Juggling Two Careers and a

Marriage." Dedication to a career, which seemed so attractive during courtship, may be a curse later when it interferes with the relationship.

For some women, time is proving that the rush for the M.B.A. and a smashing career in what was previously a man's world of banking, stocks and bonds, are hollow achievements without the opportunity to savor the human expeiences which are the best and most enduring rewards which life offers. Can cuddling up with a well-stuffed safe-deposit box be equated with snuggling down with a loving and beloved grandchild?

To savor the joys of grandparenting, one must first accept the responsibilities of parenting. The statistics noting the marked rise of later child-bearing in the Jewish community are straws in the wind. Not yet studied, but apparent from observations, are the numbers of women who, with higher education and career successes already in their curriculum vitae, are opting to make the material sacrifices needed to enable them to stay at home and rear the precious babies they have borne, at least through the babies' earliest, most formative years.

Our Jewish society must make it clear to them that we admire their decision. One young mother said, "Even my grandmother asked me if this was all I was going to do with my education." Bitterly, another highly-educated young mother exploded, "Is there any better service a Jewish woman can give to her society than to raise good Jewish children?"

It is long past time that we recognized that the answer to our suicidal birthrate is in the hands of just a small percentage of our people — the women and men from roughly 20 to 40. We must redesign our attitudes and our priorities to encourage them with financial and psychological rewards. "Homemaker" must become a proud, not a pejorative term. Men seldom have to make the choice between opting for a family and advancing a career. Often a promotion for a male employee is influenced by the stability evidenced in a strong home and family life, while the career woman's ties to young children make her less available for travel, for night work, for shifts in working schedules.

The answer of the women's movement that society must adjust to the women's needs is only half an answer, though maternity (and paternity) leave, on-site day care (one firm paid for the nanny who flew with baby and nursing mother, so that the woman might represent it at an important hearing in a different city), and flex-time shared jobs are growing concepts. We must seek, encourage and accept whatever patterns will help young women choose to bear children; and we must provide through community cooperation whatever help is needed to raise them in a two-career marriage.

A recent article in the *Jerusalem Post* pointed out that "no one will have more babies for the sake of the state, to make more soldiers, or to increase internal *aliya*. But a positive approach from the establishment would make having children easier."

We are troubled by the rising costs of university education. Have we examined how prohibitive it is for a family wishing to give a sound Jewish training to three and four children to meet these school fees (even taking into account the modest reductions usually offered for third and fourth students). In Israel, the government gives a stipend to the mother of a multiple-child family, an encouragement and a welcome, if minimal, monetary lift.

Our highly efficient Jewish Federations should be asked to come up with a pattern of rewards to encourage the growth of family size and to assure the availability—and assistance with financing, where needed—of Jewish home- and day-care for infants and school-agers, for the parent who needs and/or wants such help.

Our synagogues and Sisterhoods must undertake responsibility for changing both attitudes and financial practices in the tested pattern of the Kehillah, where the community was responsible for the Jewish well-being of each individual "from the cradle to the grave." It will require much soul-searching and budget revising, but it is "survival intensive." To start with, we must not put a dollar sign on the entrance to the synagogue door for our young people. We can finance in better ways than holding ransom the very young people who are essential to a Jewish future.

The Matter of Jewish Teaching

An earlier generation used to sing the adage, "Silver and gold may vanish away, but a good education will never decay."

Just as we must reward the homemaker psychologically and materially for the value of her work, we must realign our educational sights, adjusting them to the recognition that teaching is the most honorable profession of all. We must give it the status which will attract our ablest young people—and the recognition that will keep them in the field. Our day schools have grown, but we lack enough American-trained teachers to staff them. Even more critical is the need for expansion of and trained staffs for our day high schools, to educate our teen-agers in the most critical years of the formulation of their loyalties and their goals.

As we mechanize teaching in our religious schools, we must re-emphasize the human factor, the one-on-one, interpersonal relationships which are the building stones of memories. Only a true teacher (and this includes of course, rabbis and cantors, social workers, parents and grandparents) can *kvell* with the gratification that comes from knowing that you have influenced a child—or an adult—towards a greater sense of self, and a higher standard of behavior.

I appreciate such technical marvels as the teaching cassette for rote learning and the joy of the video record of the bar/bat mitzvah party. But the humanity developed in the teacher-pupil relationships—the love, the patience, the encouragement—are seeds which no tape or screen can plant. And the same holds true for the teaching of adults. How many people, men and women, yeshiva-trained or from completely assimilated homes, have had their lives deeply affected by quality teaching, opening new worlds of Jewish intellectuality, and personal commitment to Jewish values and practice . . . surely an area where we have not begun to utilize our potential resources. It is an area of great hunger for scattered small communities, at a distance from urban centers. In our migratory, job-related mobile society, we must meet the new challenge or lose some of our ablest young minds. This is an urgent priority to which our national and regional education agencies might well bring their creative expertise.

Setting Standards

A story is told of the late Sir Moses Montefiore. Asked how much he was worth, he answered, "40,000 pounds sterling." But of course you have much more than that!" was the incredulous response. "You did not ask me what I have, but what I am worth," the Baron admonished. "The sum of 40,000 pounds is what I have given to philanthropy this year; that is what I am worth."

In a generation which has put so much value on "things," I would pray that in the coming decades we might all pay more attention to real values. Maimonides knew well what he was saying when he placed anonymity at the top of the list of quality tzedakah. We are the poorer psychologically for the philanthropy patterns which have tied so much of the mitzvah of sharing to the mechanism of public recognition. Education to tzedakah as a Jewish standard, expected of every individual—whatever his or her income level—needs our urgent attention.

So, too, with education of our lay leadership to the obligation to follow the standards of our Conservative movement . . . ceremonial and ethical. While we surely do not advocate inspection of the pots in an individual's home, we should let it be strongly known that it is axiomatic that the person accepting the presidency of a synagogue, for example, is expected to be in attendance on Shabbat and the Festivals as well as the High Holy Days; that kashrut is a basic tenet of Conservative Judaism; that "business is business" is not a Jewishly acceptable ethic. As the leaders, so the generation. We must put our profession and our practice in alignment if we are to set examples for the young people we are influencing as they search for the way of life they will adopt.

Some small start was made at a recent conference convened jointly by Women's League, the United Synagogue and the Federation of Men's Clubs. Much more educating and formulating is needed. The three organizations are on record, but a much more positive stance and more powerful persuasions need to be developed by all arms of our movement.

We are already reaping the rewards of our investments in United Synagogue Youth and Ramah programs, with early participants now concerned parents and informed community leaders. We must recognize the value of challenging them to more, not less, so they do not go elsewhere to seek their Jewish fulfillment.

We need to ovecome through education the ghetto-inherited "double standard" view of the convert and, despite the roadblocks maneuvered by right-wing Orthodox groups, we find no reason for giving anything but full Jewish status to "Jews by choice," making use of their energies, talents and enthusiasm to move our Jewish living programs forward. A convert is a full Jew—since the time of Father Abraham and Mother Sarah.

On the other hand, we need to formalize standards for the mixed-marriage where there has been no conversion. This is especially sensitive, of course, where the mother is the non-Jew. That it is not an academic problem was demonstrated at the recent Women's League Biennial Convention when a resolution was brought to the floor asking that rabbinic authorities be requested to determine whether a non-Jewish woman, married to a Jew, might be admitted to membership in Sisterhood.

Apart from the technicality that such a member—unless denigrated with "second-class citizenship"—would be eligible to hold office and by virtue of her office to represent the Sisterhood on a Synagogue Committee or its Board of Directors, the whole question is raised of the status of the children of such a non-Jewish mother. The Conservative movement's standard is clear—the child must be the offspring of a woman who was born Jewish, or who converted. But in practice, our synagogues are groping. What do we do about the Jewish education of the non-Jewish child of the mixed-marriage? Admit to the school and then refuse—as we must—the bar or bat mitzvah rite, without a conversion of the child? Admit for a limited number of years in the hope of "reaching the mother" and then exacerbate the situation by turning the student away?

What of participation in the youth groups? In the formative years of the pre-teen and teen-ager when social relationships are beginning which often lead to permanent marital relationships, do we thus encourage interdating—under synagogue auspices? And if a synagogue decides it will accept such children in the youth group, how do you handle inter-chapter and inter-regional events where parents from other synagogues are assuming that their children will be enjoying solely Jewish mingling?

While there are, undeniably, sensitivities to consider, in our struggle for survival *is* there a choice of standard?

The "Vanishing Volunteer"?

With the advanced techniques of the ever-diminishing micro-mini chip, our time allocations have taken on different proportions. When homework and children required all of a woman's time, volunteer work outside the home was "time off" for homemakers. As powered appliances eliminated many hours of drudgery, the released time has been channeled into employment outside the home, physical fitness and personal grooming, or a return to further schooling. Volunteer work became suspect, with an assist from those portions of the women's liberation movement which declared it "exploitation" (though interestingly not so if one's volunteer efforts were devoted to their cause).

Some proponents of this point of view have seen Big Brother (in tandom with Big Sister) taking over all responsibility for "visiting the sick, dowering the bride, escorting the dead to the grave, comforting mourners, making peace between man and his fellow . . ." A robot presses the appropriate button and the computer sends out the pre-programmed response.

Somehow it is evident that this picture is coming through warped. The best of the coming generation is recognizing the emptiness of a life "possessed by possessions," surrounded by machines instead of people.

Both scientific developments and psychological awareness are having their effect. As time-saving inventions and shared responsibilities at home permit more family time, it is being recognized that our Jewish festival calendar offers the most natural of patterns for family togetherness. We can continue to pick up the fast food dinners as schedules require them. In a few places we have begun to recognize as a community the importance of ensuring that *kosher* restaurants and *kosher* fast food take-out establishments are conveniently available. The technology is there; it needs the motivation.) This is for the *wochadig* (weekday) world.

But come holidays, we are recognizing that something more personal is in order — the sights, smells and sounds which enhance our identity, reinforce pride in our heritage, give every member of the family a hands-on, living experience, feeding into memory banks the happy entries that will last long after the three dozen cashmere sweaters or the "must have" latest record or videotape (or its 3-D successor) have been discarded.

With more people living longer, we are beginning to recognize the value of inter-generational relationships rather than "the problems of the elderly parent" or "the woes of the sandwich generation." With more time at their disposal than their busy children may have, grandparents can become *living* ethical wills for their grandchildren, influencing them by practice and precept to life's true values, which we appreciate the more as we grow older.

And for the grandchildren who live at a distance? A weekly Shabbat letter, periodic phone calls, thoughtful small gifts, and visits in both directions can nurture a valuable relationship, the feeling of roots which came naturally when the aunts and uncles and cousins lived within a 40-block radius, not thousands of miles apart.

For the young family a long way from "home" or with no family home to which they can relate, the synagogue and its affiliated arms have begun to take responsibility to serve as surrogate family, the catalyst to bring together the lonely of every age in supportive, enriching Jewish living patterns — a kehillah that cares about the widow, the single young adult, the single-parent family — taking measures to see that they are part of an extended, adoptive *mishpahah*.

In every situation we have been considering, people — not things — have been both question and answer, with many of the answers appropriately provided by volunteers.

We believe that the corner has been turned. On the one hand, society is facing the fact of the value of volunteers and giving them the recognition they should have. On the other hand, the personal satisfactions and joys which come from so many avenues of volunteer work, and the many pluses it offers are being evermore widely recognized by participating individuals . . . the opportunity to pursue a variety of personal interests apart from one's regular employment; the opportunity to learn new skills in a "protected environment"; the honing of valuable techniques in interpersonal relationships in an unthreatening atmosphere; . . . the rewards are legion.

Synagogue women's groups are providing such opportunities in many ways, having long ago moved beyond the kitchen. Every aspect of women's extra-curricular interests is encouraged. There has been a marked growth of interest in *Torah lishmah,* study for its own sake, notable in the seven years and more of the Women's League classes sparked by Dr. Gerson D. Cohen, taught by Seminary faculty in New York and in Los Angeles, now developing in Philadelphia and Boston, and with further cities to be linked to the fulfillment of this dream of high-level Jewish learning for every congregant. Action for human rights and human welfare are ongoing programs of social action committees. The performance of deeds of lovingkindness — helping children, the ill, the aged, the handicapped, the poor — are also indicated.

And it is providing fellowship where women can identify with each other, communicate more openly with each other to resolve their own needs and their family needs, and make new friendships which cross generational lines. The validity of women's groups is evident in other arenas: women's professional groups, even though the women are integrated in their co-ed professional organizations; the League of Women Voters; Zionist organizations and women's Zionist organizations. In Sisterhood we share a wide common interest — we are Jewish women, concerned for individual and community commitment to Jewish values.

What is my hope in this area? That women who have not yet discovered it will find that with streamlined, business-like dispatch, the administrative portion of our meeting time can be minimal. The member who has come from one commitment and is heading for another knows that her program time here will be a quality intellectual experience with a reinforcing socializing impact.

As I come to the close of my dreams, I am reminded of the couple who announced that they had achieved a real basis of understanding. All the major decisions were to be made by the husband, the minor ones by the wife. Pressed for some specifics, it turned out that where they go for vacations, how they spend their income, what kind of house they will buy were classified as "minor." What, then, was major? What to do about relations with the Soviet Union, how to protect the environment . . .

There is no escaping the fact of such major problems to be resolved as the making of peace among the Jewish sects of our time, the safety and welfare of the State of Israel, the plight of our imprisoned brothers and sisters in many lands. Yet, I would say that our urgent need as well lies with the priorities to put our own house in order:

1. Finding the road to a peaceful pluralistic unity in our own Conservative movement.
2. Strengthening our communal support for young families so that a birthrate reversal is achieved; and offering to all segments of the community the warm experiences which answer the dual questions of *how* to be Jewish and *why* to be Jewish.
3. Giving greater recognition to the importance of the Jewish educator — of adults as well as children, keeping in mind that historically education was always a responsibility of the Jewish community, not of the individual.
4. Encouraging high standards for leadership of all organizations, recognizing that leaders should be role models of the ethical behavior which is at the heart of commitment to Judaism.
5. Giving the fullest respect and recognition to the volunteers, whose contributions of time and substance are at the core of our continuing Jewish identity, our growth and our progress

as a world movement, assuring timely, effective leadership to our people on all five continents.

With such a prospectus, we will move from a generation which has laid too much stress on *things,* to one in which we measure upward mobility in terms of how we are *using* the good things of life to make a better world.

Treasures of the Jewish Museum: Seder plate by Ludwig Wolpert, silver, ebony and glass (Frankfurt, 1930).

Torah finials by Jeremias Zobel, silver: cast, repousse, stippled, engraved and gilt (Frankfurt, 1720).

The Rabbi for Me

Jules Porter

I am what is commonly termed a "Community Leader". I have sat on the Board of Directors of my synagogue for eighteen years, including four years as Vice President, along with serving on the Board of Directors of every Conservative organization in the community at some point: Camp Ramah, Los Angeles Hebrew High School, United Synagogue of America, Akiba Academy, and I am now serving concurrently as President of the Federation of Jewish Men's Clubs, and Vice Chairman of the Congregational Cabinet of the University of Judaism. I do not mention all of my involvements to boast, but simply to establish my credentials.

Because of these credentials, several years ago, I had the honor of serving on my congregation's Rabbinic Search Committee. It was an arduous exercise, mentally, and sometimes physically fatiguing, lasting for more than two years.

At first, we saw resumes, listened to audio tapes, and viewed video tapes of at least fifty rabbis before selecting the couple we wished to interview. Yes, couple. One of our requirements was that the rabbi interviewed be accompanied by his wife.

While each couple was with us, we wined and dined them. We then had the applicant deliver a sermon, and then adjourned to question him extensively from advice on childrearing to the most complicated talmudic questions. All this was the preliminary interview. After this, five were invited back to spend Shabbat with us, and preach or teach and meet our congregation.

Our committee was large, roughly thirty members, and represented all segments of our congregation, young and old, liberal to almost orthodox, plus two members who are rabbis. At our initial meetings we were asked to list the qualities, in the order of importance, that we felt were important for the rabbi of our congregation. It became evident that our values had changed over a three-year period. Six years before, our rabbi of sixteen years resigned. He had a magnificent pulpit manner, very exciting and very dramatic. Not surprisingly then, that was judged by the Search Committee to be the foremost requirement: possessing outstanding speaking abilities. Three years later, when we were again seeking a rabbi, the foremost requirement became personal integrity, followed by warmth. Lower on the list was pulpit manner and scholarship.

During the interview process we were asked to grade each candidate on the qualities we felt important to the position. Each quality was rated—no opinion, marginal, satisfactory, outstanding. The following is the list of qualities we were asked to judge:

Age/years in rabbinate
Size of present congregation
Personal appearance
Personality/warmth
Ability to relate and communicate
Sincerity/sensitivity
Sense of humor
Stimulating speaker
Administrative experience/skills
Depth of insight
Advanced degrees and courses/publications
Fundraising accomplishments
Strength of conviction about Judaism
Ability as a teacher
Counseling/special training
Accessibility to congregation (counseling; tending to members' needs)
Interest in/involvement in school and youth
Interest in/involvement with young adults and young families
Concern about Israel and world Jewry
Involvement with Jewish community at large
Involvement with community at large
Attitude towards women's participation in the synagogue
Overall fit for the position at Sinai Temple
General comments

Quite a list! If I were ever put in the position of a rabbi, knowing in advance that I was to be evaluated on all of these various subjects, I would find it almost frightening.

While we were in the process of conducting our search for our new rabbi, we had the honor and privilege of having Moshe Tutnauer, along with his wife, Margie, act as our "Rabbi in Residence", and once again, our values changed. Who would have thought that the membership of sophisticated Sinai Temple could fall in love with a "teacher." For that is what Moshe is. He taught at minyan every morning. He taught from the pulpit. He had Torah study classes Shabbat afternoon and a Bible class on Sunday. He taught at *shiva* houses. When he was honored by the Jewish Theological Seminary and the University of Judaism with an Honorary Doctorate of Divinity, instead of delivering an acceptance speech, he handed out photo copies to the 500 people at this breakfast and taught Torah. His presence did much to heal our congregation and to begin the process of bringing us together again. So, as a result of our M&M (Margie and Moshe) experience, *teaching* moved up about six notches on our list of rabbinic qualities.

What does all this prove? To my mind, the mind of the congregant, it simply proves that if a congregation is happy with their rabbi, if they are proud of their rabbi, they will be content with that particular rabbi's personal strength.

Because of my personal involvement with the Conservative community both locally and nationally, I have been privileged to come to know many outstanding rabbis, young and old. I think back twenty years or more as to what my vision was of a rabbi. That vision was one of an older, scholarly, kind individual who is always there to hold your hand, and to preach from the pulpit on subjects that you never could quite understand. Today's rabbi is quite different. He/she is younger, and relates more to the average member of the congregation. They play tennis, golf, and perhaps are socially closer to the members of the congregation than in the past.

I look to the future and I see shining lights coming on the horizon. Young people such as our new rabbi, Allan Schranz, and Rabbis Alan Silverstein, Ron Shulman, Neil Cooper, Nina Bieber Feinstein, and Dan Gordis. I look to the past with nostalgia and I remember wonderful men of blessed memory, Jacob Kohn, Joseph Wagner, and Meyer Merimensky. Personally, I have my own qualities that I am looking for in a rabbi. There should be warmth, recognition (whether or not they are a member of the Board or a big contributor), intelligent speaking from the pulpit, a caring about all people in general, a feeling of ease at being religious, and a desire to let the children get to know him.

If someone were to ask me whom I considered the ideal rabbi, I would have to answer him with a composite of men I have known. He must have the love of Moshe Tutnauer, the intellect of Harold Schulweis, the pulpit presentation of Hillel Silverman, the writing skills of Gilbert Rosenthal, the integrity of David Lieber, the friendliness of Yaakov Rosenberg, the inspirational ability of Joel Geffen, the conceptual understanding of David Gordis, and the heart of a Jacob Kohn. That would be my ideal rabbi.

A New Image of the Rabbinate

Alan Silverstein

The Congregant's Image of the Rabbi:
A Need For a New Synthesis

The image of the rabbi in the eyes of the congregation has undergone a series of changes during the past two hundred years. As recently as the late eighteenth century, rabbis were linked to tasks as the *rosh yeshivah* (dean or principal) or *rosh beit din* (judge) rather than to any particular congregation. In rare cases, a prominent rabbi might even have been the "chief rabbi" of an entire town or city, but never was his scope limited to a single synagogue.

Such a pre-modern model of rabbinic service ended in the Jewish battles in Western societies throughout the nineteenth century to obtain the privileges of citizenship. As part of the "bargain of Emancipation," the leaders of the Jewish communities in the West sought to recast the self-image and general public perceptions regarding Judaism. Consequently, the rabbi was recast with new functions, and a new image. Like Protestant ministers in these localities, the rabbi was to be limited to one specific congregation. More importantly, the rabbi was to become the master communicator, the transmitter of ancient Judaism into a modern idiom which would be in harmony with citizenship. As a result, the image of the rabbi shifted to being rabbi as preacher, speaking to both Jews and gentiles; rabbi as scholar, publishing books and editing newspapers and journals for popular consumption; and rabbi as educator of children in a synagogue setting, with a goal of training a new generation of modern Jews.

In the last quarter of the nineteenth century and continuing into the first half of the twentieth century, a new image of the rabbi emerged within the mind of laypeople. Mirroring the successes of Harvard Law School and Johns Hopkins Medical School and a host of other rising graduate school programs, the rabbinate began to be reshaped into the dimensions of contemporary "professions." Just as physicians, attorneys, social workers, teachers, engineers and so many other earlier callings and vocations abandoned "rule of thumb" training and practices for more systematic and functional tasks, so too did the rabbinate. As part of this thrust towards professionalization, it was crucial to laypeople that the congregational rabbi transcend the subjective realm of communicator, and master more objective, easily definable responsibilities. Therefore, like clergy within Protestant and Catholic denominations, rabbis began to be accountable for "pastoral" functions — visiting congregants in hospitals, officiating at life-cycle ceremonies (births, bar mitzvah, weddings, funerals), and general counseling; as well as for a growing agenda of synagogue administration items such as scheduling educational programs, producing synagogue publications, cultivating relationships with local Christian and civic groups, etc.

The current image of the rabbi in the eyes of congregants is no longer as clearly focused as were any of the three earlier models. If anything, today's image is a synthesis of all of these earlier functions, in addition to such new tasks as promoting membership growth, serving Jewish singles, attending to the aged, providing outreach to interfaith couples, developing havurot and other means of retaining intimacy in large institutional settings. For most laypeople, the "job description" of the contemporary rabbi has become so chaotic and undefinable, that rabbinic contracts frequently avoid this highly elusive definition by referring vaguely to "all obligations usually associated with the position of rabbi of a synagogue." As a result, synagogue Search Committees, interviewing prospective rabbinic candidates, are often seriously fragmented by competing and conflicting visions of the ideal rabbinic portfolio. Some lay leaders seek a rabbi-pastor, while others long for a rabbi-preacher-communicator, a rabbi-administrator-programmer, and still others desire a rabbi-scholar-teacher. Finally, there are some laypeople whose primary goal is to locate a rabbi-membership chairman-outreach worker. Clearly, these skills are not necessarily mutually exclusive, but equally evident is the reality that no one rabbi can possibly be totally effective in all of these tasks simultaneously. As we enter the second century of the Seminary's existence, we must either train rabbinic specialists seeking to master one or several of these domains, or we must encourage the Conservative movement to redefine a realistic, desirable, and unified image for the rabbi of the future.

Women Rabbis, Younger Rabbis, American-Born Rabbis, Conservative Movement Trained Rabbis: The Pluses and Minuses of Familiarity

The negative assessment of "familiarity" is that it breeds contempt. On the positive side, "familiarity" provides a feeling of accessibility and comfort. Both of these dimensions are present in the changing image of the Conservative rabbi. Until quite recently, the image of the congregational rabbi was that of an old-world, revered father figure. A rabbi ideally would be at least fifty-five years of age, with a mature, graying and pious countenance. He clearly physically represented both an age-old tradition, as well as a tangible symbol of the congregant's image of Moses or even of God ("an old man in a long white beard"). In stereotypic terms, a "young" rabbi meant someone without gray hair, and a "modern" rabbi meant a middle-aged man without a beard. Rabbis under age forty were not to be regarded as "real" rabbis. Instead, they were psychologically viewed as "students," "rabbis in training," "assistant rabbis," "Hillel rabbis" or perhaps rabbis of isolated, entry-level rabbinic positions, experiencing an aging process prior to emergence into full congregational service.

This sense of chronological "otherness" imparted to rabbinic leadership by Conservative laypeople was further enhanced by the childhood backgrounds of the congregational rabbis. Whereas most Conservative congregants of past years had been raised in inner-city Orthodox shuls, neither they nor (in most cases) their families had ever been truly observant of Yiddishkeit. For such a laity, the suburban Conservative synagogue provided a traditional setting at times of ritual ceremonies, and yet was tolerant of the obvious non-commitment of most members to Shabbat, kashrut and holy day practices. By and large, the rabbis of such a generation, like their membership, grew up in similar urban Orthodox settings. Unlike their laypeople, however, the rabbis were generally from the few truly Orthodox and observant households of those neighborhoods, and retained their *"frumkeit"* into their adult years. Combined with formal rabbinic training, such a childhood and adolescence of piety imparted to these men, in the eyes of their congregants, ideal qualities of religious leadership as well as a sense of "otherness", of uniqueness, of difference, in their level of observance. Laypeople would often remark: "Of course, he keeps kosher and Shabbos. He is a rabbi. He grew up in a truly Orthodox environment."

Today's active congregational Conservative rabbinate is dramatically different from its predecessors, and new lay images of the rabbi are being formed. An image of "otherness," piety, maturity and paternalism is being replaced by a feeling of familiarity, comfort, accessibility and often of less respect and awe. First of all, unlike in the past, a recent Rabbinical Assembly survey indicated that the median age of pulpit rabbis is not fifty-five, but rather thirty-eight. As with lay leadership, the number of rabbis born during the 1929–1945 period of economic depression and subsequent World War is disproportionately small, while the quantity of rabbis and active laity born between 1946 and the early 1950s is exceptionally large. More and more, laypeople have begun to adjust to a new chronological image of the rabbi. Moreover, the success of Ramah Camps, USY/LTF, Hillel and Judaic Studies programs on campuses, along with the attractiveness of many suburban Conservative congregational religious settings, have produced a generation of rabbis who were raised by and large in Conservative (and sometimes Reform) households. Unlike the previous generation of rabbis, these religious leaders have become much more observant than their parents and their childhood peers, and chose the career of the rabbinate from among a wide range of professional and business vocational options. Most dramatically, the ordaining of female rabbis further reduces the sense of "otherness" of the contemporary Conservative rabbinate. No longer can the rabbi of the Conservative pulpit be expected to be a middle-aged or older father figure, nor a veteran of Orthodox, pious upbringing. Indeed the rabbi can no longer even be expected to be a male. More and more, the rabbi seems to be similar to, rather than in contrast to, his congregants. Like laypeople, the rabbi of today can be a person of any age, of any religious background (including Jews-by-Choice), and can be either a man or a woman. Unlike in the past, today's lay leaders often ask, "Why would someone from a home like ours choose to become a rabbi? What kind of job is that for a nice Jewish young person?" A demythologized rabbinate, without a sense of "otherness" is emerging.

Rabbi As Layperson: Rise in Personal Benefits and Decline in Authority

As the image of the rabbi has become demythologized, as rabbis have lost the aura of being "holy," of being father figures and gained the benefits of accessibility and of serving as religious role models for their non-Orthodox congregants, rabbis have experienced the pros and cons of being treated like laypersons. On the positive side, today's rabbis are less resented for expecting to be paid a salary, housing and a benefit package comparable to many laypeople. More and more, synagogue leaders can understand how rabbis raised in homes and communities like their own, having attended prestigious universities, and having chosen the rabbinate among a wide variety of career options, are entitled to seek reasonable comforts for themselves and their families. No longer do most congregants expect the rabbi to be supported primarily by random honoraria for life-cycle functions and other private services rendered to families and individuals. Nor do caring lay leaders express surprise when a rabbi is willing to accept a call to a larger, geographically more desirable congregation, or when a rabbi seeks to negotiate his or her compensation package. Moreover, laypeople are no longer even shocked when a rabbi chooses to leave the active rabbinate to enter the business world in pursuit of greater material rewards for personal and familial reasons.

Also on the positive side of the ledger, the demythologized rabbinate is given greater tolerance in terms of one's personal life. Whereas previous generations of rabbis were expected to provide almost unlimited efforts by the rebbetzin to serve the synagogue's needs, today's spouses of congregational rabbis are much more respected in terms of personal privacy, and in choosing in which fashion to be involved. In this context, congregations are far less likely than ever before to discriminate against hiring or retaining an unmarried rabbi, a divorced rabbi, a rabbi who is either married to a Jew-by-Choice or has personally converted to Judaism. Furthermore, there is less and less resistance to the two-career rabbinic family, even when the spouse of the pulpit rabbi is serving as part of the rabbinic staff of a different congregation or communal agency. Finally, unlike the previous generation of rabbis, today's rabbinic leaders are well respected for insisting upon a formal and written contract, including one day off per week, and four to six weeks of vacation time during the year, and of making a priority of spending time with his or her children, encouraging them to visit their rabbi-parent in the office, at services and even on the *bimah*.

The negative half of the equation of being treated like a layperson relates to the realm of rabbinic authority. The more the congregational rabbi is viewed as similar to laypeople in terms of personal, professional and familial needs, the less sanctified, protected and unique is his or her status. Such a "desanctified" image has serious implications in the context of "synagogue politics." Whereas previous generations of rabbis were often feared, and generally respected as ultimate arbiters of many aspects of synagogue management, the current generation of rabbis is challenged again and again in its authority toward decision-making, not only in administrative areas, but even in the realm of ritual policy. One of the secondary results of the grass-roots response of laypeople to the national call for counting women in a minyan and according *aliyot* to females was the revelation of the remarkable decline in rabbinic religious authority within congregational life. Throughout the 1970s and into the 1980s congregation-wide decisions concerning "women's ritual roles" often resulted from survey questionnaires, Ritual Committee and Board of Trustee debates, and a variety of other formats in which the demythologized rabbi was reduced to being a resource person, a teacher, a guide, but certainly not an authority, a *mara d'atra,* a definitive voice. As indicated by these brief reflections, the image of the rabbi in the mind of the laity is undergoing a period of uncertainty and of flux. As was true in past generations, such a lack of clarity with regard to the rabbinate is a barometer of a larger trend of ambiguity within the American Jewish community at large. Challenged by the fragmentation of the nuclear family, untraditional sexual practices, the feminist social revolution, and the demythologizing of all learned professions, the Jews of the United States are beset by contradictory currents which demand new definitions of the contemporary rabbi. As JTS, the molder of rabbinic education and style, enters its second century, may our Conservative Jewish community create a viable and effective synthesis for the rabbinate of the future.

Fifty Years Hence

Howard A. Addison

Conservative Jewry Past and Future

Projecting the future is a task to be approached with humility and trepidation. At best one can but extrapolate current trends, knowing full well that our changing world can give the lie to even the most carefully conceived scenario.

That being said, there is one assertion that can be made with certainty concerning the future face of Conservative Judaism. The sociological dynamic which carried the Conservative movement to prominence following World War II will have vanished completely by the year 2037. The large mass of second generation East European Jews who built scores of prestigious, decorous Conservative synagogues across this country's third areas of Jewish settlement will long have passed from the scene. Their children, who populated our teeming Hebrew schools in the '50s and '60s, will themselves be quite elderly if still with us at all. Therefore, if we are to discuss the future of the Conservative movement, we must realize that it will be populated by fourth, fifth and sixth generation American Jews.

In many ways this American Jewry of the twenty-first century will become more homogeneous. Years ago the various religious movements in Jewish life could be distinguished as easily by non-spiritual factors as they could in matters of doctrine and observance. Family origin, level of secular education, socio-economic status and degree of upward mobility probably played as large a role in one's movement affiliation as did strictly religious concerns. Today, as we move farther from the immigrant experience, those differentiating factors are diminishing. Fifty years from now, they will be of little or no consequence whatsoever, leaving all denominations to compete equally for the same set of Jews.

While growing more similar in those socio-economic traits which formerly differentiated the various movements, our prospective congregants of the year 2037 will differ significantly from our present parishioners and among themselves. If current trends persist, our community will continue to age with a low but constant birthrate and ever rising longevity, leading to a more even distribution of persons along the age scale. As marriage is deferred and divorce becomes more prevalent, the nuclear family is becoming rarer. Singles, single-parent families, and blended families are becoming more common. It is now more the norm that both parents in the Jewish family work outside the home, and that only one of those parents was born Jewish — a total reversal from decades past when the opposite was the case.

Not only will our future congregants be more diverse in age distribution and family pattern, but they also will be more detached from the wellsprings of Jewish tradition and from each other. Eastern Europe and Hester Street will be consigned to the history of a century and a quarter past, their common experience and holistic patterns of Jewish living to be related by texts rather than by those who lived the reality. Our high rate of mobility, with its urban exodus and sunbelt migration, will move us farther and farther away from extended family and from this continent's established centers of Jewish life. This ever-widening chasm in time and space will be intensified by a growing Jewish social distance as we continue to relocate into more scattered, smaller communities, either exurbia's rolling expanses with off-street shopping and distant neighbors or into the undifferentiated, beehive-like complexes of condominums. All of these factors will account for an increasing lack of rootedness, historical memory and socialization into the lifestyle and etiquette of the synagogue and Jewish communal life.

South Florida: A Glimpse Ahead

It is opportune that I write these reflections shortly after moving from Chicago to assume a new pulpit in South Florida. In many ways, I feel my new position is providing me with a glimpse into the future of American Jewish life.

South Florida is an area which boasts 500,000 permanent Jewish residents. Yet it is hard to call this sprawling tri-county region a Jewish community in any traditional sense. Separated by great physical distances, split among several Jewish Federations, fragmentation rather than cohesion seems to be the operative principle.

In this rapidly growing area almost everyone is a new arrival from somewhere else, providing little sense of continuity or tradition, even in a synagogue like ours which is twenty years old. An air of disruption underlies the sunshine. Many among the scores of elderly feel lonely and frustrated, cut off from family, friends and those endeavors which marked them as distinct and important up North. The young also are adrift from their primary associations and some of our Hebrew school classes contain more students from single-parent and blended homes than children living in nuclear families.

Judaism remains of some importance but must compete on a equal footing with a host of other activities for children and adults. Perhaps most disturbing is the lack of an innate feeling for what is Jewishly appropriate, a lack reflected by the incorrect assumptions which underlie almost every *shaila* (religious query) posed to me. Paradigmatic of this reality is the family who told me that they were taking their son to Israel following his bar mitzvah. The highlight of this trip would be Shavuot, when they would make a pilgrimage to Eilat to go surfing.

Our Future Challenge

What then will be the fate of Conservative Judaism fifty years from now, at once deprived of its founding constituency while facing a thoroughly Americanized, uprooted, transplanted and more loosely bonded Jewry? Some point to our static numbers and greying membership as a sign of inevitable decline. Others cite present polarization and a host of factors, some spiritual, some social, which will cause a realignment of American Jewry into two denominational camps: Orthodox and Heterodox. Under this scenario, a portion of our movement might affiliate with Orthodoxy while the majority would be submerged into Reform. I, on the other hand, feel that Conservative Judaism will have a vital role to play in the twenty-first century if we but reformulate and act on two of our most basic principles, community and authenticity.

Community

The commitment of Conservative Judaism to community as a prime Jewish value is well known. From Schechter's formulation of Catholic Israel to our early support for Zionism to our members' involvement in and leadership of Jewish organizations of every kind, ours is a movement dedicated to *Am Yisrael*.

Over the last several years our efforts in community building have taken a new turn. If the large "corporate" synagogue of the 1950s was too impersonal and cold, then we have subdivided our congregations into havurot. If our members have different educational backgrounds and spiritual needs, then we have offered not only a plurality of classes but a plurality of services as well, including traditional daily minyanim, the customary Conservative worship in the main sanctuary, beginners' services, women's prayer groups, egalitarian and creative services, and many more. Indeed, we now have interest and support groups for each age bracket and every stage of life, from nursery and youth to the single, young married, single again, elderly and beyond.

The transformation of the large "corporate" synagogue into the "department store" synagogue has had many beneficial effects. It has allowed people of like minds and like needs to find each other, to develop more intimate supportive relationships as the synagogue has reached out to serve more, diverse people in better ways. Accompanying this gain, however, has been the concurrent loss of something precious — a sense of the whole.

If the Jewry of fifty years hence will be less rooted and more dispersed, then the synagogue must take an active role in re-creating primary relationships. While much of this work can only be done in small, homogeneous groups, the need for intergenerational meeting will take on added significance. When divorced from extended family, the young need the experience and sense of continuity which the elderly can provide, while the old need the feeling of vitality and bestowed respect which only the young can offer. Not only must we program so that Nursery and Sisterhood, Young Couples and Men's Club, USY and Seniors are brought together in shared activity and task, but we must strengthen these bonds informally as well. If ours are to be congregations rather than mere collectivities, then it behooves both our lay and professional leadership to bring together people at synagogue events, at the kiddush table and in their homes who might otherwise never gravitate towards one another.

Authenticity

Combined with this new orientation towards community building must be a redefinition of Jewish authenticity for the Conservative movement. Ours was called into being as the Positive Historical school within Judaism. Perhaps the time has come for us to regain a sense of the divine which underlies the unfolding of all history.

The application of our "Historical" approach to Jewish studies has yielded a rich harvest of new insights and information concerning the plural, multifaceted development of our faith. Yet it has exposed us to certain risks as well. First among these is despiritualization, the viewing of all Jewish phenomena as resulting solely from a confluence of certain political, economic, ideological and social factors. Second is the pitfall of relativization, of seeing each decision, each epoch, each value and text as merely another manifestation of our pluralistic Jewish history with little basis for distinguishing the signal from the trivial either then or now. Finally we have opened ourselves to the threat of idolization, of making past human events and our ability to uncover and interpret them into an absolute.

What I am not proposing is that our movement abandon the gains of the last decades and march, banners unfurled, into the sixteenth century. Instead I urge that we recapture a sense of metahistory to complement and counterbalance our "Historic" Judaism. Once we have critically examined a text, we must ask a further question: How do these words amplify for us the voice which originated at Sinai? When considering matters of halakhah, we must look at each issue not only with the eyes of tradition or modernity, but primarily with an eye towards promoting devotion and faith. As each generation of American Jewry is born into greater material comfort, the need for spiritual uplift grows. As disruption and detachment due to the rapidity of change increase, we must realize that *Wissenschaft* can light the intellect's path, but does little to warm the cold, dark night of the soul.

In this, its centennial year, we must applaud the Seminary's successful efforts to professionalize, academize, and Americanize the rabbinate, cantorate, and Jewish education. Its challenge during the next half-century and beyond is to maintain the achievements of the past while seeking to further spiritualize its students and alumni. As the Seminary re-evaluates its curriculum and joins in planning continuing education for those in the field, it must realize that merely another academic course or another seminar on professional techniques won't do. Instead we need forums in which students and graduates can immerse themselves in the theology of thinkers present and past and then, by way of crystallizing their own theological orientations, be challenged to apply their insights to contemporary issues, literature, daily occurrences and even halakhic practice. We need occasions when participants can share in worship and observance and then relate to each other their reactions to the same and how these influence their approach to life situations. We need to investigate and discuss the sacred mission of the synagogue and how that can be expressed not only through worship and study, but even through the modes of our social programming and administrative styles. To these efforts we should apply the best of modern interdisciplinary studies, but we must do so in the service of faith.

As we move into the twenty-first century, we know that an ever-increasing proportion of American Jews are becoming the fourth child at the seder. Not only must they be given answers but, as importantly, they must be taught what questions to ask. If the Conservative movement is to spark their interest and elicit their heartfelt response, then its rabbis, cantors, and educators cannot merely be professionals whose profession happens to be the purveyance of Judaism. Instead, its spiritual leaders must be just that—individuals whose lives and teaching reflect their belief that there is a God in the world, allowing for our differing conceptions thereof. Only then will the Conservative movement be able to offer something sorely needed yet available in no other denomination: a searching Judaism which will be not only historically correct but existentially genuine and spiritually true.

New Allies, Renewed Goals

In carrying our dual quest for community and authenticity into the future, we can take comfort from some heartening statistics. A recent population study by the Jewish Federation of Metropolitan Chicago (October 1985) indicates that although only 44% of Chicago Jewry is now affiliated with synagogues, an additional 31% has been affiliated at a previous time. The same study indicates that 80% of all Jewish couples containing one partner who is a Jew-by-choice maintain synagogue membership. These trends, combined with the greater tendency to affiliate among those who move from one metropolitan area to another, and the higher participation rate among the elderly, give us an inkling of where our future sources of strength might lie. If the Conservative synagogue can convey a sense of the preciousness of Jewish life to a wide spectrum of age groups and welcome the newcomer from different locales and other faiths, then we will not only replenish our numbers but revitalize our activities and our faith. To do so, we will have to reorient the nature of our programs, where they occur (*e.g.*, congregation-wide programs in the synagogue combined with smaller groups at homes, condo complexes, and commercial districts) and the way we financially support our institutions (*e.g.*, graded user's fees in addition to the customary membership dues). The potential for gain, however, is definitely worth the endeavor.

Five decades hence, the initial sociological wave which thrust the Conservative movement to the forefront of American Jewish life will have abated. In a Jewish world growing ever more detached and uprooted, growing ever more polarized between indifferent antinomianism and blindly obeisant fundamentalism, the need increases for a spiritually authentic, thoughtfully searching community of Jewish religious expression. The ideology and institutional structure of our movement provides us with the tools to become that authentic, responsive community. Whether our efforts to become that movement are successful will best be judged fifty years from now.

The Talmudists by Max Weber, oil on canvas (1934).

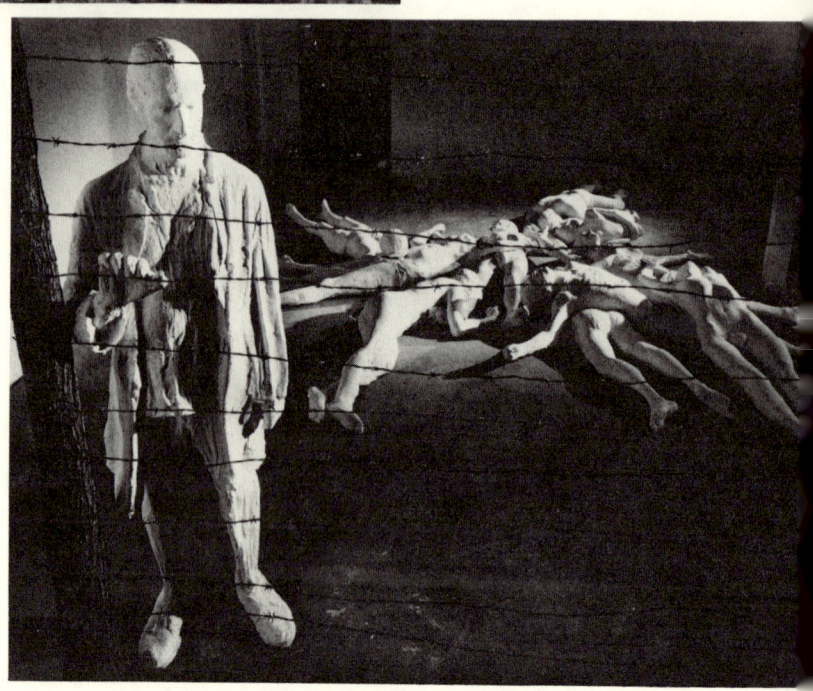

The Holocaust by George Segal, plaster, wood and wire (1982).

The Seminary and the Declining Synagogue

Elliot B. Gertel

At the risk of being labeled morbid, I must state my belief that the key to the future health of the Conservative movement lies not in the flourishing suburban congregations that grow effortlessly because of geographical desirability, but in those congregations, generally in semi-urban areas, that have declined beyond recognition from their former glory, and that seem to be in a twilight zone of endless transition and transiency. It was this intuition or, if you will, premonition, which led me to find irresistibly attractive a congregation which had declined from 600 to 196 households just before it became my first (and present) pulpit. The decline was largely the result of changes in the neighborhood (still a fine and rather expensive neighborhood, but where the public schools had fallen in quality, at least in the perception of most Jewish parents) and of internal dissensions in a merged congregation.

Ours is an urban congregation just a few minutes removed from the suburbs. The inner workings and politics of the congregation were really no different from those which occur in countless other synagogues every day of the week. Yet suddenly the rules of the game, as it were, changed. One day the borders of suburbia simply pulled away. The stalwart remnant and new leadership alike were forced into the spiritually humbling position of needing to allocate every penny and every ounce of energy for maximum spiritual, educational, and custodial benefit.

The first lesson of synagogue decline, is indeed that leadership must look upon *every* synagogue as in decline and in need of conservation. From my first interview by the congregation, I heard nostalgic talk about the hundreds of children who passed through the corridors of the Hebrew School building (now rented to other organizations). Where had they all gone? the members wondered. Where indeed? I echoed, suspecting the answer but convinced that the very process of finding out was itself an exercise in seeking the secret of renewal for Conservative Judaism.

With the help of a veteran secretary, members, newspaper publicity, old records, Hebrew School graduation lists, and numerous telephone calls, I located the 136 Hebrew School graduates, age 22 to 36, still living in the area. (Only a few were missed and later discovered.) I then interviewed them all personally by telephone, focusing on their feelings toward our synagogue—their synagogue—and toward synagogues in general. Most (more than 70% of the females and 80% of the males) had no synagogue affiliation. They intended to choose the closest, most convenient synagogue but only after they married and had children. (About half the males and a quarter of the females were single.) It was clear that to most of these alumni, United Synagogue affiliation, or a Conservative service, or Seminary affiliation, was not as important as the proximity of a temple or its social ties or its programs for children.

Surprising and painful to me was that many whom I interviewed had never even thought about what kind of synagogue—ideologically, programmatically, educationally, even socially—would fulfill their own personal needs. Even more surprising to me was that many did not know whether their parents were still members of the congregation. Most divorced themselves completely from the destiny of the congregation and from any thought about what the synagogue—their childhood synagogue—could mean in their lives today, apart from the needs of children yet unborn.

The second lesson of synagogue decline, then, and the most disturbing yet challenging lesson, is that a generation has been produced which, by and large, has not shown any loyalty to synagogue, Seminary or United Synagogue.

What is most disturbing is that this state of affairs generally reflects not the *failure* of the Conservative religious school, but its *success*. Most alumni of Conservative schools can read Hebrew, or had at least achieved enough reading ability to build on, had they made the effort. If my survey is any indication of general trends (and I think it is) many Hebrew School alumni have a good feeling about their schools. Many report that although Hebrew School was time-consuming, even burdensome in their eyes at the time, they now regard the enterprise as necessary, even beneficial. Rabbi Arthur Hertzberg observed that "despite all its inadequacies," American

Jewish education *has* played "a significant role in implanting an often deeply hidden Jewish loyalty in many younger people (and most now receive some Jewish training)."[1] Another conclusion of general application that I believe my survey yields is that Hebrew School alumni who have intermarried have, in many cases, strong Jewish feelings. Indeed, some who intermarried were among the best and most interested Hebrew School students, had close ties with their rabbis, and intermarried *not* out of rebellion, but out of love. Marshall Sklare put it well when he observed: "The Jew who intermarries . . . generally does so because he wishes to *marry* rather than because he wishes to intermarry."[2]

The predicament of the American synagogue is not that it failed but that it succeeded all too well. It has been quite effective at replicating itself—if not in ideology, or in loyalty, then in behavior patterns and attitudes. Though aware that their parents regarded the synagogue as a dropping-off point for children, many whom I interviewed declared their intention to drop their children off at the closest synagogue. Will the closest synagogue be Conservative? Or will the closest Conservative synagogue be sought out? And if there is no loyalty to one's childhood synagogue, does it really matter which synagogue is joined?

An alumna I interviewed compared our synagogue to a lonely mother waiting to get her children back. Her comment reminded me of the verse from Jeremiah read on Rosh Hashanah:

> A cry is heard in Ramah—
> > Wailing, bitter weeping—
> > Rachel weeping for her children.
> > She refuses to be comforted
> > For her children who are gone. (31:15)

The same cry is heard in many large and prosperous Conservative congregations whose children put off joining until they have children, or join a closer synagogue, or seek out a Reform temple or, occasionally, an Orthodox congregation. Recently the executive director of a thriving 900-family Midwestern Conservative congregation told me that the large Reform temples in that community banded together and formed a Hebrew High School program with the stipulation that all parents of participating youth must belong to a Reform temple. Since this program has become *the* socially desirable place for Jewish students to meet one another (though they may interdate on other occasions) some families left the Conservative congregation and joined one of the Reform temples. More are expected to do so. Is the leap from a traditional Conservative synagogue to a near-classical Reform temple that easy? Apparently, the parents really believe that the sally for Jewish socializing one night a week will prove a stronger factor in developing Jewish identity than religious ideology.

The third lesson of synagogue decline is, therefore, that if a particular service is required of a synagogue and not provided, many, if not most, American Jews feel few qualms about picking up and switching to another congregation, even if it means moving from Conservative to Reform. The survey reinforced what observers of American Judaism have long suspected: namely, that many if not most American Jews look upon the synagogue as a department store.[3] Not everyone wants the same commodity, but everyone expects the right product or service to be available when he or she wants it — or, especially, when something is required for the kids. One alumnus of the Hebrew School told me, "Young people want the synagogue to be open for them when they need it."

Given the lessons, hard-learned, stated above, the centennial of the Jewish Theological Seminary comes at a particularly crucial time. Does Conservative Judaism mean anything at all to those raised in Conservative synagogues? How do we assess its influence on the increasing numbers of outstanding USY alumni who now join Reform or Orthodox synagogues, or to those who become Reform rabbis? Does it matter that those raised in our congregations remain *Conservative* Jews, or is it enough that they are still Jews?

From the survey, from everyday experiences in the congregational rabbinate, from daydreams about the ideal synagogue that many whom I surveyed obviously don't have, I have concluded that the Seminary Centennial and indeed the Seminary itself will not inspire loyalty to Conservative Judaism unless the Seminary:

(1) assists spiritual and lay leadership in developing creative methods to popularize the approach of Conservative Judaism among members of Conservative congregations, and

(2) strengthens affiliate congregations so that Jewish spiritual, social and cultural needs can be met, not out of deference to crass consumerism (the "department store" mentality), but out of an effort to meet human needs while maintaining ritual, ethical and aesthetic

standards. The United Synagogue of America (together with Women's League for Conservative Judaism and the National Federation of Jewish Men's Clubs) and the Rabbinical Assembly are indispensable in these tasks as the arms through which the Seminary must work.

Indeed, the major function of the Seminary in concert with the national arms of the Conservative movement is to provide an ideological footing for the Conservative congregant so that sociological and geographical factors do not do as much violence to loyalty, and hence affiliation, particularly in the next generation. But, more than just loyalty to congregations is at stake. On the line is a concept of and program for Jewish religion and peoplehood.

Anyone affiliated with a Conservative congregation should have an idea of the historical approach to Judaism propounded in different ways (sometimes vastly different ways!) but with a common forum by thinkers like Schechter, Kaplan, Heschel, Agus and Gordis. Schechter's notion of "Catholic Israel," Kaplan's vision of the "evolving religious civilization," Heschel's ecstasy in mitzvah as a "way *of* God" that leads "*to* God" — these must enter the popular consciousness of the Conservative constituency just as Hamiltonian or Jeffersonian — or at least Democratic and Republican — politics are known, even vaguely, to the American public. Clever use of any electronic or printed medium, even slick blurbs from crafty public relations firms — whether on calendars, on synagogue bulletins, even on synagogue bills — are not beneath the task of such consciousness-raising. As Rabbi Bernard Raskas has been warning for decades, our synagogues individually and our movement collectively have not even begun to utilize public relations techniques for achieving institutional goals and for communicating our approach. Reasonable and tasteful means must be employed to inform our people that Conservative Judaism means obligation to historical Judaism and to the authority of our sacred literature and usages (the latter term I borrow from Dr. Gerson D. Cohen), and that to abandon Conservative Judaism is to relinquish the only continuous tradition in Jewish modernity that seeks to balance Jewish peoplehood and critical scholarship with the authority of a cumulative law and lore believed to be rooted in divine revelation.

As essential as it is that the Seminary and the other arms of the Conservative movement provide ideological footing to our congregants, it is even more necessary that they ensure the ideological viability of our congregations by advocating the legitimacy of varying practice while emphasizing the centrality of halakhah, especially of certain fundamental practices. Our members should be aware that Conservative Judaism is as committed as Orthodoxy to belief in God, as well as to ritual institutions such as the historical Sabbath, during which working, cooking, shopping, and writing, among other activities, are proscribed in favor of more spiritual pursuits such as home prayers and songs, particularly at festive meals, and synagogue worship. While there is room for different interpretation in matters of use of electricity or of the automobile, Shabbat observance remains an inviolate pillar of Conservative commitment, as does preservation of the classical order of prayer (*matbea hatefillah*) and the daily regimen of worship revolving around it. Festival observances during which men and women remain home from work and children (and especially Jewish teachers) attend synagogue instead of the public schools are also basic to the Conservative Jewish home, as are the dietary laws (kashrut). While the member of a Conservative synagogue may not presently or even shortly be able to observe all of these things, his or her commitment to Conservative Judaism should be an affirmation that these observances are the best expression of Jewish religiosity, that they hold some kind of authority over us,[4] and that they are the way that Judaism brings redemption to the world.

By publishing *A Guide to Jewish Religious Practice* by Rabbi Isaac Klein, and Rabbi Samuel Dresner's volumes on *The Jewish Dietary Laws* and *The Sabbath,* the Seminary and the United Synagogue, respectively, have fostered observance. But until these publications and future works of similar effectiveness are placed into the hands of everyone who joins a Conservative synagogue, or until their main teachings are instilled through other media than print, the job will not have been done on the local or national levels.[5]

The basic commitments of Conservative Judaism must be underscored by the Seminary and its organizational allies through competent, compassionate and *firm* guidance of individual congregations in the processes of halakhic and aesthetic decision-making. Within a single congregation there may be an historic pattern of traditionalism or of more eclectic ritual usages. The Seminary, Rabbinical Assembly and United Synagogue should organize panels sensitive to both the histories of congregations[6] and to the halakhic guidelines evolved by the Committee on Jewish Law and Standards. Such panels should, obviously, include local historians, experts in the history of Conservative congregations, and perhaps even local sociologists, and should be able to interpret these factors clearly for local lay groups, and to work with them on the graceful and effective definition of local usages. It should be made clear to congregations that while one cannot compromise on basic Jewish Law such as dietary regulations and the prohibition of cooking or working on Shabbat, the alternatives in halakhic practice in such matters as the role of women in the minyan or the use or non-use of instrumental music at Shabbat services or receptions, must be chosen by each congregation out of deference to a number of factors: majority wishes, congregational traditions, and the role of that particular congregation in the local community and in the Conservative movement.

The process itself would provide a solid lesson on *the need for and parameters of a mature recognition of plurality within a single Conservative congregation.* Different families of diverse interpretation of Jewish practice and ideology can and do feel strong ties to a single congregation. Any social, ideological or geographical factors that militate against the continuity of the generations within a given congregation must be fought squarely and creatively. The one-generation congregation is a mockery of everything our tradition teaches about respect for the elderly and outreach to the young. But unless our synagogue leadership and our laity at large can achieve enough grounding in Conservative approach to appreciate plurality and to distinguish between halakhic and aesthetic decisions — then stubbornness, inflexibility and the ignorance and closed-mindedness that breed them will drive away thoughtful, searching members of the next generation who seek creativity and sensitivity rather than acrimony and double-dealing at board meetings and in the entire decision-making process in synagogue politics.

Our movement allows for diversity of practice (as does classical Judaism) and this requires great maturity within each *individual* congregation. If, for example, a given congregation is very traditional by consensus and by historical role in the community, it should probably remain traditional, but might allow an egalitarian group to meet regularly in an alternative service and then, at regular intervals and at times when the minority group require the sanctuary for life-cycle events with a large attendance (b'nai mitzvah, baby namings, *aufruf* celebrations, etc.), they should lead services in the main sanctuary in *their* style so that the general congregation, by participating, can demonstrate that the alternative approach is not merely *tolerated,* but is indeed *recognized* by the mainstream congregation as being a legitimate minority interpretation of Conservative Judaism in that particular synagogue body. I think it is fair to observe, however, that the Conservative congregations with the most gracious and mature ideological sharing will be those where the alternative groups meet least frequently and join the majority group and offer alternatives at the main service most frequently.

Such a shared ideological climate within individual Conservative congregations is essential not only for the strengthening of congregational identities and of the movement in general, but for creating the kind of atmosphere that would challenge younger generations and make them more sensitive to the nuances of Conservative ideology. The United Synagogue, the Rabbinical Assembly and the Cantor's Assembly, together with Women's League and Men's Clubs, should establish programs to nurture the kind of synagogue leadership and synagogue board that can create this synagogal climate.

On the ideological and programmatic levels, *how* an issue is debated within a single congregation or community will influence the continuity of that congregation or community as much as the halakhic or ethical component of the debate itself. At the bottom line, joining a Conservative synagogue should mean more than just signing a check. It should mean commitment to certain standards of observance (or at the very least, in the short run, an affirmation of certain observances as the goal of synagogue life) as well as commitment to religious pluralism within the halakhic guidelines of the Conservative movement.[7]

Last but not least, the cultural standards of the Conservative synagogue will determine whether the generations can be stimulated aesthetically into appreciation of Jewish concepts, of authentic Jewish song, and of a compelling synagogue art and architecture. Especially in the realm of Jewish music, the province of the cantor, there is a responsibility to choose the most authentic and the most artistic (and, one might add, the most straightforward) cantorial and congregational melodies for prayer and celebration. While we don't always find the old piety in our congregations (though a goal of synagogue life remains loving acquaintance with our liturgy and with our ritual and ethical mitzvot, and fervent observance of them), good taste and a willingness to experiment with newer (but authentic) sounds must prevail over the trite and the outworn if we are to retain aesthetically discerning constituents.

In my own urban congregation, we have been able to grow considerably and to stem the tide of decline with innovative programs, a small community Hebrew School, and utilization of the talents of members. The local Solomon Schechter Day School community has enriched us immeasurably. But whether we or any other Conservative congregation can endure in the long run depends upon what guidance the Seminary and the arms of the Conservative movement will offer us *now* in preserving Conservative ideology and in enhancing the individual's cultural and social ties to the congregations that transmit it.

NOTES

1. Arthur Hertzberg, *On Being Jewish in America* (New York: Schocken, 1979), pp. 219-220.

2. Marshall Sklare, *America's Jews* (New York: Random House, 1971), p. 201.

3. See Marshall Sklare, "The American Synagogue: From Supermarket to Boutique," *Proceedings of the Rabbinical Assembly* (1975).

4. See Robert Gordis's comments on "Catholic Israel," in Seymour Siegel with Elliot Gertel, eds., *Conservative Judaism and Jewish Law* (New York: The Rabbinical Assembly, 1977), pp. 50-77, and in Gordis, *Understanding Conservative Judaism* (New York: The Rabbinical Assembly, 1978), pp. 53 ff.

5. It should not surprise us, furthermore, that according to at least one survey, the young people raised in Conservative homes who were most likely to join Conservative synagogues are those whose parents observed the dietary laws. See Charles S. Liebman and Saul Shapiro, "Survey: The State of Conservative Judaism," *United Synagogue Review* (Winter 1980), pp. 8 ff.

6. On the value of congregational histories for determining the character and trends of congregations, see Elliot B. Gertel, "From Beth Tefillah to Beth Midrash—Learning From Synagogue Histories," *American Jewish History* (March 1985).

7. On religious pluralism as a "conservative" value, see Elliot B. Gertel, "Is Conservative Judaism—Conservative?" *Judaism* (Spring 1979).

School children at the Jewish Museum's archeology exhibition. (Spring 1987).

Between Two Worlds, or Why the Peacock Doesn't Fly

Benjamin Edidin Scolnic

Conservative Judaism, in reaching this centenary landmark, may now be challenged to demonstrate its effectiveness as a religious movement. Clifford Geertz's famous definition will provide a starting point for our discussion:

"Religion is a system of symbols which acts to establish powerful, pervasive, and long-lasting moods and motivations in men by formulating conceptions of a general order of existence and clothing these conceptions with such an aura of factuality that the moods and motivations seem uniquely realistic."[1]

A religion attempts to impress a world-view on its adherents, to give them a view of reality and the meaning of life. To do anything short of this is merely to skirt the edges of a religion's purpose. Merely to say that one should perform this or that observance, without a successful transmission of the symbolic world in which that observance is meaningful, is insufficient at best. Even if the adherent performs the action himself, he may not be able to transmit the necessity of doing the ritual to the next generation.

Conservative Judaism, in attempting to reconcile the symbolic world of traditional Judaism with the symbolic world of modernity, has, for the most part, been unable to establish the desired moods and motivations in its adherents because it has not clothed its conceptions with the necessary "aura of factuality." We must consider the notion that the current approaches of Conservative Judaism do not sufficiently emphasize the basis of the religion, the performance of ritual. Ritual, Geertz reminds us, is where everything comes together: "In a ritual, the world as lived and the world as imagined, fused under the agency of a single set of symbolic forms, turns out to be the same world."[2] Judaism's insistence on the constant performance of ritual is not arbitrary or accidental; it is the constancy which keeps the Jew within the symbolic world.

The challenge facing our movement in the next decades will be whether or not we can turn Conservative Jews into Conservative Jews. In the lifestyles of both our lay leadership and our "High Holiday Jews," ritual is accorded a low priority. Rituals are often seen as unconnected to a person's belief in God or to his identification as a Jew. It is my fear that our rabbis and scholars have contributed to the de-emphasis of ritual by our noble but naive attempts to make Judaism relevant to the non-ritualistic members of our synagogues and by our deconstruction of the "myths" of the past.

Conservative Judaism's intellectual foundation is the historical study of Judaism as an evolving, religious civilization. If asked about the future, we will usually think about the next evolutionary steps to be taken. While Kaplan's definition of an evolving civilization was based on Darwin's theories, more recent work has questioned and refined these theories in ways which should be examined by all who would use the metaphor of evolution to explain religious development. Two items from the current debate, from the updated understanding of evolution, are those which have been called "overshooting" and "punctuationism."

"Overshooting" means that evolution sometimes goes too far. It is "like the case of a jammed switch, stuck in the 'on' position."[3] My favorite example is the peacock, which has been called "the most magnificent" of birds. The peacock evolved its ostentatious tail covered with the eye-like patterns called ocelli; it spreads its splendid plumes like a fan. This is all very beautiful, and the peahens find the peacocks very attractive. Each peacock has a harem of four or five females. But the peacocks rarely fly; even when in danger, they run. That is, as Leviticus would agree, an abnormal situation for a bird. Sometimes one can go too far in making oneself attractive, so far that one is untrue to one's basic self. It was not necessary for the peacock's evolution to go so far; the peahens could be attracted without such magnificent displays. Conservative Judaism has always played the peacock, spreading its fan in order to be attractive. But attractiveness should not be the primary goal; the goal is to synthesize, in a meaningful way, the two worlds in which we live.

"Punctuationism" means that evolutionary development does not always happen gradually through the accumulation of minute differences but that the gradual trend is "punctuated every now and then by a sudden jump." Judaism's development in history is too often taken to mean merely that we can keep on changing things because things have always been in a process of change. In terms of an aerial historical view, this may be true, but it might be more correct to talk about limited periods of significant change surrounded by much longer periods of quietude when the emphasis was on the seemingly permanent. To get down to cases: Let the 1950s through the middle of the 1980s be remembered as a time of great change, of Lieberman's addition to the Ketubah, of permitting electricity and riding to shul on Shabbat, of the inclusion of women as full participants in our religious community. The case of women's rights in Judaism is an example of what Stephen Jay Gould means when he says "that change occurs in large leaps following a slow accumulation of stresses that a system resists until it reaches its breaking point."[4] But evolution does not allow for constant leaps. Therefore, let this next generation be one of consolidation of the gains, of the development of the seemingly permanent. If the fundamentalist sects of the various religions around the world have one thing in common, it is their reaction to modernity. Too much change at a rapid rate can be frightening and unsettling. One becomes unsure of one's footing. This is contrary to some very basic religious impulses.

Again, the basic religious need is involved with ritual. Religion and its rituals require the "aura of factuality." But it is not only the rapid change which undermines the "factuality" of Conservative Jewish ritual.

One is reminded of the now-famous story cited by Gershom Scholem, at the dramatic end of the already-classic *Major Trends in Jewish Mysticism,* about the Baal Shem Tov and his spiritual descendants. When the Baal Shem Tov had a difficult task to perform, he would go out to a certain place in the forest, light a fire, say a prayer, and the task would be done. In the next generation, they did not know how to light the fire, but they knew the place in the forest and they said the prayer; the wish would be fulfilled. In the next era, they could not light the fire, they did not know the prayer, but they could still go to the correct place in the woods. In the last generation, Rabbi Israel of Rishin says: "We cannot light the fire, we cannot speak the prayers, we do not know the place, but we can tell the story of how it was done." And this would be enough to ensure the fulfillment of the task.

This is a very beautiful story, and it describes our state of affairs today, but it is, unfortunately, overly optimistic in its conclusion.

Most people, in the vacuum of understanding which is the fate of the last generation, will simply stop telling the story. But more, even if the story is told, it will be deemed insufficient for the completion of the task. People will listen, say it's a nice story, but will be more interested in many other stories which they have been told. They don't believe that tasks are fulfilled in this manner, and so they listen to the story with some amusement. They hear scholars say that the wonder-workers were really crazy to begin with and the whole story is undermined. They no longer believe that one place is more sacred than another, so the idea of a special place in the forest makes no sense. They no longer believe in the efficacy of prayer or the type of observance exemplified by lighting a fire. They do not believe that any of the previous generations actually accomplished anything by the ritual in the woods.

There is a severe, fundamental mistake here: Most of us do not understand the meaning of ritual, of "how it works." The truth is that it works in one reality even as it does not work in another.

Most modern Jews do not understand the important concept which Jonathan Z. Smith calls "incongruity."[5] The symbolic world of ritual orders life and tells us how life should be. The real world is often in disorder and tells us how life is. A believer will find many incongruities between the two worlds. Someone who understands religion will spend his life thinking about the incongruities from within the circle of faith and ritual action.

Judaism has been amazingly adept in dealing with some of the real or apparent incongruities by reinterpreting its symbolism without destroying the symbolic world. The history of Judaism is a history of such reinterpretation, but the key to the success of our religion has been the respect paid to the past. The boundaries of Sinai have been extended, but only so we can remain at the foot of the mountain. And the mountain is still covered by a cloud.

History and Interpretation

Between the myth as it has been transmitted and history as it "really happened" is an area for reinterpretation and thought. The author/editor of I and II Kings, considered to be part of the Deuteronomic school, viewed the history of the period from the perspective of a well-defined ideological system. Each king is judged on an absolute scale based on rigid criteria. Of great concern is the king's relationship to the Temple cult in Jerusalem. As we read, we are led to wait for the king who will carry out the centralization of cultic worship. The prophecy in I Kings 13 even names the king for whom we are waiting, Josiah. After centuries of war and idolatry, he finally appears (II Kings 22). He is the great king who does in fact centralize worship. He is the ideal king who has been taught from an early age to have great respect for the past, for ritual, for God. "There was no king like him before who turned back to the Lord with all his heart and soul and might, in full accord with the teaching of Moses; nor did any like him arise after him" (II Kings 23:25).

But a terrible thing happens to Josiah on the way to the fulfillment of his greatness. In a story of only one verse, we learn that Josiah sides with the "king of Assyria" against the Pharaoh Necho and is killed at Megiddo. We are given no information about why he participates in this war, nor why he supports the Assyrians. We are left to wonder not so much about the historical situation, which we can reconstruct, but about the ideological framework of Kings, which has just fallen apart. The Chronicler understands our problem, and has the Pharaoh warn Josiah not to interfere in the war, for he (Necho) is only carrying out God's will. Josiah marches out anyway, "heedless of Necho's words from the mouth of God" (II Chr. 35:20ff). In other words, Josiah dies because he has not obeyed the word of God. In Chronicles, then, reinterpretation and elaboration of the story keeps the framework of reward and punishment intact.

The more interesting fact is that the author of Kings, who does not have the Chronicler's elaboration, still shapes his work according to a framework which he knows will fall apart at its climax. Centralization finally takes place, but the victory is short-lived; it will not be long before the destruction of the Temple and the exile of the people.

What we have here is a lesson in the incongruity of myth. For the author of Kings, the myth holds, the interpretation of history holds, centralization is still the key. He has faith not only in God's justice but in the ability of those who come after him to comprehend what he may not. After long reflection, a new understanding of Josiah's fall will be found. In the meantime, the framework remains intact.

The relationship between myth and history here is analogous to that between the world of ritual and what we call the "real world." It is crucial that the symbolic world stay intact in order for it to be reinterpreted in later generations.

Now let us complete the story of the generations after the Baal

Shem Tov. All of a sudden, a group appears which claims that it knows the way to the place in the woods. A larger group follows. The task is fulfilled; the task is interpreted and reinterpreted. Actually, the task is not fulfilled, but it does not matter to those who are there: they are standing in the right place.

Emboldened by this success, the leaders light the fire; they then claim to know the secret meditation and say it. They are powerful leaders; a great movement grows around them.

Left behind are those who are skeptical about the efficacy of ritual and the validity of belief. They do not understand what all the fuss is about. They still do not believe that there is a special place in the forest, or a secret meditation, or a fire worth lighting. The people in this category may identify with those who follow the observance, and they may feel some sentimental attachment or aesthetic appreciation for the ritual action, but they will not participate themselves.

Most people who call themselves Conservative Jews are in the category of those who will not light the fire. The leadership has its own intellectual problems, for it has been overwhelmed by the myth of historicism to such an extent that it may not be able to see the symbolism as eternal. The leadership remains embarrassed by revelation, shy about theology. But worse, in creating a product that they think will sell to those who do not care about ritual, they often call rituals "customs," and laws "standards."

In a movement where most of the adherents do not themselves light the fire, the leadership is often content to walk around the edges of the forest. Here again, a story may help, this time from India about the coming of Alexander the Great:

"It was Calanus, we are told, who lay before Alexander the famous illustration of government. He threw down upon the ground a dry and shrivelled hide, and set his foot upon the outer edge of it; the hide was pressed down in one place, but rose up in others. He went all around the hide and showed that this was the result wherever he pressed the edge down, and then at last he stood in the middle of it, and lo! it was all held down firm and still. The similitude was designed to show Alexander that he ought to put most constraint upon the middle of his empire and not wander far away from it.[6]

The "middle of the empire," the basis of any religion, is its ritual. Again, this is where the two worlds, the world as it should be and the world as it is, meet. Walk around the edges and nothing stays firm. Ritual allows one to find a place on which to stand and view the world.

That place is an opening into the other world, an opening into the sacred. Conservative Judaism must provide openings into the sacred, its synagogues must be centers not so much of bingo, basketball and bake sales as for the breakthrough of the sacred into real life.

The Creation of the Sacred

The Bible records many breakthroughs of what we moderns might call the unrepresented into real life. The breakthrough, the revelation at Mt. Sinai, means not that we should study Torah as literature nor as pleasant advice, but as the basis for our beliefs, as the real thing. The Sinaitic texts are the witnesses to the revelation of God's will. The participation of the people at the foot of the mountain was the key. It still is. Participation is still the basis of a two-way covenant. That the records of the events bear strong signs of multifacetedness is natural and very appropriate to the covenant relationship. The people really did participate. The people of later generations continued to participate. Historically speaking, those who widened the boundaries of Sinai were saying: "We have seen the breakthrough of the unrepresented into life and we call this Sinaitic revelation." This is true in halakhah and it is true in apocalyptic works as well. To talk about the Oral Law as a myth which was created by the rabbis does not do full justice to what may have been a much less self-conscious perception of their role as creators than we like to assume. Theirs was not an intellectual dishonesty but a belief that they too were witnesses to the breakthrough of the Divine Will. And they preserved the aura of factuality.

Seeing the Torah in this light, we can interpret. We can use our tools of criticism which show evolution and growth and pluralism within the Torah.

But we must emphasize the breakthrough nature of the Torah, the sacredness. The Bible is not just literature. The Torah is not just fossils and relics. It is the essence of our religion.

What We Must Conserve

The Baal Shem Tov was the master of the good name. Conservative Judaism must be worthy of its good name. We are not just conserving heritage. We are not just conserving standards. We are conserving the sacred world which was created at the physical and the metaphorical Mt. Sinai over the course of the centuries, which was transmitted to our people through the witness of the Torah and the power of our rituals. We must be worthy of our name.

In the next decades, we should not spend our energies in acrimonious debates over the next change and the one after that. If we follow the current evolutionary path, we will remain the peacock, an extraordinarily attractive bird which rarely flies. This is not to say that the peacock cannot fly; it can, its flight is "strong and labored." But if we remain dressed in the colorful plumage of pluralism, we must find ways to take to the sky, to the sacred world which is the essence of religion.

We return to Geertz's definition of religion. Conservative Judaism is a system of symbols, maintained from the past, which is eternal and meaningful; it is a system that connects us to the sacred world, it is a system through which we can view the general order of existence. The sacred world would become realistic if we would perform the rituals which create the "aura of factuality." We have been in a "punctuated equilibrium" with the switch for change locked at "on," and our claims of factuality, which we usually call "authenticity," have been dismissed, even by our own people.

It is rather strange that such an educated group of people should understand so little about the nature of religion. One goes to the sacred place, lights the fire, and says the prayer, not to accomplish a magical feat but in order to understand the world as it should be as opposed to the world as it is. And if the two sets of "facts" of one's existence seem at odds, that is a natural consequence of living inside two realities. We live inside and outside both of the realities; life is meaningful and always fascinating.

Most Conservative Jews only live inside the world as it is. The task before us is to teach them about the world as it must be.

NOTES

1. "Religion as a Cultural System," most recently reprinted in *The Interpretation of Culture*, (New York: Basic Books, 1973), p. 90.
2. *Ibid.*, p. 112.
3. Gordon Rattray Taylor, *The Great Evolution Mystery*, (New York: Harper and Row, 1983), p. 29.
4. "The Episodic Nature of Evolutionary Change," in *The Panda's Thumb* (New York: Norton, 1980), pp. 184–85.
5. In various essays, including "Map is Not Territory," in *Map is Not Territory: Studies in the History of Religion* (Leiden: Brill, 1978), pp. 289–309.
6. *Op. cit.*, p. 102, in an essay called "The Wobbling Pivot."

Some Notes on the Future of Conservative Judaism

Elliot Salo Schoenberg

Communal Needs

My second son, Ariel Isaiah, was born on a Shabbat morning. Cathy and I were delighted at the birth of a boy and began to prepare for a Shabbat *brit milah* at my congregation. The Orthodox *mohel* informed us that he would not be able to walk the distance to our suburban home; that he could not stay over at a kosher congregant's home because of his kashrut observance; and, for spiritual reasons, he needed to *daven* in an Orthodox synagogue. We could not drive to his home for the mitzvah because, according to his definition, that would violate Shabbat. The *mohel*, in essence, forced me to choose between his religious needs—his observance of Shabbat within an Orthodox community, and mine—the timely circumcision of my son. He added that "he would be happy to do the circumcision early Sunday morning if we still desired his services."

The experience taught me many things. I learned that there are very few Conservative *mohalim* and that Conservative rabbis and Conservative Jews, for the most part, are dependent on the Orthodox community for the performance of many basic Jewish rituals.

Our subjugation to the Orthodox is not limited just to *brit milah*. The Orthodox are the exclusive kashrut supervisors on a national level and the predominant kashrut supervisors on the local level, even though Conservative Judaism differs, in some cases, over what is kosher and what is not. In most places, the communal *beit din* is Orthodox. Conservative Jews are likewise dependent on the Orthodox for use of the local mikveh, whether for regular monthly use or for conversion.

The Conservative movement must now come of age and take responsibility not only for our own synagogues but for communal institutions as well. We need to train a new generation of Conservative Jewish *mohalim*. On a local level, we need to train a generation of *mashgihim* (kashrut supervisors) and then to organize *hashgahah* (supervision) of food producers, eating establishments and bakeries under the supervision of Conservative rabbis. Conservative rabbis should establish a network of local religious courts. Not only would these courts deal with conversions and divorces; the rabbis involved could be trained as mediators to address community conflicts as well. Every major Jewish community should have a mikveh, controlled, operated, and supervised according to the regulations set by the Committee on Jewish Law and Standards. Only by developing Conservative communal institutions will our movement come of age.

Educational Needs

Quality Jewish education of tomorrow — a pressing need for our children — requires community schools. Synagogues will have to divest themselves of local control of afternoon religious schools and turn their energies and resources toward creating and organizing communal educational endeavors. Individual synagogue schools do not have enough quality teachers. Only a few good teachers are available and the various synagogues in a community are competing against each other for them. When we fragment the already limited resources, every synagogue loses. With the small student population remaining stable, only a community school can afford to provide the best, broadest, and most flexible curriculum. A pooling of resources can provide the brightest, the average, and the learning disabled with a Jewish education geared to their respective needs.

The Synagogue

Religious schools and synagogues are today inextricably bound together. Many congregants join synagogues only as a requirement for enrolling their children in synagogue schools. If there were only a local Hebrew school, the argument could be made, these people might never join a synagogue. This challenge could be met simply by requiring family membership in a synagogue as a prerequisite for entrance into the community school. Underlying this membership dilemma is a more serious question, however. What will become of the synagogue if it is no longer, to use a business analogy, the holding company for its major subsidiary, the afternoon religious school?

Without the burden of religious school, the synagogue may soar to new heights and turn to new purposes. Without the financial drain and space requirements of a religious school, synagogues may venture into currently uncharted territory. The synagogue may truly become a caring community that responds to the spectrum of communal needs. A synagogue may provide Jewish day care for the toddler population, or an after-school program for elementary and junior high or middle school students. The elderly now make up an ever-increasing percentage of our population, creating a chronic shortage of programs and facilities for them. Synagogues can provide care, shelter and programs for senior adults. The synagogue lends dignity to singles events and should be a source of programs for singles. (Synagogues might even become a center for hospices and the care of the terminally ill.) The rabbi and the congregation give a Jewish perspective to support groups and could provide services to the handicapped, recently bereaved and others desiring the company of similarly tested souls.

Without the burden of a religious school, the synagogue can turn to serious adult education (Talmud Torah) for adults. We must begin to see the synagogue of the future as a center for sophisticated, intellectual and cultural programs. It could be the local University of Judaism whose purpose is to stimulate, challenge, and enlighten adults.

Finally, the synagogue of the future should concentrate on spirituality. In this high-tech age, our people are turning back to religion and to tradition. The synagogue must become a place where the religious quest may be taken seriously. There are many who assume that thinking about God is for theologians, rabbis, even children, but not themselves. The truth is we all think about God. He is on our minds and in our hearts. Every Jew is capable of a relationship with God. In fact, Judaism demands it from us. The synagogue of the future must become a place where the pursuit of holiness and the quest for a relationship with God are given the highest priority.

Limits of Ideology

Every year my synagogue and I give an orientation to the parents of next year's *b'nei mitzvah*. One of my subjects is having a kosher reception. Most of my congregants have never kept or no longer keep kosher. In my impassioned speech I talk about the religious nature and purpose of the bar/bat mitzvah and the moment of education this special occasion provides:

"On a day-to-day basis one may not keep kosher. But what is the family's attitude to the dietary laws in specific and the obligations of Jewish tradition in general? Let this *simcha* be an occasion where your family celebrates its love, respect and the wisdom of our tradition."

The speech more often than not has its desired effect.

What is the benefit? If our congregants will not observe halakhah every day of their lives, let us persuade them to embrace the Conservative Jewish lifestyle at moments of transition and special occasions throughout life. If our congregants will not observe halakhot at home, let them observe them in and around the synagogue. Congregants may not *daven* regularly at minyan with tefillin, but we could encourage them to do so on special days of the year, like a birthday or anniversary. Talmud Torah may not be a central mitzvah for a family as a whole, but the congregation can design a program so the twelve months preceding a bar/bat mitzvah become a period of concentrated study in order to transform the ceremony from a morning event to a year-long process. Perhaps we should suggest that a trip to Israel is the perfect 25th wedding anniversary gift.

The best method of closing the gap between congregant and halakhah, and between rabbinic observance and lay observance, without compromising on our ideals, is to create an awareness of moments of greater spiritual involvement and opportunities for greater openness of tradition. The role of the rabbi is to nurture, utilize and even to manufacture these moments and opportunities for his congregants.

The Authority of Women Rabbis

A woman rabbi tells the story of a young boy in her congregation five years ago. She is the only rabbi the boy has ever known. One day the boy turns to his father, and asks, "Can boys be rabbis too?"

It is of vital concern that women rabbis be allowed to establish themselves. Male colleagues need to respect and accept women rabbis. This may be difficult for more veteran rabbis and it may threaten some younger ones, but we need to say up front that women ordained as rabbis by the Jewish Theological Seminary and/or accepted for admission to the Rabbinical Assembly are rabbis in the fullest sense of the term. They should not be labeled for or pigeon-holed into select professional positions.

Both the Seminary and the Rabbinical Assembly must monitor

and encourage the progress of women rabbis. A new dean for women in the rabbinical school could serve as advocate, adviser, and role model for our female colleagues. The Rabbinical Assembly, for its part, should organize a committee chaired by a male to help resolve issues that will inevitably develop: maternity leave, part-time positions, and the like.

It may very well be that full acceptance of women rabbis may take an entire generation. The generation that knew only male rabbis as spiritual leaders may have to die and a new generation be born, exposed to, taught by, and influenced by both female and male rabbis, for all anxiety and novelty to dissipate. By the time the new generation is born, our movement will be blessed with many talented and learned rabbis and scholars, some of whom just happen to be male.

Women Rabbis as Center of Strength

Several women rabbis have repeated a similar story to me. A woman seeks them out for advice, counseling, or a wedding arrangement, and appreciatively concludes, "Thanks for listening. I'm glad I could speak to another woman." Women rabbis add a whole new dimension to rabbinic job definition and potentiality. For those women who prefer to distance themselves from male authority figures, including rabbis, and for those women who cannot identify with what they believe to be a patriarchal and sexist religion, women rabbis can serve as a sign inviting them back in to explore the heritage they abandoned. They will nurture and inspire both men and women to identify ever more strongly with our tradition.

Egalitarian Tradition and Change

What affect will the legitimation of women rabbis have on our laity?

Over the course of the next twenty years we will see a quiet growth toward egalitarian ritual observance by our women. More and more, women do not want to be exempt from positive, time-bound mitzvot. More and more, women will see themselves as Jewish leaders and will want to avail themselves of more Jewish responsibilities. Ordaining women as rabbis was not only a struggle over halakhic questions. It was also a victory over psychological obstacles. Now that the greatest hurdle is behind us, the change in women's roles in society will also nudge the egalitarian ritual evolution along. Traditional women who attend Shabbat services will begin to wear a tallit and kippah. Observant women who frequent the daily morning minyan will don tefillin. Women who would not attend minyan because they did not "count" will eventually come because now their presence may very well make possible the recitation of Kaddish. That there will be women who will not participate in these mitzvot, as there are men who do not participate in them, is not pertinent to the argument. What is important is that women will help create a fully participatory egalitarian Jewish tradition.

Electronic Media

Perhaps the greatest challenge our movement faces and the hurdle that may provide us with the means to our greatest impact is mastering the electronic media. Rabbis of the future must have television skills. They will occasionally be called upon to be a guest on a television show. They need to know how to present themselves and their tradition in the very best light. At the very least, the Jewish Theological Seminary should provide rabbinical students with a basic introduction to electronic media communications. Fortunately, the Seminary is close to the television center of the world, many of whose leading lights are Jewish. Guest speakers and instructors could provide an enlightening experience for the next generation of rabbis. It would give the next generation of rabbis a sense of familiarity with the strange and complex world of electronics they will eventually meet.

The Rabbinical Assembly should create a committee to coordinate, share, distribute, and disseminate media material to colleagues. Just like the expansion of services committee now collects and distributes sermons, *divrei Torah* and other interesting and useful printed materials, a new media committee would provide the energy, the effort, and above all the leadership to teach rabbis the best ways to utilize and benefit from the electronic media. In the field, colleagues are already producing many wonderful, creative, and thoughtful media projects, but usually in isolation. The influence of their wonderful programs should not be limited to one small geographic area. With a little strategic planning and coordination, we could organize a national video production network. For example, one rabbi and his synagogue could produce one media project a year on cable television. The Rabbinical Assembly media committee could select the topics—

for instance, Jewish holidays — and organize twenty rabbis and their congregations, each having the responsibility and commitment to produce a tape on one holiday or one aspect of the holiday. The Rabbinical Assembly media committee would then collect the twenty tapes and make them available for national distribution to every Conservative congregation. In a very short span of years, we could have a complete cable and home video library on the holidays graded from preschool through high school and beyond. Each succeeding year another topic would be chosen for development. The technology is already in place. The resources are available in every community. The vision has been created. What is needed is the leadership to organize the project.

Finally, I would suggest one more move — one that is both imaginative and expensive, yet having the greatest potential: A television studio for the joint use of the Jewish Theological Seminary and the Rabbinical Assembly to be housed on the Seminary campus in New York. We need to think about ourselves and our jobs differently, not only textually, not just orally, but visually. Not only should our scholars write popular as well as learned tracts, but they should share their material visually with our laity as well. Television will make this possible. There are a great many conferences, lectures, and programs convened at the Seminary that many rabbis, for financial or other reasons, are not able to attend. All these events may be videotaped and made available for distribution to the R.A. Many Christian denominations — the Methodists, the Southern Baptists, and several Catholic dioceses — have already established studio facilities.

To make the vision a reality, we need to take the next steps along practical lines. Rabbi Barukh of Medzibozh taught, "Every person is a vessel taking into itself whatever the owner pours into it, wine or vinegar." Broadcast television, original access programming on cable, video tapes, and tape recordings are the vessel. The content of the program is the liquid that is poured in. Nationally produced programs of the first order, along with locally produced cable television of Judaic content is the "sweet" wine. May the Conservative movement and Conservative rabbis pour the wine and may our communities and Conservative congregations enjoy its taste.

The Contributors

Kassel Abelson is President of the Rabbinical Assembly, and Rabbi of Beth El Synagogue in Minneapolis.

Howard A. Addison is Rabbi of Temple Beth Israel, Greater Fort Lauderdale, Florida. He taught Jewish Thought at Fordham University, Kent State and Spertus College of Jewish Studies. He is a member of the Editorial Board of *Conservative Judaism,* and serves on the Conservative movement's Commission on Ideology.

H. A. Alexander was ordained by the Jewish Theological Seminary and holds a Ph.D. in Philosophy of Education and the Humanities from Stanford University. He has served on the education faculty and as director of leadership development at the Jewish Theological Seminary, and was director of the Mador Leadership Training program and professor in residence at Camp Ramah in California. Dr. Alexander is presently Assistant Professor of Philosophy and Education, and director of Lee College at the University of Judaism in Los Angeles.

Bradley Shavit Artson, JTS class of '88, is the author of *Love Peace and Pursue Peace: A Jewish Response to War and Nuclear Annihilation,* published by the United Synagogue. He and his wife, Elana, are the Residence Advisors for the Seminary's undergraduate dorm. He is an *ex officio* member of the RA Social Justice Committee.

Emily D. Bilski has been with the Jewish Museum since 1978, where she is currently an Associate Curator. She was the curator of the recent exhibition, *Art and Exile: Felix Nussbaum (1904–1944),* and author of its accompanying catalog. Her future projects include exhibitions on the theme of the golem in the visual arts and a retrospective of the 20th-century German artist Ludwig Meidner.

Debra Reed Blank entered the Rabbinical School in 1984. She received her B.A. in Religious Studies from Indiana University, and attended graduate school at the Hebrew Union College in Cincinnati. She later received an M.S. in Library Science from Columbia University and has worked as a Judaica librarian at the YIVO Institute and Hebrew Union College – Jewish Institute of Religion in New York City.

Eugene B. Borowitz is Professor of Education and Jewish Religious Thought at HUC-JIR, New York, and founder and editor of *Sh'ma* magazine. He taught at the Seminary in its Comparative Judaism course from 1969-72. He has also served as visiting professor at Temple, Princeton, Columbia and Harvard Universities. Rabbi Borowitz is the author of numerous studies in Jewish theology and ethics and has published ten books in these fields.

Burton I. Cohen is National Ramah Director and Assistant Professor of Jewish Education at the Seminary. Dr. Cohen's 40-year affiliation with the Ramah movement began as a camper during the first Ramah season in 1947. His Ramah experience led him to study for the rabbinate and toward academic and professional work in the field of Jewish Education.

Aryeh Davidson is Assistant Professor in the Department of Jewish Education at the Jewish Theological Seminary and principal of the Seminary's Prozdor High School. Dr. Davidson is currently engaged in research on religious development across the life span.

Elliot N. Dorff is Provost and Professor of Philosophy at the University of Judaism, where he has directed the program of rabbinic studies since 1971. Rabbi Dorff has also served as a lecturer in the law schools of UCLA and the University of Southern California. He is the author of *Jewish Law and Modern Ideology; Conservative Judaism: Our Ancestors to Our Descendants;* and, with Arthur Rosett, *A Living Tree: The Roots and Growth of Jewish Law* (forthcoming).

Amy Eilberg, JTS class of '85, was the first woman ordained by the Jewish Theological Seminary. She currently serves as the Jewish Chaplain at Methodist Hospital of Indiana and as the Community Rabbi of the Jewish Welfare Federation of Greater Indianapolis. A member of the Rabbinical Assembly's Committee on Jewish Law and Standards, she is also the proud mother of a baby daughter, Penina Tova Eilberg Schwartz.

Theodore Friedman has lived in Jerusalem since 1970. He is past president of the Rabbinical Assembly and a frequent contributor to *Conservative Judaism* magazine.

Elliot Gertel is Rabbi of Congregation Beth El Kesser Israel in New Haven, Connecticut; a member of the Editorial Board of *Conservative Judaism* magazine; and the co-author with Rabbi Seymour Siegel of two books, *Conservative Judaism and Jewish Law* and *God in the Teachings of Conservative Judaism.*

Robert Goldenberg is Associate Professor and Director of Judaic Studies at the State University of New York at Stony Brook. Rabbi Goldenberg has published several studies relating to the thought, literature, and early history of Rabbinic Judaism. His present research concerns the nature and basis of rabbinic authority in the Jewish community. Dr. Goldenberg is currently serving as Chair of the National Havurah Committee.

Neil Gillman is Associate Professor in Jewish Philosophy at the Jewish Theological Seminary. He is completing a book in Jewish theology, to be published in 1988 by the Jewish Publication Society, for use in adult education classes.

Leonard Gordon, ordained by the Jewish Theological Seminary in 1985, is Visiting Instructor in the Integrated Program in Humane Studies and the Jewish Chaplain at Kenyon College. He is completing a doctorate in Religion at Columbia University.

Arthur Green is President of the Reconstructionist Rabbinical College. Ordained by the Jewish Theological Seminary in 1967, he received his Ph.D. from Brandeis University in 1975. His books include *Tormented Master: A Life of Rabbi Nahman of Bratslav* (Alabama, 1978) and the recent *Jewish Spirituality* (Crossroad, 1985–87).

Edward L. Greenstein is Associate Professor in Bible at the Seminary and chairs the department. Author of numerous monographs, articles, and reviews, he is co-editor of *The Hebrew Bible in Literary Criticism* and author of the forthcoming *Essay in Biblical Method and Translation*. He has been editing the *Journal of the Ancient Near Eastern Society* since 1974 and is associate editor of *Prooftexts*.

David Weiss Halivni is Professor of Talmud and Classical Rabbinics in the Department of Religion at Columbia University. He taught Talmud at the Jewish Theological Seminary from 1957 until 1986.

Reuven Hammer is Dean of the Jewish Theological Seminary's Jerusalem Center, Neve Schechter, where he also serves as Assistant Professor of Talmud and Rabbinics. He served as chairman of the founding committee of the Seminary of Judaic Studies and as its first Director. He is the author of *The Other Child in Jewish Education* and the translator of *Sifre on Deuteronomy*.

Barry W. Holtz is Co-director of the Melton Research Center and Assistant Professor of Jewish Education at the Jewish Theological Seminary. Dr. Holtz is the editor of *Back to the Sources: Reading the Classic Jewish Texts* (Summit Books).

Paula E. Hyman is the Lucy Moses Professor of Modern Jewish History at Yale University. From 1981 to 1986 she served as the Dean of the Seminary College of Jewish Studies at the Jewish Theological Seminary. She has published widely in modern Jewish history and in Jewish women's history. Co-author of *The Jewish Woman in America,* her latest book is *The Jewish Family: Myths and Reality* (co-edited with Steven M. Cohen).

Francine Klagsbrun has written more than a dozen books for adults and young people, including *Married People: Staying Together in the Age of Divorce* and *Voices of Wisdom: Jewish Ideal and Ethics for Everyday Living.* Her articles have appeared in such magazines as *The New York Times Book Review, Newsweek, Ms.,* and *McCall's.*

Benjamin Kreitman has been the Executive Vice-President of the United Synagogue of America since 1976. He has served on the faculty of the Jewish Theological Seminary of America as a visiting professor of Rabbinic Law and on the faculty of Brooklyn College as a visiting professor of Judaic Studies.

Franklin D. Kreutzer is currently International President of the United Synagogue of America, to which he was elected in 1985. A native Floridian, he is active in the Greater Miami secular and Jewish communities. A noted attorney, Mr. Kreutzer has served as Special Assistant Attorney General from 1975–1978, and is presently a Dade County Personnel Board Hearing Examiner and Dade County Circuit Court Master-Guardian-Commissioner. He has also served as President of the Greater Miami Hebrew Free Loan Association (1970–79) and as President of Temple Zion—Israelite Center.

Morton M. Leifman is Vice-President of the Jewish Theological Seminary where he is also Dean of the Cantors Institute—Seminary College of Jewish Music, and Assistant Professor of Liturgy.

Anne Lapidus Lerner is Dean of List College at the Jewish Theological Seminary and Assistant Professor of Hebrew Literature. Her publications include *"Passing the Love of Women": A Study of Gide's "Saül" and Its Biblical Roots* and "Who Hast Not Made a Man: The Movement for Equal Rights for Women in American Jewry."

Lee Levine is a professor of Jewish History and Archeology at the Hebrew University in Jerusalem where he has been teaching since 1971. He has written numerous books and articles on a variety of subjects including the ancient synagogue, the Pharisees and rabbis. Dr. Levine also teaches at the Jewish Theological Seminary's Jerusalem campus, Neve Schechter. In addition to his academic work, Dr. Levine has been active in the Masorti movement in Israel. He was among the founders of Ramot Zion Synagogue on French Hill, Jerusalem (1973), of the Masorti (Tali) School in Jerusalem (1976), of the Masorti movement (1979) and of the Israeli Conservative Rabbinical School (1984).

David L. Lieber is Vice-Chancellor of the Jewish Theological Seminary and has been President of the University of Judaism since 1963.

Joseph Lukinsky is Professor of Education at the Jewish Theological Seminary, Professor of Religion and Education at Teachers College, Columbia University, and Professor of Education at Union Theological Seminary. He has written extensively on curriculum development and moral education.

Ivan G. Marcus is Professor of Jewish History at the Jewish Theological Seminary. A graduate of Yale College, he is the author of *Piety and Society: The Jewish Pietists of Medieval Germany* (1981), is writing a one-volume history of the Jews for Scribner's and is translating *Sefer Hasidim* for the Yale Judaica Series. Rabbi Marcus and his wife Judith, a practicing pediatric hematologist/oncologist, live with their four sons, Yuval, Magen, Sasson and Ehud in New Rochelle, N.Y.

Rela Geffen Monson is Professor of Sociology at Gratz College, and Chairman of the Faculty. Dr. Monson is a Fellow of The Center for Jewish Community Studies.

Yochanan Muffs is Professor of Bible at the Jewish Theological Seminary. Rabbi Muffs is the author of *Studies of the Aramaic Legal Papyrii from Elephantine*, "His Majesty's Loyal Opposition," "Joy and Love in Ancient Israelite Literature," "God and the World," and other studies.

David Novak is the Rabbi of Congregation Darchay Noam in Far Rockaway, New York and Visiting Associate Professor of Talmud at JTS. He is Adjunct Associate Professor of Philosophy at Baruch College of the City University of New York, and Vice-President of the Union for Traditional Conservative Judaism as well as Co-ordinator of its Panel of Halakhic Inquiry.

Michael Panitz is a doctoral candidate in Jewish History at the Jewish Theological Seminary; rabbi of Temple Beth Israel of Maywood, New Jersey; and a member of the Editorial Board of *Conservative Judaism* magazine. He is currently a member of the Theological Department of St. Peter's College, Englewood Cliffs.

Jules Porter is International President of the Federation of Jewish Men's Clubs. A long-time member and past vice-president of Sinai Temple in West Los Angeles, he currently serves as vice-chairman of the Steering Committee, Congregation Cabinet, University of Judaism, as well as a member of the Board of Directors of the United Synagogue of America, the World Council of Synagogues, the Foundation for Conservative Judaism in Israel, and the Jewish Theological Seminary of America.

Ronald D. Price is the first Executive Director of the Union for Traditional Conservative Judaism. Prior to his appointment in 1985, Rabbi Price served as spiritual leader of Congregation Ramot Zion in French Hill, Jerusalem. From 1977–80, Rabbi Price was Assistant Dean of the Rabbinical School of the Jewish Theological Seminary.

Joel Rembaum is Rabbi of Temple Beth Am in Los Angeles, California and former Associate Professor of Jewish History and Dean of Undergraduate Studies at the University of Judaism. He is a member of the Executive Council of the Rabbinical Assembly and is Co-Chair of the United Synagogue Committee on Commitment and Observance.

Yaakov G. Rosenberg is Vice-Chancellor for Development at the Jewish Theological Seminary. He serves on the faculty as Lecturer in Professional Skills and is Rabbinic consultant to the Department of Pastoral Psychiatry. He spent 29 years in the congregational rabbinate, prior to returning to the Seminary in 1978.

Gilbert S. Rosenthal is Rabbi of Temple Beth El in Cedarhurst, New York. He teaches Senior Homiletics in the Rabbinical School of the Jewish Theological Seminary. He has written and edited nine books including *The American Rabbi* and *Contemporary Judaism: Patterns of Survival*. He is Vice President of the New York Board of Rabbis, past Vice President and trustee of the UJA-Federation of Jewish Philanthropies of New York. He is a member of both the Executive Council and Administrative Committee of the Rabbinical Assembly and chairs that organization's Publications Committee.

David G. Roskies is Associate Professor of Jewish Literature at the Jewish Theological Seminary. He is co-founder and editor of *Prooftexts: A Journal of Jewish Literary History*. His book *Against the Apocalypse: Responses to Catastrophe in Modern Jewish Culture* was awarded the Ralph Waldo Emerson Prize by Phi Beta Kappa. He held a Guggenheim Fellowship in 1985–86.

Joel Roth is Associate Professor of Talmud at the Jewish Theological Seminary and Chairman of the Rabbinical Assembly's Committee on Jewish Law and Standards. He is the author of *The Halakhic Process: A Systemic Analysis*.

John S. Ruskay was appointed Vice President for Public Affairs of the Jewish Theological Seminary in 1985. Previously, Dr. Ruskay served as Education Director of the 92nd Street Y; Executive Director of the National Jewish Conference Center; and Education Director/Executive Director of the Society for the Advancement of Judaism.

Raymond Scheindlin is Provost of the Jewish Theological Seminary, and Professor of Medieval Hebrew Literature at the Seminary. His most recent book, is *Wine, Women and Death: Medieval Poems on the Good Life,* published by The Jewish Publication Society.

Elliot Salo Schoenberg is the Rabbi at Temple Aliyah of Needham, Massachusetts and a member of the Editorial Board of *Conservative Judaism.* He is the executive producer of "Aliyah," a syndicated cable television show and founder of The High School of Jewish Studies. His articles have appeared in *Conservative Judaism, Religious Education, Reconstructionist* and *Sh'ma.*

Ismar Schorsch is Chancellor of the Jewish Theological Seminary. He succeeded Gerson D. Cohen in the summer of 1986, the beginning of the school's centennial year. He is Rabbi Herman Abramovitz Professor in Jewish History.

Benjamin Edidin Scolnic is the Rabbi of Temple Beth Sholom in Hamden, Connecticut. He recently received his Ph.D. in Bible from the Jewish Theological Seminary where he will be Visiting Assistant Professor in 1987–88. He has also taught at Yale University. Dr. Scolnic is on the Editorial Board of *Conservative Judaism,* and is President of the Connecticut Valley Region of the RA.

Miriam Klein Shapiro is Education Specialist for Westchester of the Board of Jewish Education of Greater New York and Educational Director of Camp Ramah in the Berkshires. She holds a DHL in Bible from the Jewish Theological Seminary.

Alan Silverstein is Rabbi of Congregation Agudath Israel in Caldwell, New Jersey and a member of the Editorial Board of *Conservative Judaism* magazine.

Jacob J. Staub edits the *Reconstructionist* magazine and directs the Medieval Civilization Program at the Reconstructionist Rabbinical College. He co-authored, with Rebecca T. Alpert, *Exploring Judaism: A Reconstructionist Approach* and co-edited, with Jeffrey L. Schein, *Creative Jewish Education: A Reconstructionist Perspective.*

Gordon Tucker is Dean of the Rabbinical School at the Jewish Theological Seminary and Assistant Professor of Jewish Philosophy. He is the Director of the Louis Finkelstein Institute for Religious and Social Studies and a member of the Rabbinical Assembly's Committee on Jewish Law and Standards.

Samuel Weintraub, JTS class of '87, held special student internships in interreligious affairs through the American Jewish Committee and in work with the intermarried through the Jewish Theological Seminary and the

Leonard E. and Phyllis S. Greenberg Foundation. Professionally, he hopes to "bring Torah-healing to a perplexed people and a troubled planet." He is the son of Rabbi Lewis A. Weintraub, JTS '44, and the brother of Rabbi Simkha Weintraub, JTS '82.

Selma Weintraub is Immediate Past President of Women's League for Conservative Judaism. She is an Honorary Vice President of the World Council of Synagogues, a member of the Chancellor's Leadership Cabinet of the Jewish Theological Seminary, a member of the Executive Committee of the Jewish Braille Institute and of Mercaz. Her present Women's League assignment is National Chairman for Branch Conferences. A resident of Hartsdale, N.Y., she has been a member of the Board of Temple Israel Center in White Plains for many years.

Jack Wertheimer is the Joseph and Martha Mendelson Associate Professor of American Jewish History and Director of the Archives of Conservative Judaism at JTS. He is the author of *Unwelcome Strangers: East European Jews in Imperial Germany,* and editor of *The American Synagogue in Historical Perspective* (forthcoming).

About the Editors

David Wolf Silverman is Chairman of the Editorial Board of *Conservative Judaism* and Rabbi of Temple Beth Zion-Beth Israel in Philadelphia. Rabbi Silverman holds a doctorate in philosophy from Columbia University. He has served as President of Spertus College of Judaica in Chicago and has taught Jewish philosophy at several universities and colleges, including Fordham University, New York University, Bryn Mawr, and the Jewish Theological Seminary, where he also was Chairman of the Philosophies of Judaism department. He has authored, edited and translated dozens of works on religious thought as well as on religious life in America. He is married to Ziona Silverman, is the father of three daughters and a son, and has one grandson.

Nina Beth Cardin, JTS class of '88, is a former managing editor of *Conservative Judaism* and a current member of its Editorial Board. She is also Coordinator of Publications for CLAL, The National Jewish Center for Learning and Leadership. Prior to entering rabbinical school, Ms. Cardin co-founded and directed the Jewish Women's Resource Center, now a project of the National Council of Jewish Women, New York Section. She is married to Rabbi Avram Reisner and is the mother of three sons.